To the Garys:

With love and
gratitude
for all of
your encouragement —

Mara

CRIMEA IN WAR AND TRANSFORMATION

CRIMEA IN WAR AND TRANSFORMATION

MARA KOZELSKY

OXFORD
UNIVERSITY PRESS

OXFORD
UNIVERSITY PRESS

Oxford University Press is a department of the University of Oxford. It furthers the University's objective of excellence in research, scholarship, and education by publishing worldwide. Oxford is a registered trade mark of Oxford University Press in the UK and certain other countries.

Published in the United States of America by Oxford University Press
198 Madison Avenue, New York, NY 10016, United States of America.

CIP data is on file at the Library of Congress
ISBN 978-0-19-064471-0

1 3 5 7 9 8 6 4 2

Printed by Sheridan Books, Inc., United States of America

For Crimea

CONTENTS

———◦◦◦◦———

ACKNOWLEDGMENTS

———

BEFORE I COMPLETED WORK ON my first book, I began gathering material for this one. In the course of more than fifteen years' research, I have accumulated many debts of gratitude. Archivists and fellow scholars in multiple Russian and Ukrainian archives have been extraordinarily kind and helpful. I am particularly indebted the staff of the State Archive of the Autonomous Republic of Crimea and the Russian State Historical Archive. Librarians at the Crimean Tatar Ismail bey Gasprinsky Library in Simferopol and at TAURICA supplied me with a variety of support. One of my favorite places in the world is the rare book room at the Russian National Library in St. Petersburg; it has been a privilege of my career to work there.

The University of South Alabama has generously supported multiple trips to Crimea and Russia in a tight budget climate. Deborah Cobb and Rebecca Young at the University of South Alabama Marx Library have gone to spectacular lengths to supply me with research material; I could have not written this book without their kind assistance. Harvard's Davis Center for Russian Studies has also facilitated access to research materials, as have the Slavic librarians at the University of Illinois. Harvard Map Collection granted permission for several images used in this book. The Anne S.K. Brown Military Collection, at Brown University Library, granted permission for the cover image.

Many generous colleagues have inspired me with their insightful feedback whether in conversation at the archives or in numerous meetings of the Association for Slavic East European and Eurasian Studies and the Southern Conference of Slavic Studies. Others have read portions of this manuscript. Ekaterina Zakharova's fine copy-editing of footnotes and technical assistance with Russian transliterations helped me smooth rough edges. I especially would like to acknowledge Lucien

J. Frary, David R. Stone, Larry E. Holmes, David M. Goldfrank, and the anonymous readers of my manuscript, whose excellent suggestions helped me produce a better book. Idil Izmirli opened up a new world for me in Crimea. Chuck Veit taught me about the salvage operation at Sevastopol and generously shared his research with me. I am grateful to Nancy Toff, who saw promise in the early manuscript and encouraged me to write with broader audiences in mind. Thank you to the team at Oxford University Press, and Newgen KnowledgeWorks, especially Shalini Balakrishnan, for such dedicated assistance in the production process. My colleagues in the History Department, the Department of Modern and Classical Languages and Literatures, especially Nicholas Gossett in the Russian Program, and everyone affiliated with the Center for War and Memory at the University of South Alabama are simply spectacular. My immediate and extended family has been with me every step of the way and fortified me through long, lonely stints of research. Most of all, I would like to thank my husband, Richard Hunter, for his constant support.

NOTE ON TRANSLITERATION

A MODIFIED LIBRARY OF CONGRESS system is used for rendering Russian and Ukrainian terms. To facilitate smoother reading for an Anglophone audience, I have omitted the single prime representing the soft sign in Russian geographic and personal names, thus for example spelling Симферополь as Simferopol. Similarly, I have used conventional English spellings for the large cities referenced in this work, including Odessa (Odesa), Nikolaev (Mykolaiv), and Kiev (Kyiv), and I employ traditional English language renderings for names of the Russian Tsars and other well-known Russian historical figures.

Crimean personal and place names are often difficult to depict accurately as places and people adopted hybridized spellings indicative of the peninsula's diverse Turkic, Greek, Armenian, Ukrainian, German, and Russian heritage. Many Tatar and Greek clerks in Crimea poorly knew Russian language, while few Russian officials understood *kirimtatar*. Often unfamiliar with local geography, itinerant military commanders and imperial bureaucrats confused Crimean villages, towns, rivers, and landmarks. In these challenging circumstances, I have recorded local villages and local personal names as accurately as possible.

Unless otherwise noted, dates are given according to the Julian calendar Russia followed until the after the Revolution. As appropriate, I have given old style/new style dates for significant events, such as for the Battle of Alma (September 8/20, 1854).

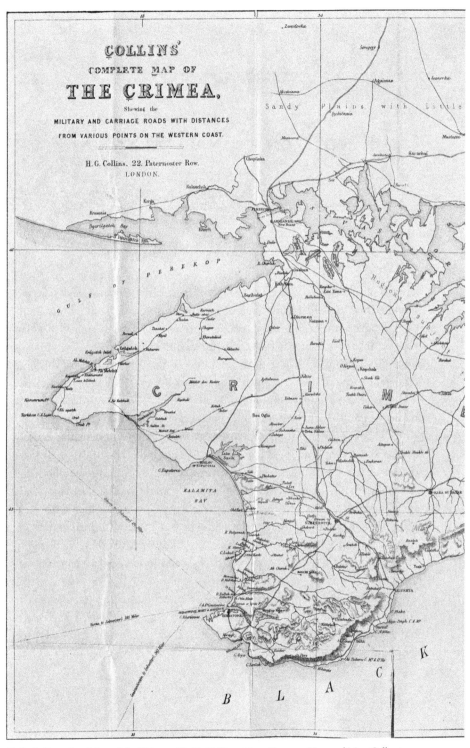

Collin's Complete Map of the Crimea, H. G. Collins, 1854. *Courtesy Harvard Map Collection.*

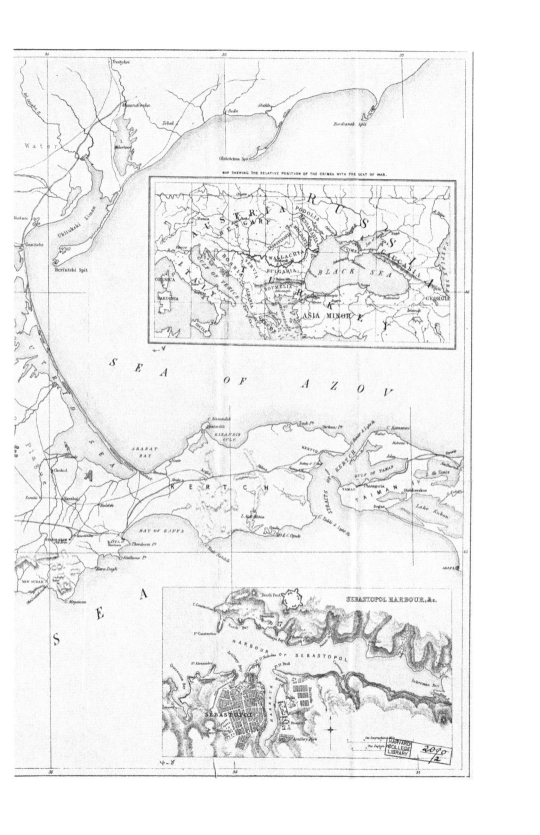

MAP SHEWING THE RELATIVE POSITION OF THE CRIMEA WITH THE SEAT OF WAR.

SEA OF AZOV

SEBASTOPOL HARBOUR, &c.

HARBOUR OF SEBASTOPOL

SEBASTOPOL

Introduction

"OH WAR, WAR! THE DETAILS of it are horrid!" wrote Light Brigade survivor George Paget, as he picked his way over horse carcasses and human corpses strewn on the road toward Sevastopol.[1] He, like many soldiers, struggled to find words for the utter devastation they encountered in a land seared by violence. Nearly 170,000 men perished in Sevastopol alone, many scrambling over muddy, bombed-out bastions. Even more died in cholera's sweaty, gut-wrenching grip. Throughout the war's multiple theaters, Russia lost 400,000 soldiers, with a death toll greater than all the Allied armies combined.[2]

Crimean civilians experienced each of the war's terrible phases beginning with Russia's mobilized homefront. They endured violence of cannon-fire and battles. Civilians starved along with the soldiers and remained homeless after peace was declared and armies left. Everyone sacrificed. Some fled. Others remained, too poor, and less commonly too patriotic, to leave. Apart from a few unscrupulous profiteers, most people suffered, and countless people died. The decimation of Crimean animals was severe in the extreme, and the same can be said for the natural environment. War devoured every vine, tree, or blade of grass in its path. Broken and irreparable despite millions of rubles dedicated to its reconstruction, Crimea had changed inexorably by the time savagery had run its horrific course. Russia, too, had changed, in ways war's champions likely neither anticipated nor desired. A different Crimea and a different empire emerged from the rubble. With a focus on the toll of violence in Crimea, this book examines the grim, transformative nature of war.

3

The violence unleashed on Crimea came as a shock to this tiny and remote corner of the empire. A small, diamond-shaped peninsula on the northern shore of the Black Sea, Crimea is roughly 17,000 square kilometers (about 10,500 miles), about the same size as Massachusetts in the United States, and a fifth the size of England. Russia annexed the space in 1783. After, Crimea existed on the outskirts of imperial politics, its inhabitants mainly allowed to live as they had done for hundreds of years. Tatars professed Islam and followed Sharia in their own courts.

On the eve of war, most inhabitants spoke *kirimtatar*, a Turkic-sounding language, and still dressed in Ottoman fashion. Men wore comfortable shirts tucked into baggy trousers that gathered at the ankles, and colorful sashes around their waists. Headgear similar to turbans or the fez, along with traditional outer robes, often completed their ensembles. Women covered their bodies typically to the wrists and ankles in form-fitting gowns. They wore veils, but left their faces and necks exposed to the sun.

More than 50,000 Greeks and Armenians had lived peacefully among the Tatars for centuries. Many had adopted the Tatar manner of speaking and dress, as had several thousand Crimean Jews, called *Krymchaki*, and Karaim, the latter a confessional group who followed the Torah but not the Talmud.[3] Travelers passing through Crimea often could not distinguish one ethnic or religious group from another.

Muslim Nogai Tatars inhabited the plains north of Crimea and west of the Caucasus. Whereas many Crimean Tatars had some European heritage, the Nogai Tatars were more closely connected to the Mongolian and Turkic groups of Central Asia. And although Nogai and Crimean Tatars shared some cultural institutions, the two groups had descended from different parent states and had gone through unique historical paths before and during Russian rule.

In the decades after annexation, Russian mandates slowly altered the region. Catherine the Great created the province's capital city, Simferopol, on the footprint of the Crimean Tatar town of Aqmescit. The Khan's palace in Bakhchisarai became an elegant monument to the once formidable Crimean Tatar state, whose raids regularly penetrated Moscow in the reign of Ivan the Terrible. To the north, Russia settled the nomadic Nogai Tatars in villages, creating three districts in the mainland (Berdiansk, Melitopol, Dneprovsk) and five districts in Crimea (Evpatoria, Simferopol, Yalta, Feodosia, Perekop). Together these districts formed the province of Tauride.

Like many borderland regions, Tauride had become a space of shifting identities and allegiances.[4] The population of the province rose to 650,000 by the mid-nineteenth century, although few Russian bureaucrats and landowners took up residence among the Tatars.[5] German Mennonites, invited by Catherine the Great, and Russian settlers, many of whom had dissented from the official Church, built communities among the Nogai.[6] As one might expect, Crimea's diverse groups comingled in the larger population centers, where people interacted regularly for trade, and city councils might have Tatar, Russian, Greek, and Jewish members.

Nevertheless, Tatars remained the majority population in Crimea, and many villages consisted only of Tatars. Tatar *sarai*, vine-covered palaces hewn of limestone blocks and connected by a maze of airy loggias, blended seamlessly into the landscape. Turrets of 1,600 mosques rose gracefully from towns and countryside, interspersed with a few Orthodox onion domes and ancient synagogues. Hauntingly beautiful calls to prayer echoed in the valleys, and old Tatar customs prevailed.[7] Crimea was a quiet, peaceful place, far removed from the stress of the bustling imperial cities and the advances of the industrial age. It was a place that time had forgotten, or so it had seemed.

No one expected the sleepy seaside villages of Crimea to become the primary battleground of Russia's deadly war, and the sudden concentration of European, Ottoman, and Russian armies in September 1854 shook the peninsula to its core. Literally overnight, armies doubled Crimea's population. Ensuing violence turned local farms into battlegrounds, and mosques and churches into storage depots for weapons. Verdant river valleys became mud pits; temporary military bases and combat hospitals cropped up in the plains. Soldiers pressed peasants living at subsistence levels into labor brigades and requisitioned their food. Invading armies consumed animals that retreating Russian troops had failed to slaughter. As the fighting wore on, many Russians in the war zone questioned whether Tatars had sympathies with their Ottoman co-religionists and therefore labeled the entire Tatar population as traitors. Thousands of Tatars were forcibly ejected from their homes before humanitarian impulses prevailed.

Beyond the destruction wrought on the local population, war fundamentally altered nature and landscapes. Soldiers dug shelters and burrowed trenches through the soil. Like ants, they heaped the earth into mounds and built barricades from existing natural resources. Death polluted rivers and poisoned wildlife. Artillery fire destroyed Crimea's ancient and medieval heritage, including the remnants of Roman fortifications and Byzantine cities. Ugly barracks were hastily erected in their place. Cemeteries replaced pastures, and mass graves were dug into formerly life-sustaining gardens. No war in Russia, not even the 1812 campaign of Napoleon and the burning of Moscow, had been so expensive or so destructive.

The Allied attack upon Crimea lasted eighteen months. Enemy armies continued to occupy Crimean cities and towns through demobilization in May 1856. It ranked among the longest enemy invasions in the history of the Russian empire.[8] The war named for Crimea in actuality waged across the globe. Nearly 8,000 kilometers (nearly 5,000 miles) as the crow flies separated the siege of Sevastopol on the Black Sea from the bombardment of Petropavlovsk on the Pacific. Navies fought in the Black Sea, the Azov, the Baltic Sea, the White Sea, and the Pacific Ocean. Ethnically and religiously diverse peoples constituted each combatant's imperial armies.

The Crimean War was also the first major violent conflict of the industrial era, for which "there [was] no precedent in History" in the words of General M. D. Gorchakov, penned while he was considering whether to abandon Sevastopol in August 1855.[9] Steamships, long-range guns, sea mines, rail, and telegraph provided new tools of violence. Cutting-edge scientific research revealed rigorous standards of sanitation as the key to containing epidemics. Nursing and battlefield medicine reached new levels of sophistication. Photography captured these developments for mass-consumed media at home. Disease and death rates among soldiers appalled eyewitnesses, although no one undertook a serious effort to calculate the loss of life among civilians near the battlefields.[10]

Florence Nightingale and the "Charge of the Light Brigade" have become icons of this war, as have the photos of Roger Fenton and William Russell's exposés in the *Times* (London). More recently the remarkable contributions of Mary Seacole, a battlefield nurse who traveled to Crimea from Jamaica, have come to light. Karl Marx's career took a substantial leap forward when the *New York Tribune* contracted him as its European war correspondent. In Russia, the Crimean War produced a cadre of nurses known as the Sisters of Mercy, who performed feats no less daring than did Nightingale and Seacole. As Immanuel Nobel exploded sea mines in the Gulf of Finland, Russian writers Leo Tolstoy and Konstantin Leontiev served in Crimea. Tolstoy was a captain in Sevastopol, and Leontiev a medic in Kerch.

The war also produced F. K. Zatler, the first Russian theorist of logistics. As the chief military officer in charge of provisioning the Russian army in Sevastopol, he organized supply during the hungriest years of the conflict. After the war, Zatler became a pariah, the face of Russian suffering, and the scapegoat for defeat. Spending several months in jail and more than a decade in disgrace, he wrote prolifically about food and war.[11] At a critical moment in the transition toward modern warfare, Zatler sounded the alarm bell against total war, although he did not use that term.[12] Even though the tsar formally rehabilitated him in 1869 and returned him to service working on the military portion of Russia's Great Reform, Zatler remained a controversial figure at the time of his death in 1876.[13]

In many ways, Zatler and Tolstoy took the same lesson from Crimea.[14] Both men understood war in its details. For Tolstoy war was an aggregate of individual experiences. For Zatler, wars were won and lost according to the amount of food in soldiers' backpacks, or a sudden change of weather. Neither romanticized violence, and both ridiculed the notion of military genius. Much like Tolstoy's caricatured General Kutuzov in *War and Peace*, Zatler argued that war operates according to its own internal logic and outside the control of men. It moves with the force of a hurricane; once it hits land, it can spiral into any unpredictable direction.

Contemporary British estimates placed costs of the Crimean War at 340 million pounds sterling, nearly half attributed to Russian war spending. The figure did not include requisitions, nor "suspension of industry, the ruin of commerce, bankruptcies, the enforced idleness."[15] The Allies waged economic warfare, blockading Russian ports to stem the flow of trade; they deliberately destroyed factories and farms on every shore they approached.[16] Altogether 2.3 million Russian men bore arms during the Crimean War, or about one-tenth of male agricultural workers between the ages of eighteen and fifty. War decimated the economy, especially agriculture.[17] Russian ministers and men of war, many of whom served in 1812, concluded that the Crimean War was the most expensive war Russia had yet fought.[18] The Russian economy went into a deep tailspin for more than a decade. As the imperial economy recovered and the state boomed into the industrial age, civilians from the war zone and Crimea especially were still picking up the pieces well into the 1870s and 1880s.

After the war, Tsar Alexander II acknowledged Crimea's utter destruction. "Our heart sympathizes with your suffering, your wounds," he announced in an imperial proclamation. "We express our sincere appreciation for the sacrifice made for the Fatherland's sacred cause."[19] He promised to put the Crimean peninsula, and the province of Tauride to which it was attached, on the path to recovery. Subsequently, the Russian government embarked upon the largest war recovery effort undertaken in the Russian empire. Charities and state agencies gave millions of rubles in relief, while government ministries offered interest-free loans and alleviated tax burdens.

Aid fell well short of local needs. In 1857, Crimean winemakers produced only one-fourth their prewar volume, and agriculture did not resume prewar production until the 1870s.[20] The peninsula's shipping industry had collapsed after Russian generals scuttled merchant vessels in the entrance to the Sevastopol Bay and the Kerch Straits.

Beyond Crimea, northern districts of Tauride descended into poverty following attacks on the Kinburn fortress in the west and along coastal towns on the Azov Sea toward the east. Diversion of virtually all residents from normal occupations to support the military, from mobilization in 1852 through Russian demobilization in 1857, had drained the provinces of the southern Russian empire, now southern Ukraine, for decades.

War journalism brought violence into distant homes; during the war, a new brand of dark tourism attracted spectators to battlefields. After the war, Sevastopol featured in Mark Twain's European odyssey.[21] Recording his impressions in *Innocents Abroad* (1869), he wrote: "Ruined Pompeii is in good condition compared to Sebastopol [*sic*]. Here, you may look in whatsoever direction you please, and your eye encounters scarcely any thing but ruin, ruin, ruin!—fragments of houses, crumbled walls, torn and ragged hills, devastation everywhere! It is as if a mighty earthquake had spent all its terrible forces upon this one little spot."[22]

A radical change in Crimean demography exceeded the shocking alteration of the landscape and the wreckage of local commerce and production. Nearly 200,000 Tatars, approximately two-thirds of the peninsula's population, abandoned their homeland at the war's end.[23] Tatars left their homes and livestock, and sold their property at a fraction of its value. They relinquished their status as subjects of the Russian empire and bid farewell to the land of their ancestors. The Crimean Tatar departure plunged the peninsula, already wasted from the war, into the deepest crisis of its history since the Russian annexation of the region in 1783. As an observer of the Tatar exodus reflected, "emigration of an entire population always impoverishes the country, and in this case indelible traces will remain for decades."[24] Already brutalized, the peninsula sank even deeper into despair.

Even though belligerents fought mostly on the soil of the Russian empire, histories typically cover the war from the British perspective. Few books in the English language describe the Russian experience of war, especially outside Sevastopol.[25] This book, therefore, seeks to shed light on the civilian experience. It focuses also on military-civilian policy. Areas of interest include the nature of the Russian home front; the war's impact on Crimean peoples and landscapes; and Russian postwar recovery efforts.

The Crimean War was the biggest test of post-Napoleonic military reforms, and the first major conflict fought on Russian soil after the establishment of the Third Section, Nicholas I's secret chancellery of police dedicated to internal surveillance.[26] The war exposed weaknesses in army provisioning, food policy, and war financing, the models for which began to change during the war itself.[27] Conventional scholarship suggests that civil society either did not exist in Russia or developed after the Great Reforms. A closer look at charity networks and other home front activities during the war calls such assumptions into question.[28] Beyond expanding knowledge about the Crimean War, an important subject in itself, this book enhances our understanding of Russian military and social policy in the *longue durée*.[29]

In terms of the war, vast quantities of archival documents remain unexploited. Vital questions remain. For example, what happened during the war that prompted serf emancipation? What linked the war to the reshaping of the judiciary system, the reconfiguring of industry and commerce? The frequently invoked cliché of Russia's "humiliating defeat" does not match the historical reality.

Instead, Russia conceded to peace talks only after a major victory at Kars. It gained more territory from the war than it lost. Further, Russia contravened treaty clauses that prohibited a Black Sea Navy when it sponsored a steam-based merchant marine equipped with state-of-the-art military technology. Moreover, the predominant contemporary narrative of the war was not one of humiliation, but rather, persecution.[30] The war was a great catalyst of change, and scholars have yet to probe fully the many-dimensioned consequences of the conflict on the course of Russian history. In seeking to understand the costs of war to civilians and landscapes, this book contributes to answering these questions in large and small ways.[31]

Civilians were at the center of the Crimean War. Without voluntary and involuntary civilian support, Russia could not have fueled the war effort. Yet, "The least powerful participants in armed conflict suffer the most," claim Daniel Rothbart and Karina Korostelina in *Why They Die*.[32] This is certainly true of the Crimean War, where combatants perceived civilians as either instruments or impediments. A primary line of inquiry thus analyzes the evolution of military management of civilians through various stages of war. Related themes include the implementation of martial law, food policies, the use of irregular forces, and state violence against imperial subjects. This book also explores the struggle to reestablish civilian life against the backdrop of demobilization.[33]

The Crimean War was a transitional and transformative conflict in terms of Russian culture and policy. Multiple and conflicting approaches to population management divided Russian bureaucrats and military leaders. Relentless violence fueled anti-Islamic sentiment and amplified dangerous administrative philosophies. Combined with growing fear of internal enemies, the Crimean

War accelerated the end of religious toleration. The derogatory term *kulak*, which many readers might associate with the First World War, the Russian Civil War, or Soviet collectivization, appeared in this era to describe people perceived as hoarding food or speculating on food prices while the masses went hungry.[34]

Scholars contextualize the Stalinist deportations in a longer history of forced migrations derived from Social Darwinism, colonial policies of the late nineteenth century, and a pathological fear of internal enemies extending into the Tsarist period.[35] During the First World War, as Peter Gatrell and William Fuller have shown, the military resettled borderland populations and blamed minorities for defeat.[36] But the origins of these practices date to the Crimean War and pre-Reform imperial laws. Russian civilian and military officials cast Tatars as "internal enemies," exploiting rising anti-Islamic sentiment to justify moving Crimean Tatars from their homes. Others evoked laws and customs pertaining to moving serfs. While reform-minded individuals like the Minister of State Domains, P. D. Kiselev, had been trying to limit the practice, forced migration was nothing new; the state and nobility had been relocating small and large groups of people according to whim for centuries.[37]

The extensive categorization of peoples through statistics gathered by the military did not play the same role in Crimean violence as in the postwar conquest of the Caucasus, or in the First and Second World Wars.[38] Instead, statistics and tools of categorization actually *impeded* forced relocation, as civilians used Tsarist-era privileges attributed to respective social categories (merchant, clergy, and nobility) to resist the contraction of rights based on religious or ethnic designations. Thus, for example, local bureaucrats proved reluctant to eject Tatar nobility and merchants from their homes, but eventually accepted that relocation of state peasants accorded with Russian tradition and law. Checks and balances built into the Nicolaevin ministerial system, moreover, prevented the sort of ethnic cleansing that ensued in the Caucasus under Alexander II.[39]

Nevertheless, Russian wartime civilian policy had changed. Many officials during the Crimean War did identify Tatars as enemies of the state and recommended deporting the entire population. This book interchangeably uses the terms "forced relocation," "evacuation," and "deportation" to describe the removal of Tatars from the coast, a conscious deployment of terminology that reflects shifts in policy or differences in thinking among officials. Thus, for example, agents associated with the Ministry of State Domains used language of resettling or relocating, while military officers typically employed terms evocative of removal, exile, and deportation.

The apogee of the movement to deport Tatars occurred when Alexander II managed the war, and not Nicholas I, the tsar usually credited with hardline oppressive policy.[40] Alexander II and his Great Reforms, contemporaries and historians have suggested, represented the forward thinking of his day.[41] Yet, this progressivism apparently contained dangerous seeds of social engineering that unfolded in the settlement of the Caucasus as well as Crimea. Punitive population policies and "spy mania" evident in the Crimean War gathered momentum through the late Tsarist and Soviet periods, while the portrayal of Tatars as collaborators with the enemy reappeared later in Soviet demonization of loyal Tatars as Nazi sympathizers.[42]

As much as the Crimean War marks a transition in Russian military management of civilians, it also marks a transition in Russian policy toward Islam. More specifically, we might call the Crimean War the end of toleration in the empire of the tsars. Catherine the Great had developed a limited policy of toleration following the annexation of Crimea that allowed Tatars cultural autonomy in exchange for loyalty to state institutions.[43] The rise of Orthodox nationalism under Nicholas I challenged religious toleration in the Russian Empire, however, and set the foreground of anti-Islamic attitudes and exclusionary tactics during the Crimean War.[44] Increasingly, Russian policy makers referred to Tatars neither as state peasants nor Tatars, but "Muslims," and projected unfounded anxieties about Islamic temperament and tendencies upon them. This book operates under the assumption that language matters and dangers associated with identity labels are particularly apparent in times of protracted violence.[45]

Finally, this book is a study of the relationship between war and the social construction of landscapes.[46] Russian imperial narratives had cast the diamond-shaped Crimea as the jewel in the crown of Catherine the Great. Crimea's stunning mountains plunging into glittering sea vistas captured the imaginations of Russians living in snowy St. Petersburg, as did the eclectic architecture reflecting the peninsula's ancient Greek, Roman, Byzantine, and Ottoman eras.[47] During the reign of Nicholas I, biblical scholars pinpointed a small seaside town near Sevastopol, Chersonesos, as the location of the tenth-century Slavic Prince Vladimir's baptism.

According to legend, Prince Vladimir's conversion brought Slavs from paganism to Christianity, from the darkness to the light. By the nineteenth century, biblical scholars and historians alike began to cast the medieval prince as the founder of the Russian state.[48] The Allied invasion of Crimea in 1854, particularly the French base camp in Chersonesos, brought what had been obscure Orthodox Christian narratives into the Russian mainstream, where they have persisted through the Soviet period to the present. Thus we can say war changed Crimea *writ large:* its topography, demography, architecture, and identity.

Crimea's transformation through home front, war, and recovery is chronicled in the hidden literature of war. Tatars who protested their arrest, exile, or deportation; monks who conducted liturgies as bombs fell around them; and civilians who fled invasion or fought to remain in their homes supply the essence of this book. Letters and reports from harried officials provide a second point of entry. Local bureaucrats knit society and state together through the war, and many became refugees themselves. Their exchanges with superiors in the distant Ministries of Finance, State Domains, and the Interior make for poignant reading. Though Crimean bureaucrats initially discussed the plight of others, they shared their own tales of survival as the war continued. Thousands of reports from generals, field commanders, intendants, quartermasters, the war minister, and the tsar also prove indispensible for understanding military-civilian policy as well as the flow of war over Crimea.

During the course of many years, I gathered material in multiple trips to archives in Crimea, Ukraine, and Russia. I tried to be as precise as possible when identifying letter and report writers, but this has been no simple matter. Local, district, provincial, and imperial officials in both the civilian and military administrations changed in rapid succession throughout the war. Thus, from 1854 to 1856 three different men governed the territory Catherine the Great named New Russia (M. S. Vorontsov, N. N. Annenkov, and A. G. Stroganov). Another set of three administered Tauride (V. I. Pestel, N. V. Adlerberg, and G. V. Zhukovskii). Leadership of armed forces in Crimea also changed three times (A. S. Menshikov, D. E. Osten-Sacken, and M. D. Gorchakov). Many lower-ranked officers and bureaucrats died during the war. The lucky ones transferred out of the war zone. Officials themselves often did not know to whom they were writing, a problem exacerbated by shockingly slow postal communication. A significant portion of policy appears to have been formulated by interim appointees who remained unnamed. Thus, in the absence of a clear indication of writers' identities, I employ generic titles rather than specific names.

War began in 1852 for Crimea with Russian mobilization. At first, Crimean civilians experienced war nearly the same as in other parts of the empire, as a distant home front. They gave money, time, labor, and material goods to the Russian military. Unlike predominantly Orthodox regions of the empire, however, Crimean Muslim civilians struggled under pressures of holy war rhetoric. Crimea's experience as a home front set the stage for the peninsula's later experience as a battlefield, namely the implementation of martial law, and local performance of international religious conflict.

I

Mobilizing the Home Front

WAR PULLED TAURIDE INTO ITS funnel cloud well before it drenched Crimean shores in blood. Eight months prior to the official declaration of hostilities, Prince M. D. Gorchakov received a secret order to prepare Russian forces for battle. Diplomatic talks between Russia, the Ottoman Empire, and European powers had come to a stuttering halt during November and December of 1852. Multiple issues were at stake. The tsar protested the Ottoman Empire's suppression of Montenegro's bid for independence, and still smarted from lost access to holy places in Ottoman-controlled Jerusalem.

When negotiations broke down, Tsar Nicholas ordered his army to the borders of the empire.[1] War Minister Prince V. A. Dolgorukov sent the Thirteenth Artillery and Infantry to Simferopol where, he promised, "they could be quickly dispatched to Sevastopol."[2] In April 1853, Crimean residents made space for the Fourteenth Artillery in Aleshka.[3] Russian soldiers streamed through the dusty postal roads toward Crimean ports, where they feasted on Tatar bread and drank Tatar wine. There they waited, readying themselves for war.

After months of mobilization and half-hearted negotiation, Tsar Nicholas announced war on October 20, 1853. His manifesto explained that Russia crossed into Ottoman territory "to defend the Orthodox faith in the East."[4] He repeatedly expressed sympathy for Christians living under Ottoman rule and wrote to Prussian king Frederick Wilhelm IV that he waged "war neither for worldly advantages nor for conquests, but for a solely Christian purpose."

He lamented that only Russia fought for the freedom of Christians living in the Ottoman Empire and asked, "Must I be left alone to fight under the banner of the Holy Cross and to see the others, who call themselves Christians, all unite around the Crescent to combat Christendom?"[5]

Debates about the war's origins were heated at the time and remain contested today; then, as now, critics rarely accepted the tsar's statement at face value. Alternative explanations for the causes of the war include Russian and British imperialist designs upon the territory of the Ottoman Empire, nationalist agitation in the Balkans, hawkism, and diplomatic blunders.[6] Still, the importance of religion should not be underestimated.

Religion was fundamental to the causes of the war and to the local experience of the war. Religious disputes over access to and maintenance of pilgrimage sites occupied the central stage of international politics for years, as did the place of Christian minorities in the Ottoman Empire. Orthodox charity networks sprung up to help Greek and Slavic "brethren of the faith," believed to be oppressed in the Ottoman Empire.[7] Once war began, official Russian newspapers latched onto religion to rally support for the war effort, while readers answered with poems dedicated to "Orthodoxy, the Tsar, and the Fatherland." International religious tensions widened existing cracks in Crimean society, splitting the Muslim and Christian communities ever further apart.

Nonetheless, the imperial model held together for a time as Crimea's diverse population echoed performances of patriotism throughout the empire. Martial law, its codes recently rewritten according to the latest theories of military science, organized their generous donations to the war effort. Had military extraction been reasonable, Crimea's precariously balanced society might have survived intact. As it happened, military demands disregarded civilian needs and set the stage for the terrible crisis to come.

Martial Law

The Russian war ministry placed Tauride, and Crimea with it, under martial law (*voennoe polozhenie*) on November 19, 1853. Martial law governed the province until August 7, 1856, nearly a year after the fall of Sevastopol and several months after the April 1856 armistice.[8] In accordance with the 1846 Military Regulation, an imperial order granted Naval Commander Prince A. S. Menshikov the powers of a regional commander-in-chief.[9] Effectively a commander-in-chief for a defined territory, the orders of a regional commander-in-chief (henceforth "commander") superseded those of civilian administrators within his territory. Commanders gave orders in the name of the tsar and had the right to communicate directly with the tsar and the war minister.[10]

The theory of absolute authority ascribed to commanders in the Military Regulation rarely accorded with reality however. Once the war began, Menshikov still had to negotiate with civilians and government agencies to accomplish his goals, while civilian leaders under martial law remained uncertain about new limits placed upon their authority. Further, Menshikov competed with other commanders posted elsewhere for favor of the tsar and resources from the war minister.

The same directive that placed Tauride under martial law gave extraordinary powers of regional command to General D. E. Osten-Sacken for the southwestern provinces of Kherson and Bessarabia. The Russian Senate placed Ekaterinoslav (to the north of Tauride) and Taganrog (to the east) into martial law under the leadership of Don Cossack Hetman General of Cavalry M. G. Khomutov, on February 16, 1854.[11] Khomutov eventually assumed authority over Crimea's shore on the Azov Sea. His territory included the eastern Crimean peninsula: Feodosia, Kerch, and the Arabat Spit.

Given that the war opened over Russian and Ottoman competition for the Danubian Principalities, the tsar and his advisors expected violence to remain localized around what is present-day eastern Romania and southern Moldova. Thus, martial law in Tauride, Kherson, Bessarabia, and Ekaterinoslav through September 1854 principally served to organize food and supplies for the military.[12] Russia's northern and western provinces bordering the Baltic Sea, Austria, and Prussia went into martial law in March of 1854 after it became apparent that France and Britain were entering on the side of the Ottoman Empire.[13]

Real power in the military resided with the war minister, Dolgorukov, in St. Petersburg, who held the tsar's ear. Dolgorukov advised in matters of military policy, general strategy, and supply. General Field Marshal Prince I. F. Paskevich managed the men on the ground. He prioritized areas of defense and advised about placement of forces. Prior to the 1846 Military Regulation, an earlier code in 1836 had divided military command between the war minister in St. Petersburg and the General Field Marshal. The war in Crimea subjected the 1836 and 1846 codes to an acid test, demonstrating among other things the weakness of divided command.[14] During the war, the field commanders and war ministry often worked at cross-purposes and competed for the tsar's attention.

In any case, Paskevich questioned Austria and Prussia's neutrality, and so insisted on keeping the large First and Second Armies on the western borderland. On the active front near Silistra and Varna, Gorchakov headed Russia's southern army (parts of the Third, Fourth, and Fifth Armies). In the Caucasus, Russia had approximately 140,000 soldiers and Cossacks who had been waging a war of conquest against the mountain tribes to fight against the Ottoman army around Kars.[15] Thus, although Menshikov commanded the Russian Navy in Crimea and exercised extraordinary authority in his own territory, he was nevertheless merely a local commander. As such, in the fall of 1853 and spring of 1854, Menshikov primarily organized the flow of troops from Russia's interior through the port cities of Crimea.

A mobilizing Russian army was a city in motion. Officers, soldiers, doctors, cooks, musicians, tailors, wives, and children comprised its vast train.[16] Many of the larger units traveled with their own brothels as well. All of these people needed food and shelter, and the bulk depended upon the military for clothing or equipment, and transportation. Through an elaborate operation, Menshikov extracted resources from local communities to support arriving soldiers.

Food and supplies traveled from civilians to the military through local and imperial provision committees. Before the war, the Crimean capital city of Simferopol was one of six strategic provision sites in the empire.[17] Given its location, Simferopol became a natural distribution point for goods transiting from the mainland through the Crimean port city of Feodosia.[18]

During times of peace, civilian administration ran the committees, which supplied the army posted along the borderlands, and purchased goods in accordance with market prices and civil law.[19] In times of war, the military assumed direct control over provision committees; it could set prices and use *kvitantsii*, or receipts that functioned as "IOUs." Hypothetically, these receipts entitled civilians to reimbursement at some near or later date for goods or services supplied to the military. In the words of Dominic Lieven, the receipts functioned as a sort of "forced loan," which the government repaid at the end of the Napoleonic War.[20] As the Crimean War ground on, however, these receipts became meaningless pieces of paper. In most cases, the military stopped handing out receipts altogether and just took what they wanted from civilians without payment or record.

The Crimean War became the first major test of Russia's revamped military provisioning system in a domestic combat situation. Tsar Nicholas I and his ministers had carefully studied Russia's experience in the Napoleonic Wars as well as other militaries in Europe to construct a state-of-the art military supply chain. Their careful planning supported the military in the smaller colonial wars of Nicholas I's reign well enough. The provisioning system could not cope, however, with the unprecedented scale of war in Crimea. The system's collapse led to the utter exhaustion of the Crimean peninsula and surrounding territories, and ultimately to the surrender of Sevastopol. Shortcomings in the provisioning system deepened burdens upon the local populations already evident during mobilization. Provision committees in Kiev, Odessa, and Simferopol especially struggled to meet the needs of a transient population of soldiers. In the underpopulated and underdeveloped cities of the southern empire, quartermasters likewise encountered difficulty in finding space, whether houses, apartments, or cleared fields, where the commanders and their men could sleep.[21]

Charity and Obligation

While violence unfolded on the sea or distant battlefields, Crimean civilians indirectly experienced war through donation and requisition. At the beginning of the war, the tsar encouraged Russian civilians to donate to the cause and constructed elaborate ceremonies around gifts pouring in from various regions of the empire. Similarly to Alexander I's invocation of patriotism during the Russian campaign of 1812, Nicholas I and his cabinet prevailed upon Russian subjects' patriotism to volunteer money and goods for the war effort.[22]

Russian periodicals like the official St. Petersburg publication *Severnaia pchela* (The Northern Bee) regularly reported donations, as did the military papers *Russkii invalid* (Russian Veteran) and the paper for the navy founded by Commander of the Admiralty Grand Duke Constantine, *Morskoi sbornik* (The Naval Journal).[23] Products of the regime rather than a popular press, these journals were among the only sources of information about the war. Despite tight censorship, subscriptions expanded during the war years as Russia's small reading public became eager for news.[24] In addition to highlighting Russian victories, these journals published correspondence accompanying subjects' gifts to the war ministry. Often published letters expressed the donor's love for "Orthodoxy, the throne and the fatherland" and were followed with a statement of gratitude from the tsar. The tsar's statement typically indicated where the money or material would be spent, whether for wounded soldiers of lower ranks, widows and orphans of military personnel, hospitals, or soldiers and sailors who fought in specific campaigns.

Victories frequently inspired a flurry of donations, especially the Battle of Sinope (November 18/30, 1854). In this pivotal battle, Russian naval forces under the command of Admiral P. S. Nakhimov soundly defeated the Ottoman navy. Inspired by news of the victory, a fish merchant from Yaroslavl mailed a poem to Grand Duke Constantine, along with 25 rubles for "distributing to one or multiple sailors wounded in battle."[25] Russia's destruction of the Ottoman fleet at Sinope motivated France and Britain to enter the war the following spring. The imbalance in the battle was shocking; Ottomans lost more than 1,800 sailors to Russia's 35. More controversial in the European press, Nakhimov inexplicably fired upon civilians in the town of Sinope. Such details were not reported in Russia, which instead celebrated Russia's naval and moral superiority. The Grand Duke sent the small monetary gift to Menshikov and published the poem in his naval journal.[26]

Larger gifts also poured in. Students and faculty members took up collections for orphans, widows, and wounded soldiers. Elite donors sent in varying amounts, from 300 rubles to 3,000 rubles with stipulations for where they would like the money to go.[27] Smaller donations were often applied toward disabled veterans, while the larger donations, such as a gift of 2,500 rubles from an Odessa merchant, were directed toward military commanders for use in the field.[28] Members of the St. Petersburg Yacht Club raised 3,000 rubles and requested that the money be distributed among the lower ranked sailors who served in the battle of Sinope.[29] Beyond helping people in need, these efforts laid foundations for voluntary associations and charity networks following the Great Reforms and through the First World War.[30]

Separate from monetary charitable donations, civilians gave according to obligations assigned to their social estates. As opposed to Western European states with well-developed banking industries and diverse tax bases, Russia devolved military expenses directly to the population. Specific social groups, whether serfs or state peasants, merchants and craftsmen, provided the recruits, taxes, labor, and materials to support Russian forces. As a condition of their rank, nobility served in the officer corps.[31] Russia had followed this system from the age of Peter the Great if not before. In 1812, Alexander I created provincially based regiments raised from the peasants, organized and paid for by the nobility, and equipped by the merchant populations.[32] During the Crimean War, Nicholas I and his war ministry followed a similar pattern of recruitment and funding, framing traditional estate obligations in appeals to patriotism and requests for donation.

At the beginning of the war, obligations were comparatively light. Russia fought only the Ottoman Empire and violence unfolded in an occupied territory rather than within imperial borders. Obligation transpired more in the manner of a strong recommendation or a special tax, and was still cast in the language of donation. Thus, for example, Dolgorukov alerted the Moscow merchants to fund military hospitals. According to reports in *The Northern Bee*, the merchants distributed a sign-up sheet at their assembly for members to pledge contributions. They raised more than 500,000 rubles, prompting the tsar to issue a special proclamation to be read at an elaborate ceremony. On the day of the event, a gilded carriage arrived at the door of the merchants' hall. Accompanied by his footmen, a grandly attired delegate carried the tsar's document on a velvet cushion into a packed room. As merchants listened to the edict granting tax relief in exchange for the "donation," their eyes "shone with sweet tears."[33]

Another example of civilian obligation involved the Tambov nobility's presentation of 500 horses for the cavalry. Functioning as an instructive narrative for other groups, an article in *The Northern Bee* documented the nobility's gift from the beginning to the end. According to the article, the marshal of the Tambov nobility received official notification of need from the Ministry of Interior on November 2, 1853, and so immediately alerted landowners in all districts under his jurisdiction. Through good management and foresight, praised the article's anonymous author, the Tambov nobility managed to fulfill their donation in twenty-eight days.[34] An accompanying vignette depicted patriotic unity binding nobleman and serf in support for the war:

> When the manifesto about war with Turkey was read in the parish churches of the villages belonging to Tambov Province, a large number of peasants gathered around the marshal of the nobility at the end of the liturgy and prayer service. Here he explained to them the causes of the war and donation, how it might help the faithful sons of the fatherland, and added: "If the tsar wished to call up the militia, then I hope that you are not left behind, and that we together go into battle for the Orthodox faith, for the tsar and Fatherland." Suddenly the crowd threw themselves at his feet and cried "We are prepared to leave everything, to go to war wherever the Tsar orders!"[35]

The author of this article concluded, "suffice it to say such examples demonstrate the might of Holy Rus under the Orthodox scepter of our Tsar!"[36]

Rather than portraying Russian subjects as fulfilling defined obligations, *The Northern Bee* transformed the Tambov experience into a donation made willingly for the Orthodox faith and the fatherland.[37] To be sure, many Russians gave to the war voluntarily. The small gift of twenty-five rubles and poem exemplifies an individual moved by patriotism to donate to the cause. However, the other meaning of the term *pozhertvovat'* ("to sacrifice") might be more appropriate for much of the donation that fueled the war. Equally, the state's view of "donation" might simply have been an expectation that subjects would willingly fulfill the obligations assigned to them before they were forced.

Crimeans contributed to the war effort in a similar manner as the rest of the empire. Not foreseeing a long course of war on their own shores, Crimean residents, whether peasants, foreign colonists, or aristocrats, gave deeply to the army that passed along their postal roads en route to the Black Sea. They gave thousands of bottles of wine, countless carriages full of hay and horses to pull them, tons of grain, hundreds of sheep, oxen, and fowl. The Tolstoy estate donated several tons of hay; the Evpatoria nobility donated meat, water, hay, and salt; the Simferopol nobility gave 750 rubles; Armenian merchants in the town of Armenian Bazaar (Armiansk) hosted an engineering division twice for dinner and once for lunch.

Tatars who lived along the thoroughfares and near the transit stations gave tremendous amounts of wine and food, enough to sustain 16,000 passing soldiers. Tatars also contributed physical labor, whether loading carriages or driving wagons. Four Tatars in Melitopol risked their lives to transport soldiers across the river in severe winter weather. Early on, colonists from Melitopol donated 1,000 horses with wagons, and 200 sheep. The Muslim Spiritual Society of Simferopol offered up 460 carriages.[38]

Nogai Tatars in Melitopol and Berdiansk gave among the largest of gifts. Initially they had proposed donating 120,000 bushels of grain from their private stores and community reserves. Their contribution was so substantial it alarmed Kiselev, the Minister of State Domains, who cautioned peasants to keep more for themselves.[39] A long-term advocate for reforming serfdom, Kiselev sympathized with the Nogai peasants who had not yet recovered from the livestock epidemic and harvest failure of 1847–1848.[40] Much to Tauride Governor V. I. Pestel's chagrin (the governor was eager to assume credit for the Tatars' gift), the Nogai followed Kiselev's recommendation and reduced their contribution.[41] Tsar Nicholas I approved the donation, expressing his "gratitude and recognition."[42]

The Tauride governor, who was the brother of the Decembrist P. I. Pestel, adopted the language employed by the tsar to characterize Crimean donation when he boasted to Menshikov in May of 1854:

Residents from all places through which the military passed, forgot their various different provenances and merged together in one Russian family to greet, transport and feed the soldiers. The nobility, the merchants, the citizens, the state peasants, the Russians, the Nogai, the German colonists, outdid one another with overflowing hospitality and eagerness to assist the comfort of the marching soldiers. I smile when thinking that, despite all of its diversity (*raznoplemennost'*) in this circumstance . . . there is not a more purely Russian province in Russia than Tauride.[43]

Whether Crimean residents supported the war effort from patriotic zeal, from obligation, or from feelings of vulnerability (many were Muslims and foreigners in an empire at war), we do not know.[44] Nevertheless, contributing to the war at this stage, while significant, was much less burdensome than the terrible requisitioning that came later.

The Structure of Giving

When talks with Britain and France started to break down, and a prolonged war appeared immanent, the Simferopol Provision Committee tasked with procuring and distributing food for the military enlarged its sphere of activities in the winter of 1853–1854. Along with the existing depot in Sevastopol, several other provision committees formed in key locations in Crimea and northern Tauride, including Karasubazar, Bakhchisarai, Kerch, Perekop, Genichesk, Berislav, Melitopol, and Arabat. Simferopol and its offshoots relied upon a combination of special levy upon the civilian populations and contributions from Menshikov's budget to provide food.[45] From July 1853 forward, local police tracked market prices of grain, and the amount of grain merchants held in reserve. The police also reported transportation costs for moving grain between cities.[46]

Despite careful planning reflected in the military code of 1846 and the earlier code of 1836, the system proved inadequate to manage incoming and outgoing supplies. In the case of the Nogai donation, neither the provision committees nor Menshikov had the wherewithal to transport grain from the Tatars' remote villages in Tauride's northern provinces to Simferopol. Menshikov pushed the peasants to deliver the grain themselves, a monumental undertaking given the costs and pace of travel. The peasants reluctantly agreed to transport the grain up to 160 kilometers (about 100 miles), "for a fair price . . . provided the roads are passable."[47]

As the seasons changed from winter to spring, a new problem arose pertaining to milling. Neither the military nor the Simferopol Provision Committee had the ability to transform large amounts of raw, unrefined wheat and rye into a bread product soldiers could consume. At the end of April, Menshikov requested the peasants mill their grain as well as transport it.[48] Busy with planting and exasperated by yet another demand, the peasants demurred. The Ministry of State Domains interceded again, demanding the provision committee take responsibility for transporting and milling the grain.[49]

By now, Britain and France had entered the war. Extraction of food took on new importance, as did the role of the Simferopol Provision Committee. New waves of recruits for the tsar's army began arriving in the peninsula en route to the Black Sea, and Simferopol had to feed them all. The provision committee proposed establishing additional depots at Berdiansk and Melitopol to serve Cossacks who had been dispersed along the northern seashore under the command of Hetman Khomutov. Any grain not needed by Cossacks could be distributed to stores in Crimea's interior.[50] Mindful of the peasants' obligation to their own farms, Kiselev's agent in Crimea stipulated deliveries would have to wait until October or November, after the harvest.[51] An enlightened bureaucrat who had served in the area from 1851, E. F. von Bradke emphasized that peasants had neither sufficient resources to make their own sacks nor the means to purchase the cloth.[52] In the end, the provision committee hired "sackmen" to provide sacks and haul the grain. Sackmen in Crimea developed a reputation of dishonesty and graft as they later carried in the First World War and the Russian Revolution.[53]

Such problems were endemic for the entire military and grew as the war continued.[54] The military office in charge of logistics, called the intendancy after the French model, estimated supply needs. The chief intendant conveyed final orders through the military general staff to the war ministry. The war ministry in turn interfaced between state and civilians to fund and supply the committees.[55] This set up a triangular process of negotiation between the central government which organized provision, the military who consumed provision, and the civilian population who willingly and unwillingly supplied resources. In practice, the process often resulted in underfunding and understocking of the provision committees, confused channels of communication between all parties, exploitation of local population, corruption in the military intendancy, underfeeding and entrepreneurship of soldiers.[56]

Funding the provision committees also proved challenging. Anticipating the entry of France and Britain on the side of the Ottoman Empire, Dolgorukov ordered Menshikov to assist the Simferopol Provision Committee with supplying soldiers and sailors traveling through Feodosia to the theaters of violence in the Danube and the Caucasus. In other words, Dolgorukov asked Menshikov to maintain the needs of all forces passing through Crimea, when Menshikov operated on a limited budget intended mainly for Sevastopol. By February of 1854, the Simferopol Provision Committee complained to

Dolgorukov that Menshikov had not given them the means to meet their obligations.[57]

After pressure from the center, Menshikov eventually released some 15,000 rubles to the Simferopol Provision Committee, an amount inadequate to purchase butter, salt, wine, vinegar, and beef for the whole of the Black Sea Fleet under his charge.[58] The rank and file suffered the flaws in the system with unabated hunger, and the question of funding the provision committee returned. Simferopol sent in repeated requests to the war ministry's centralized provision department for an infusion of 100,000 rubles to fund the military passing through Crimea, and simultaneously sought monies from Menshikov. At last on June 17, Menshikov wrote to Dolgorukov, claiming he "decidedly did not have at his disposal the kind of funds from which to loan the committee 100,000 rubles." Moreover, Menshikov argued 100,000 rubles fell well short of military needs. He asked Dolgorukov to communicate "with whomever" necessary in order to disburse funds quickly to the provision committee in Simferopol.[59] This awkward triangulation of supply persisted through the war. The chief result was that soldiers turned to the Crimean countryside to satisfy their hunger.

Beyond the provision committees, Menshikov worked with civilian administrators to safeguard local monies and make contingency plans for evacuating local governments in case of attack. As talks with French and British diplomats soured in February 1854, Governor Pestel received orders from the Russian Ministry of Finance and the Governor General of New Russia to closely consider areas under his jurisdiction vulnerable to attack, and to plan as necessary the "transfer of sums, books, and affairs belonging to the bureaucracy of Tauride to a safer place."[60] Menshikov precipitated the order, having heard that Feodosia alone had more than 300,000 rubles in its treasury.[61] While everyone hoped war would not reach Crimea, the civilian and military leaders nevertheless took a first step in preparing for war by evacuating key accounts to Simferopol. From April 1854, local bureaucracies in Evpatoria and Feodosia held only enough currency to conduct business for one month.

Around the same time, Tsar Nicholas I issued an order to strengthen all fortifications in Tauride. Admiral M. P. Lazarev's plans for Sevastopol would have made the fortress among the strongest in Russia. Begun in 1834, Lazarev's ambitious project was never finished and fortifications on the south side of Sevastopol were particularly weak. Aware of Sevastopol's vulnerability, Menshikov had requested additional forces multiple times. In a letter to Dolgorukov, Menshikov stated, "At the present, Sevastopol is the decisive point that will settle the question about our influence in the East."[62] Reluctant to dispatch forces from the Bessarabian border, the tsar ordered Menshikov to improve Crimean roads around Sevastopol and to finish building the bastions.

Subsequently, Menshikov lobbied Dolgorukov for funds to complete construction on Sevastopol fortifications, money that never came. In August, Dolgorukov released some money for labor and materials, but too little came and too late. Sevastopol engineers estimated they needed a constant stream of three hundred carts of stone and sand, along with 1,700 general laborers and 2,000 stone masons to build walls between the third and fourth bastion and fortify the redoubts.[63] The army could easily find general laborers among the local prison population, but finding skilled stoneworkers was a constant problem of the war. Masons were in demand along all of Russia's borders for repairing or expanding forts. The tsar did not concede the need to prioritize Sevastopol until the enemy appeared in Evpatoria Bay (September 1/12, 1854) and then, after the Russian defeat at the Battle of Alma (September 8/20, 1854).

In a similar manner, the tsar ordered Cossack commander Khomutov to strengthen defenses along the Azov Sea. Khomutov lobbied for money and material to fortify the Pavlovsk fortress that guarded the Kerch straits. In addition to increasing the supply of guns in the fortress, Khomutov proposed purchasing a fleet of old merchant vessels that could be sunk between the straits to prevent the enemy from sailing or steaming through Azov waters. Kerch residents raised nearly 30,000 rubles for this project. Money for the ships went into Khomutov's coffers along with a contribution from the war ministry, but the amount, Khomutov later argued, was still inadequate for the number of ships needed to block 4 kilometers (about 2.5 miles) separating the straits. In May 1855, the enemy took Kerch and the Azov Sea without any opposition, a matter that became the subject of an official inquiry.[64]

Orthodoxy and Islam at War

Evolving military and political events spurred the tsar's urgency to restore forts across Russian imperial borders, including those in Crimea. Several conferences over the winter months of 1853–1854 kept diplomats and generals walking a tightrope. Each phase of the talks shifted war plans. In February 1854 General Paskevich wrote his field commanders to prepare for a larger conflict.[65] He predicted the likelihood of the French landing 40,000 men and the British 10,000 men in what is present-day Bulgaria. Altogether, Paskevich anticipated a total of 100,000 European and Ottoman troops arrayed against 66,000 Russians (four infantry divisions totaling 56,000 soldiers and 10,000 cavalry). "Our situation would then already be quite serious," Paskevich concluded.[66]

Moreover, Paskevich feared Austria, as well as Piedmont-Sardinia, might join forces with the British and French.

From the beginning, Russian nationalists met the war with tremendous enthusiasm and cast the conflict in religious terms. Even if A. S. Khomiakov later interpreted Russia's performance in the war as a sign of Russian backwardness, his poetry before 1853 cast Slavic bids for independence in providential terms.[67] The ardently nationalist historian M. P. Pogodin even advocated Russia to take Istanbul, writing: "Here is our purpose—Russian, Slavic, European Christian! As Russians, we must capture Constantinople for our own security! As Slavs, we must liberate millions of our older kinsmen, brothers in faith, educators, and benefactors. As Europeans we must drive out the Turks. As Orthodox Christians, we must protect the Eastern Church and return to Saint Sophia its ecumenical cross."[68] Entrance of European powers on the side of the Sultan only elevated Russian Messianism.

In the poem "Ura!" the Russian patriotic writer F. N. Glinka castigated France and Britain for siding with the Ottoman Empire against not just Russia but all of Christendom. In exchange "for bread and salt, and our friendship," he wrote, "we were given Symbols of the Quran." The stanza continues: "You entered into Turkish service, and abandoned Christianity!" Only the Russian Empire stands "with Christ and for Christ!"[69] Anticipating the West's break with Russia from the first rumors of war with the Ottoman Empire, Glinka had composed the poem in the summer and fall of 1853. Russian censors delayed publication until January 1854, after it had become apparent that Russian talks with France and Britain would fail. Like most patriotic literature of the era, "Ura!" appeared first in the semi-official paper *The Northern Bee*, and then in regional newspapers and pamphlet form.[70]

The Russian Orthodox Church, which had advocated Russian intervention on behalf of Orthodox Christians during the Greek War of Independence in the 1820s, supported the war.[71] Moscow Metropolitan Filaret remarked, "Really, this might be a biblical struggle, a fight of the people of God with the heathens, if only it were less infected with the usual heathens of the West. . . ."[72] Archbishop Innokentii in Odessa, whose see included Crimea, similarly portrayed the war as a crusade, a holy mission ordained by God and Russia's one destiny: "This affair of Christianity, is in the hands not of people, but of God. Russia accepted the challenge, made not in words, but of fire and sword. . . . Millions of our brothers in faith wait, like a holiday, for us to rescue them. . . ."[73] The depiction of the war as a religious conflict between Christianity and Islam appealed to many Russian nationalists, and became a trope of war propaganda. Broadsides, poems, and proclamations emphasized the religious nature of the conflict.[74]

Karl Marx was a regular correspondent for the *New York Tribune* during the Crimean War. His articles covered all aspects of war from parliamentary debates to battles; his portrayal of events left a deep legacy. For Marx, the entrance of European powers on the side of the Ottoman Empire heralded a new, secular age. After having searched carefully for a "purely ecclesiastical view" of the conflict in the European press, he claimed to have found only a handful of pamphlets.[75] Instead, the European masses and their parliaments, like the Mississippi River, "rolled onward a tide of opinion" against autocracy and the old age of religion. He saw the cooperation of Ottoman and European powers as an important step in historical progress, the dawning of a new era in which individual conscience trumped religious authority.[76] Marx did acknowledge the persistence of religious rhetoric in Russia, but he believed Russian elites entered war for economic, expansionist reasons, invoking religion only to manipulate feelings of patriotism among backward peasant masses.[77]

Whether or not Russia's elite believed their own rhetoric (evidence suggests the tsar did), religion made its way into the internal discourse of the war and into Crimea.[78] In June 1854 Menshikov signed his report, for example: "We lay down our lives in a desperate battle for the defense of Holy Rus and her Orthodox affairs."[79] Marx was right: religious nationalism rallied Orthodox believers to support the war effort and comforted Russian soldiers in the battlefield. It also imperiled Muslim subjects of the Russian Empire who happened to live near the primary theater of violence. After France and Britain entered the war, nationalist memory of 1812 became a popular motif in the Crimean War. Russian leaders took pleasure in pointing out that Russia had defeated Napoleon in 1812, and would defeat his nephew, Napoleon III, in 1854.[80] Still, religious motifs of the Crimean War remained salient.

In many ways, the notion of an Orthodox holy war stemmed from the tsar's personal piety.[81] A devout Orthodox Christian, Tsar Nicholas I believed that "the state was to serve God, not God the State."[82] His religious interpretation of state power infused the policies of his regime, demonstrated in the official nationality platform "Orthodoxy, autocracy, nationality," formulated by Minister of Education Count Sergei Uvarov in April 1833.[83] Yet Russia's elevation of Orthodoxy as the religion of state and basis of imperial identity conflicted with Russia's diverse, multi-confessional population. The Crimean War sorely tested Russia's confessional policies and emphasized the contradictions that engaged Russian officials in endless debate before, during, and after the reign of Nicholas I, and which occasionally led to violent suppression of non-Orthodox faiths.[84] Ongoing questions about toleration and assimilation lay at the heart of the problem.

In Crimea, where war eventually settled, holy war rhetoric took a particularly profound toll as the peninsula's majority Muslim population became associated with the enemy by virtue of a shared Islamic faith. Many Russian civil and military administrators located in or near the war zone came to view Islam as inherently violent and fanatical. As in the Caucasus, the spread of anti-Islamic rhetoric in Crimea had terrible consequences including collapse of the uneasy peace between Muslim and Christian populations. [85] Even at this stage of war, when violence remained hundreds of kilometers away, religious nationalism in the Ottoman and Russian capitals resonated on the peninsula.

Muslims in Crimea responded to Orthodox war rhetoric with demonstrations of loyalty to the Russian throne. The spiritual leader of the Muslim population in the province of Tauride, Mufti Seid-Dzhelil-Efendi, led the effort. Catherine the Great created the position of mufti and the Muslim Spiritual Assembly for Crimea after annexing the peninsula in 1783.[86] The Assembly paralleled the Holy Synod, the official governing body of the Russian Orthodox Church established by Peter the Great.[87] Meant to offer religious autonomy in the context of Russian imperial practice, the Assembly incorporated Muslim clerics into civilian administration and invested authority in the mufti, who became the leading Islamic cleric. In addition to supervising Muslim clerics, the mufti oversaw mosques and their *vakif* (non-taxed landholdings), and was responsible for religious schools and other religious Islamic institutions.[88] During the Crimean War, the mufti played an important role liaising between the Russian state and Muslims in Crimea.

Unlike the Orthodox leader, whose allegiance to Russia (as well as that of his flock) was taken for granted by the ruling elite, the mufti realized that an Orthodox holy war placed his Muslim community in a fundamentally awkward position. Crimean Tatars had cultural and historical linkages to the Ottoman Empire. They spoke a Turkic language and their religious practices (while retaining some syncretic traditions reminiscent of Crimea's pagan and Christian past) had much in common with Anatolian Islam. Crimean Tatars had volunteered to fight in Ottoman armies in previous Russian–Ottoman conflicts, while several waves of Crimean Tatars had migrated to the Ottoman Empire in the recent past, including Crimea's former ruling dynasty, the Giray clan.[89]

In January 1854, as most Russians resigned themselves to the inevitability of a protracted conflict, the mufti issued a statement in *The Northern Bee* to all Muslims under his spiritual jurisdiction, later republished in *Russian*

Veteran. Part call for Tatars' allegiance and part demonstration of loyalty for Russian readers, the mufti's words reveal the complex set of pressures upon local Muslim populations living in a Christian state conducting a holy war. Consistently through his statement, the mufti emphasized that Tatars prospered under Russian rule. "If poverty has befallen us," or "illness, hunger, poor harvest," the mufti stated, the tsar "dispatched medicine to heal the ill, released bread to the hungry, even gives us animals for plowing. He defers taxes. What government has such care for its people?" The mufti's praise for the tsar was lavish. The highest praise was reserved for matters of faith. "Christians and Muslims live throughout the globe," the mufti stated, "but only in Russia is there religious toleration."[90] Repeatedly, the mufti referenced the freedom to practice faith. He emphasized that the tsars granted Muslims many rights, the most important of which was to "understand cases according to Sharia."[91]

Multiple, intersecting themes are present here, including the assertion of Tatar prosperity under Russian rule, special privileges granted Muslims, and religious toleration. Some Tatars had indeed created successful lives in the Russian empire, particularly the landed Tatar nobility who maintained or expanded their estates under Russian rule.

Yet, the experience of the landed elite differed dramatically from that of their poor relations. The majority of Tatars on the peninsula experienced a sharp decline of freedoms and status under Russian rule.[92] By the mid-nineteenth century, wealthy landlords had encroached upon small Tatar landholders. Many Tatars had been alienated from their property and lived as strangers in their own lands.[93] Tatars of lower estates and education did not know Russian and did not understand Russian law. They became dependent upon the arbitrary will of Russian landowners and the bureaucrats.[94] It is hard imagine that the mufti was insensitive to the erosion of Tatar status, yet it is possible that the mufti, like many in powerful positions, had been lulled by the complacency of his own and his elite peers' success, or had adopted Russian attitudes toward the lower social estates.

Similarly, the mufti's comments about religious toleration ring somewhat hollow. Although Catherine the Great espoused toleration as a foundational principle, Nicholas I's nationality platform had shifted the balance between Orthodoxy and other religions, and the practice of Sharia in Muslim courts was soon to end. In Crimea, like Kazan, Muslim populations had the right to adjudicate crime committed by members of their own faith communities and administer punishments according to Sharia, or Muslim law.[95] Participation in the courts required an oath to the Quran and the tsar. On the eve of war, some Russian administrators questioned the courts' loyalties and in 1855 they shut them down.[96]

The mufti exhorted Tatars to serve the tsar in the spirit of Tatar mobilization during 1812. Tatars had formed a national militia during the reign of Catherine the Great. Organized by Potemkin in 1784, three divisions headed by members of leading Tatar families protected postal roads, policed the peninsula, guarded the forests and salt lake in Saki. In the Russian-Ottoman War of 1787–1792, six Tatar divisions served in Chernigov; they were disbanded upon Catherine the Great's death in 1796. Later, Tatars successfully petitioned Alexander I to form a cavalry modeled after the Cossack structure. Tatars supplied their own horses and weapons, and selected their own officers. They also operated under Islamic law.[97] In his call to the Tatars, the mufti celebrated the Tatar heroes of earlier eras, including the leaders of the four Napoleonic regiments named after Crimean districts they represented: Balatukov (Simferopol), Khunkalov (Perekop), Abdula Aga Mamaiskii (Evpatoria), and Murza Shirinskii (Feodosia).[98] Here, as elsewhere, the mufti reminded non-Tatar readers, as well as his own followers, of Tatars' history of service to the Russian Empire.

Many Tatars answered the mufti's call, including the Nogai who proposed their gift of grain as an expression of loyalty to the government and from a "desire to fulfill their war obligations and legal demands." Through the spring, summer, and fall of 1854, the Ministry of State Domains' local agent von Bradke had been locked in an argument with the Tauride Governor Pestel about the mood of the Tatars.[99] He repeatedly maintained Tatars were loyal to the Russian throne; Pestel was less sure.[100]

The Crimean Tatar Squadron continued their service to the tsar through the Crimean War. Formed at the end of the Napoleonic Wars, the Crimean Tatar Life Guard Squadron consisted of three regiments. Two regiments served continuously in St. Petersburg, and one reserve regiment was based in Simferopol. The reserve regiment trained locally and relieved members of the Squadron in St. Petersburg upon retirement or temporary leave. The Crimean Tatar Squadron fought on the Turkish border in 1828, and had acquired a building in St. Petersburg in 1846. When war broke out with the Ottoman Empire in 1853, the St. Petersburg regiments defended Kronstadt, while the third reserve regiment in Crimea served under General-Lieutenant Ryzhov.[101] By March of 1854, twenty-two Tatars "of lower ranks" had begun to prepare for their new post in St. Petersburg. In accordance with Russian military policy, Tatar villages supplied their warriors with horses, hay, uniforms, boots, and salaries.

Crimean Tatar nobility, who retained the old khanate titles of bey and murza, similarly answered the mufti's call with a profound expression of loyalty.[102] *The*

Northern Bee and *Russian Veteran* published their statements as well. These Tatar noblemen and community leaders emphasized that their people had lived under Russian rule for seventy years and "had never violated their sacred oath of allegiance" to the Russian tsars. Tatars, they wrote, recognized that their success was due to the generosity of the tsar, and any youth who questioned Tatars' position under Russian rule met with "shame and reproach." Tsar Nicholas I responded to the petitions that he had never doubted the Tatars' devotion.[103]

War changed local landscapes from the first moment of mobilization, even before the declaration of martial law. Transient populations created make-shift living quarters in Crimean villages and cities. War's widening vortex extracted precious food and supplies from Crimean civilians and their northern neighbors in Tauride even as violence unfolded hundreds of kilometers away. In Crimea, army provisioning and religious identities acted upon each other to produce cataclysmic consequences for the Crimean Tatar population.

As a Muslim population, Tatars held "second among equals" status in the Russian Empire. Russian law granted Islam and its adherents toleration, yet official nationalism formulated during the reign of Nicholas I cast Orthodoxy as a core element of what it meant to be Russian. During times of peace, Muslims could prosper in the empire. Many groups practiced Sharia and maintained distinct cultural traditions, while simultaneously adapting certain Russian customs. Resource scarcity introduced by the war quickly exposed the limitations of "second among equals" status.

When the provisioning system collapsed after the war moved to Crimea in the fall of 1854, local Muslim residents who happened to share the same faith as the Ottoman enemy became convenient targets for blame. As Russian forces lost ground to the invaders and soldiers died of hunger, desperate men blamed Tatars for sabotaging war efforts and withholding food. From the imposition of martial law in 1853, when Crimea was merely a distant home front, Tatars felt dramatic pressures from the provisioning system and brewing religious conflict. They responded by making a concerted effort to demonstrate their loyalty to the regime with gifts of money, labor, and grain. Unresolved tensions between the Russian state's religious policy on one hand and the need to mobilize Muslim population for the home front on the other persisted through the First World War.[104]

Finally, the Crimean experience at this stage has much to tell us about the functioning of the Russian government at different levels, the nature of martial law, and the logistics of local operations. Ostensibly, martial law gave Menshikov absolute authority over Tauride. In reality, Menshikov negotiated extensively with other imperial bureaucracies and the civilian population. Nor did he exercise much influence in St. Petersburg. Instead, he lobbied for attention from the war ministry to fund his projects at the most basic levels. Even before the main theater of violence moved to the peninsula, military authority had already broken down, as did the uneasy alliance between Christians and Muslims living in Crimea.

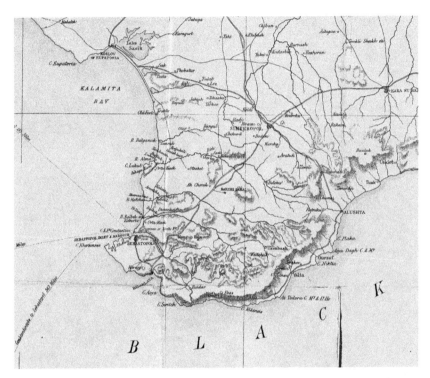

Collin's Complete Map of the Crimea, H. G. Collins, 1854, detail of the west coast. *Courtesy Harvard Map Collection.*

2

Crimea under Attack

ON THE CRISP, CLEAR MORNING of September 1, 1854, a sailor from Tarkhankut arrived in Evpatoria with frightening news of enemy warships following in his wake. His warning gave the people of the town a few hours to make the crucial decision of whether to run or face the enemy. City officials caused widespread dismay when they packed up important documents, gathered their families, and fled.[1] Once the warships had become visible from the shore, Evpatoria's wealthy residents followed suit. As these caravans exited the city, taking horses and wagons with them, they abandoned middling and poor residents to a hostile invasion. They also passed thousands of villagers streaming in on foot from the opposite direction, heading straight toward the danger lurking off the city shore.

British, French, and Ottoman armies disembarked at Evpatoria and nearby Kamysh Bay before proceeding to Sevastopol. Estimates of Allied forces at the time of invasion range from 61,000 to 80,000 men.[2] Menshikov, in contrast, had 37,000 soldiers grouped around Sevastopol. Another 20,000 sailors manned ships and naval bases along the Crimean coast, 5,000 of whom were posted at Sevastopol. To the east, in Kerch-Enikale, the Cossack General Khomutov commanded 20,000 men to protect the straits and the entrance to the Azov Sea.[3] On the surface, these numbers seem sufficient to thwart the Allied landing. However, because Kerch and other fortresses in Crimea such as Kinburn needed protection, only Menshikov's force, which was half the size of the Allied power, was available to defend the southwest coast and Sevastopol.

As a naval city, Sevastopol had reasonably good defenses and a sea-faring population readied for warfare. Wives and children of the sailors manning the Black Sea Fleet and priests who followed them into battle were also more prepared for war than the average imperial subject. If nothing else, they had access to military rations and could call upon military resources for evacuation. East of Sevastopol, the Greek Battalion spread along the Balaklava bay. These Greeks descended from ancestors who had participated in the Russian-Ottoman Wars under Catherine II. In reward for their service, Catherine's erstwhile lover Potemkin had settled the Greek refugees outside of Sevastopol and granted them a military status similar to the Cossacks.

Early on, the Balaklava Greeks had suppressed Tatar resistance to Russian rule. As relations between Russians and Tatars normalized in the first half of the nineteenth century, the Balaklava Greeks worked as border guards and built roads in Crimea. Some volunteered to fight in the Greek War of Independence.[4] On the eve of the Crimean War, the Greek population of Balaklava numbered just over 1,000 men and women. Of those, only 240 were soldiers and 60 were officers.[5] A few had served alongside Cossacks fighting in the Caucasus from the early 1840s. For most, however, warfare was a distant memory grandfathers shared with grandsons. Nevertheless, the Greeks of Balaklava were quicker to adapt to war than the civilian population who lived outside Sevastopol along the eastern and western coasts, and the interior of the peninsula. This diverse population of rural Tatars, Armenians, Jews, Greeks, Russians, and foreign colonists had been left defenseless.[6]

When the invasion came, some residents of Sevastopol evacuated with the help of Tatar cart drivers. Others threw themselves into preparation for war. People who stayed were either directly connected to the military or engaged in the business of war. Soldiers and sailors set immediately to reinforcing the bastions, while merchants began a prosperous trade with the intendancy. Women and children contributed as well, helping in the construction of batteries and parapets.[7]

Virtually overnight, engineers transformed the entire city into a military camp, and as such, its experience has been well documented in Tolstoy's *Sebastopol Sketches* and numerous secondary works.[8] As Russian historian M. I. Bogdanovich wrote in 1876, "Sevastopol will remain in the memory of the people for a long time."[9] Sevastopol has loomed so large in accounts of the Crimean War, many people have forgotten the European and Ottoman Allies landed first in Evpatoria. The successful occupation of the city enabled them to lay siege to Sevastopol. Evpatoria gave the Allies a stable base of operations and a steady supply of goods and food that prolonged the war.

The Allied invasion of Crimea's western coast also exposed major weaknesses in Russia's ability to manage civilian populations during war.[10] Menshikov's evacuation orders focused on local government offices, with a goal of preserving imperial papers and treasuries. In compliance with Russian policy, he ordered local officials and guards to destroy or remove any foodstuffs that might fall into enemy hands. The end result was disintegration of public order in the absence of a functioning bureaucracy, and rupture between some Tatars and the Russian imperial state over food.

The reason that Crimea was so poorly prepared for war has been the subject of much speculation; as commander in Crimea at the outbreak of war, Menshikov became a convenient target for blame. In an age of growing literacy and an evolving meritocracy, Menshikov received his position as head of the Navy based on his noble birth and proximity to the tsar. Sevastopol's Admiral M. P. Lazarev, who unsuccessfully advocated replacing wooden ships with iron-clad steam vessels, described his superior as "not a 'Navy man.'"[11] Others criticized Menshikov for acquiring his knowledge through "studying . . . some books for several months while in the country side."[12] During the Crimean War, Menshikov commanded Crimean army and naval forces, and received numerous commendations, but he had never fought in battle, had never even served as a sailor or soldier.[13] He was, as Soviet historian E. V. Tarle suggests, simply inexperienced.[14]

American Civil War General George McClellan toured Crimean War battlefields in 1855. Witnessing the devastation of Sevastopol first-hand, McClellan anticipated Tarle's point of view: "I . . . can not resist the conviction that the history of his operations will but present another example of the impropriety of intrusting [sic] military operations to any other than a professional soldier."[15] Interestingly, McClellan emerged from the U.S. Civil War with a reputation no less damaged than Menshikov's.[16]

Those who surrounded Menshikov in the summer months of 1854 described him as an apathetic aristocrat, cavalier about the war and unconcerned about the fate of his serf-soldiers.[17] In the months leading to the invasion, Menshikov had received various communications alerting him to the possibility of an enemy siege of Crimea, which Tarle argues he disregarded. It appears, as Sevastopol engineer and war hero E. I. Totleben concluded, that Menshikov "really did not foresee the siege of Crimea by the enemy armies."[18]

Attribution of blame to Menshikov offered his contemporaries an easy, plausible explanation for Russian failure and prevented accusations from spreading out more widely or vertically.[19] The portrayal of Menshikov as a bumbling aristocrat, a symbol of privilege and ineptitude of the Tsarist regime, also served Tarle well, who as an official historian in the Stalinist Soviet Union had to write within acceptable Marxist parameters.[20] To give Tarle his just due, his 1943 depiction of Menshikov can also be read as an excellent piece of dissident writing, as skeptical Soviet readers might have seen in Menshikov's denial of the enemy invasion of Crimea an implicit parallel to Stalin's paralysis in the face of the German invasion of 1941.

Points of the Enemy Attack

The Russian failure to prepare Crimea for war was not Menshikov's fault alone. In the decades before the Crimean War, the Russian government had devoted only a small portion of its budget to the navy, and then prioritized the maintenance of the Baltic Fleet over the Black Sea Fleet.[21] Neither was Menshikov a feeble-minded sycophant. Menshikov openly disagreed with the tsar on naval strategy in the Baltic. When Tsar Nicholas proposed placing small groups of Russian ships along the Finnish and Russian coast, Menshikov dissented, arguing that division would weaken the fleet. He further impressed upon the tsar that Russia's large sailing fleet was no match for British screw-propeller ships.[22]

Tsar Nicholas wrote to Menshikov in June asking for his view of Crimea's ability to withstand an invasion. Specifically, the tsar wanted to know which of Crimea's main port cities of Feodosia, Kerch, Evpatoria, or Sevastopol the enemy was most likely to attack.[23] In an interesting analysis, Menshikov described the characteristics of potential targets, all of which became involved in the war in some way or another and so are worth reviewing here. One of the larger harbor towns in Crimea, with a population of nearly 8,500, Feodosia was the seat of the easternmost district by the same name. Historically an Armenian city with an Armenian monastery and fourteenth-century ruins surviving from the Genoese Republic, Feodosia still had a diverse population of Tatars, Armenians, Greeks, and some Russians on the eve of war. Catherine the Great temporarily made Feodosia her home. Feodosia was, and remains, a showcase Crimean city with museums, vineyards, fountains, and government buildings.[24]

Feodosia, Menshikov wrote, could not be a "foundational foothold" of an enemy attack for although the port had an excellent channel, it did not have a sheltered harbor. Ships would be too vulnerable to Russian canon. The city itself would be very hard take. Feodosia, moreover, had an insufficient water supply to maintain a large force. Menshikov noted that even the Russian garrison posted there had difficulty securing water. Finally, the mountains surrounding Feodosia made any overland effort to join with Sevastopol impossible.[25] Kerch, concluded Menshikov, was a more likely location of an attack.

Located on the eastern peninsula of the Crimean diamond, Kerch sits on a sparkling natural bay. Small peaks along the shoreline offer expansive views of the harbor and on a clear day, one can see across the straits to what is now Taman, Russia, a peninsula that juts out from the mainland located north of Sochi. Together, the peninsulas upon which Kerch and Taman are located form a natural barrier to the Azov Sea. The ancient Greeks recognized Kerch's strategic location and over the centuries had built cities atop its rolling hills. After annexing Crimea, Russia followed in the Greeks' footprint. In the first half of the nineteenth century, Russian tsars granted Kerch the status of *gradonachal'stva,* the name given to a town or city, independent of provincial administration. The *gradonachal'stva* received resources directly from St. Petersburg, and its territory included the surrounding environs. On the eve of war, Kerch had a population of more than 20,000 and one of the more active harbors in Russia's Black Sea border.[26]

"Without a doubt," wrote Menshikov, "it would be more practical for our opponents to try to control this point." From Kerch, he argued, the enemy could break through to the Azov Sea. Still, he pointed out, enemy attackers would encounter several obstacles. Careful generals would avoid any kind of overland invasion between Feodosia and Kerch, as the road connecting the two cities traversed more than 80 kilometers (i.e., more than 50 miles) blocked from view of the Sea by mountains. Every step forward would require battle. Further, Menshikov pointed to General Khomutov's forces in Kerch, writing "to lay siege to such a significant number of soldiers" would be inconvenient and would not permit a sudden disembarkation. The element of surprise would be lost. For this reason, Menshikov advocated maintaining Khomutov's large force in Kerch-Enikale to repulse an enemy attack. He also advocated reinforcing the old Turkish fortress at Enikale, and observed that the requested arms had not yet arrived.[27]

In Menshikov's view, the western portion of the peninsula from Evpatoria to Sevastopol was the most likely target of an enemy attack. He fairly accurately predicted the course of the enemy invasion soon to come. Specifically, he wrote, "The enemy might occupy and fortify Evpatoria, establish a foothold, with a goal to achieve its main objective, namely: *destroying our flotilla in Sevastopol.* This, of course, is the aim of any enemy attack in our region."[28] Yet Menshikov did not believe the Allies would or could abandon their positions in

Adrianople and Varna for an immediate invasion of Sevastopol. Only if Austria were to enter the war on the side of the Allies and occupy the Principalities, in his view, would the Allied forces relocate the 50,000 or 60,000 men necessary for a full-scale attack on Crimea.

Should the Allies wage war on Crimea, Menshikov knew himself to be woefully underprepared. He counted 22,700 bayonets and 1,128 sabers among soldiers and cavalry, and 36 light guns at the batteries. He could also call upon 600 reserve Cossacks. The Allies had every advantage, in numbers, weapons, and choosing a point of attack. Menshikov doubted the enemy would open battle on the Sea. Instead, given "their significant superiority over our forces, [they] will lead an attack on the seashore."[29] He further reiterated that the Allies would not attack Sevastopol directly; it was too well protected. Rather, they would land elsewhere, "in Evpatoria for example," or the bay of Chersoneses, and attempt to flank the flotilla. Sevastopol itself, Menshikov maintained, was sufficiently well fortified to withstand a temporary attack, but not a focused siege from a large army, or a bombardment from the harbor. Under these circumstances, Menshikov delicately asked the tsar for one more brigade in Crimea to protect the shore and balance enemy numbers. Menshikov also asked for two or three additional battalions to be spread between himself and Khomutov.[30]

Menshikov's June 1854 report to the tsar is remarkable for many reasons. Most evidently he clearly understood Crimean vulnerability and could antici-pate an enemy's likely military strategy. From this point of view, the traditional portrayal of Menshikov as a vain, bumbling, and ill-experienced aristocrat whose ineptitude put Crimea on a path of disaster seems in need of revision. Instead, Menshikov's report accurately predicts the flow of war over civilian areas. The attack did begin in Evpatoria. It proceeded overland to Sevastopol and eventually made its way around to Kerch for an assault on towns lining the Azov Sea.

Although (as it turns out) Menshikov produced a fairly comprehensive picture of a potential enemy attack, his was one of many predictions of doom the tsar and Dolgorukov juggled. The tsar feared many potential points of attack along the Black Sea: Anapa and Novorossiisk, Akkerman and Odessa, or Nikolaev. Commanders posted in many different regions in the Caucasus, the Baltic Sea, the White Sea, and the Pacific coast sent in similar reports of impending disaster in the event of invasion. With similar language they requested an additional array of forces. Large by European standards, the Russian army was simply inadequate to manage the needs of the massive borders.

In the 1850s, Russia's army consisted of 930,000 regulars and 240,000 irregulars.[31] Only a very small percentage of this number was assigned to Crimea. Instead, nearly 500,000 men patrolled the interior of the empire; 200,000 men served in the Caucasus, and 300,000 soldiers stayed in the west and the north to protect the lands around the Baltic Sea and Poland.[32] Persuaded by Paskevich of the imminent threat of a Prussian and Austrian invasion, Dolgorukov resisted fortifying the south. Until the death of Tsar Nicholas in February/March 1855, Paskevich's anxieties over an attack through central Europe dominated military planning.[33]

Another reason Russian military analysts failed to appreciate Crimea as a target is that, with few exceptions, Crimea was not then perceived as having any great strategic value. Before the war, most Russians considered Crimea a remote, underdeveloped backwater of the empire. Desert covered much of the northern reaches of the peninsula. Mountains rose from the barren plains and stretched toward the sea, making overland travel impractical. Crimea's arid, rocky soil was inhospitable to agriculture. Its residents engaged mostly in craft industries like hand-woven textiles. A few wealthy Russian landowners had built estates along the shoreline, but these were not so productive as to attract invaders.

A couple of exceptions to Crimea's rural isolation existed, including Sevastopol. By 1829, city registers included nearly 30,000 residents.[34] Before the war, Sevastopol had grown to include a military hospital, several thousand private homes, and buildings for military staff and local government. Still, the citadel that became the focus of the enemy siege was not yet fully purposed. Much of Sevastopol resembled a massive construction site on the eve of war while the main Black Sea Fleet ported in the more established and better protected inland bases on the Bug River at Nikolaev and on the Azov Sea.

Apart from the heavy investment in Sevastopol and Kerch in the 1830s and 1840s, the Russian government allocated a few other resources to Crimea. The New Russian governor general, M. S. Vorontsov, had established viticulture in Crimea as a main industry. More than three million vines grew along Crimean shores.[35] He also funded construction of thoroughfares connecting Simferopol with Yalta and Alushta.[36] Nevertheless, roadworks were still so primitive, and Russian concerns about Crimea so minor, that the government had not attempted any military maps.[37]

Crimea's poor road system prohibited enemy penetration as much as it created obstacles for Russian defense. Preexisting postal roads, some quite ancient, criss-crossed the peninsula and intersected in Simferopol, the provincial capital. Evpatoria sat 62 kilometers (almost 40 miles) to the west of

Simferopol, while Kerch was more than 200 kilometers (about 125 miles) to the east.[38] A slow southern road established by Vorontsov traveled in a semicircular fashion out from Simferopol to Alushta, Yalta, and then east to Sevastopol for a distance of 150 kilometers (93 miles).

The primary access route to mainland Russia stretched from Simferopol in the west to Perekop in the north.[39] Because Perekop was located at the top of the Crimean diamond, at the point in which the peninsula attached to the mainland, contemporaries often described it as the gateway to Russia. The road between Evpatoria and Perekop was one of the most heavily trafficked before the war due to salt mines in neighboring Saki, which supplied the valuable commodity to Moscow and St. Petersburg. Another thin highway traveled the eastern shore of Crimea, connecting the Kerch straits with the district of Melitopol on the Azov Sea.

In the interior, only narrow dirt paths criss-crossed the peninsula. These roads had evolved over centuries through rugged terrain and were principally utilized by Tatar and Greek merchants familiar with shortcuts and eroded trails. Few roads could accommodate more than a single cart, and navigating mountain crags could be arduous.

According to R. A. Chodasiewicz, who fought on both sides of the war:

a Tatar village is one of the worst obstacles that can present itself to the maneuvering of troops, because the streets are narrow and crooked, but chiefly because Tatars and Nogais are in the habit of digging large funnel shaped holes before their houses where they store their grain. These holes are generally covered over with planks and a thin layer of earth, so that cavalry or artillery would be thrown into utter confusion if they were to attempt to advance through a village with obstacles like these.[40]

The American merchant John Codman, who operated in Crimea during the war, noted by November 1854 that it could take a full day to walk 4 kilometers (2.5 miles). Travelers had to pick their way through treacherous clay roads clogged by animals that had died in their tracks.[41] Travel from one town or village to the next located only a few miles apart took longer in carriages loaded with wheat or handicrafts than by foot. At the height of the war, the chief intendant complained of provisions traveling at a rate of half a kilometer an hour, while thousands of troops, supplies, and wagons waited for weeks to pass through the bottleneck at Perekop, the so-called "gateway to Russia."

On the other hand, the same layout served to protect the Russian mainland from an invading army. Enemy armies who occupied and laid siege to

Crimean coastal cities had little chance of crossing rough mountain passes or poorly constructed roadways to access the interior. Thus, after taking Evpatoria in September 1854, or even Sevastopol in September 1855, the Allies never advanced on nearby Simferopol, the seat of administrative power.

Rather than Crimea, Russian military analysts perceived Nikolaev and Odessa as more strategic targets on the Black Sea. Nikolaev was the larger and historic naval base, the center of ship construction on the Black Sea, while Odessa was the southern boomtown. As early as 1818, Alexandre Langeron poetically observed that "Odessa, still in its cradle, is already a flowering city. . . ."[42] With fewer than 2,500 people in 1795, Odessa's population had increased to 35,000 well before Langeron's famous comments, and had tripled by 1848, reaching over 90,000. Only fifty-five years after its founding, it had become the third largest city of the empire.[43] Outside of Odessa and Nikolaev, the war ministry allocated few resources along the expansive Black Sea shore. Mainly Russian forces concentrated in Poland along the Austrian border waiting for a war that never came, and in Bessarabia, the Caucasus, and then to a certain degree the Baltic, where war was actively being fought.

From the beginning of French and English entry into the war, Russian military leaders and war ministers could only guess at enemy strategy. Paskevich assigned the Sixteenth Division to Ekaterinoslav, where it was to stand as an auxiliary force to defend Nikolaev in case of attack. By February, however, Osten-Sacken managed to persuade Paskevich that Odessa was more vulnerable. Consequently, Paskevich ordered the Sixteenth Division to relocate due west, to Voznesensk. From Voznesensk, the Sixteenth Division could march southeast to Odessa or southwest to Bender, in Moldavia.[44] Ultimately Crimea, and not Odessa, needed those men. Perhaps the real problem, as Gorchakov lamented at the end of the year, was the immense Russian border. The more than 30,000 kilometers (nearly 19,000 miles) of coastline, the 20,000 kilometers (about 12,500 miles) of land borders, and the hundreds of cities, towns, and villages presented too many potential targets.[45]

Further, Russian military leaders could not be sure Allied European and Ottoman forces intended to remain at Sevastopol. Instead, Russian commanders debated through the fall of 1854 whether the enemy would set sail for Odessa. Commanders placed in Bessarabia had difficulty shifting their sights toward a different front. Accordingly, Gorchakov suggested to Napoleonic War hero and infantry general A. N. Liders on September 7th that whether or not the Allies were successful in Crimea, they might soon return to the mouth of the Danube or lay siege to Odessa.[46] As the Allies disembarked in Evpatoria, Gorchakov urged Liders to fortify the fortress in Izmail at the border of present-day Ukraine and Romania. As the Anglo-French force launched a cannonade on Sevastopol, Paskevich continued to fear Austria's entry into the war, and a joint Austrian-Ottoman invasion in Bessarabia. Until November 1854, even March 1855, an Austrian invasion seemed quite a real possibility.[47]

Uncertainty over enemy strategy presented a tremendous challenge for Russian military commanders. A careful parsing of debates between Paskevich, Gorchakov, Menshikov, Liders, Osten-Sacken, and others has much to tell us about the challenges of Russian defense, the nature of the war, and the management of Russian military at the highest levels of command, subjects about which we have only the most general impressions in relation to the Crimean War. These debates provide the context for understanding Crimea's underprepared defense.

In early July, Menshikov received intelligence the Allies planned to relocate 50,000 or 60,000 men from Varna to Crimea, with intentions of laying siege to Sevastopol. A cholera epidemic raged in southeast Europe; more men died from the disease in Varna than from battle. The disease traveled to the region with the French Army from Marseilles. Trapped in the Marseillais's quarantine, Codman depicted a city of ceaseless funerals, overcast by gloom and despair. Men fell to their knees in the street, writhing with agony; others fled to the country, where thousands perished under the relentless, scorching rays of the sun.[48]

Cholera derives from a bacteria produced in feces-contaminated water. People infected with cholera painfully pass out of life, sometimes within six to twenty-four hours. Victims experience intense dehydration, severe bowel cramping, waves of nausea and diarrhea. British doctors in Varna chronicled a death rate of 68 percent; nearly three-fourths of the 7,000 men who died in Varna. Twice as many remained in the hospitals, infected with the disease. Most did not to recover.[49] At the end of July several hundred men died daily from the disease. French soldiers erupted into cholera riots, a phenomenon that had occurred in 1831–1832 in London, St. Petersburg, and undoubtedly elsewhere. Fearing he would lose control over his men, Marshal (Jacques Leroy de) St. Arnaud prepared to depart.[50]

Although most observers expected the Allied fleet to move the war to Odessa, including Codman, Menshikov asked the commander of forces in Bessarabia, Gorchakov, to relocate immediately the Sixteenth Division to Perekop along with additional artillery. Gorchakov dispatched the division but proceeded cautiously. Unsure whether the tsar would grant approval, and unsure how Austria would interpret a reduced Russian force, Gorchakov also reinforced Russian forces in Focşani, a small village on the border between

Moldavia and Wallachia.[51] On July 20, Menshikov reported that the large invasion about which he had been warned had not occurred; still, he noted that several ships from the Allied fleet had appeared in Crimea, possibly for reconnoitering.[52]

By August, more signs that the Allies planned to leave Varna appeared, and while Tsar Nicholas began to contemplate Crimea more seriously as a possible location of conflict, he still worried the enemy might instead wage war on Novorossiisk, Anapa, or Abkhazia.[53] At the end of August, Menshikov shared intelligence depicting several disasters striking the Allies in Varna. Reports taken from "two Austrians, two Neapolitans, two Greeks, and one Serbian skipper" who had arrived in Kerch from Constantinople and Varna on separate trade missions gave the same information. A fire devastated the French camp in Varna, destroying two-thirds of the city and the majority of French provisions. In addition to fire, the skippers all confirmed that a severe cholera epidemic cost the lives of thousands of French soldiers and the contagion had spread to Istanbul.[54] Although it was the fire and the cholera epidemic that ultimately led the French and English to leave Varna for Crimea, Menshikov took heart at the Allies' misfortune and hoped the British and French would pass back through the Bosporus and return home.[55]

The April Invasion

Enemy ships appeared off Crimean shores for the first time in April 1854, some five months before the landing in Evpatoria and the subsequent siege of Sevastopol. But even then, military commanders did not plan for war. Instead, they feared more for Odessa, which had been subjected to heavy bombardment. On April 9, French and English ships steamed into Odessa harbor. At 4:00 that afternoon, the Allies informed General Osten-Sacken of siege conditions and presented him with a demand to relinquish all ships. The Russian general refused. At 6:30 a.m. the next day, nine enemy ships, including a 54-gun, opened fire. The poorly armed city returned volley. Cannon and gunfire lasted for twelve hours and resulted in a few fatalities on both sides. Apart from several fires close to the harbor, Odessa itself emerged relatively unscathed.

The Odessa bombardment was important for several reasons. First, it indicated the Allies' willingness to bring the war to Russian territory. Hitherto, the war had chiefly revolved around Silistra, Dobrudja, and Varna, where the Allies had set their main base. Battles proved indecisive, yet men died by the hundreds each day. St. Arnaud, to whom Louis Napoleon entrusted France's eastern forces, in particular argued that the Allies needed a decisive victory on Russian soil.[56]

Second, the ill timing of the bombardment during Orthodox Easter fueled the Russian perception of the conflict as a holy war. M. V. Iuzefovich, a Russian nationalist who later became known for his opposition to the emergence of an independent Ukrainian identity, speculated, "it seems that we stand upon a threshold of a new period in Christianity," a time in which European powers had no respect for the Christian calendar.[57] For many Russians, the bombardment carried indisputable religious symbolism, a point that church publicists repeatedly emphasized.[58] Later, Europeans distanced themselves from the act of war. British Admiral Hamelin claimed that the Russians had opened fire first, and the Allies' return volley was aimed only at Odessa's battery, while "the town, and the mercantile harbor (where were lying a great number of ships of all nations) had been respected."[59]

In this climate of heightened religious tension, enemy ships anchored off Crimean shores. Apart from giving money and goods to the war effort, Crimeans had been bystanders in this war. For most, the war had been something that happened to other people in a land far away. Suddenly, the unexpected had happened, and Crimeans found themselves thrust into an international conflict that had little to do with their everyday lives. Evpatorians lined the jetty, watching as the harbormaster and his agents sailed out to the Allied ship for parlay. One can imagine how frightening it would have been for them to see what happened next: enemy officers boarded the Russian vessel. They took the Russian crew as prisoners, and set the ship on fire.

An eyewitness to the event, an official in the Evpatoria magistrate's office, V. S. Rakov, wrote that the sight of the burning ship signaled to local populations an immanent and terrible invasion. Aware of the Odessa bombardment of several days before, Evpatorians feared their city would be next. People wept openly in the street and scrambled to evacuate. Those on horse rode toward Simferopol. Others left Evpatoria on foot. The poorest of the refugees spent the night in the open road, where they slept under the stars, vulnerable to thieves and other criminals. As it turned out, the panicked exodus proved unnecessary. The Allies did not disembark in Evpatoria, nor at any other Crimean city. Instead, the ships sailed further up the coast to put animals to pasture; the burnt Russian vessel and the imprisonment of its crew constituted the net loss of this April invasion. Evpatorian residents trickled back to their homes, many much the poorer for their emergency evacuation. Inhabitants resumed business as usual.

From April through September, residents in Crimean towns and villages could see enemy ships traveling the shoreline en route to the Caucasus. People eventually became accustomed to the sight of enemy ships to the point of "joking about their recent panic."[60] Although most Crimeans settled back into their routines over the summer, a few government agencies were prompted to consider an emergency plan. On April 18, Menshikov issued provisional evacuation orders.[61] Concerned principally with administrative and treasury matters, Menshikov's evacuation plan required cities on Crimea's coast to remove all treasuries and important court documents to the interior should Allied forces return.[62] Emergency protocol further required grain either to be evacuated or destroyed so it would not fall into the hands of the enemy.[63] Menshikov also assigned a few irregular Cossacks to protect strategic spots along the shoreline.

Menshikov's orders inspired a flurry of exchanges between several Crimean districts and the provincial center in Simferopol. District officials in Dneprovsk, the eponymous capital of the westernmost province in Tauride, asked whether bureaucrats should evacuate with treasuries and their documents, or remain in their posts. The question proved crucial to managing (or mismanaging, as the case may be) the population once the war came to Crimea. Pestel replied to Dneprovsk with a statement that subsequently circulated through the other districts. He wrote, "local officials must stay in the towns at their desks and be occupied with fulfilling their obligations for as long as they can; in situations in which the enemy has already opened military activities, this becomes a matter for the Military Authority and officials should act according to that decision."[64]

Pestel's directive followed the terms of the Military Regulation of December 5, 1846, specifically clauses 20 and 1078 that invested absolute authority in the person(s) of the commander during wartime. During times of peace, according to the military regulation, the commander had neither jurisdiction over civilian governors nor civilian affairs. His only responsibility in relation to civilian authority was to report abuse of power to the tsar. Martial law, in contrast, changed the relationship between civil and military government instantaneously.[65] In November 1853, Crimea had been assigned to Menshikov's command, but the prince had done little to prepare the civil administration for war.

Although meant to ameliorate local anxiety, Pestel's statement introduced new ambiguities. His order for bureaucrats to "stay in their places as long as they can" became subject to individual interpretation, dependent upon the level of risk an individual was willing to take. How to evacuate, and with what resources, received no elaboration. Moreover, Pestel no longer saw himself as the province's highest authority; rather he saw himself as implementing the will of the commander. Yet Menshikov made decisions regarding the local population only in relation to military strategy, and not civilian welfare.[66] Confusion shared between Menshikov, Pestel, and their functionaries was not so unusual in the Russian empire where civilian and military jurisdictions often overlapped.[67] The intensity of violence over the next year placed new strains on Russian bureaucracy in Crimea. The fluid, flexible system that may have worked in times of peace collapsed under the burdens of war.

The exchange with the Dneprovsk district exposed another weakness in the Military Regulation, which did not specify a process for shifting power from one bureaucracy to the other. Thus, as the Allies landed throughout Crimea in September, many local administrators abandoned their posts before the military authorities could fill the void. Crossed lines of communication and conflicting orders plagued Crimea from the moment of the enemy invasion through the end of the war.

Naturally, local officials who read Pestel's circular were not concerned with parsing the whys and wherefores behind the ambiguity. They just wanted guidance. Rakov described his office in despair. In the event of an attack, the office had been told "to evacuate on the road to Perekop, with all files." Yet, they were also ordered to conduct business as usual. "Receiving such a line of orders," he wrote, "we did not know to whom to turn for good advice, as it seemed to us the sheep were being tossed to the wolves." Without clear leadership and direction, he and the magistrate secretary decided "to pack up boxes and be completely ready to evacuate."[68]

From July, with enemy warships sailing and steaming along the Crimean shore with greater frequency, the Tauride administration revisited the question of evacuation, this time debating measures for people living in coastal areas presumed the most vulnerable to attack. Some Russian administrators in Crimea questioned whether the "appearance of Turks . . . among the Muslim population" might test loyalties and so proposed relocating coastal Tatars into the interior. But officials remained "completely divided in manner of thought" on the issue, and so delayed a decision. The Ministry of State Domains opposed relocation on multiple grounds. Primarily concerned with peasant welfare and maintaining domestic order, ministers also cautioned against disrupting agricultural production during war.[69]

The degree to which the general Tatar population knew of government schemes remains unclear. Certainly some Crimean Tatar landowners occupied positions in local bureaucracies and so would have been aware of debates surrounding mass relocation. A few Tatar servants may well have turned their attention to conversations that involved the fate of their people as well. However it happened, rumors spread from Yalta to Evpatoria during the late summer of 1854 that the Russian government planned to relocate coastal Tatars.

The September Invasion

After months of stalemate between Allied and Russian forces on the western shores of the Black Sea, St. Arnaud again sent ships along Russia's Black Sea coast to research potential siege locations. Crimea had been one of many proposed locations for attack; Napoleon III desired to move the war to Russian shores, while British officials wanted to test the Navy's new state-of-the-art steam fleet against Russia's star fort at Sevastopol. Vastly overestimating the fortress as the bastion of Russian power in the south, an article in the *The Times* advocated Sevastopol's destruction as early as June.[70]

The French military historian César de Bazancourt, who accompanied the Allied expedition, similarly inflated Crimea's strategic value for his readers: "The Crimea, by its almost central position in the Black Sea, commands at once the shores of Asia, the mouths of the Danube, and the entrance to Constantinople from the Bosporus."[71] As the crow flies, Crimea is located 500 kilometers (310 miles) from the Danube. It is 600 kilometers (nearly 375 miles) from the Bosporus, while the nearby Georgian coast could hardly be counted as the "shores of Asia." Typically ignorant of the lands beyond the Elbe, many nineteenth-century French and British readers would have accepted Bazancourt's embroidery at face value. Exaggeration of Crimea's strategic value justified the attack and may have masked the Allies' decision to leave Odessa in peace, a city with heavy British investment and a large aristocratic French enclave.[72]

When fire devastated Varna in August, St. Arnaud at last committed to decamp. The departure was abrupt; the French and English still knew very little about the northern Black Sea coastline. "This grandiloquent expedition to the Crimea with six hundred ships and sixty thousand soldiers, with three siege trains and nobody knows how many fieldpieces, instead of being the deliberate result of skillful movements, prepared scientifically long beforehand," wrote Karl Marx for readers of the *New York Tribune* in October 1854, "is nothing but a hurried *coup de tete* undertaken to save Leroy Saint Arnaud from being massacred by his own soldiers [during the cholera riots]."[73]

Ships steamed from Varna toward Crimea at the end of August.[74] Timothy Gowing, a sergeant-major of the Seventh Royal Fusiliers described the awe-inspiring sight of 800 ships charging across the Black Sea: "Each steamer towed two transports; a part of the fleet was in front, a part on either side, and part behind us . . . it seemed as if no power on earth were capable of stopping us." For Gowing, the voyage was "truly a source of delight to the proud and war-like feelings of a Britain." In his world above deck, colorful regimental flags festooned the ships, and flapped loudly in the wind. Military bands played marches and national anthems. Gowing's memory contrasts starkly with Lady Duberly's record of groaning cholera victims rolling in her ships' fetid holds.[75] It took the flotilla about a week to reach Crimea, and another few days scouring the coast between Sevastopol and the Tarkhanut Peninsula to decide where to put anchor.[76]

On September 1, 1854, Menshikov sent the tsar an ominous dispatch announcing the beginning of the war in Crimea: "The enemy navy on this day approached the Crimean shore and now is in view of the bay with 106 ships. On this date, there is no doubting they are planning to disembark, but the place of siege is still not determined. Our military meanwhile is concentrated on the space from Kacha to Alma."[77] After months of waiting and speculation, fears of an enemy invasion in Crimea had come to pass, and it soon became clear that the enemy intended to take Evpatoria first as Menshikov had predicted.

When the Allies sailed their first ships into Evpatoria's harbor the majority of city residents did not immediately flee as they had done in April, but stood in their balconies and clambered on their roofs to get a better view.[78] Having been accustomed to the sight of enemy warships off their shores, and remembering the needless expense and difficulty of the April evacuation, many people were hesitant to pack up and flee a second time. Crimean Tatars from the countryside poured into the city and thronged the streets and quay waiting for the ships to arrive. By 2:00 p.m., Allied ships crowded the bay, masts rising out of the water like trees in a forest. Riggings clanked as seamen took down sails. Smoke from the steamships filled the air.[79]

N. Mikhno, a civil servant placed in Simferopol, recalled a similar reaction in the provincial capital. Hearing rumors that the Allied flotilla had anchored up and down the western coast, Simferopol residents ascended a nearby mountain in Bukhta. From the peak, residents saw vast plumes of smoke spiraling from the enemy ships moored off the seashore, which at the closest point to Simferopol was only about 40 kilometers (25 miles) away.[80]

In Evpatoria, curiosity gave way to anxiety as the enemy flotilla grew ever larger, and villagers arrived from the countryside. During the April invasion the Muslim and Christian population had fled together. By September, the sense of common purpose had evaporated. Christian observers commented that Tatars milling in thousands on the quay appeared energized, rather than fearful, at the prospect of an Allied landing. In contrast to the invasion in April, "Now was the opposite; from all districts [Tatars] crowded to hurry to Evpatoria where they happily met their co-religionists."[81]

Rakov writes of a growing division between Muslims and Christians: "At this time on the jetty of Evpatoria, literally the whole city began to gather, young and old, and Jews and Russians, and Karaim, and Greeks of all estates were here." The Tatars, he wrote, "composed a separate, entire large group. . . . They stood, whispering among themselves and vigilantly looking around." That they were there to conspire with the Allies, he argued, "could not have escaped anyone, so that in the end, residents became more frightened of them, than the enemy."[82] Evpatoria's city police force, composed of Muslims and Christians, struggled to keep order on the quay, efforts at dispersing the crowd having failed.[83] While he did not remark on the mood of the mob, an officer in the British headquarters staff, Lt. Col. Somerset John Calthorpe, noted that an "immense crowd" had gathered on the jetty.[84]

Around 5:00 p.m., two enemy officers with a translator disembarked on the quay. Silence settled over the throng as people strained to hear the translator read a proclamation announcing the intention to take over the city. The proclamation assured residents they would not be harmed if they remained in Evpatoria. A Cossack commander and the harbormaster were the highest-ranking officials in Evpatoria following the city administration's evacuation. They pushed through the crowds to greet the delegates.

They confirmed through the translator the Russian military did not have forces posted in Evpatoria to oppose the enemy invasion. Evpatoria, they repeated, was left at the invaders' mercy. When the delegates returned to their ships, the villagers returned to their farms. Residents brooded late into the dark night, pondering their fate at the hands of the enemy and debating whether they should stay or go.[85] Remaining city officials, meanwhile, sent a courier to Simferopol to inform Pestel that Evpatoria had been taken.[86]

The Cossack commander followed standing orders to transfer his men to Simferopol in the event of an invasion. Knowing the light guard was insufficient to defend Evpatoria from invasion, Menshikov did not want his men, horses, and weapons falling into the hands of the Allies. At dusk, the Cossacks gathered in Crimean markets and bought all the fruit, bread and other supplies they could carry. They should have fulfilled Menshikov's orders to remove or destroy the grain, but they did not have enough wagons; the city administrators who had evacuated earlier in the day had commissioned them all.[87] Neither did they have enough wagons to transport wounded soldiers convalescing in Evpatoria's hospital, and so left behind thirty-eight Russian soldiers who could not walk under their own power.[88] The hospital administrator similarly hurried to leave Evpatoria, and made no provisions for the wounded and the ill entrusted to his care.[89]

It is in this manner that civil and military authorities quickly, and in the judgment of many Russians, selfishly and cowardly, abandoned the city. They took with them all the wagons they could muster and food they could buy in the market. The militia, the hospital staff, the city magistrate, the district court, and eventually, the last of the local police, left Evpatoria. Without having had clear procedures, they dispersed in confusion.

Some offices relocated to Perekop and Armenian Bazaar in the north, and others established themselves closer to Simferopol in the west. For days authorities had thought the magistrate's files had been lost, only to discover that the secretary had funded their removal to his mother's estate in Aleshka for safekeeping. When Evpatoria officials arrived in Perekop and Simferopol, they found those cities empty of local authorities, who had evacuated elsewhere.[90] Religious figures such as the priests, the rabbis, and the *khatibs* were among the few local authorities who stayed to help civilians.

In the wake of the authorities' departure, it seemed to many that those with privilege left behind the poor and the weak, sending waves of anger through the city and through the peninsula.[91] In reality, many of the civil servants who left Evpatoria, Perekop, and Simferopol did so at the orders of governor Pestel. Pestel had written to the New Russian General Governor N. N. Annenkov (who had taken over from Vorontsov in March 1854) that he had ordered evacuation of files and treasuries in areas located within a 25-kilometer (15.5-mile) radius of the enemy landing.[92] After the war, the Russian Senate investigated Pestel for dereliction of duty; Pestel claimed in defense he had merely followed Menshikov's order to remove critical personnel, "files and papers, as well as monies with documents and books . . . to a safer place."[93] Moreover, the bureaucrats of Simferopol had returned by September 11, as soon as it became apparent that the French and British did not plan to advance on Simferopol.[94]

Civil servants as a rule evacuated themselves, their families, and often their departments without any support from the imperial government. Most continued in their jobs either remotely or in place without pay for the duration of the siege of Sevastopol. Low-ranking Crimean civil servants especially bore the brunt of the war. Along with the poorest civilians, they suffered through cholera epidemics and hunger. They were plundered or killed by raiders.[95] Thus, while civil servants became targets of criticism during and after the war, they were themselves victims of violence.[96]

The military followed a similar laissez-faire attitude toward civilians elsewhere in the empire during the Crimean War. In Kola (Mumansk), for example, the local military commander requested artillery for batteries and gunboats to defend Archangelsk but received instead 100 antiquated muskets. With too few men and supplies, the commander ordered Kola's inhabitants to prepare their own defense, and to "think for themselves what ships may visit them and what could prevent them from repelling the unwelcome visitors."[97] British forces set fire to Kola in August of 1854 and burned it to the ground, along with many cities along the Crimean coast.

During the first few days of the siege in Evpatoria, only a handful of low-ranking civil servants remained to keep the peace with an invasion unfolding. These state servitors, many of whom were Tatars as well as Russians, were drastically understaffed with no supporting justice system, nor police chief. In the dawn hours of September 2, Evpatorians woke up to an eerily quiet city. Residents representing all of Evpatoria's diverse population, Tatars, Russians, Greeks, Armenians, and Karaim, strolled empty streets taking stock of available foodstuffs. In hushed tones, they discussed their futures with those who remained.

At noon, a British admiral, two other officers, and a translator disembarked and called upon the local authority. This time, he spoke with Feodor Kostiukov, a local ranking bureaucrat in the police department. The admiral demanded of Kostiukov that residents provide the Allies with local currency, several thousand loaves of bread and several hundred sheep. Kostiukov handled this delicate moment as well as he might. He deflected. "I am a minor *chinovnik*," he said, "without authority to fulfill demands of that magnitude." In any case, he told them, Crimea's terrible harvest the previous year meant stores were empty. His hands, he said, were tied.

Unconvinced, the British admiral asked Kostiukov to call up shopkeepers and bakers from the vast crowd of spectators. Kostiukov dutifully consented. He turned to the crowd, and purposefully asked the merchants to cooperate with the desires of the admiral, while (according to the local priest whose memoirs record this moment) giving them secret signals to resist. The merchants, the majority whom were Tatars, threaded through the spectators and entered into careful discussion. After pausing to consider the request, or at least giving the appearance of considering how the request might be fulfilled, the merchants concluded it was impossible.

Having dismissed Kostiukov in disgust, the admiral called upon the local priest, and finding little satisfaction there, located the harbormaster who had handled the first day's communication. The harbormaster reiterated

Kostiukov's response, but with a harder line. "We cannot enter any kind of agreement with the Allies," he said, "without informing our authorities. Equally we cannot open such conversations with people on these subjects and we do not have the right." Furthermore, he emphasized the effect of evacuation. "All people have left and the city is empty," and "therefore in Evpatoria, you will not find any kind of provisions. Take the city if you want, and if this is what you do, then the remaining residents will leave." He reiterated the point: "Do what you wish, but you will find in Evpatoria only empty homes."[98]

While the harbormaster engaged the English officer, Kostiukov made a last effort to fulfill Menshikov's standing orders to destroy stored grain with water. In April 1854, Evpatoria had a reserve of more than 480,000 bushels of grain. Following Menshikov's orders of April 18 that grain "belonging to private people in the event of an invasion of the enemy military should be quickly removed from Evpatoria or destroyed," some grain had already been transferred to Simferopol's Provision Committee. However, more than 180,000 bushels remained in the coastal town, as there were too few carriages available to transport the remainder.[99] Thus, Kostiukov rounded up a small number of the civil servants and about eighty day laborers, hired transportation, and set out to destroy the grain.[100]

In an effort to satisfy the demands of the military, Kostiukov unintentionally ignited a wave of panic. Weather conditions had indeed produced a poor harvest in the summer of 1854, while Evpatorians had already given generously to the Russian military along with the rest of the peninsula the previous spring. Consequently, the people who were too poor to evacuate were also particularly dependent upon the community supply of grain.[101] British staff officer Calthorpe had reported upon his arrival in Evpatoria that "the inhabitants were badly off for food, and the Tatar population almost starving."[102] Without the grain, many would not survive the winter. As rumors of Kostiukov's intention to spoil the grain spread through the town, resentment toward Russian administrators surged. Before Kostiukov could execute his plan, a band of Tatars supported by enemy infantry seized him. They took Kostiukov's crew, including Tatar and non-Tatar civil servants and local police as prisoners, eventually sending them to a prison in Istanbul.[103]

Kostiukov thus became one of Crimea's first prisoners war, while Menshikov's critics blamed the prince for allowing a large quantity of grain to fall into the hands of the enemy, or, as one man put it, to "to give [the enemy] the gift of a guarantee of 60,000 army provisions for four months."[104] Kostiukov survived the war and returned to Crimea in the fall of 1856. One of his first acts as a reinstated civil servant involved presenting the Ministry of Internal Affairs a carefully itemized expense report detailing the money he spent in his thwarted efforts to spoil the grain, in total, 172 rubles. More than twenty-five people, including various government officials, a rabbi, and local Greeks, signed Kostiukov's statement.[105]

Throughout the war, civilians of all ethnic and religious backgrounds came into conflict with the Russian government over the grain policy. In December, after the Russian government had restored some semblance of order on the peninsula, it had begun to investigate alleged crimes of the local population, including the failure to destroy or transport food that could fall into enemy hands. Thus, for example, the Yalta district court reported that an Evpatorian from the Karaim population, Scholem Babovich, had a large amount of grain stored in Alushta and Gurzuf "but has not done anything demanded of him." With sailors on enemy ships threatening to disembark, the Yalta commander fretted that the "enemy could at any moment use the provisions of wheat," and demanded that Babovich be tried as a criminal. Babovich's defense survives, and gives important insight into the problems faced by civilians. "This last year has completely ruined me," he wrote, and "this grain consisted of my last means of support." At the time of police inquiry, he was located in Simferopol, in the grip of typhus. Without means of transporting the grain and without compensation for it, he argued that he would be completely impoverished.[106]

Neither Russian civilians nor military officials were equipped to save the food for use of the military, much less the civilian population. "Apart from one company of Cossacks, there are no militia available to move such a large amount of wheat," the Yalta officials worried. Rather than destroying the grain, as Kostiukov had attempted in Evpatoria, the Yalta officials offered it to any person who had the means to collect it. Several different people in January, including merchants, villagers, and people of Greek, Russian, and Tatar heritage, carted off the wheat in small quantities. The sensible handling of the grain, distributing it rather than destroying it, may have gone far in preserving fragile civil peace in Yalta. As for the Karaim merchant, Russian thinking had changed after the conclusion of war. Once treated as a criminal, Babovich's case was transferred to a war relief committee in Odessa, where sympathetic authorities considered compensating him for his losses.

Other areas of Crimea were not so fortunate in keeping their grain stores. The Crimean population of all ranks and ethnicities continued to resist demands to destroy grain as the war continued.[107] In 1855, the peninsula plunged into a massive substance crisis, but food had already become the wedge between the Russian military and the civilians.[108] In Evpatoria, where the local government evacuated and the Cossack guard emptied food and supplies from local markets, it is no surprise that some Tatars sought help from the Allies to ensure survival. Following Kostiukov's arrest, the last remaining police officials waited until night to escape "further into the steppe."[109]

Evpatoria remained under Allied control from September 1/13 through the declaration of peace in March 1856.[110] Russian forces attempted to liberate Evpatoria only once, in February 1855, in a storm that failed dramatically.[111] Many residents, Tatars and non-Tatars, decided to not to evacuate, choosing instead out of necessity or desire to weather the war in their homes. Rakov survived the war by moving between Evpatoria, Simferopol, and his nearby family estate at Mairyk. His memoirs do not provide too much detail about life in Evpatoria after the first days of the enemy invasion, but he does suggest that residents slowly adapted to enemy occupation. For example, a local woman married a Polish officer who served the Allies. She used her personal connections to secure good treatment of war prisoners.[112] We also know from British staff officer Calthorpe that the Allies carried cholera with them to Evpatoria. Dozens died from cholera on the ships en route to Evpatoria, and the disease spread rapidly through the civilian population.[113] By October, a cholera epidemic swept through the Tatar population, with death tolls due to disease, deprivation, and starvation rising into the hundreds.[114]

Of greater concern to Russian authorities than civilian health or ill treatment at the hands of enemy forces was the question of Tatar mutiny. Following the Tatar break with Russian authorities over the grain, rumors of the Allies inciting Tatars to insurrection circulated the peninsula. Refugees flooding into Simferopol and Perekop brought news of Tatars ransacking Russian estates, blocking roads in and out of Evpatoria, and providing Allies with food and other resources. Chaos erupted in the spaces bordering enemy-occupied zones. Criminals roamed the countryside, as vigilantes punished the innocent.

"A Panoramic View of the Principal Forts & Towns on its Shores, the Peninsula, Town, & Straits of Kerch, & the Whole of the Seat of War." *Stannard & Dixon*, 1855.

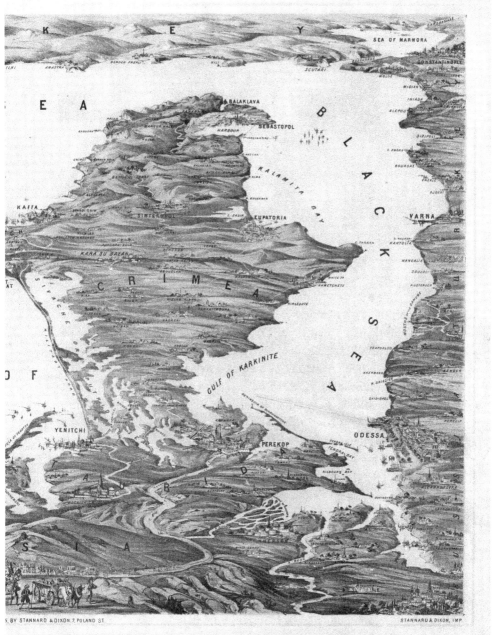

RES, THE PENINSULA, TOWN & STRAITS OF KERTCH, & THE WHOLE OF THE SEAT OF WAR,

ISTHMUS & TOWN OF PEREKOP, THE MILITARY ROAD ACROSS THE PUTRID SEA.
RABAT & ANAPA, & EVERY PLACE OF NOTE & INTEREST IN THE BLACK SEA & THE SEA OF AZOF.

3

Tatars and Cossacks

AS THE ALLIES DISEMBARKED IN Evpatoria, the large Russian army remained several weeks' march away near the far borders of Bessarabia. Russia's aging Black Sea Fleet was no match for British and French steamships; it could neither meet the Allies in the open water for battle nor risk sea transport of soldiers.[1] Despite being woefully outmatched, Menshikov felt he had little choice but to confront the Allies to prevent their penetration into Crimea's interior. On the banks of the Alma River, a force of 55,000 French, British, and Ottoman troops squared off against 35,000 Russians. Russia, in the words of British cavalryman George Paget, "was utterly licked."[2] As it turned out, the Battle of Alma (September 8/20) was bloody for both sides, resulting in 5,845 casualties for Russia and 4,300 for the Allies. Paget's superior officer was less sanguine, reflecting "another such victory, and England will not have an army."[3] Nevertheless, the Allies' performance at Alma opened the march on Sevastopol, and it was evident to everyone in Crimea that Sevastopol was not prepared.[4]

After Alma, Allied troops traveled south toward the naval city, crossing the rivers Kacha, Belbek, and Chernaya, and the Tatar farms and orchards that lay in between. Chaos gripped the civilian population living on the western half of the peninsula. Simferopol absorbed refugees from the areas on the coast under attack. People living in Simferopol panicked, and hurriedly prepared for a fast exit from Crimea. People feared the worst from the invading armies: plunder, violence, rape. In the hours after defeat, civilians rushed markets for food and

transportation to aid evacuation; their desperation caused prices to rise exponentially within hours. In one day, currency lost half of its value, and the cost
of a closed-carriage ride to Melitopol rose to 200 rubles, or a full year's salary
for low-ranking civil servants.[5] More crowded open wagon transport cost 100
rubles. Only the very wealthy could afford emergency evacuation.

At 7:00 a.m. on September 10, refugees and residents met in the city square
for the long march out of Crimea. Three hours later, thousands of civilians
thronged the road leading away from the city. Some rode in carriages, but most
walked on foot. Dogs barked at bleating sheep and lowing cows, the animals
contributing to the din of loud, nervous jabber and the creak of wagon wheels.
Bands of armed men, some Cossacks and gendarme agents, others reserve militia, marched at the head and tail of a several-kilometer wagon and pedestrian
convoy. By noon, Simferopol was deadly quiet; only the very poor and very
stubborn remained, governed by a skeleton organization of low-level police
officers and non-essential government personnel.[6]

Amid panicked evacuation, rumors of the Tatar insurgency were particularly
acute, as Russians speculated about the size of the mutiny in Evpatoria and
the source of discontent. Many Russians blamed the Tatar rebellion on Islamic
fundamentalism. Locals began to use the terms "Christian" and "Muslim"
interchangeably with "Russian" and "Tatar," a conflation often found in
church correspondence before the war, but not usually in civilian or military
documents. Rumors flew through Crimea that the Ottoman Pasha told local
Tatars to round up all Christians to be killed.[7]

Residents who lived alongside each other for years did not know whom to
trust. Widespread violence and theft swept through town and country.[8] Roving
bands of criminals plundered landed estates and harassed travelers on major
thoroughfares. Murder rates soared; two Karaim merchants were murdered in
the countryside near Yalta in September.[9] All the while, Allied blockades cut
Perekop off from Evpatoria, Simferopol, and Sevastopol. Convoys of artillery,
clothing, and food destined for Sevastopol waited outside Perekop, as roads
remained impassable.[10]

Chaos in western Crimea was further compounded by Menshikov's decision to move all military support to Sevastopol and surrounding access points,
Pestel's decision to evacuate the government from Simferopol, and the local
administration's decision to leave Evpatoria. For two weeks, the highest Russian
authority in the western peninsula was the army's postmaster, V. I. Charykov,
stationed in Perekop. Finally, the Russian government, which was slow to accept Crimea as the new front of the war, assigned irregular Cossack forces to
patrol civilian areas. Arriving in Crimea from fighting Muslim tribes in the

Caucasus, Cossacks resorted to the brutal tactics they used in fighting the so-called Lion of Dagestan, Imam Shamil, and his guerilla forces.[11]

As the Allies made their approach to Sevastopol, distrust and uncertainty over who was the enemy ruled western Crimea. Cossacks had not been given clear orders or even sustenance from the Russian military and so unleashed a terror campaign among local villages. They plundered the estates for provisions, beating and arresting Tatars who protested. Many were deported to Russia's interior with neither a trial nor a word to their families. Allied forces that were camped in Evpatoria, meanwhile, pressed civilians living along battle lines ever more for supplies. Ruin of local inhabitants grew at an exponential pace. For those civilians who remained trapped in the crosshairs of war, Crimea became the place of suffering, of punishment, and of the dead.

The Tatar Mutiny

Russians began to speculate about the "mood of the Tatars" from December 1853 when rumors spread of a French emissary promoting a holy war against Russia. Several months later, a German newspaper published an account of an Ottoman agent attempting to incite Tatars to a national or religious rebellion. Ottoman officials had assiduously avoided holy war rhetoric given its alliance with Western powers and denied the allegation.[12] Instead, as historian Candan Badem has pointed out, some Ottoman clerics depicted the war as a *jihad* against Russia.

In September 1853, more than thirty Ottoman religious leaders submitted a petition to Ottoman officials that repeatedly referenced the Quran. They urged waging *jihad* and chided the Sultan for taking counsel from French and British advisors.[13] Ottoman and Crimean merchants were frequently in each other's ports for trade before the war; it is not hard to imagine that the *ulema*'s statements found an audience among some Crimean Muslims living on the other side of the Black Sea. Moreover, the Tauride mufti's caution in January that "idiotic thoughts are punished by God, idle words are punished by the Tsar," suggests that a few Tatars may have expressed sympathy with the Ottoman Empire or otherwise may have murmured disobedience.[14]

Before the Allies landed in Crimea, they attempted to reach Muslim groups of the Caucasus. British agents in particular aimed to draw Shamil into a holy war against Russia, while Bazancourt lists a delegation of fifty Circassian chiefs reviewing the French camps in Varna in July. Wary of unfulfilled promises and Westerners who manipulated Islam for political purposes, Shamil and his Circassian deputy Muhammad Amin avoided the Allies, choosing instead to

concentrate upon their own anticolonial struggle. Unfounded fears of collaboration between Circassians and Allies nevertheless fueled speculation about
Crimean Tatars.[15]

Rumors of a French emissary in Crimea may have had some element
of reality, for the French had recruited Mussad Giray, a descendant of the
Crimean Tatar ruling dynasty. The Giray clan had ruled Crimea for centuries
prior to Russian annexation, and had fled to the Ottoman Empire at the end
of the eighteenth century. For the following decades, the Girays served as
administrators for the Ottomans in the Balkan Peninsula and entered into
military service. At various times, the Ottoman Empire formed regiments
and cavalries from Crimean Tatar émigrés. Crimean Tatars fought against the
Russian Empire under the Ottoman flag in the Napoleonic Wars, the Russian-
Ottoman War of 1828–1829, and again in the opening of the Crimean War.[16] In
this way, the Crimean Tatars followed a pattern established by Greek, Serbian,
and Bulgarian nationalists who joined Russia to fight against the Ottomans in
the many Russian-Ottoman Wars.[17]

Mussad Giray himself was stationed in Varna when the war between
Russia and the Ottoman Empire opened. According to Hakan Kırımlı, Giray
persuaded the French to allow him to foster a Crimean Tatar rebellion. Within
a week after disembarking, the French dispatched Mussad Giray back to the
Balkans, considering his job complete. They praised Giray for his efforts, and
after the war, the French awarded him with a medal.[18]

One memoir of the Allied invasion of Evpatoria describes Allied agents
circulating through the cafes and calling Tatars to stage an uprising against
Russia.[19] The Allied regime announced Evpatoria's independence from Russia
and promised protection to civilians who assisted them. They appointed a guard
from local men who principally blocked roads leading out of Evpatoria.[20] The
British staff officer Calthorpe mentions having a "Tatar spy" on board, while
Lord George Paget, who landed in Evpatoria at the beginning of September,
described Tatars approaching ships to sell provisions.[21] "Here we are at last,"
Paget commented in his journal, "landed in a *friendly* country, the contrast
being evinced to us here and Bulgaria remarkable. They bring us everything
and appear glad to see us." [22]

A Cossack reconnoitering mission of September 21 reported Tatars working
with Allies to set up stone barricades separating Evpatoria from Perekop and
Simferopol. Further, the Cossacks reported about 1,000 British and French
soldiers garrisoned in the city under heavy guard. Ottoman soldiers (described
as "Arab cavalry" in the Russian report) occupied surrounding villages where
they united with Tatars.[23] In the first few days, Allies arrested Tatar and Russian

authorities who professed loyalty to the Russian empire. They created a new local administration under an Ottoman Pasha and a Polish officer identified only as Tokarskii who had participated in the 1833 uprising in Kiev.[24]

Charykov wrote to the governor general of New Russia, Annenkov, that "Tatars met [the enemy] with cries of joy. They arrested all of the city police and there and then allied with the English. . . . [They] rushed into the outskirts of the city to steal from the Russians, [both] peasants and landlords." The post-master forwarded rumors of Tatars armed with scythes and guns leading Allies to food and supplies in area estates.[25] By the end of the week, Charykov noted, the mutiny had spread west to the post road between Simferopol and Perekop. In early October, Baron V. S. Korf, who led the Uhlan regiment in the west of the peninsula, reported Tatars fighting alongside the Allies in a skirmish near Chorgun and Traktir Bridge.[26]

While some Tatars clearly supported the Allies, many did not. The Tatar head of police in Evpatoria described a divided community with few options in occupied territory. He wrote his superiors in Simferopol about a village near Evpatoria refusing to hand over a deserter. They announced "now there is a new authority and new law." Elsewhere, Tatars searched the countryside for local civil servants to hand over to occupying authorities. Yet he was careful to point out that not all Tatars supported the Allies, stating there were "clearly innocent Tatars" on one side, and on the other, Tatars of various estates assisting the Allies.[27] Like many of his Tatar countrymen who had the means, he fled Evpatoria for Simferopol.

Given evident contradictions in many sources about the size and nature of Tatar collaboration, it is useful to recall the terrible conditions of war in which allegations of insurrection were composed. Evpatoria officials fled shortly after the destruction of the grain and so his impression of the mutiny was limited to the chaotic period surrounding the initial invasion. Other memoirs had been composed years after the event; the devastation of war and the need to make sense of it colored recollections.[28] One memoirist's bitterness toward Tatars crops out repeatedly, and characterizes Tatars as "predisposed toward robbery by nature."[29] The same writer (who happened to be a priest) describes Tatar suffering from the cholera epidemic as just punishment for believing the "empty promises of the Allies" and their "thoughtlessness in betraying Russia."[30] Such evident and continuing anger requires a cautious interpretation indeed.

While some Tatars worked with the Allies, whether motivated by religious considerations, resentment against Russia, or hunger, other Tatars in Tauride went to great lengths to distance themselves from the mutinies occurring in Evpatoria, Perekop, and later Yalta.[31] Because Lord Paget moved out of the stronghold in Evpatoria on the march to Balaklava, his journal offers no further discussion of friendly Tatars willing to sell goods. Instead, he describes foraging for food and taking supplies from burned and abandoned buildings. In one instance, a British foraging party captured a Tatar prince, whom they interrogated at length. The captain became convinced the Tatars "intend[ed] to throw us over if they had the chance."[32]

Codman, the American merchant who traded in Crimea during the war, argued that the British vastly overestimated Tatars' desire to rebel. The British, according to Codman, imagined Tatars to be "the abject slaves of the Czar," eager for liberation. British agents found instead that "patriotism was as ardent and self-sacrificing among the inhabitants of the Crimea as among those of any other lands that they had before endeavored to conquer."[33]

Although Russian authorities later came to blame Tatars en masse for their mutiny, many others believed Tatars had remained loyal. Thus, for example, General R. I. Knorring wrote to Annenkov, in mid-September, that "Only part of [the Tatars] are being obstreperous and committing robbery; most of them tried to save [materials] from falling into the hands of the English and French as they could."[34] The civil servant Mikhno, who spoke the Tatars' language and was raised with Tatar servants, suggested in the absence of any Russian obstacles to the invasion of Evpatoria that Tatars were easy subjects of enemy propaganda. Mikhno noted that while a few Tatars collaborated with the enemy, all the villages on or near the western coast of Crimea were occupied. Willingly or unwillingly, the locals by necessity had to cooperate with the Allies.[35]

Later, a nobleman petitioned Russian authorities in defense of Tatars on his estate who were suspected of collaboration. According to his statement, approximately 500 French cavalry entered his estate while he was in Simferopol. They demanded one hundred cattle from his workers, and when the Tatars in the village refused, the French took two young boys prisoner. French soldiers presented the boys' families a letter stating demands for their return, but it was written in French, which no one in the village could read.

The Tatars dispatched a horseman to Simferopol to ask the nobleman to help them decipher the message. The next day, the French returned and stole hay, cabbages, and other food and supplies from the village.[36] After the declaration of peace, the nobleman petitioned Gorchakov to secure the boys' release, which was achieved in May of 1856. These Tatars, the nobleman asserted, did not give the French hay and cabbage, the crime for which they were accused. Rather they had defended his property and their own.[37] Such voices of reason became dimmer as the war continued.

Usually, documentation of Tatar experience during the invasion was shaped exclusively by the military or police. Surveillance records are often more reflective of the fears of authorities than the realities on the ground.[38] Here, the nobleman's testimony offers an important alternative narrative to that which runs through most police files from the era. The French plundered the estate and took hostages to secure provisions. Tatars had a good relationship with the local landlord who was in turn sympathetic with their plight and worked on their behalf. Even Rakov describes Tatars in Evpatoria who protected the Christian population as they could.[39]

The Cossack Deployment

By mid-September, another rumor reached Perekop that Shamil had landed on the coast of Feodosia with 70,000 Circassians. "That is probably not true," Charykov wrote to Annenkov, "but worries the people and excites the Tatars."[40] The absence of reliable information was fueled in large part by the near total absence of government authority. Daily, often several times a day, Charykov wrote to higher authorities pleading for a civil authority to manage affairs in the absence of the evacuated local bureaucracy, and Cossacks to patrol the roads. Charykov specifically requested "an appropriate General Police-master which would preserve postal and transport communication between Sevastopol, Bakhchisarai, Simferopol, and Perekop." Due to unprotected roads and uncertainty of the unknown, contractors bound for Sevastopol were turning back to Perekop with goods they were supposed to have delivered to the military.[41] Later, Charykov pressed Annenkov to appoint an independent command of one hundred Cossacks to oversee military and other traffic in the Crimean peninsula.

In a letter to General Annenkov dated September 13, Charykov bitterly complained about Menshikov "having only one goal, to protect Sevastopol." Charykov also lambasted governor Pestel, who "lives as if sick and carries the shame of his desertion." Even the "clever ones do not take any active measures for halting the roaming of the Tatars." Worse, no single authority took any action to protect the roads to Bakhchisarai and Simferopol. The only reason the enemy did not penetrate further, in Charykov's mind, was either cowardice or their inability to believe that Crimea had been left so vulnerable. "In the present moment, all of the western regions of the peninsula are left to the will of God."[42]

Archbishop Innokentii, one of the few people who had rushed into Crimea rather than out of it, became stuck at Perekop. He added his voice to Charykov's, blaming the government's evacuation for the disorder. The archbishop wrote to Annenkov: "The authorities first served as the shameful example of this panicked evacuation, even from Perekop, which was not in danger. All local government transferred to Berislav, without entrusting city administration to anyone. From here—the Crimean Gate to Russia, the city is completely without leadership and almost empty."[43] Both the archbishop, who was the highest spiritual authority in the southern Russian Empire, and the postmaster, the only remaining official in the western part of Crimea, pressed New Russia's governor general to restore civilian administration and a policing force.

Despite the peninsula's evident distress and pleas for help from the few officials left to manage local affairs, Russian leaders were slow to respond. Partly, this is because news took so long to reach St. Petersburg; telegraph lines did not reach Crimea until 1855. Others believed the landing in Crimea masked designs upon Odessa or Nikolaev, targets of greater strategic value.[44]

Nikolaev commander General Knorring, for example, expressed sympathy with Menshikov's position but did not consider relocating his men or materials there. Rather than offering to send his own men, whom he needed to protect his own base, Knorring washed his hands of the problem, writing, "I do not know from where the Prince expects reinforcements." Optimistically, he suggested that a small reinforcement would suffice, since cholera and the fire at Varna had already weakened the enemy. He did acknowledge that his men, particularly those with kin and estates in and around Sevastopol, did not share his confidence. "They have lost everything!" Knorring wrote. "We are trying music on the Boulevard to inspire them, but are not quite successful!"[45]

Refusing to budge the two big Russian armies posted at the Prut and Bug rivers, which protected Russian positions in the Danubian Principalities and Odessa and Nikolaev, respectively, the tsar finally assigned a regiment of Don Cossacks to assist Menshikov in Sevastopol. In an age of war and empire, all belligerents in Crimea employed irregular forces. The Ottomans drew upon Kurdish and Circassian irregular soldiers called *bashi-bozouks*, the French pressed zouaves from Northern Africa, and the British, peoples from throughout its empire. Notoriously undisciplined and mercenary, irregular forces contributed to the general looting and civilian-directed violence in all fronts of the war.[46] In Crimea, Cossacks were the most prevalent irregular force.

Coming from outside the regular Russian military and with no counterpart in the West, Cossacks were a "martial estate"; they descended from frontiersmen and retained certain privileges of self-administration in exchange for military service. They could be called up at any moment. They supplied their own horses and saddles and, usually, their own arms and provisions.[47] Over the late eighteenth and nineteenth centuries, the state had gradually integrated Cossacks into regular military structures. It had standardized military rank and published field regulations for Cossacks. Only in 1879, however, did the state rename "the Main Administration of Irregular Forces" to "the Main Administration of Cossack Forces." Cossack experience during the Crimean War prompted this change.[48]

Organized into fourteen cavalry divisions and eighty-three regiments, Cossacks constituted nearly one-tenth of Russian armed forces in the Crimean War and approximately two-thirds of Russia's cavalry. Of these, Don Cossacks (i.e., those Cossacks based along the Don River) accounted for 40 percent of the Cossack army and 50 percent of the Cossack cavalry and played a particularly active part in the Crimean campaign. They were posted initially in Kerch and the northern shores of the Azov Sea under Khomutov, where they were the only military units patrolling the eastern areas of the Crimean peninsula.

In the Caucasian theater, Cossacks helped Russia achieve victory in the Battle of Kars.[49] In Crimea, Cossacks patrolled the external boundary of the enemy-occupied territory. They provided intelligence on Allied movement, conducted raids on Allied camps, and harassed Allied scouts. Cossacks also implemented orders given by Menshikov to destroy civilian food supplies near enemy positions.[50]

Understanding that access to food and supplies was necessary to sustain an invasion, the Russian military followed a scorched earth policy when it could not remove provisions located close to enemy lines. Menshikov gave the Cossacks an official order to destroy grain reserves and hay in villages near Allied-occupied zones at the beginning of September.[51] Subsequently, they spent much of October cutting a swath of destruction from the Salt Lake in Saki to the northern district outside Perekop. They rode into villages in groups of twenty or thirty, flashing their sabers and rifles. Against the horrified protests of local villagers, they drove away herds of sheep and set silos on fire.

On October 6, for example, Cossacks and Uhlans raided a Tatar village on the outskirts of Evpatoria. They had been searching for a large field gun reportedly left unattended. Commander Korf assigned a group of twenty men and two officers to take the weapon. Upon arriving at the scene, the group discovered the gun had already been removed. They followed tracks to the edge of the city where they "cut through a crowd of Tatars dozens deep," in search of the gun. They found instead a group of French soldiers with whom they exchanged fire. In the end, the Cossacks did not capture the gun. They did, however, take two Tatars prisoner and drove away more herds of cattle, horses, and sheep.[52]

Tatars and Cossacks often came into armed confrontation over food. On October 7, a group of Tatars attempted to sneak back into their Cossack-controlled village to rescue grain about to be burned. A Cossack and Uhlan squadron, in the official Russian record, routed the Tatars, killing eight men, wounding ten, and capturing two.[53] Shortly after their arrival in Crimea, the Cossacks formed a military commission for Tatars suspected of treason. They issued orders to arrest Tatars riding on horseback, and forbade Tatars from carrying guns. These actions met protests from local residents and officials, and unfolded with little coordination from regular military staff.

From September through the end of the year, Cossacks arrested hundreds of Tatars, many of whom they sent on to Ekaterinoslav. Charges ranged widely. A handful of Tatars had been arrested for serious charges, which included being "capture(d) with the enemy [who] were being expelled from the city"; "overpowering a *chinovnik* [a low-level bureaucrat of the Russian empire] who remained under arrest by the Allies"; firing guns upon Cossacks; supplying the enemy with food; "talking with Turks"; and "attempting to unite with the Sultan." By September 10, the Cossacks claimed to have uncovered thirteen conspirators at the center of the Tatar rebellion in Evpatoria, whom they identified based on testimony given by Emir Ali Osman.[54]

In addition to those arrested for alleged war crimes, Cossacks detained several Tatars for plundering estates belonging to Crimea's European and Russian landowners, including Rakov. The majority of arrests were for much more nebulous charges relating to having pamphlets in Turkish languages, simply possessing guns, or "leading sheep away from herds."[55] These men were treated as war criminals, removed to military courts without word to their families, and dispatched to Ekaterinoslav.

The arrests produced a flurry of appeals and petitions from local villagers to Governor Pestel, demanding to know why and where their relatives had been taken. Although restoring Tatars to their families was a process that often took years, Tauride governor Pestel wrote to the Cossack commander demanding an immediate end to the indiscriminate arrest of Tatars, which would only "produce dangerous consequences." Pestel insisted only those "Tatars and Russians" who "have committed an offense, stolen or in general clearly violated order" be taken under arrest. The commander repudiated the charge, claiming his men did not harass civilians, and (in reference to this case) arrested only three Tatars who had galloped through a checkpoint without stopping.[56] In October, when Pestel once again protested the indiscriminate arrest of Tatars, the commander claimed he was only following orders.[57]

In another case, as belligerents were still counting the dead from the Battle of Alma, Cossacks arrested a Tatar man in his seventies, Selim Ahmed, whom they accused of assisting the Allied march toward Sevastopol. Selim Ahmed lived in the path of Allied foraging, near the mountain between Sevastopol and Bakhchisarai named after Thomas MacKenzie, a Scottish naval officer who served in the Black Sea Fleet founded by Catherine the Great. Some seventy years after MacKenzie died in Crimea in 1785, the farmstead became the site of skirmish between Russians and Highlanders.[58]

The day after the Allies marched through the area and destroyed Selim Ahmed's house and confiscated his belongings, a Cossack patrol followed in pursuit. When Cossacks demanded information about the movement of the Allied military, Selim Ahmed explained he had nothing to share. Still he agreed to take the Cossacks, who did not know the local terrain, through the MacKenzie foothills. After failing to find any Allied soldiers, the Cossacks accused Selim Ahmed of collaboration and deliberately leading the men astray.[59] They arrested the village elder on the general charge of "ill will," or "ill intentions," a generic crime with which Tatars repeatedly were charged through the course of the war.

Following his arrest, the elder man was dispatched to the Simferopol prison, from where he was sent to Kursk and toward the end of the war, the city of Kherson. "From 23 September 1854, having lost my home, being in my seventies and with five years faultless service as an appointed head of the village," Selim Ahmed wrote in a petition to the New Russia governor general in 1859, "I was made to suffer [even though] I was completely innocent."[60] In 1860, Russian authorities arrested him again, after he returned to his village without having received permission to travel there or to recover his property.[61] Selim Ahmed seems an unlikely conspirator, but his story was all too common.

Located on the Vorontsov Road near Balaklava, the Chorgun area endured plundering from Allies, Cossacks, and even the Balaklava Greek regiment. Quite often, civil servants intervened with the military on behalf of Tatars and other civilians terrorized by Cossacks. Thus in 1856, the Simferopol civil government specifically protested abuse of innocent villagers at the hands of criminal Cossacks. In this case, a few armed Cossacks of the Kandirov regiment and the Volunteer legion of Nicholas I beat a Tatar *kadi* nearly to death for refusing to relinquish his oxen.

Later, the Cossacks returned, wielding their whips and demanding that the village produce several young men for unspecified crimes. When residents attempted to protect their relatives, a Cossack sliced a man neck to shoulder with his sharp sabre. Outraged by the death, the villagers turned the tables and took the Cossack under arrest with intentions of presenting him to authorities for trial. The Cossack leader to whom they protested did not acknowledge the Tatars' position, and instead dispatched the villagers to the police in Bakhchisarai.[62]

At least some Russian authorities were aware of Cossack behavior. Landowners such as Aristide Reveliotti brought charges against the Cossacks in the Simferopol court. In this case, Reveliotti accused the Cossacks of stealing more than two tons of hay. His charges against the Cossacks dragged through the court system until 1858, and possibly later.[63]

A secret gendarme report at the end of September 1854 described the pitiful state of Crimean villages: "All villages located near camps where our military has passed through are completely empty, all gardens are destroyed, estates have been robbed, all within them killed or destroyed, even burned by the Cossacks, whose sphere of plunder [includes] misappropriation of carriages. . . ." The chief cause of Cossack ill behavior, according to the author, is that "the military is sent to forage in surrounding areas, and they can take everything without obstacles, and of course in these circumstances, they steal."[64] Unlike the regular army, the gendarme report continued, the Cossack regiments had no provisions officer, nor connections with local police "who could procure food from rural landowners under receipts." Instead, the Cossacks provisioned their ranks through looting, such that "property in Crimea is completely ruined by our military" if not by the enemy.[65]

In the wake of Russian anxieties about Tatars in Evpatoria, innocent Tatars who tried to protect property of their landowners often took the blame for Cossack pillaging. Russian authorities imprisoned four Tatars for looting the Bernadaki estate in the village of Totman. Located at the western border of the Evpatoria district, the village of Totman was closer to the Cossack encampments than the Allies. These Tatars, according to the charges brought against them, distributed grain from the estate to local villagers, stole as many as seven hundred sheep and confiscated the estate's horses. Cossacks had arrested them in September 1854, and these men remained in the military prison system through 1856.

Throughout their imprisonment, the Tatars maintained their innocence. They insisted that the bailiff who had managed the estate was busy transferring valuables to a safer location in Samov, and had authorized them to distribute the grain to villagers. In turn, the villagers of Totman had promised to either reimburse the landlord after the war, or would pay in kind after a good harvest.

The bailiff also requested the Tatars to lead the horses and sheep to Samov. Before they could carry out his orders, however, Cossacks arrived to requisition wagons, and according to the Tatars' testimony, plundered the estate. When they protested, the Cossacks arrested them based on orders to "arrest all Tatars on horses." They presented the Tatars to the police in Perekop, accusing them of "stealing from the estate, looting it, and in general of rebelling and plundering." The police officer accepted the Cossacks' allegations at face value and did not listen to testimony from the accused, the bailiff, or the peasants of the estate.[66]

In August 1856, the postwar governor of Tauride reopened the Tatars' case. A representative from the governor's office noted that crimes alleged or committed during the war could not be properly researched. In this case, he argued that the robbery of the Totman estate occurred "during the chaos arising from the war circumstances." The Tatars, he said, had been prosecuted without evidence and there was no reason to believe them to be guilty. He ordered their release."[67]

Cossacks also arrested Tatars for carrying guns. In February 1854, the Ministry of Internal Affairs ordered police in Simferopol to compile a list of gun owners, not for confiscation, but to assess residents' ability to defend themselves. The police had compiled a list of 211 individuals possessing gun licenses across Simferopol's diverse population of Tatars, Russians, and Greeks.[68] Eight months later, it had become a crime for Tatars (but not Russians, Greeks, Armenians, or other Christian populations) to openly possess weapons. Some of the lists of registered gun owners fell into the hands of Cossacks, who then searched homes and confiscated private arms.

In October 1854, a Tatar official appealed the arrest of his father and uncles in a petition to Governor Pestel, a petition that also contained statements from peasants of the Yalta district. Three men, ranging in age from sixty-three to seventy-three, had never committed any crimes and were legally registered gun owners. Two of the men carried old muskets for hunting, and the third, guns he inherited from his father who had served in the Napoleonic Wars.[69]

Cossacks were not the only group subjecting Tatars to what appeared in most cases as arbitrary arrest in September; so were local police and militia, the latter of whom consisted mainly of Russian and Greek veterans who spontaneously mobilized when the enemy disembarked. Evidently, these men had fallen under the dangerous sway of rumor and began to suspect all Tatars of crimes and collaboration with the enemy. Governor Pestel wrote to the Simferopol City police on September 15, arguing that Tatars were generally calm and peaceful citizens, protected by law as were Russians. Pestel commanded the police to arrest only "those Tatars, or Russians, who steal, or who generally clearly disrupt order."[70]

At the end of September and the beginning of October, Tatars on the coast began to leave their homes. Some Tatars had been captured by the Allies for having Russian sympathies, some voluntarily attached themselves to the Allies, and still others had fled alongside Russian populations to a safer location. A police officer wrote to authorities in Simferopol for a decision on the property of Tatars who had fled to the enemy. These people had left behind items from their homes, and grain and hay in the field. How, he wanted to know, should abandoned Tatar property be managed?[71]

Similarly, an officer noted in a letter to the Tauride governor that robbery of empty Tatar villages called *auls* had become quite serious. Remaining local residents, whom he identified as Greeks, Armenians, and "even a few local officials" led away livestock and resold Tatar belongings in Perekop. His regiment was tied up in maintaining order around the rear of the Evpatoria blockade and could not be spared for policing abandoned Tatar property. He advocated that anyone arriving in Perekop, Simferopol, or elsewhere with Tatar property from Evpatoria be arrested.[72]

On October 6, 1854, the Tauride Muslim Spiritual Assembly passed a resolution denouncing the mutineers. It began by referencing the event: "Information has revealed that a number of Muslims in the Tauride province taking an oath to the Tsar of Imperial Russia to be faithful subjects, violated the oath, and many have already passed over to the enemy who has appeared on the borders of Russia in the city of Evpatoria." The resolution continued in no uncertain terms: "Breaking the oath is strongly forbidden, by Russian and equally by Islamic law." The statement gave a long discussion of the severe punishments for disloyalty according to Sharia, which included amputating the hand and foot, and even the death sentence.[73] Here, the Tatar Muslim Spiritual Assembly unequivocally cast its support behind the Tsar and the military, and clarified that it would prosecute any Tatars proven to be traitors.

The Nogai Tatars who occupied the northern parts of the Tauride province in the Dneprovsk, Melitopol, and Berdiansk districts also expressed their disproval of Tatar actions in Evpatoria. Their petition, issued one week later, clarified their loyalty to the tsar: "Located more than seventy years under the scepter of the Great Tsar of Russia, the Nogai feel themselves to be fully happy in their status and wish to show their gratitude and recognition for the generous care of the government, and together with this to show how separate they are from those ill-intentioned and ungrateful Crimean Tatars who demonstrate a friendly disposition to the enemies of Russia. . . ."[74] They concluded their petition by emphasizing that the "Nogai do not have any kind of relationship with the ill-willed Crimean Tatars" and reiterated their oath "to the throne and the fatherland."[75]

Menshikov forwarded the petition to the tsar, who proclaimed his gratitude for the Tatars' expression of loyalty.[76] Convinced that the mutiny of a few did not characterize the attitude of the entire population, Tsar Nicholas I agreed that the Muslim Spiritual Administration should carry on as it always had, including trying Tatars accused of crimes.[77] The tsar's commitment to the Tatar Assembly was significant in light of his 1833 reform expanding the authority of military courts in peace and war.[78] In the fall of 1854, therefore, the Tatar Spiritual Assembly presided over cases of treason according to local custom. For example, the Tatar Spiritual Assembly heard a case about a Muslim man who had been caught trading hay and sheep with Ottoman soldiers by the Russian advance guard. The man's possession of Ottoman coin was raised as evidence against him. Finding the prisoner guilty, the Tatar Assembly assigned a punishment of thirty-nine blows, which the court said accorded with Islamic law for treason.[79]

The so-called Tatar mutiny has been a subject of speculation from the moment the Allies landed in Evpatoria. The evidential record remains highly problematic. Panic and uncertainty infuses sporadic documentation of the invasion of Evpatoria. With few exceptions, Tatars left behind neither manifestos nor proclamations, and professed their innocence under interrogation.[80] By March of 1855, some three hundred Crimean Tatars had formed into volunteer regiments recognized by Ottoman officers. Another 150 Tatar volunteers served under the French.[81] While it is evident that some Tatars sided with the invading powers, these numbers fell well short of Russian estimates of a Tatar insurrection composed of 14,000 or 50,000 men.[82]

At the end of the war, a special government investigation concluded that the Tatars were victims of war, rather than collaborators.[83] This is true. But the perception of Tatar insurrection is also important for understanding Menshikov's decision to forcibly relocate Tatars from the coast to the interior.

In his classic account of the Crimean War, Alexander Kinglake offered an impression of Crimean Tatars formed from his survey of official British documents and memoirs. The Crimean Tatars, Kinglake concludes,

> found themselves unaccountably marshalled and governed, and involuntarily taking their humble part in the enterprise of the Western Powers. Many of them wore the same expression of countenance as hares that are taken alive and thus looked as if they were watching after the right moment for escape; but they had fallen as it were into a great stream, and all they

could do was wonder, yield and flow on. There were few of those captured lads who had the strength to withstand the sickness and hardships of the campaign. For the most part, they sank and died.[84]

The Tatar position, as Kinglake suggests, became more tenuous as the war progressed, just as the label of collaborator ill fits. In the absence of Russian protection, civilians in the path of the enemy advance had few choices available to them. Those who could afford to evacuate left along with Russian authorities. The vast majority of Tatars, however, were poor state peasants with no funds to leave, and following Cossack confiscation of guns, no weapons with which to fight. Survival for the majority, therefore, meant making an uneasy peace with the invading power, a power that along with Russian forces stripped Tatars and other peasants of food and livelihood. As the war ground on, Menshikov showed little understanding of or sympathy with Tatar's untenable position. Instead, he feared Tatars were a dangerous fifth column. Together, Menshikov and the new military governor who had replaced Pestel, N. V. Adlerberg, orchestrated a deportation of Crimean Tatars from the Russian coast. Before the relocation of Tatars, however, the peninsula plunged even further into the abyss of war and hunger.

Three Tatar laborers dig a trench outside a British regimental magazine, while four others rest. It is unknown whether these men were conscripts or volunteers. *Photograph by Roger Fenton, 1855. Royal Collection Trust / © Her Majesty Queen Elizabeth II 2018.*

4

Civilians in the Line of Fire

WHEN THE ALLIES CUT EVPATORIA off from Sevastopol and Simferopol, a dark curtain fell over the western Crimean coast; what happened behind it remained a mystery until the end of the war. How people survived, who lived, and who died, became a matter of speculation as did who collaborated or resisted. Families despaired over losing contact with loved ones. Anxious peasants risked their lives sneaking across the Cossack line to pull up the last of their harvests. Lacking reliable information, suspicious government agents imagined widespread Tatar spy networks along the coast.

Silence from western Crimea blanketed the critical postal route through Perekop. In 1853, telegraph lines connected St. Petersburg and Warsaw, Moscow and Kiev. Menshikov had proposed lines for Sevastopol, Ochakov, and Nikolaev in 1854, but these were not completed until 1855.[1] Rather than traveling directly via Perekop, news from Sevastopol to the mainland now went through Melitopol, a slow, circuitous, route along Crimea's eastern villages.[2] Tsar Nicholas I only learned that the enemy occupied Evpatoria nearly twelve days after the invasion.[3] Still, the threat of Prussia and Austria joining the Allies grew stronger as the war continued, and so Tsar Nicholas refused to move his large 1st and 2nd armies from the Polish border.

If the tsar and Paskevich were concerned about Austrian invasion through Poland, Gorchakov remained committed to holding his line in Bessarabia.[4] It was only on September 5th or 6th that Gorchakov became fully aware of the occupation of Evpatoria and ordered Liprandi and his 16,000 men to march from Ukraine to Crimea.[5] But Liprandi and his men had to march several hundred kilometers to reach their post, and so Menshikov and the sailors of Sevastopol faced the Allied siege practically alone. The failure to take decisive action in Crimea caused consternation on the battlefield and among nationalists in the empire.[6]

Following Russia's defeat in the Battle of Alma and the Allied occupation of Evpatoria, Menshikov anticipated the fall of Crimea. He sketched the hopelessness of Russia's position in a letter to Annenkov:

> [The] enemy with all their forces surrounds Sevastopol; meanwhile the Turkish Pasha in Evpatoria issued a proclamation to Tatars calling for general rebellion; if it succeeds, all communication from Crimea could be cut, what is more, in the Evpatoria district, Tatars have already begun to rebel. Given my present means it is difficult to combat the enemy and one wonders whether it is possible to hold on to Crimea.[7]

The outlook for the Russian military was indeed dire. Short on men and supplies, Menshikov had ample reason for pessimism.

St. Petersburg conceded that the winds of war had shifted east by the end of September and so expanded Gorchakov's military authority. In addition to managing the military in Bessarabia, Gorchakov became Commander in Chief over Podolia, Kiev, Poltava, Kherson, Ekaterinoslav, Kharkov, and the northern part of the Tauride province to the Perekop isthmus. Menshikov retained control over three-fourths of Crimea, including the western shores with Perekop and Evpatoria, and Sevastopol, Balaklava, and Yalta along the southern coast. The war ministry treated Kerch-Enikale, the large peninsula jutting off the eastern side of the Crimean diamond into the Black Sea as its own discrete unit, and attached it to the authority of the Don Cossack Hetman, Khomutov.[8]

In this manner, the three military commanders divided Tauride between them: Gorchakov in the north, Khomutov in the east, and Menshikov in the south. Gorchakov's expanded authority enabled him to orchestrate movement of divisions across southern Ukraine and, conversely, to call them back to Bessarabia should the need arise. Under his guidance, war-weary soldiers traveled eastward out of Bessarabia. They marched hundreds of kilometers to Perekop, a journey that easily consumed two weeks in good weather.[9] The fording of a river took a full day as cavalry led nervous horses through rushing waters and porters carried food, weapons, and baggage often in treacherous conditions. Soldiers traveling from Bessarabia typically passed through Odessa, where they consumed local food and received blessings from the archbishop.

A sermon commiserated with the tired soldiers: "You have not had long to rest from your labors and feats in the Danube!"[10]

Just as soldiers were slow to trickle into Crimea, so was gunpowder. After receiving multiple dispatches from Menshikov, an official in the war ministry assured him they were taking "the utmost decisive measures to speed up the transport of gunpowder to Sevastopol."[11] The chief obstacle to timely transport, the official confessed, was that few carriages were designed for needs of mass, heavy transport. Instead, civilian carts, such as those requisitioned from the Jewish community of Tulchin, could at most travel 80 kilometers (50 miles) over a twenty-four hour period.[12]

On the surface, dependence on civilian wagons and livestock for the war effort reduced military expenditure in peacetime. Further, martial law and custom enabled the tsar to mobilize all civilians and their property for the war. While not always efficient, the Russian military could count on the full resources of the empire and occupied territory. Yet, as became quickly apparent, exploitation of civilians for the war wrecked local economies wherever the military extracted resources; the Tulchin community, for example, likely never saw their wagons again. Repeated requisitioning, moreover, could generate discontent, as it did later in Kiev and Crimea.[13]

Given transportation difficulties across awkward terrain, the gunpowder arrived in mid-November, much too late to assist in the battles of Balaklava and Inkerman. A disgusted Menshikov quipped that there were three things to know about the war minister's relationship to gunpowder: "He does not smell it; he does not make it; and he does not send it to Sevastopol."[14] Waiting on supplies, Menshikov borrowed some gunpowder from Khomutov. Kerch was not yet under attack; Khomutov undoubtedly concluded that helping Menshikov to hold the Allies in the western peninsula was a worthwhile risk to take. The transfer of the gunpowder was dutifully accounted for at every stage with beautifully sealed, finely appointed *kvitantsii* (receipts), a nicety that soon dropped off as the war worsened.[15]

Sevastopol

The loud boom of the September 8 cannonade in Alma echoed across the valleys to Sevastopol. When the last cannon fired around 4:30 in the afternoon, the city anxiously waited for the victory announcement. Reports of defeat sent Sevastopolians into panic.[16] Leaving behind hundreds of wounded soldiers who soaked the battlefield with blood, the Russian retreat from Alma was hasty and chaotic. Men fled in different directions. Fearing that the

Allies might penetrate further in Crimea, Menshikov himself did not know where to direct his army. He veered first toward Bakhchisarai to protect the road between Sevastopol and Simferopol, before returning to the Belbek and Kacha rivers north of Sevastopol a few days later.[17] Poorly patched-up soldiers dropped by the side of the road, unable to trudge any further. Chodasiewicz passed "numbers of these unfortunate men, who cried out . . . for water to quench their intolerable thirst, while others begged hard to be put out of their agony by a speedy death."[18] As the Allies marched onward, Admiral V. A. Kornilov enacted Menshikov's standing orders to sink older Russian vessels in the city harbor. Not knowing where Menshikov was with the army, Sevastopolians descended into despair as they watched ships burn and sink to the sea floor.[19]

Contemporaries widely criticized Menshikov following the battle of Alma. Charykov blamed Menshikov for focusing single-mindedly on Sevastopol at the expense of Evpatoria and Perekop, while the men at the Sevastopol garrison accused Menshikov of abandoning the city. No one was more critical than Admiral Kornilov, who wrote in his diary: "Had I known he was capable of such betrayal, then of course I never would have agreed to scuttle the fleet." Rather, he would have tested his outnumbered and aging ships in an open sea battle.[20]

Viewing Sevastopol after its destruction in 1855, the American observer McClellan offered Menshikov rare sympathy, stating that the only reasonable course of action was "to remain in position at Sebastopol, and act according to circumstances as soon as the allies showed their hand." He also approved of the sunken ships in Sevastopol's main harbor, which had kept the Allied flotilla outside the bay. Nevertheless, McClellan's voice joined the chorus of those who second-guessed Menshikov. He suggested that "the Russian general should have annoyed and harassed [the Anglo-French forces] by day and night, by unremitting attacks by his Cossacks and other troops," as well as sinking a few vessels in Balaklava harbor. McClellan also wondered why Menshikov did not blast the Balaklava cliffs until they tumbled into the sea, thereby preventing the Allies from disembarking.[21] Few people at the time, including McClellan, appreciated that Menshikov had lacked crucial support from St. Petersburg, and he'd had neither men nor artillery to spare. Thankfully, Menshikov had never considered McClellan's other idea of blowing up Balaklava's beautiful cliffs for the sake of war.

Instead, Menshikov had called every resource he had to Sevastopol and the road to Bakhchisarai. He assigned protection to the critical artery connecting Sevastopol with the rest of the empire, and put the city's defense in Kornilov's, Nakhimov's, and Totleben's hands; admirals Kornilov and Nakhimov led the soldiers and sailors while Totleben, an engineer, completed fortifications. Everyone young and old worked at frenzied paces to finish construction of the bastions. One eyewitness recalled, "People gave up their horses to carry gunpowder and earth; children dragged shovels; women carried water and food."[22] Other women joined the men, digging earth for the bastions. At the beginning of October, civilians and soldiers under Totleben's direction had constructed three main lines of defense around the city. The first consisted of the fortress, bastions, and redoubts connected by trenches and foregrounded by mines, spikes, and pits. Troops were stationed around the surrounding second line for artillery fire; behind were dugouts and shelters for the reserves.

It took several weeks for Allies to reconnoiter the area and set up bases in the nearby towns of Chersonesos and Balaklava; nearly a month passed from the Battle of Alma before the first major bombardment of Sevastopol. On October 5/17, Allied forces bombarded the city from 6:30 in the morning until nightfall. "Blood inundates the ground, but the dead are instantly replaced by the living," Bazancourt wrote. Dead bodies, suffocated, burned, or blown by bombs into the air, scattered around the ground and in the blasted batteries. The dead mingled with the living, all faces darkened by smoke and fire.[23] When sounds of cannon faded with the setting sun, Russian residents rushed out to help soldiers rebuild fortifications. The next day, the Allies were surprised to see the batteries and parapets restored. Russian casualties from the first bombardment were significant. More than sixty-eight men died; 221 soldiers and sailors were wounded along with two officers; and another thirty-seven men received concussions. Kornilov was among those who perished.[24]

One of the many stories to come out of the bombardment was that of a local resident famously known as "Daria of Sevastopol." Daria was a seventeen-year-old girl, daughter of a Sevastopol bureaucrat, and worked as a laundress at the camps. During the first bombardment, she fearlessly ran out on the battlefield with her linens in hand and set to cleaning and wrapping the warriors' wounds. In other words, before Florence Nightingale landed in Scutari, the young Russian woman had pioneered battlefield medicine in Crimea. The Grand Duke awarded Daria with medals and gifted her with 500 rubles promising another 1,000 when she married. Subsequently she worked alongside Russian nurses known as the Sisters of Mercy established by the Grand Duchess Elena Pavlovna.[25] Today Daria is immortalized in the famous panorama in Sevastopol and is the only woman depicted among the male pantheon on the exterior of the building.

Balaklava

Before the British fired upon Sevastopol, they set up a base camp in Balaklava. The famous Battle of Baklava (October 13/25) actually occurred in a deep valley north of the town along the Vorontsov Road in the intersection of three small villages populated principally by Greeks and Tatars: Chorgun, Kadi-koi, and Kamary. The Battle *for* Balaklava was a much smaller affair in September between a small band of residents defending their homes against the overwhelming British Army.

The little town of Balaklava is a strategic, picturesque place. Over the millennia, crashing waters of the Black Sea cut a long and deep finger-like bay into steep limestone cliffs. In the Soviet era, the military hollowed tunnels into the harbor's hills for nuclear submarines to submerge without detection from satellites. Centuries prior, Greeks built a city around the harbor during the Byzantine era, as did the Genoese who built a fort on the cliffs in the fourteenth and fifteenth centuries.[26] Balaklava remained a Greek enclave through the Russian Revolution of 1917, repeatedly replenished by Greek-Ottoman refugees during the Russian-Ottoman wars of the eighteenth and nineteenth centuries.

The Balaklava Greeks had participated in Russian conflicts from the 1780s forward, and marshaled up a special unit during the Crimean War. In quiet periods, they performed a variety of tasks for the Russian Empire. For example, they acted as border patrol along the stretch of the Black Sea coast from Sevastopol to Sudak, and built new roadways. They also enforced the quarantine when the plague hit Sevastopol in 1829.[27] In return for their service to the Russian empire, the government awarded the Greeks with plots of land throughout surrounding hills.

The Balaklava Greeks had a mixed history with Crimean Tatars. They interacted on a regular basis; travelogues are rich with anecdotes of Greeks, Armenians, and Tatars working and recreating together. Yet, the Greeks also acted as informants for the Russian government and subdued Tatar unrest.[28] According to some observers, Balaklava Greeks nurtured resentment against the Ottoman Empire through the 1840s, and transferred negative feelings to local Tatars. In the words of French geographer Victor Amanton, "This transplanted Greek colony, which is in the middle of a Muslim population is possessed of the highest degree of hatred for the Muslims from whom they fled, and contributes to the irritation of the subject [Tatar] population, which is still an enemy in Russia today as it was from the first day of the conquest."[29] Balaklava, in other words, was one of many flashpoints of ethnic conflict in Crimea.

Estimates of the Greek population vary. Russian census takers reported Balaklava Greeks around 2,500, but an Englishman who toured Crimea during the Crimean War put the Greek population of Balaklava and surrounding villages close to 8,000.[30] In addition to the ancient Byzantine church, Balaklava was home to one of Crimea's largest and oldest monasteries. On the eve of war, St. George housed the Black Sea Fleet's priests during peacetime, and was headed by a Greek abbot. The archbishop had established there, near the village Kadi-koi, a small monastic community, a *skete*, in the name of St. John the Baptist on springs locally revered for their holiness and proposed that St. George become a center of Crimea's Orthodox revitalization.[31]

Balaklava's admirable harbor in such proximity to Sevastopol appeared to be a perfect spot for British admirals, who quickly chose it as the base of their camp. Lady Frances Isabella Duberly, an officer's wife who spent the war in Varna and Crimea, described the harbor as seeming completely land-locked: "Through a fissure in the cliffs you can see just a number of masts; but how they got in, or will get out, appears a mystery."[32] Although British admirals appreciated Balaklava's harbor, they knew nothing about the village or surrounding cliffs. Without maps or reliable intelligence, British forces learned firsthand about the surrounding terrain on the march from Alma.

By the time British soldiers made camp in Balaklava, the landscape had already been poisoned by war. Picking his way carefully over wounded men whose blood seeped into the ground, and others who fell to cholera and dysentery, Paget describes a horrific scene. Horses lay strewn about the road. He spotted one horse suffering a slow death, writhing in pain from a shot to its flank. Here, as in Evpatoria, Russian forces spoiled the grain and damaged wells. Hunger drove roving bands of soldiers to harvest unripe fruit from vines and orchards, for good crops had already been consumed or destroyed and livestock slaughtered. Flames devoured wooden structures, while many of the region's clay brick buildings crumbled in ruin.[33]

Avoiding the guns positioned in the south of Sevastopol, British forces cut around the north of the city on a road that led toward Bakhchisarai. Sun dazzling off Sevastopol's white limestone buildings could be seen as soldiers passed over the northern hills. They pillaged a convoy of refugees: soldiers turned over trunks to steal the valuables, and took men and women as prisoners. Most villages they passed through, such as the Greek settlement of Kadi-koi, however, were already deserted, and houses had been emptied of anything useful.[34] As many as fourteen British soldiers per day died on the road to Balaklava, victims of cholera. On September 13/25 they finally arrived.[35]

Like Evpatoria, Balaklava had been abandoned by the Russian army. Only local residents, the 110-member Greek battalion under the leadership of M. A. Manto, remained to resist the thousands-strong British army marching over land and the twenty ships docking in the bay. The *Balaklavtsy* fired from the ruins of the Genoese Chembalo fortress until they exhausted their small supply of weapons. At the end of the brief battle, the British captured Manto, six officers, and sixty soldiers, all wounded in battle.[36] A mine exploded as Allies attempted to cross the barricades into Balaklava, wounding and killing some thirty men. According to Russian reports, Allies suffered nearly 200 casualties trying to take Balaklava.

Upon surrendering Balaklava, the commander begged Lord Raglan's intercession on behalf of women and children who had fled into the hills where (in the words of one eyewitness) they encountered "an enemy more terrible and merciless . . . hunger and cold nights of approaching fall."[37] They were allowed to return briefly to their homes and husbands. British and Russian eyewitness accounts agree that commanding officers promised Balaklava residents safe passage and preservation of property. In the Russian account authored by V. Zelenkevich, however, the enemy failed to keep their word.

Women were harassed, to what degree he did not say. People found "dresses and valuable things destroyed, furniture broken," while the most valuable items had been hauled back to the ships. Icons were torn from the walls and tossed into the streets. Hungry soldiers ransacked kitchens and almost immediately slaughtered the hens and sheep for food.[38]

As the Allies moved into Balaklava, John Snow made medical history in England when he linked the origins of a deadly cholera outbreak to London's Broad Street Pump.[39] Scientists debated the merits of his hypothesis for decades. On the eve of war theories abounded, the most prominent being that cholera was a *miasma*, an unpleasant vapor in the air. Others hypothesized that cholera traveled in meat or vegetation. Believing cholera traveled in grapes, one of the French commanders had his men cut down Crimean orchards, and burn the vineyards. By nightfall, berserk soldiers had dismantled the terraces and trampled even the kitchen gardens. "In this manner," writes Zelenkevich, "the *Balaklavtsy* suddenly became destitute, without means for existence, and were in complete fear for their lives."[40]

The French, British, and Ottoman invaders spread similar destruction around nearby villages. Residents who fled into the woods following the initial attack returned to their homes a few days later looking for food and shelter, only to find empty cupboards, broken windows, and damaged roofs.[41]

Calthorpe simply acknowledged that some brigandage occurred, for which he blamed the French.[42]

British and French invaders also took over the monastery of St. George on September 14, 1854, and quickly transformed it into a base of operations. While the abbot had already evacuated with the monastery's valuables into the Russian interior, several monks remained to protect the chapel. For months, diocesan authorities pressed civil and military officials for information about the monastery.[43] In early February, the monks sent a letter through the French commander, stating, "Thanks to God, all are alive and healthy."[44] A year later the archbishop received a second correspondence from the monastery bearing similar news.[45] After the war, the naval monks and all other brothers associated with St. George Monastery received medals for defending Sevastopol, and in "Memory of the War of 1853–1854."[46]

Immediately after the seizure of Balaklava on September 15, 1854, the British left a small garrison in the town and set up a base of operations about 4 kilometers (2.5 miles) from Malakhov Kurgan. They built small redoubts near Kadi-koi, the village Kamary, and the Spiliia mountain, stationing there 4,350 Ottoman and British soldiers. The British also used Balaklava as base from which to raid local towns and countryside for food and supplies, and disembarked in Yalta, where they robbed the city and surrounding estates, including Massandra, known now for its rich, ruby port, and Livadia, then Vorontsov's main estate in Crimea.[47] Many of the Tatars displaced by invading armies and Russian forces lost their land in this area, never to regain it.[48]

Menshikov waited several weeks for reinforcements to arrive. Until then, he could do little more through the month of September than hold the road connecting the northern side of Sevastopol with Bakhchisarai. He achieved a small victory when at the beginning of October, A. E. Rakovich and his men took Chorgun, a small village north of Balaklava on the Vorontsov Road.[49] Finally, Liprandi and 12,000 men marched into Crimea, allowing Menshikov to plan his attack. With the goal of securing the road and hemming in the Allies along the coast, the Battle of Balaklava opened on the morning of October 13/25.

The Battle of Balaklava is best known for the ill-fated charge of the Light Brigade. Immortalized in the poem by Tennyson, the Light Brigade left an impression even upon on the Russian priests who reported that the foolhardy Scottish cavalry "fought like lions," because "up to the last of them were drinking."[50] Casualties at Balaklava were limited to fewer than 1,500 for all sides combined. It was decisive inasmuch as Menshikov re-established Russian control over Crimea's interior and hemmed the Allies around the coast. As the enemy invaders, many of whom were desperately hungry, retreated from the valley, they pillaged local villages and butchered civilians caught in their path.[51] In the aftermath of Balaklava another wave of refugees fled their homes "flow[ing] like lava" on the road to Bakhchisarai.[52]

By December 1854, picturesque Balaklava had become a macabre reflection of its former self. Starvation, murder, and disease decimated the Allied camp. Dead bodies of horses and men littered the quay. Lady Duberly's wondrous image of Balaklava had changed into something gruesome:

> We are on board ship moored close to the shore in a harbor that so often stinks from the vast numbers of sick and wounded that it makes me retch— dead bodies only recognizable from a thigh bone or an arm floating round the ship, a sight so horrible that it seems to stop the current of one's blood. On the quay, ankle deep in wet mud . . . you stumble over a dirty bundle that looks like a sack, it is a dead Turk in a blanket put down in the mud. All the time the rain goes on, hard and ceaseless. Out of the town in the middle of the road, throwing up the mud like a fountain spurt, is an artillery horse kicking in his death struggle.[53]

Inkerman

Hoping to build upon his victory at Balaklava, Menshikov launched an attack on Allies at Inkerman on October 24/November 5. A vast plain bordered by cliffs on one side and the Chernaya River on the other, Inkerman had been populated from ancient times; before the war, its lace-like caves dotting the cliff face attracted archaeologists from across Europe. Orthodox scholars believed Inkerman was the location to where the first-century Roman Pope Clement had been exiled, and that Byzantine Christians hid in Inkerman's caves during the iconoclast period. The Russian Orthodox Church established a monastery there only a few years before the war. Monks who remained in their posts as bureaucrats fled were eyewitnesses to the war, and reported the presence of enemy military in the valley from September 11/23, three days after the Battle of Alma.[54]

Following the Battle of Balaklava, additional reinforcements arrived in Crimea. Menshikov's forces had swollen to 107,000 men, not including sailors, which made Russian forces 30 percent to 35 percent larger than the combined forces of the Allies, who numbered 71,000.[55] On Inkerman's hilly terrain, the Allies and Russians were evenly matched with approximately 50,000 men each.[56] The battle that began at dawn on 24 October/November 5, 1854, raged for twelve hours. Through a series of miscalculations, miscommunications, and underpreparation (the Russian commander Dannenberg had not even visited the battle site), Russian forces lost the day.[57] Russian defeat at the Battle of Inkerman devastated Russian morale, and enabled the Allies to settle in their positions along the coast for the winter. The battle devastated the civilians living in the area, their homes plundered or destroyed.[58]

Undeterred, the British troops settled into their base of operations in the Bay of Balaklava. The French camped in Chersoneses, and Ottomans retained their position in Evpatoria. Together, the Allies surrounded Sevastopol, which remained short of gunpowder, coats, boots, and medical supplies. The battles of Alma and Balaklava clarified for Gorchakov that the enemy intended to make war in Crimea. In October, he ordered the commander of the Fifth Army and Cavalry, Liders, to begin crossing the Danube.[59]

Contrary to the conventional wisdom at the highest levels of imperial administration, Gorchakov had begun to doubt an Austrian invasion. Writing to Liders from his muddy post in Kishinev, Gorchakov argued that the latest intelligence indicated that Austria would not enter the war during the winter.[60] Eager to relocate his men from Moldova to reinforce Crimea, Gorchakov nevertheless expressed some concern that Ottomans might mount an attack should Russian forces leave their position.[61] Meanwhile, Menshikov descended ever further into despair. The inconsolable commander in Crimea saw no chance of Russian success against the European invaders and fully anticipated the immanent collapse of Sevastopol.[62]

Although the Allies mostly focused on Sevastopol, as fall turned to winter, enemy ships also brought the war to other parts of the peninsula. Local residents sent in a flurry of reports about ship sightings off the coast of Yalta, Feodosia, and Kerch. Occasionally, the enemy disembarked to roam local villages in search of food and loot. Only a force of nature could hinder the Allied advance, or so it seemed. Many devout Russians believed God had finally answered their prayers when a hurricane (the term contemporaries used) hit Crimea in November. The storm eroded trenches around Sevastopol, grounded ships, and sank others with medical supplies, food, and ammunitions. Although hundreds of men died in the storm, the loss of material goods, such as coats, hats, boots, and gloves was far more damaging to the British, who were desperate for cold-weather supplies.[63]

Consequences of Enemy Occupation for the Local Population

If the battles of Alma, Balaklava, and Inkerman distressed Russians in Moscow and St. Petersburg, they were devastating to the local population in Crimea.

Refugees continued to flee from the Crimean coast. After the Battle of Inkerman, the centrally located Dormition monastery in Bakhchisarai became a waypoint for many of the Orthodox refugees evacuating Sevastopol, Evpatoria, Balaklava, and surrounding villages. The archimandrite remarked, "The enemies, like locusts, surround Crimea, and squeeze the cities, causing people to flee. Not wishing to judge the runners [*bezhentsy*, i.e., refugees], I nevertheless have to ask, to where will they run?"[64]

Refugees from Evpatoria, Sevastopol, and coastal villages spread diseases of the military beyond the battleground. The cholera epidemic during the Crimean War had originated with the French army in the ports of Marseilles and Toulon, who then transported the disease to the theater in Dobrudja. When they left for Crimea in September, they brought the disease to new ground.[65] It took some time for the Russian Military Medical Department to catch up with the changing nature of the war, just as it had taken the army months to transition to Crimea as the new battlefield. But by late November 1854, the war ministry established facilities in Simferopol and a new doctor, N. I. Pirogov, arrived from St. Petersburg to assume direct control over medical activities at the front.

Pirogov is widely acknowledged for advancing Russian medicine through the war; Tarle includes the doctor in the pantheon of Crimean War heroes, and indeed doctors were among those who received medals at the end of the war.[66] Pirogov finished his surgery program in St. Petersburg in 1841 and gained his military experience in the Caucasus. In 1854–1855 he organized battlefield medicine, and his work evolved into a foundational study of military medical service. In addition to discussing treatment of war wounds, surgery, and amputation, Pirogov provided an extensive analysis of treating cholera.[67]

Pirogov was appalled at the unhygienic conditions in which wounded soldiers were kept. Extreme need combined in epic proportions with indifference, ignorance, and dirtiness, he observed in a letter to his wife. In two small barrack rooms of a temporary hospital between Simferopol and Bakhchisarai, 360 men stretched out on the floor "head to toe one after the other, without spaces, without order, without differences between dirty fetid wounds and the treated."[68]

Pirogov blamed Menshikov for the status of military medicine in Crimea, and became one of the commander's most bitter critics. Whereas Vorontsov regularly visited the wounded Russian soldiers in the Caucasus, distributing medals and money, Menshikov, he complained, came only once, and only to visit a general. Pirogov depicted Menshikov as a terrible leader, unconcerned with the fate of his soldiers, writing, "Please Lord, let all of this be untrue, and Menshikov be made, really, a great man of history. I desire this from the bottom of my soul, because I wish to see Sevastopol in our hands; but it is true that the soldiers do not know their commander, and the commander does not care for his soldiers."[69]

The young doctor established quarters on the south side of Sevastopol, where he spent his mornings working on medical administrative matters and visiting patients. In the afternoons, he took a boat to hospitals on the north side of the bay. While Pirogov's main responsibility involved supervising medicine for the Russian armed forces, his orders and those of his colleagues had some effect on the local population, particularly in relation to controlling epidemics.

On the eve of Pirogov's arrival, the Medical Administration asked Governor Pestel to appoint a quarantine space for refugees and military personnel. Police records show a few people dying from cholera in Simferopol in October and November, but reported incidents tapered off by January.[70] As Pirogov prepared Crimea for medical emergencies in the spring, the Medical Department demanded that northern Sevastopol be cleaned of "all impurities." This included, above all, clearing dead corpses and animals that had been left to decompose openly in streets. Orders specified that the dead should be buried six feet underground in a high, dry area away from homes and water supplies. The Medical Department gave additional instructions regarding burial of corpses from the Battles of Alma and Inkerman still on the ground and ordered all places marked by death to be scrubbed with bleach and chlorine.

Beyond death and disease, civilians lost their property and means of survival. Forty-year-old Selim Murza Dzhankichev had a small estate in Tarakhanlar, a village located in the Simferopol district near the Battle of Alma. He was married twice over; his first wife was close to thirty, and his second, twenty years old. With them, he had a son and daughter. At the orders of the Russian military, he and his family fled in advance of the enemy occupation of Birliuk, a little hamlet near Tarakhanlar.

Like many Crimean residents forced to flee at a moment's notice, Dzhankichev left everything behind, and "barely had time to leave with [his] family." The invading military robbed his estate of grain reserves, hay, furniture, linens, and kitchen utensils. Soldiers dismantled wooden and stone fences around the gardens, ruined the house and destroyed the orchards. "Without help from the government," Dzhankichev wrote to authorities in Simferopol after the war, "I cannot find hope to rebuild." He estimated his total losses at 3,000 rubles.[71]

An old Tatar settlement, Chorgun was about 16 kilometers (10 miles) north of Sevastopol; after annexation, Catherine the Great granted a large estate in the village to a Russian-Greek family by the name of Mavromikhaili. The family patriarch, P. S. Mavromikhaili, had fought among the Greeks in an uprising against the Ottoman Empire during the Russian-Ottoman wars at the end of the eighteenth century. Later Mavromikhaili became a key advisor to Duke (Armand-Emmanuel) Richelieu, the first Governor General of New Russia, while one of his daughters sat for a portrait painted by Ukrainian poet Taras Shevchenko.[72] On September 14, 1854, the enemy had occupied Chorgun and stolen everything in sight. The Mavromikhaili sisters (their father had passed away) evacuated in advance of the enemy occupation and spent much of the war serving as nurses in Sevastopol. Before the war, their estate was valued at 132,000 rubles. It contained orchards, vineyards, forests, and sheep, with annual output of 10,000 rubles. But the war ruined everything: "The house and all agricultural buildings were completely taken apart and destroyed, the fruit orchards and vineyards were razed."[73]

In the same village, a fifty-seven-year-old Bakhchisarai merchant shared a home with his thirty-year-old wife, his two-year-old son, and his centenarian mother-in-law. He too lost everything: stores of winter wheat, rye, and barley; furniture, silver, and "all moveable property." He estimated his losses at 1,635 rubles, an amount that would not have covered the expense of evacuation, or relocation, much less rebuilding a home that had taken decades to establish.[74]

Sevastopol and Balaklava were nearly completely ruined; residents reported razed orchards, uprooted vineyards, destroyed businesses, and bombed-out homes.[75] General Mayor N. de Antony, who spent the war serving the engineering group building dry docks in Sevastopol and camps, lost his Sevastopol-Balaklava estate to enemy invasion. Enemy forces destroyed his 15,500 vines and 450 fruit trees, which once produced an annual income of 2,000 rubles. A stone house of five rooms and a wooden ceiling covered in clay tile had been reduced to rubble, as was external storage buildings. All hay, wine, and grain had been completely consumed.[76]

At the behest of the Tauride governor in December 1854, police tallied the number of Orthodox Sevastopolians who had been displaced by war to Simferopol. They counted more than forty families, evenly headed by men and women. Of the forty, eight were widowed with children and thirteen were wives of officers or civilians working in Sevastopol. The men included merchants and townsman, and lost property ranged in value from 30 rubles at the bottom strata to 17,000 rubles at the top. Overwhelmed with managing the needs of the military, Simferopol had little to spare for refugees.

After some debate between military officials and the local government, officials decided only soldiers' wives could receive benefits.[77] Russian civil and military administrations' inability help these families boded poorly for the future, for at this stage of war, most of Sevastopol's poor could still live in the city. Six months later, relentless bombardment in Sevastopol, Kerch-Enikale, Genichesk, and elsewhere produced a refugee crisis of epic proportions.

Many Crimeans could not afford to evacuate and remained in their homes to weather the European invasion and Russian occupation. A vignette from Tolstoy's *Sevastopol Sketches* portrays the precarious existence of civilians caught in the crossfires. A poor sailor's widow lamented as cannon fire fell around her: "The women who had husbands and money all moved away . . . but here— oh misery me, the poorest house in the neighborhood, and they've blown it up, too. Look at him blazing away, the devil! Lord, Lord!"[78]

In a bustling harbor, European and Ottoman Allies greet each other alongside a short railway connecting ships in Balaklava with supply stations in Allied camps. The British Army had the technological advantage during the Crimean War, and built the railway shortly after they had disembarked. *W. Simpson, artist; Paul & Dominic Colnaghi & Co., May 24, 1855.*

5

The Feeding Ground

THE WINTER OF 1854–1855 WAS deathly cold. British soldiers weathered freezing temperatures without greatcoats, 25,000 of which sat in a ship at the bottom of the sea, capsized by the November hurricane. Other ships lost masts, rudders, and precious cargos of food or gunpowder. Icy gales swept away tents and crashed ships on the rocks. More than 1,000 men drowned. The frost on Christmas Day (as marked by Catholics and Protestants) killed one Englishman in the trenches, while dozens of unsheltered horses and work animals died from exposure.[1] Russian soldiers fared no better. They too waited for sheepskin coats that had not arrived. Food prices soared; a quarter of a pound of sugar more than tripled to 1.75 rubles. Crimean wine, which was 1 ruble in the fall, cost 9 rubles after the New Year. For another ten days as 1854 turned to 1855, Russian soldiers had no bread.[2]

Mutiny loomed. In angry tones, a commander wrote to his superiors about flu and other epidemics raging in Cossack regiments. Underprepared for winter, men died because they still dressed in their summer uniforms. Men and work animals alike starved.[3] Conditions worsened through January, prompting the same commander to issue a public statement read in front of all Cossack regiments and batteries. The statement harshly criticized the Russian military establishment for satisfying personal gain over the needs of their men. The order (*prikaz*) was shared widely with thousands of angry, hungry warriors posted in Crimea, and read as follows:

> There is no doubting the valor of the military. The chief problem is provisioning people and horses. True, in this corner of the region, the Authorities meet huge obstacles in acquiring wagons. But really the Commander in Chief could easily feed all the cavalry in Crimea with the Intendant's ability. . . .
>
> All of Rus, from the wealthy to the poor donated what they could for general success. Regimental Battery and Squadron Commanders! I appeal to Your unwavering patriotism: forget personal gain for the sake of our general glory. . . . Let the first priority be to feed our soldiers and sate our horses. From the impossible we make the possible, and then with God's help, we will faithfully defeat the enemy.[4]

Indicting Menshikov and his chief intendants, the Cossack commander blamed his superiors for the day-to-day suffering of the rank and file.[5] Relentless hunger kept Russian soldiers on the razor's edge of mutiny, and the crisis in supply ultimately cost Russia Sevastopol. It most certainly deepened the schism between military and civilians throughout the southern Russian Empire and shaped life in Crimea for the duration of the war. When the military failed to provide, Cossacks and soldiers turned to the civilians for food. Breakdown of supply, inadequately clothed men, starving horses and soldiers, the threat of mutiny and peasant rebellion, in other words, the day-to-day experience of war prompted Russia's Military Reforms, and not "humiliating defeat" as so many scholars have proposed.[6]

War fell upon Crimea like Gargantua and Pantagruel at feast; the entire peninsula became the feeding ground. The feeding and supply of an army during battle is decisive.[7] Bread, and not strategy, wins a war, theorized F. K. Zatler. As the Crimean general in charge of organizing supply, Zatler wrote from experience.[8] Provisioning the army in Sevastopol became the biggest challenge of the war, as more soldiers concentrated in Crimea than the peninsula's entire prewar population. In 1848, Tauride contained fewer than 650,000 people, half of whom lived in Crimea, with about 54,000 horses. Seven years later, the population of the peninsula swelled with 300,000 soldiers and 100,000 horses. Human and equine population had doubled.[9]

The enemy positioned along the coast besieged the cities of Evpatoria, Balaklava, Sevastopol, Yalta, and Feodosia. Plundered and bombarded, these cities quickly became empty shells. The towns of the interior—Simferopol,

Karasubazar, and Bakhchisarai—anchored the Russian defense. Residents gave up their homes and schools to hospitals and officers' quarters. Local industries ceased prewar activities and transitioned to mass production of food, barracks, and furnaces. All grain, livestock, oxen, horses, and carriages funneled from the most remote corner of the province of Tauride to the military hive in the interior. Crimean merchants entered into the war's command economy, and all operated at a steep loss.

Hospitals

From the outset of the war, Simferopol and the constellation of interior towns became the way station for the sick, the wounded, and the dying. The first six months of conflict in Crimea produced more wounded and ill than one year of the Danubian campaign.[10] The scale of the conflict was much larger than the military commanders and the war ministry had imagined; only four military hospitals existed in Simferopol, Feodosia, Kerch, and Sevastopol before the Allied invasion. Anticipating a possible naval battle on the Bosporus, Governor Pestel had created another small hospital in Bakhchisarai during the spring of 1854. Together, these hospitals had 3,000 beds for an army of 52,000 men, a ratio deemed sufficient for peacetime; only two of three beds had adequate supplies for the wounded and ill. The battle of Alma (September 8/20) soon clarified the need to enhance medical facilities. More than 3,000 Russian soldiers were wounded; and nearly one-third of them were left on the battleground.[11] Following Alma, the military rushed to relocate hospitals and medical staff to Crimea. Gorchakov's vast command allowed him to boost medical facilities in Crimea within one month.

Nevertheless, September proved to be a terrible challenge. Crimean infrastructure simply could not support the needs of the military's many divisions. Following the Battle of Alma, the medical department entered the competition for wagons. One medical officer complained to the general in charge of supplies in the beginning of October that the wagons he had ordered a week earlier to transport patients from Simferopol to Kherson had not yet been delivered. "I apply personally everyday to the head of the province [Pestel], and receive promises," the commandant complained, "but still there are no wagons." Upon asking Pestel when the wagons will arrive, the officer heard the same answer: "It depends!"[12]

The governor's equivocation did not reflect indifference; far from it. Rather, Pestel sent courier after courier through Crimean villages, one more remote than the other looking for carts that had not already been donated or drivers not already pressed into service. His couriers returned bearing news of over-tired civilians and ransacked villages. The resulting inability to transport wounded soldiers from the battlefield meant that many men died who might otherwise have been saved, while corpses rotted above ground because there was no one available to remove the dead for burial. Locally, the military's utter monopoly over transportation meant civilians had no efficient way to tend to their own business. Especially, they could not transport their harvest to the mills or, later, sow seeds of a new crop.

In contrast to Alma, Russian medical staff managed Balaklava well enough. Hostilities resulted in fewer than 700 injuries, and the army had prepared for far worse. With 6,800 wounded, the battle of Inkerman was another matter. Beyond inadequate space for incoming patients, medical staff grappled again with too few wagons and transport animals. When Pirogov arrived eighteen days after the battle of Inkerman, he found more than 2,000 soldiers who should have been operated on immediately after the battle lying in dirty material.[13]

Space also came at a premium. Hospitals, transfer stations, and operating rooms occupied private homes and public buildings, even courtyards. When a bomb destroyed the naval hospital, a makeshift space was created out of Sevastopol's Noble Assembly. The dance hall served as triage, where bloody men lay on the floor between once-gleaming marble columns and the unlucky underwent medical butchery in the billiards room.[14] In Simferopol wounded and sick men had beds in thirty different public buildings as well as in the homes of a few residents.[15]

The Russian Military expanded medical staff by pulling young students from their medical programs. Konstantin Leontiev, the poet and Slavophil, was among this generation of students. For Leontiev, the war was a grand adventure. Twenty-three years old, he self-educated in the Idealist tradition popular in Russia during the first half of the nineteenth century. Leontiev had developed a friendship with the famous novelist Ivan Turgenev, and took to heart the words of poet Nikolai Ogarev, who had asked, "What do I want?" and answered, "Everything in all its fullness."[16] The short poem expressed the yearning desires of a melancholy generation, eager for experience, and eager for change.[17]

Leontiev grew up hearing about the daring feats performed by his elders in the war against Napoleon. For Leontiev and many in his generation, no other experience, except perhaps love, was as meaningful and transformative as war. Like many who served in Crimea, Leontiev embraced the opportunity to prove himself. He had also dreamed of seeing Crimea, which had been steadily growing in Russian nationalist imagination during the reign of Nicholas I. He wrote: "For three years in a row in Moscow before the war, I always thought about Crimea. . . . I also thought about war; I was terribly frightened that in my lifetime there would be no kind of large and serious war. And to my joy, I came to see at once both of these different things together—Crimea and war."[18]

Initially posted at a military hospital at the fortress in Enikale (about 12 kilometers, or 7.5 miles, from Kerch), Leontiev labored non-stop from 8:00 in the morning until bedtime. Disappointed he had not been sent to Sevastopol, Leontiev initially saw a very different, quieter side of the war than Pirogov or Tolstoy. Nevertheless, he often cared for 200 patients a day, many of whom had served in Sevastopol.[19] Before breakfast, Leontiev studied curriculum assigned by his final medical course.

In Moscow, he wrote, he had only removed "the cold, dead leg of an anonymous corpse under the kind and intelligent supervision" of his professor in the predictable environment of the school's anatomy theater. In the fall of 1854 in Crimea, the young Leontiev performed surgery for the first time on a live person. He vividly recalled confronting the desperate faces of living, breathing men, and slicing "a large knife through warm, vital flesh of a soldier's thigh, and the flood of live, hot, blood."[20] Four of his seven amputees survived, a rate he considered successful. Whereas Tolstoy devoted his later writing career to the experience of war in various ways, Leontiev did not; although he described the war as transformative in his memoir, he otherwise wrote very little about it.[21]

No less than men, women felt the call of duty and honor. The Russian battlefield nurse Ekaterina Bakunina told one general, "If I had been a man, then I would have long had the honor to serve under his [the general's] leadership; when the call came for women, I could not refuse."[22] Bakunina read about British and French nurses in 1854 and advocated for the formation of the Sisters of Mercy. She served from 1854 to 1860, with posts in Sevastopol, Simferopol, Bakhchisarai, and Kronstadt. "Really could it be possible all this has happened," she asked writing her memoirs four decades later, "and I saw it all?"[23]

Through the winter of 1855, the medical staff created a network of hospitals between Sevastopol, Simferopol, Odessa, and Vosznesensk. November and December proved to be important months for military medicine, as the military pulled more resources in and invited foreign doctors. Americans had arrived to work in Crimean hospitals as early as March 1854.[24] By February 1855, more forces concentrated in Crimea, bringing the army to 160,700 men. The eight hospitals of Crimea held 16,400 patients. More than 12,000 suffered from epidemics spread in enemy camps and among the civilian populations. Cholera and typhus were constant concerns.[25]

Crimean residents gave their homes to the army for the quartering of the sick and infirm. The Simferopol Quartermaster listed eighteen private residences housing 1,000 men. Records indicate that people of all Crimea's ethnicities gave up their homes: one Tatar civil servant put eighty beds in his home, as did Crimean Jews and Karaim.[26] The medical staff placed thousands of wounded soldiers in the care of Crimean Mennonite colonies and created new hospitals in Perekop and Karasubazar.[27]

Food

Food constituted a crucial point of interaction between the military and civilian population, yet Russian law, as recorded in the Military Regulation of 1846, provided only general guidelines. The 1846 Regulation vested military personnel with special authority, and was the law to which military personnel referred when issuing orders in areas they occupied. Few civilians, however, would have been familiar with the content of the Regulation. In March 1854, as St. Petersburg went under martial law, the editors of *The Northern Bee* translated the dense code into language readers could understand. The goal of this fascinating article was to educate Russians about their new, war-time obligations and so is well worth reviewing here.[28]

Principally, the article emphasized the enhanced powers of the military commander. Civilians owed support to the military, the author explained, in the three main areas of transportation, hospitals, and provisions. The military had the legal right to hire transportation, whether carts for convoys, or rafts for water routes. Under orders from the military commander, residents also had to prepare hospitals and care centers for hurt or sick soldiers.

The article in *The Northern Bee* laid out a process local communities were to follow, but which quickly broke down in Crimea. Ideally, local officials inventoried existing produce at the local, district, and provincial levels, which they then submitted for review to the regional commander. The commander then established new prices for food that balanced market availability and military consumption. He also set rent for homeowners who quartered soldiers. Finally, the regulation stipulated that "in situations of extreme need" soldiers themselves were allowed to take provisions directly from residents provided they left a receipt.[29]

In short, martial law placed civilians at the mercy of the appointed military commander. Civilians could not set prices, nor could they demand payment

for food. As one might imagine, the imposition of military law in the provinces could be as arbitrary or illogical or as sensible as the leader vested with its
authority. Further, even without the laboratory of war, it is evident the broad
powers Regulation granted the military could lead to a wide number of abuses.

In Crimea, food extraction and preparation unfolded in lopsided negotiation between the military, civilians, and different government agencies.
Procuring, transferring, and preparing food involved the office of military command, whether the commander or his agents, the governor of
Tauride, and various representatives from other Russian bureaucracies,
including the Ministry of Internal Affairs, Ministry of State Domains, and
the Ministry of Finance. Together, military and civilian bureaucracies engaged in a complex operation that began with the fall harvest and ended
with bread and *sukhari* in the soldiers' hands. Conflict more than cooperation characterized food interaction as each group fought for the interests
of their respective spheres.

The Russian military food chain in the nineteenth century began with
grain, not the product of that grain (i.e., bread). In an age before refrigeration,
chemical preservatives, and rapid transportation, food had to be made freshly
and in the immediate proximity of soldiers. Rather than working with single
corporations to provide complete meals as do modern militaries, nineteenth-
century food procurement stretched from farm to table. Transforming the raw
food into a consumable product assumed critical importance, and civilians
near the war zone became bakers for the Russian military. Considering the military had instantly tripled Crimea's population, however, farm to table meant
importing raw grain from hundreds of kilometers away.

Within two weeks of the enemy invasion in September 1854, Menshikov's
staff ordered local provision committees to organize the preparation of *sukhari*.
Similar to croutons or dry toast, *sukhari* resists mold longer than fresh bread
and so had a better chance of arriving to the soldiers unspoiled. Unlike British
hardtack, however, Russian *sukhari* is made with yeast, which limited its shelf
life and presented a challenge for Crimean bakers accustomed to unleavened
breads.

Almost immediately, townspeople reported they did not have enough
kitchens to make *sukhari*, nor did bakers have enough fuel to keep ovens in
continuous operation. The engineering brigade had requisitioned all manner
of logs for building barracks and the camps took remaining woodpiles for
their own fuel. Simferopol kitchens also competed with artillery brigades and
hospitals for wagons and quickly found that transporting weapons and patients
took priority over food.[30] Tasked with producing 5,000 bushels of *sukhari*, the

town Bakhchisarai managed to bake their *sukhari*, but could not deliver the product because the military had already commissioned their wagons.[31]

For these reasons, local bakeries took weeks to meet the growing needs of the expanding military in Crimea. Particularly after the Battle of Alma, the sudden influx of military placed a very heavy burden on Crimean supply systems. The bottleneck of provisions sent a wave of panic among the rank and file, while intendants sought to supply their respective divisions through whatever means possible. Panic turned into anger when commissioners finally delivered, and quite late, wagons full of soggy, moldy bread. Alarm spread through the troops as did the words "the soldiers have nothing to eat; the soldiers are without *sukhari*."[32]

As kitchen and bakery production normalized, residents of Crimea and the province of Tauride supplied the grain, the kitchens, and the labor. Local residents also paid costs of the operation. In Simferopol, for example, wealthier merchants and nobility contributed 1,000 rubles to support baking. In this way, all strata of Crimean society contributed to the war effort, willing or unwillingly performing their obligation. Under direct oversight of the civilian bureaucracy and police, which organized the collection of flour from the committee stores and distribution to residential kitchens, Crimean residents harvested and milled the grain, delivered grain and wood to kitchens, baked bread, and paid for it. [33] Local carpenters built furnaces and ovens so more Crimean residents could be drawn into the baking process.[34]

Not all places complied with the order to make bread or *sukhari*. The Karasubazar city council (*duma*) claimed, for example, it could not fulfill the demand for *sukhari* because the residents of Karasubazar were not ethnic Russians. They did not know, he wrote, "how to cook yeast bread, and due to this inexperience, are in danger of spoiling state flour."[35] The *Novorossiiskii Kalendar* (New Russian Calendar) for 1848 lists the population of Karasubazar at more than 12,000 people, predominantly Tatar and Armenian (twenty mosques and four churches), while Pirogov described finding only one Ukrainian in a city of up to 15,000 Tatars when he visited a hospital there during the winter.

A very old Crimean city dating to the Mongol era, Karasubazar also had one of the largest *Krymchak* populations, or native Crimean Jews who dressed similarly to Tatars and spoke a Turkic language.[36] Most likely, this Tatar, Armenian, and Jewish population made and consumed lavash or traditional Tatar unleavened breads and had little practical experience working with yeast. In mid-September, two weeks after the enemy invasion, the veteran group (presumably deputized by the police force) tasked with gathering provisions pressed Karasubazar again, this time for feeding the Don Cossack regiments. The city stated its willingness to support the efforts to make *sukhari*, provided the veterans brought in twenty-five experienced bakers.[37]

Crimean residents continued to provide grain and bread for the military through the end of the war. Many were forced to abandon their regular activities in service of food production, and had their homes and livelihoods ruined as a result. While some military agents behaved responsibly toward local property, many did not. Thus, the home of a Tatar merchant in Simferopol and business had been transformed into a bakery for one of the hospitals in the fall of 1854. Upon conclusion of peace and evacuation of wounded, the hospital had given him a receipt, which he presented to the quartermaster for compensation.

Rather than reimbursing the merchant for two years' worth of damaged property, capital investment, and production, the quartermaster exploited the opportunity of an open kitchen. He transferred the merchant's property to the "lower ranks" of the Minsk regiment, which turned the kitchen into a boiler house. The Minsk regiment destroyed the property, burned wooden doors, and stole, lost, or ruined the tools.[38] The merchant's experience was reflected widely across the peninsula. Still, the majority of urban residents in Simferopol, Bakhchisarai, Karasubazar, and other central towns with Russian hospitals and provisions activities fared better than villages in the war zone patrolled by the Cossacks.

Villages between Crimea's interior cities and the coast had become a no man's land. Villagers tried to eke out survival against a backdrop of Allied–Cossack skirmishing. They endured enemy raiding and Cossacks who requisitioned supplies for themselves and the soldiers at Sevastopol.[39] Rarely did Cossacks issue receipts. Lacking a steady supply of food for themselves or their horses, Cossacks continued to plunder, and the rate increased several-fold in the cold winter months. On December 5, the German colony at Kronenthal reported, for example, that the Cossack cavalry stole oats and barley. The Cossack commander ordered his men to be punished, and stated that they had acted "independently." Their immediate superior was also penalized for failing in his supervision.[40] By February 1855, however, as the Cossacks died in large numbers from exposure and malnourishment, their commanders turned a blind eye toward unlawful foraging.[41] Starving and cold, these men roamed the Crimean countryside in bands of ten, twenty, and thirty men, stealing anything they needed to survive. Tatars who resisted were hanged or arrested as traitors.

Transportation

In addition to space and supplies, transportation became a major drain on civilians and a constant source of anxiety for civil servants and military men alike. Arriving at Perekop from St. Petersburg after traveling 4 kilometers (2.5 miles) an hour on the leg from Kharkov, Pirogov found the postal station to be little more than an ill-used shanty. Built to accommodate imperial correspondence and small trade, it could not cope with thousands of soldiers and their supplies moving in and out of the peninsula. Its windows had been broken, the floors were dirty, and Pirogov's party waited half the night for a set of hungry horses to be fixed to his wagon. Still, he commented, the experience in Perekop "was golden, in comparison with that which we encountered in Crimea itself."[42] In the depth of the winter it could take two weeks to travel the 60 kilometers (37 miles) between Sevastopol and Simferopol due to the terrible roads, inadequate horses, and over-taxed drivers.[43]

When the war was still in the Danube, Crimeans donated horses and oxen to help transport troops from the interior to the ports in Feodosia and Sevastopol. After the Allied landing, however, the military demanded that residents give even more. In mid-September, Menshikov turned to the Governor of Tauride with a demand for wagons. Subsequently, Governor Pestel asked the German colonists of Tauride and residents of Feodosia for help. Feodosia sent forty carts, while Mennonites in Melitopol contributed nearly 300 wagons. These particular wagons transported military patients to Simferopol hospitals.[44]

Menshikov further ordered state peasants, the majority of whom were Tatars, to supply 1,000 horses. Drawing upon a formula previously established by the Ministry of State Domains, military intendants requisitioned one horse per thirty peasants, and one in eight from the Muslim clergy. District authorities were to work with two or three elected members of each village and the *kadi* to organize the selection. Officers gave villagers who lost horses receipts in the amount of 35 rubles for a horse without a saddle and 40 rubles for a horse with a saddle, and placed copies of receipts with Menshikov's chancellery.[45] In the fall, official records noted that Tatars had given nearly 2,500 horses and 943 saddles. Yet, such a number reflects only the initial wave of work animals Crimean civilians provided the military. On March 5, 1855, the Tsar officially recognized Crimean Tatars for their "laudable gift to the Throne and Fatherland."[46] To feed animals, Crimeans donated millions of pounds of hay, which still fell well short of military demand.[47]

The very large sacrifice of local communities amounted to a drop in the bucket of the military's needs. As the army grew in Crimea during October, November, and December of 1854, so did the need for animals. The intendancy

estimated the need for horses at 14,000 for the regular cavalry; 6,500 for artillery; 14,000 for Cossacks; 3,000 for higher officers; and another 3,000 beasts
of burden. Altogether, the army used on a *regular* basis some 44,000 horses
and 2,400 oxen.[48] The demand for animals grew so quickly that agents for the
intendancy simply took horses from villagers or bought animals on the black
market. Tatars from unoccupied parts of the Evpatoria district issued an official
complaint in October after Cossacks had confiscated their horses and later sold
them to the Lieutenant of the Light Infantry connected with Korf's *wagenburg*
(a mobile military camp) outside of Sevastopol. Civil authorities in Simferopol
wrote to the lieutenant's superior, demanding the return of the Tatars' horses,
but it is unlikely that the horses and their masters ever reunited.[49]

Feeding war animals proved as taxing as procuring them. Together horses,
oxen, and Crimean camels could consume 10,000 tons of hay per month, and
in one day, up to 360 tons. The military animals very quickly consumed all
available Crimean straw and grass once they arrived. Oxen and horses pulled
3,500 carts from the north of the Tauride province to Sevastopol just to feed the
animals. The hay estimates did not include, moreover, the fodder needed by the
work animals that brought supplies to Crimea's borders.[50] The competition for
straw and hay was so contentious that the military placed fodder under strict
guard to prevent soldiers from stealing it for their starving horses.[51]

Animals were among the biggest casualties of the war; beyond the dangers
of the battlefield, horses and oxen stumbled, fell, and broke legs on Crimea's
terrible roads in large numbers.[52] Many more suffered starvation and exposure.
In summer months, distressed cavalries who had no other options left their
horses to stand long hours in the sun. Cossacks watched helplessly as their
beloved, under-nourished horses sweated under the scorching rays until they
spilled blood and molted like birds.[53] Dead horses rotted on the roads unless
soldiers dragged them to the side.

After the Battle of Inkerman alone, 357 horse carcasses piled up along the
road to the Chernaya River. Soldiers threw lime on the carcasses, hoping the
oncoming winter would arrest decay.[54] On the road between Sevastopol and
Duvanov a space of about 16 kilometers (10 miles), it was not uncommon to
come across ten, fifteen, even twenty horses dropped from exhaustion on the
roadside.[55] The intense cold of the winter and the hurricane of November
worsened conditions for the animals. In British camps, pitiful cavalry horses
"attempted to stay alive by eating canvas covered with mud, old socks, blankets,
saddles and even one another's manes and tails."[56]

In December 1854, F. K. Zatler, who was visiting Crimea from his post
in Bessarabia, forecast a year's provision needs for Crimea's army of 100,000
men. Stores on the peninsula located close to the military (i.e., 55 to 200

kilometers, or about 35 to 125 miles) anticipated receiving approximately 308,220 bushels of grain and an additional 10,314 bushels of oats at the beginning of January. Outside the peninsula in the northern districts of Tauride, stores had another 510,000 bushels of grain and 13,500 bushels of oats. Such an amount was to be supplemented with an additional 1,500,000 bushels of wheat and 110,000 bushels scheduled from surrounding provinces. The difficulty, he wrote, stemmed from transportation. There were not enough wagons on the peninsula to move all the grain from its origin to stores in Simferopol, Karasubazar, and Sevastopol. Moreover, movement of grain between Simferopol and Bakhchisarai required six to fourteen days of travel, and from Perekop to Simferopol, easily two weeks.

To feed Sevastopol, Zatler suggested food convoys needed to travel unceasingly between Perekop, Simferopol, Bakhchisarai, and Sevastopol. Without wagons and drivers for hire in Simferopol, however, it was likely that the army would experience shortages. Moreover, couriers often had to wait several days at postal stations for increasingly scarce horses, which then traveled at a rate of 5 kilometers an hour on clogged roads.[57] One could walk from Simferopol to Sevastopol more quickly, in other words, than a wagon of grain could travel. Poor Crimean roads and transportation impeded the military through the end of the fall and the beginning of the winter. Costs of gunpowder, bread, and vodka grew daily, while cost of transport expanded at an even faster pace.[58]

Wagon drivers found Sevastopol overwhelming; the city was constantly in motion and under fire. Parapets crumbled only to be resurrected somewhere else. Buildings daily collapsed into rubble. Under these conditions, addresses were hard-to-impossible to pin down. Drivers spent days searching for addressees, enduring terrible roads, often under fire, while horses went hungry. Eventually the drivers either found the addressee and delivered the goods in terrible condition, or simply sold the lot.[59]

Consequences for Civilians

Between September and December, military obligations had impoverished Crimea, a place where most people lived at or just above subsistence level. The Bakhchisarai town council petitioned the governor of Tauride for relief in light of the dramatic increase in transportation and quartering obligations for the military.[60] Hosting the military had "emptied the town of grain stores, hay, and ruined livelihoods based on transportation, orchards and vineyards," they wrote. For those reasons, the townspeople argued that they could not pay the a new tax imposed by the military, and asked instead whether the military might take wood from the city forest as payment in kind. This wood, the petition underscored, had been the property of Bakhchisarai residents from ancient times and spread over 1,000 acres.[61] In 1854 the city remained principally Crimean Tatar, and the signatures to a person on the petition were in the old Tatar language.

Other villages and cities in Crimea suffered similar or worse depletion. By year's end, four months of battle, disease, and army encampments had taken its toll. In villages around Perekop, dry weather and excessive demand created a shortage in the water supply. Wells that once flowed continuously had been drained to mud. By March, Cossacks established a guard over water, limiting villagers' access to two draughts a day.[62] The civilian population throughout the entire province dropped nearly 30,000 from its prewar high.[63] The death rate from cholera, especially around areas occupied by the enemy in Perekop and Evpatoria, was still unknown, while the massive exodus of Tatars had not yet begun. Murder increased four-fold among Crimean inhabitants according to local crime reports, much of it the result of interfaith violence.[64]

Animals, oxen and horses particularly, died in terrible numbers. Like men, many animals died in battle. Lt. Col. Calthorpe described the wounded horses as one of the "most painful things" about the Battle of Balaklava. He wrote:

> Some of the poor creatures went grazing about the field, limping on three legs, one having been broken or carried away by shot; others, galloping about screaming with fright and terror. At times, some would attach themselves to the Staff, as if desirous of company; and one poor beast, who had its nose and mouth shot away, used to come in amongst us, and rub its gory head against our horses' flanks; he was ordered to be killed by one of the escort.[65]

Soldiers slaughtered horses and oxen in the hungriest days of the war. Other animals perished from overwork and undernourishment.[66] A report at the end of the war calculated the number of Tauride animals that had perished from exhaustion (see Table 5.1). Moving provisions was more taxing for animals than moving soldiers. More than 35,000 oxen and 12,000 horses died hauling food and hay.[67]

The war devastated Crimean landscapes, agriculture, and livestock. Enemy and Russian armies razed forests for firewood, barracks, and bulwarks.[68] The year before had been an exceptionally hard growing season, with a long, dry fall and cold, hard winter. Freezing temperatures had already killed off many animals and crops during the first half of the year, and in the second half of the year, the Allies destroyed Crimean vineyards and orchards. The nascent

Table 5.1 Dead Working Livestock, May 1, 1854–April 1856

Tauride Districts	Died Transferring Military			Died Transferring Provisions			Total		
	Horses	Oxen	Camels	Horses	Oxen	Camels	Horses	Oxen	Camels
Crimea									
Simferopol	648	2,436	—	284	2,796	—	932	5,232	—
Perekop	1,755	2,362	160	779	1,220	255	2,534	3,782	415
Feodosia	11	160	—	230	2,240	—	241	2,400	—
Evpatoria	892	2,294	—	143	466	—	1,035	2,760	—
Northern districts									
Berdiansk	102	33	—	5,344	1,6933	38	5,446	1,6966	38
Melitopol	296	186	—	1,056	2,022	—	1,352	2,208	—
Dneprovsk	301	372	—	976	1,299	70	1,277	1,671	70
Total	4,005	7,843	160	8,812	17,176	363	12,817	3,5019	523

Source: GAARK, f. 26, op. 1, d. 20938, l. 75.

tobacco industry, which had been developing between Yalta and Simferopol, and around Evpatoria and Perekop, also collapsed in 1854. Heavy obligations to transport the military took Tatars away from the harvest. Leaves withered on the stock.[69] Grain scattered in the field, and that which had been gathered waited to be milled. In other words, not only had the war consumed available food, it had interrupted the fall harvest and prevented stockpiling provisions for the coming winter.[70]

Throughout Crimea and the province of Tauride, local business suffered tremendously to the point of collapse. Merchants in Sevastopol, Yalta, and Evpatoria in December of 1854 petitioned for tax and duties amnesty, arguing that the war had brought ruin and terminated trade.[71] Evpatoria officials renewed their request in June 1855. The request listed a diverse group of Tatars, Karaim, and Russians, in the first, second, and third guilds. Typically tax relief required presentation of evidence and accounting, but because many of the merchants had evacuated following enemy occupation, argued the Evpatoria treasury, "the taxes cannot be paid, and other merchants will not be able to renew their dues personally." The officials asked that the Evpatoria merchants be released from providing evidence, while retaining their status and ranks.[72] Two months later, the New Russian Governor General petitioned the

Ministry of Finance to extend tax relief and exemptions to Kerch, Berdiansk, and Feodosia.[73]

Concerns raised by Crimean merchants reflected complex issues pertaining to precarious social status as well as financial survival. Russian tradition and law freed merchants from the burdens placed upon serfs: soul tax and military service. Merchants occupied a privileged place in Russian society. Unlike nobility, who inherited a stable status determined by birth, merchant status depended upon their financial success. Enterprising serfs could pay their way into guilds willing to accept them, just as merchants who failed to pay their guild fees could be expelled.[74] Financial ruin during the war meant merchants could be reduced to serfdom.

As local businesses collapsed in the first weeks of the war, a new crop of merchants entered Crimea to trade with the military. Many were Jews from Poland and Bessarabia who, through peculiarities in Russian law, were uniquely licensed to travel and sell within certain perimeters of the war zone. These men filled a necessary function in the market, and provided officers and soldiers with items that could not be had locally or through the military, such as razors, shoes, and food. Their well-established trade networks extended beyond the plagued military requisition routes through Ekaterinoslav and Kherson.

Anti-Semitism rose sharply in the form of negative caricatures of Jewish merchants, and Jews, like Tatars, were blamed for withholding grain, horses, and services. Tension further developed between local religious and ethnic groups because Russian law organized imperial subjects according to identity markers with attendant rights and privileges. On the surface, Russian subjects were organized into four main social estates: nobility, clergy, townspeople, and serfs (state and private-owned). These groups were further legally divided into so-called natives or ethnic Slavs, "non-Russian national minorities [*inorodtsy*] and foreign-born nationals [*inostrantsy*]," who were in turn sub-divided into hierarchies of estate.[75] Thus, for example, population registers for Crimea divides the Russian population into groups of nobility, clergy, townspeople, and peasant, and within that, the townspeople are divided into the merchant societies of the 1st, 2nd, and 3rd guilds.

It has been argued that the categorizing of the Russian population rendered imperial peoples vulnerable to state exploitation.[76] This was indeed the case in Crimea, as statistics assisted the state in determining which population group to lean on for requisition. Moreover, Crimeans themselves were hyper-aware of differences in legal privileges or exemptions based on group identity. During the war, a few local Crimean guilds competed with one another for military contracts, which led one malcontent to complain that the Simferopol Provisions Committee made "nefarious deals with Jews for delivery and transportation of provisions, and refused to contract any of the loyal Russian suppliers."[77] Reduced to poverty and powerless to resist demands of the military, Crimea's diverse population began to turn on each other.

From Menshikov to Gorchakov

Tsar Nicholas I died of influenza on February 18, 1855. His name was consigned to history when the civil bureaucracy and the military took an oath to his son, Tsar Alexander II, nearly two weeks later. Hope for peace traveled through Sevastopol city streets, but it quickly became apparent that Alexander II planned to continue the war started by his father. By then, Menshikov had retreated to Simferopol to recover from a severe gall bladder infection. Pirogov, who had become circumspect in his criticism of Menshikov after he realized his confidants might have loose lips, became bold once again. "We would all be very glad," he wrote to his wife, "if Prince Menshikov upon becoming better, did not return to Sevastopol."[78] Daily command of the military passed temporarily into the hands of Osten-Sacken.[79]

In an order dated February 28, Menshikov announced to his men that Tsar Alexander II had relieved him of his responsibilities so that he could recover his health.[80] The tsar subsequently appointed Gorchakov as Commander in Chief of the Army and Navy for all of Crimea on February 20, 1855, granting him authority over Kerch as well.[81] The general took over from Osten-Sacken on March 10.[82] Privately, Menshikov expressed relief, writing to the tsar of his transfer of power to Prince Gorchakov, "I take it as a sacred duty to share with him everything I know, not only with complete transparency, but also with feelings of friendship which have united us since childhood."[83]

The disaster of provisions in Crimea was widely known and one of the many failures of the war attributed to Menshikov. While a convenient scapegoat, Menshikov was in many ways hostage to circumstance. The active military had increased from just over 100,000 men to 300,000 during the fall of 1854, and provision needs had grown faster than the either the military or civilians could supply.[84] This is not to say that Menshikov could not have made better decisions or advocated more actively in the war ministry for an increased budget. Rather, war had expanded into a small space wholly unprepared to accommodate it. For the short time he held the reins of war in Crimea,

Osten-Sacken had made an effort to address corruption and complaints from the civilian population, but he could do little more in the space of a month than issue empty warnings. Change did not come, therefore, until Gorchakov arrived in Crimea.

Arguably, the biggest challenge facing Gorchakov in March was neither the Allies, nor the cholera that had done so much damage in the fall of 1854. Rather, it was the crisis of supply. The majority of Gorchakov's commands in his first month in Crimea addressed the provisioning system. His very first order, issued even before he announced his authority over the eastern part of Crimea that had formerly belonged to Khomutov, increased the allotment to the Cossacks serving in Evpatoria.[85] Numerous other commands in March addressed corruption in the intendancy and soldiers' unlawful requisitioning from Crimea's civilian population.[86]

Differing from Menshikov, Gorchakov opposed scorched-earth tactics. "In my opinion," he wrote weeks before he assumed Menshikov's command, the military "must not be ordered to set homes on fire, not in the cities, and not in the villages in the path of the enemy's advance." Although many commanders had seen the burning of Moscow as the cause of the French army's demise, Gorchakov argued that the sacrifice was too great. The edge gained from deliberate destruction of district and provincial cities was not worth the disadvantages.[87] Gorchakov later elaborated his position. Destroying farms, homes, and food would leave civilians vulnerable *and* alienate them from the Russian cause.

Gorchakov cleaned house in the Crimean intendancy as one of his first items of business. He staffed the office with his own men who had conducted war in the Danube.[88] F. K. Zatler, who had run all operations of the intendancy for the 4th and 5th armies out of Kishinev replaced Vunsh as the chief intendant in Crimea.

Born in Finland and educated in the school for orphaned children of military servitors, Zatler had had a long career in the Russian army. He had participated in the Russian suppression of Poland in 1831 and had worked in military bureaucracy until his transfer into the intendancy under General Paskevich in 1846. He had received awards and promotion for ensuring smooth provisioning of the Russian army during its invasion of Hungary in 1849. Upon the opening of the Crimean War, Zatler led the provisioning operations in Kishinev, based directly under Gorchakov's sphere of authority. Learning of the collapse of provisioning in Crimea, Zatler left his post in Kishinev to review affairs on the peninsula. He submitted a report to Menshikov in December with recommendations for improvement. Those recommendations lay dormant until Gorchakov brought Zatler more permanently into the Crimean theater.[89]

As the chief intendant for the army in Crimea, Zatler's responsibility involved securing a steady supply of food for soldiers. A chart compiled by Zatler's office gives a sense of the soldiers' diet and the amount of food and livestock soldiers and their officers were expected to consume between March and June (see Table 5.2).

In addition to flour, oats, vinegar, salt, and vodka, the intendancy had to consider firewood and transportation, including oxen for pulling the carts and fodder needed to sustain them. Never before, not even during the Napoleonic Wars, had the Russian intendancy been tasked with organizing such a mass quantity of food for such a large military. Nevertheless, Zatler concluded that imperial stores within a 500-kilometer radius had enough stock and that local provision committees could cope with transporting the food to the gates of Crimea. Once the food reached Perekop and Melitopol, however, Zatler argued that food would become stuck, and rot in place as it had done during

Table 5.2 Estimated Supplies Needed for the Southern Army, March–June 1855

Item	Amount
Wheat	5,760,000 bushels
Groats	540,000 bushels
Vodka	7,488,000 liters
Vinegar—for three months	2,160,000 liters
Pepper—for three months	30,562 pounds
Salt—for three months	2,608,000 pounds
Oats—for the full year for 68,146 cavalry horses and 30,000 transport horses	8,400,000 bushels
Hay—for the full year for 68,146 cavalry horses and 30,000 transport horses	18,777,600 pounds
Straw—for the full year for 68,146 cavalry horses and 30,000 transport horses	29,991,054 pounds
Firewood	272,640 meters
Oxen (calculated on the basis of 1 per 360 pounds)	140,000
Carts (in ideal conditions)	132,621

Source: Table modified from Zatler, *Zapiski o prodovol'stvii voisk v voennoe vremia*, 1: 253.

the winter. Food, in other words, was not the challenge; transportation was. The Russian military had only about 7,000 carts at its disposal, and needed 125,000 more. Moreover, if by necessity the food for the military was to come from outside of Crimea, the labor of transport fell to residents of Tauride, who were pressed into mandatory service.[90]

Zatler's report also explored the problems of foraging and pricing. Foraging, Gorchakov had stated in an edict, had "attracted [his] particular attention." Because the military had failed in the feeding of its soldiers, most had turned to "foraging," a broad term meaning (in the context of Crimea) procurement of food outside the rationing system. At best, foraging referred to the purchase of items at market prices, and at worst, the arbitrary seizure of goods and services from local residents. Zatler's agents compiled evidence for what had become common knowledge among all inhabitants (permanent and transient) of Tauride: food prices had risen dramatically without adjustment in the treasury for inflation. The result was that soldiers starved from constant shortages, while the treasury operated at a loss. Moreover, the arbitrary seizure of residents' resources had completely exhausted the peninsula.[91]

By winter, Tatars no longer had the ability to feed their animals, as the military had requisitioned all hay and barley from their fields, and so sold their work animals to the soldiers to be consumed as food.[92] Through the fall and the winter, the military had eaten their way through military transport animals; more than two-thirds of Crimean military and civilian work animals had been slaughtered for food.[93] Gorchakov further became incensed at rumors that the military had not only pressed civilians into transportation obligations without pay, but had done so for long periods of time, without regard to civilian livelihoods. He forbade the practice and demanded immediate release of any civilian conscripts.[94]

Gorchakov expressed dismay at the state of the peninsula, which had been wrung out like an old rag. "Never is it possible, in a time of war, for the military to count on foraging for its needs," he argued. Foraging drains the region, he insisted, and leads to ruin. In drawing from the province for sustenance, the military had drawn until nothing was left in the land, neither produce nor fertility. Gorchakov insisted in multiple, separate orders that the military should resort to foraging *only* in cases of extreme need. Moreover, soldiers must not forage independently but should extract resources from the war zone through a carefully controlled process. He ordered a central authority to organize extraction and set prices according to real value.[95] Such a policy aimed to eliminate war-profiteering and to cap exorbitant inflation.

Henceforth, Gorchakov demanded that unit and regiment heads carefully monitor prices, plan for the needs of the military, and communicate provision emergencies to his staff. He discouraged dependence upon civilian modes of transportation, which had already been stretched to the point of collapse, and expressly forbade the arbitrary requisition of supplies from civilians. In the event that the military had to draw upon civilian labor or resources, workers were to be fairly compensated. Gorchakov set prices for civilian transportation, which, he noted, had risen completely out of proportion. He promised quick and certain punishment for any violation of policy, whether one attempted to bypass the chain of command in procuring goods or overburdened civilians with labor obligations.[96] In short, Gorchakov crafted a new policy for Crimea characterized by reduced dependence upon local resources, controlled prices, and tight supervision over foraging.

Gorchakov also set the rations budget for military captives and volunteers appearing in Sevastopol at 22 silver kopeks per twenty-four hours, and 15 silver kopeks outside Sevastopol through Perekop.[97] He raised the prices the military would pay for meat. Reflecting the growing expense of food as one approached Sevastopol, he set a tiered pricing structure: 2 rubles for thirty-six pounds of meat outside of Crimea (in Dneprovsk, Melitopol and Berdiansk); 2 rubles, 40 kopeks in Crimean interior (around Simferopol, Bakhchisarai and villages in between); and 2 rubles 60 kopeks for Sevastopol and the coastline up to Bakhchisarai. Further, Gorchakov imposed a series of regulations designed to prevent the military from consuming working livestock. He stipulated that all oxen procured by the military intendancy for meat rations must come from *outside* Crimea, and have careful documentation showing the origin of sale.[98] It should be noted that Crimean civil officials who remained in their posts experienced the same dramatic rise in food prices but did not have the same support behind them.

Despite intentions to improve the system, Zatler's intendancy, like that of his predecessor in Crimea, failed the soldiers and the civilians during the remainder of the war. Inflation tripled, and then quadrupled. A sack of flour costing 3.7 rubles in Tauride in 1854 surged to 12 rubles by 1856; hay rose from 28 kopeks for thirty-six pounds to 1.5 rubles.[99] Starvation and shortage shot through the army. The army in turned squeezed the civilian population, which had nothing left to give. A din of criticism emerged in the Russian periodical press immediately after the war, and anger over failures in Crimea shifted from Menshikov to Zatler. Allegations of corruption in the intendancy were particularly acute. Tsar Alexander II ordered an official investigation spearheaded by General Adjutant Prince V. I. Vasilchikov, who had won distinction during the siege of Sevastopol for reestablishing order among military supply chains.[100] In response to his critics, Zatler compiled one of the most detailed and eloquent discussions of military provisioning in its era.

The problem, according to Zatler, was the nature of the war. The Crimean War was the largest war Russia had ever experienced. During Napoleon's invasion of 1812, the Army had amassed and fed 125,000 men for an engagement that lasted six months, from June to December. With the exception of Tarutino, the army had moved constantly, which spread the sphere of its provisions over a vast space. Food did not need to be imported long distances and communities had time to recover. The army moved toward food; food did not move toward it. But the arrival of war in Crimea, he wrote,

> was entirely unexpected, in the very worst time of year, in September 1854, before the *rasputitsa* [impassable road conditions due to weather], and continued two falls, two winters, two springs, and only one summer, and finished in March 1856. The military completely stripped the Tauride peninsula in October [1854], and after, they concentrated in Crimea almost for two years, on a very small piece of land, separated from grain-producing provinces by 400 kilometers of steppe. Moreover the military was two times larger than that of 1812.[101]

"Obviously," Zatler concluded, Crimea and surrounding areas under these conditions "must have been exhausted much more than the provinces through which our military traveled in 1812. . . ."[102]

At the beginning of 1855, the General Governor of New Russia, Annenkov, attempted to redress the exhaustion of Crimea, and took care to widen the gathering of materials from Kharkov, Voronezh, and Kursk. To a lesser degree, he included Kiev, Podolia, Poltava, Ekaterinoslav, and Kherson, provinces that had already given substantially to the military when the war was near Bessarabia.

Annenkov also lobbied the Committee of Ministers to introduce relief measures and benefits for state peasants of the peninsula, particularly refugees from Evpatoria, Sevastopol, Balaklava, and Yalta. He further asked about relieving peasants from taxes, arrears, and reduction or cancellation of various state obligations. The tsar approved Annenkov's request at the end of January and released 500,000 silver rubles for the governor of New Russia to apply at his own discretion to the needs of Crimean peasants, many of whom wound up in Nikolaev, Kherson, and Odessa.[103] Later, the tsar released another 1,400,000 rubles for refugees.

Further, Annenkov secured distribution of emergency grain supplies to residents of Tauride. In February 1855, the Committee of Ministers purchased 1,200 bushels of wheat for distribution to evacuees from coastal towns. Some of this grain was to be given out as loan and some was to be sold in rations. The ministers stipulated that loans were to be given only in extreme circumstances with a three-year limit, the first two years without interest. In April of 1855, the Ministry of the Interior approved loans for all peasants living on land-lord estates, with a reserve based in Simferopol.[104] The ministry continued to issue loans for food, and to organize distribution of grain reserves for civilians living near the war zone. However, these measures were reactive, taken at the height of crisis, rather than proactive efforts to forestall hunger. Moreover, as Ministry officials later conceded, the military consumed most of the emergency preserves intended for civilians.

"War cannot be fought without food," Ina Zweineger-Barielowska opens her aptly titled book *Food and War*.[105] Food supply and food shortage plagued the Russian Army and all belligerent parties during the Crimean War. Food became such a crisis that the Russian government instituted a commission to study army supply in 1855 and subjected Zatler to a criminal investigation immediately after the war.[106] The problem was not the military's alone, however, but was shared by the civilian population at the eye of the storm.

As Zatler subsequently argued, the Crimean War was a new type of war, one characterized by mass armies and entrenchment. Steam, rail, and telegraph had been introduced, but the technology was yet too undeveloped to make a difference in the vast Russian Empire. Answering critics who proposed that the intendancy should have organized a railroad to transport food from the interior, as had the British in Balaklava, Zatler argued that such was impossible. The technology was too new, the empire too vast, and the borders too broad. In this sense, he suggested, Russia was less a victim of backwardness than its bulk. Military leadership had planned for a war in the Danube that might spread to the western borderland; no one had anticipated its relocation to Crimea. And in only one season, war drained Crimean resources. The terrible logjam of goods had begun, and every item coming into Crimea was given to Sevastopol.

Two small groups of Sardinian soldiers survey a small mosque and narrow aqueduct stretching across the Chernaya (Black) River before battle. The bucolic scene contrasts with the ensuing slaughter that left thousands of corpses in the fields and river. *Aqueduct of the Tchernaya (Sardinian Picket), Lt. Col. Andrews, J. Sutcliffe lithograph, 1855.*

6

People's War, or War against the People?

COMBINED WITH DEFEAT IN INKERMAN, winter's hunger produced hysteria across the peninsula. Many Russians began to scapegoat military failures and the subsistence crisis on the local population. Rumors alleged that Crimean Tatars collaborated with the enemy and hoarded food. Seeking to prove Tatars' innocence, the Tauride mufti advocated the creation of a Tatar militia. He believed Muslims could restore good faith with their fellow Russian subjects and the tsar by joining Russians on the battlefield. He encouraged Tatars to follow the example of thousands of Russian peasants who had volunteered for service in temporary militia from the start of the Crimean War.[1] The mufti swung conditional approval from Tsar Nicholas I, the New Russian Governor General Annenkov, and officials in the Ministry of the Interior. Told to refrain from sharing his plans among the Tatar community before securing final approval from the military, the mufti nevertheless sent an announcement to local *kadi* and *mullahs* throughout Crimea.[2]

In his call to his spiritual flock, the mufti addressed the Tatar mutiny in Evpatoria. He argued that Allied agents manipulated Tatars' historical and religious affinity with the Sultan for their own nefarious intentions and wanted to use Tatars as weapons in the war. Rebellious Tatars had become victims of propaganda, he said, casting a shadow over the much larger population of faithful subjects. He enjoined Tatars to redeem their people in the eyes of the tsar and Allah by fighting for Russia. The mufti invoked the Napoleonic War, when Crimean Muslims had lain their lives down for Russia. Once again, he argued, Tatars "must go bravely to the defense of our Fatherland and courageously resist the enemies," . . . "and only then can we prove our love and respect to the law of the government and public order."[3]

Despite the mufti's best efforts to will the militia into being, the Tatar militia never materialized.[4] Instead, government authorities placed Tatars under surveillance and initiated a forced migration of Tatars along the coastline. Winter peace talks between Russia and the European powers had broken down, and the bombardment of Sevastopol had begun anew in the spring.[5] With little warning or time to pack their belongings, men, women, and children were deported from the border of the occupied territory.

The quick change between the tsar's permission for Tatars to form a militia and their deportation into the interior reflects the constant tension between various wartime Russian civilian policies. The Russian government pursued multiple approaches to managing populations living along the war zone, each of which placed needs of the military over the needs of civilians. Some of these efforts, such as the creation of military districts (*voennye okrugi*), became the foundation for postwar reform. Resource extraction was paramount.

Another set of questions revolved around whether the military could *trust* civilians. Could the government motivate peasants to fight a *narodnaia voina* (partisan warfare—literally, "people's war") against the enemy as in 1812? Or, would the population collaborate with the enemy? Russian opinion divided.

Men like Baron A. E. Wrangel, who became the District Military Commander (*voenno-okruzhnoi nachal'nik*) in western Crimea, and Count N. V. Adlerberg, the military governor who replaced Pestel in Simferopol, viewed Tatars en masse as traitors. They argued in multiple reports that Tatars were conditioned by their faith to side with the Sultan and believed that Islamic law allowed Muslims to murder Christians indiscriminately.

Other Russian officials, like Gorchakov, had a much more nuanced view and may have envisioned relocating Tatars as an emergency evacuation. Finally, some Russian officials, like the Minister of State Domains, Kiselev, and his agent in Crimea, von Bradke, actively campaigned on Tatars' behalf. The first proposal to relocate Tatars appeared in July 1854, even before the enemy landed in Crimea. These men managed to forestall the forced migration for a time. Of course, their efforts may have meant little to those innocent Tatars arrested for crimes they did not commit, or who lost everything when they were ejected from their homes.

Partisan Warfare and its Dangers

The Russian military's conflict over *narodnaia voina* stemmed from lessons learned during Napoleon's invasion of Russia. In 1812, peasant partisan warfare was matched in equal part by peasant rebellion. Russian military leaders, particularly Lieutenant-Colonel Denis Davydov, encouraged the use of peasant militias to disrupt enemy lines and harass transportation networks. Davydov encouraged peasant militias to capture French scouts, and fight guerilla warfare. However, even as Russian officers began organizing militia, some peasants turned their arms against local landlords and agents of Tsar Alexander I. Rumors spread among the Russian peasantry along with the advancing French troops that Napoleon planned to free the serfs. Western provinces in Belarus and Lithuania experienced the most peasant disturbances, but uprisings also occurred in Tver, Perm, and near Novgorod. In Penza, Russian serfs who had been drafted into Russian forces as temporary militiamen overthrew their commander. Believing entry into regular infantry would result in freedom at the conclusion of the war, these militiamen demanded to be sworn into the army as regular soldiers.[6]

In the decades that followed, Russian military theorists debated the utility of partisan warfare, comparing the example of organized peasant militias in Russia against the spontaneous guerilla warfare exemplified by the Spanish population during the Peninsular War (1807–1814). Russian experimentation with partisan warfare in the 1828–1829 Russian–Ottoman War also provided critical context for military debates.[7] At the outset of the Crimean War, Tsar Nicholas I revived the debate about *narodnaia voina,* asking his generals for their perspectives. Gorchakov's response, delivered while still organizing the military effort in the Danubian Principalities, reveals a pragmatic philosophy mired in the slippery language of empire.

Gorchakov advocated limited use of partisans guided by local police forces. While civilian officials evacuated papers and treasuries to a safer location, police should remain in their places to protect the mail. If necessary, police should deputize and arm the most capable people in the villages. In ideal circumstances, the local population could assist in capturing enemy spies and couriers; driving off the livestock; removing or destroying reserves; and destroying mills, bridges, wells, and roads. Gorchakov saw a role for adolescents as well. Under the supervision of an elder, he suggested that young men could secretly observe enemy maneuvers, ascertain the sizes of enemy forces, intercept couriers, and the like.[8]

The general also envisioned a critical role for clergy, who should stay in their posts just as the police. He recommended that the government should:

> Inspire all clergy with acts of loyalty to the throne and hatred of the enemy;
> clarify for parishioners that it would benefit everyone to expel the enemy,

and there is an obligation of each and all to harm the enemy, to resist him in all possible ways, to deprive him of food, to resist providing convenient means of transport, to seize small units and bands; to assist Russian military as needed; and finally to take small enemy parties under guard and present them to Russian military couriers. . . .[9]

While Gorchakov believed that the Russian government would find the most support among the Orthodox clergy, he also initially advocated that similar instructions be given to the "foreign faiths" in the line of enemy invasion.

In Crimea, Orthodox priests played a visible role that belied their small percentage of the population in Crimea. Orthodox priests stayed in their posts longer than most bureaucrats, and provided regular intelligence about movement of Allied troops near their parishes.[10] After the war, the Crimean Orthodox clergy received medals for their activities, an honor not extended to their Muslim counterparts, who were eager to form a militia.[11] Clergy posted in remote borderland villages in the Baltic Sea and White Sea played similar roles, acting as agents of military intelligence and in the case of the Solovetsky monastery, invoking their medieval militaristic heritage.[12] In theory, his instructions should have included Muslims, and in Tauride, the mufti was ready to fill the role prescribed by Gorchakov. But in practice, the Russian military—Gorchakov included—rejected Muslim and partisan assistance.

Despite recognizing the utility of partisan warfare, and having developed a fairly comprehensive vision for its management, Gorchakov ultimately opposed drawing upon partisans for the Crimean War. Partisan warfare, he argued, should only be invoked in cases of extreme need and not in areas prone to peasant uprisings. Peasant resistance had begun in different parts of the empire as early as 1854 in response to recruitment, and continued to grow through 1855. The largest uprisings occurred in Kiev and Voronezh.[13]

Peasants in nine of twelve districts in Kiev rebelled against local authorities after a call to arms published by the Holy Synod in February 1855 emphasized the religious nature of the conflict and invoked peasant memories of 1806 and 1812.[14] Government agents pinpointed the origin of the uprisings to an over-zealous local priest who allegedly read an 1806 manifesto to his parish that he had dug out of church archives. The proclamation promised Ukrainian peasants attached to noble estates they could transfer into Cossack status if they signed a military roster. Rumors of freedom in exchange for service quickly spread through many villages and townships.

During Holy Week, 700 peasants gathered outside the gates of a noble estate in one village. In another, a discontented crowd of 3,000, armed with old muskets and farm implements, demanded release from their seigniorial obligation.[15] In both cases, district police fired upon the crowd; dozens of peasants were killed and many more were injured. Another major uprising occurred in Korsun, when 4,000 peasants refused to work on their local landlords' estates claiming they had been transferred to Cossack status after signing up to serve in the war. On this occasion, eleven peasants died. The peasants' behavior, wrote the official charged with investigating the event, was caused by excess drunkenness brought on by the religious feast.[16]

Undoubtedly aware of the peasant disturbances in Russia's western provinces, Gorchakov saw little role for partisan warfare in 1855. A People's War in 1812, Gorchakov argued, had a place in those provinces on the left side of the Dnepr, where the people naturally had feelings of faith, loyalty to the throne, and hatred of the enemy. Further, the governors of those provinces, in Gorchakov's view, had worked efficiently to channel popular support for the Russian military. Local authorities in the provinces under attack in the Crimean War, however, were not nearly as reliable; many in Bessarabia and Crimea had resisted the order to destroy food.[17] Such policies, he argued, caused tremendous schism between the military and the local population.

In the same series of reports, Gorchakov addressed the issue of food and population relocation. He argued that Russian forces should destroy only surplus food, rather than food needed by civilians to survive. He further cautioned against moving people against their will. If evacuation became necessary, he argued, people should not be forced out into the wilderness but instead should be relocated to a safer place through a sensible and methodical process.[18] Here, Gorchakov expressed sensitivity to civilians that was rare among his counterparts, including awareness that moving people too quickly would induce or enhance poverty.

The Crimean War presented a very different environment for partisan warfare than the Napoleonic invasion. Napoleon's march on Moscow struck at the heart of Russia. During the Crimean War, in contrast, the enemy attacked the imperial border. Bessarabia, Gorchakov pointed out, had a population mainly consisting of Moldavians, Bulgarians, and Germans. In Crimea, Tatars were the majority population.

To leaders evidently still quite concerned about an Austrian invasion, Gorchakov responded, "The primary population [in Podolia, Volynia and Kiev] is of the Orthodox faith and of Russian origin, but the nobility and middle class consist of Catholics and Poles." There was little to no hope of rallying the Poles of Ukraine behind the Russian throne. If the Poles (due to their Catholicism) had a dislike for Russian rule, the tribes of Moldavia, according to Gorchakov, were "sluggish by nature."[19] Gorchakov transferred skepticism about partisan warfare to Crimea, for it was he who ultimately rejected the idea of a Tatar militia unit.[20]

Military Districts

Instead of Tatars fighting for the Russian tsar, as the mufti had advocated, Russian authorities pursued a program of oppression and surveillance as outlined in secret instructions initially formulated for Bessarabia, instructions which proposed creation of military districts. Scholars have previously associated the emergence of the "military district" system in Russia with the suppression of the Polish rebellion of 1863 and the postwar Miliutin military reform, rather than the Crimean War.[21] Intended to alleviate burdens of the commander in chief, the military district commander held extraordinary powers of civilian and military administration in their respective territories.[22]

In Crimea instructions describing Military Districts circulated to Menshikov in the fall of 1854 and chiefly focused on resource procurement, preservation of order, and observation of the local population.[23] The military district commander acted as the chief liaison between the local population and the military. In times of war, he took over war-related policing duties such as the arrest of army deserters, undocumented itinerants, and black-market merchants. The instruction further required district commanders to track secretly civilian attitudes toward Russian authority and as necessary to take civilians under arrest.[24] In order to carry out responsibilities in Crimea, the military district commander was assigned military police and small Cossack brigades.

In addition to managing order and tracking disposition of the local population, military district commanders recruited translators, clerks, and accountants from the civilian population. The commander was to support building military hospitals, help armies find accommodations, procure transportation as needed, and supervise the construction of paths, barracks, and wagons. As necessary, the district commander had to outsource labor to the local population. In short, military district commanders had significant influence in the region to which they were assigned. Their reports and attitudes informed Russian policy at higher levels.

Wrangel assumed control as the District Military Commander for Evpatoria and Perekop in the fall of 1854, and reported directly to Menshikov. A Russian-German, blonde and big-boned, Wrangel had come to Crimea from the southern Caucasus, where he had served from 1839 in suppressing local tribes. In July 1854, he led 5,300 men in a successful assault on Ottoman forces nearly four times that size in the city of Baiazet.[25] When war moved to Crimea, Wrangel became the commander on the ground tasked with settling chaos around Evpatoria, and took the order of surveillance to heart. He attached less significance, however, to the other responsibility stipulated in Annenkov's instructions, which was to resolve complaints between local residents and military ranks as peacefully as possible.[26]

Stemming from the state's practice of pushing accommodation, labor, and supply onto the population, military-civilian conflict occurred frequently. Troops stationed in forts throughout the empire imposed huge burdens upon local populations who had to feed soldiers, often in times of lean harvests. Soldiers crowded villages and towns. Often underpaid and undernourished, many of these men and their families stole from their peasant hosts for survival. High rates of drunkenness disturbed social order. A well-managed military unit could invigorate a local economy, but poor management introduced crime waves and oppression. Peasant resistance to military demands in the form of individual acts of violence or mass rebellion was not uncommon.[27] The prolonged nature of violence in Crimea and the drastic shortage of supplies created a hostile environment for military-civilian interaction. Some military officials, including Menshikov and Wrangel, perceived removing local inhabitants as the solution.

Deportation Forestalled

Military-civilian policy in Crimea evolved with shifting war conditions, but also had much in common with policy articulated in other theaters including around the Danube, the White Sea, and the Baltic Sea. Military authorities organized civilians into labor forces and enlisted civilian support in procuring provisions and apartments. Military authorities formed militia units among the Christian populations and tracked the disposition of local inhabitants, focusing mostly on Tatars. However, civilian policy in Crimea was left up to Menshikov to interpret and implement and was informed by constant, unabated fears of Tatar mutiny, anxieties that emerged well before the Allies landed upon Crimean shores.

The idea to deport Tatars from the coast first arose during the summer of 1854. In July, local officials in the provincial seat approached the local agent of the Ministry of State Domains, von Bradke, about relocating Tatar state peasants to a separate province. Von Bradke, in turn, circulated the proposal to

Kiselev. Russian law permitted state and gentry to move serfs from one region of the empire to another. Before Kiselev assumed control over the Ministry of State Domains in 1837, resettlement policies evolved haphazardly according to different perceived needs of different regions of empire. Over the course of the late 1830s and early 1840s, Kiselev had passed a series of reforms aimed at rationalizing resettlement and crafting a policy attuned to peasant welfare.[28]

The minister emphasized that any relocation of state peasants must be conducted according to procedures established by Russian law, including consideration for the peasants being moved as well as for the communities to which they would be relocated. Ultimately, Kiselev rejected the proposal to relocate Tatars because officials in Crimea had included gentry-owned peasants in the proposal.[29] Tauride had among the smallest populations of gentry peasants anywhere in the empire, for Catherine had restricted spread of serfdom to New Russia.[30] In particular, she forbade nobility from attaching Crimean Tatars to their estates. Yet, she did attach Tatar free agriculturalists to the legal status of state peasants.[31]

In essence, Kiselev (whose authority may not have exceeded the military's) stalled the proposal on a technicality. As Minister of State Domains, he had jurisdiction over state peasants, but not privately owned serfs. More importantly, here and elsewhere Kiselev demonstrated a commitment to basic human rights, and activated any Russian law he could to support his program.

On the heels of the Allied invasion in September, Menshikov reopened the issue of Tatar deportation and proposed using Cossacks to remove Tatars living on Crimea's western coast. He designated a wide swath of territory for Tatar relocation, stretching from the Perekop Bay southward through Sevastopol. Relocated Tatars would be resettled north of Perekop into the steppe.[32] Governor Pestel agreed it would be beneficial to make a show of punishing those Tatars who were clearly guilty of collaborating with the enemy and urged Menshikov to make the decision quickly.

Pestel further pointed out that the military would be moving approximately 20,000 people dispersed among four townships (*volosts*) and nine village societies and proposed that Tatars be removed 25 kilometers (15.5 miles) from the seashore. He argued against relocating Tatars above Perekop, which was populated by Nogai Tatars, who, he insisted, remained loyal to Russia. Instead, he suggested removing the Crimean Tatars to a completely different province. Finally, Pestel expressed concern about the cholera and typhus epidemics that had begun to spread through semi-abandoned Tatar villages. Whether his concern was for the Tatars or for the military that would be relocating them was not entirely clear.[33]

Menshikov responded with an official order dated September 30 "to deport as quickly as possible all Tatars in the seaside residences from Perekop to Sevastopol itself to the Melitopol district." A small city north of the Sea of Azov, Melitopol had become the evacuation center for Crimea's government offices and a waypoint for refugees. The horse and oxen of those Tatars slated for relocation could be seized without reimbursement, he suggested, and allocated to the military for pulling wagons and transporting the wounded. Likewise, Tatar sheep and cattle could be distributed to the soldiers for food. Menshikov asked Pestel to relocate the Tatars "quickly, and to rush the settlement of Tatars as much as possible."[34]

Menshikov's proposal circulated northward to Tsar Nicholas I in St. Petersburg, who again tasked the Minister of State Domains, Kiselev, with researching and/or organizing the transfer of Tatar state peasants.[35] At this stage of correspondence, government documents referred to Tatars generally as "residents of the Muslim faith," rather than the pre-war terms of "Tatar," "Nogai Tatar," or "Tsegany Tatar," or otherwise the more common categorization of peoples by estate (nobility, merchant, state peasant, etc.) regardless of ethnicity or confession. Whether serfs, free peasants, merchants, or nobles, Tatars were now indiscriminately grouped together and described as "Muslims." Before the war, social identity (i.e., noble vs. peasant) held more weight than confessional designations, but this had begun to change.

Kiselev had resisted the relocation of Tatars in July. It appears he attempted to do so again in October 1854 despite pressure by the military leadership. In accordance with the tsar's wishes, Kiselev sent an agent from St. Petersburg to assist the local state councilor in Tauride. He tasked them both with researching local conditions and coordinating with the Ministry of War a safe and legal transfer of state peasants. The two men quickly returned a report listing a number of objections. Based on their conclusions, Kiselev argued that the approaching winter made it too late to move families to the interior of the province. Even just quartering Tatars in refugee centers in border provinces Ekaterinoslav and Kherson was problematic, for district officials had already complained about overcrowding, a rising itinerant population, and general disorder.[36]

Kiselev raised new questions about funding resettlers (*pereselentsev*) through their transfer and temporary quartering. Menshikov's proposal, he pointed out, called for taking Tatar livestock for the military without reimbursement or a scheme to feed resettled peasants. When Kiselev requested that Menshikov cover Tatar expenses from military coffers, Menshikov referred him to the Ministry of Finance. The problems with Tatar relocation, Kiselev argued to

Tauride governor Pestel, were many, and needed resolution before "the project could move forward."[37]

Kiselev's man in Crimea, state councilor von Bradke, protested that an indiscriminate population transfer would include innocent Tatars who "remained in a peaceful, faithful relationship with the government and fulfilled their land obligations on the estates where they lived." He suggested that perhaps guilty Tatars could be relocated but cautioned that it was extremely difficult to determine guilt. A special commission requiring his participation would need to be created, but he was too busy organizing food for the military.

In addition to the issues surrounding guilt and innocence, von Bradke raised several arguments against deportation based on logistics. Such a population transfer would be a tremendous operation requiring many carriages, and a huge supervisory role by the military, both of which the war could not spare. Removing Tatars from the war zone, moreover, could harm Russia's position, for the military "receiv[ed] at present carriages and other benefits from peaceful residents." Finally, von Bradke argued that the weather made any mass relocation untenable, and suggested that, at the very least, authorities wait until the spring before undertaking such a measure.[38] In the fall of 1854, the Ministry of State Domains had won the battle. On December 9, Tsar Nicholas I ordered an end to the "project."

Deportation Implemented

Outside of Evpatoria, Tatars and the Russian military worked closely together through the fall and winter of 1854–1855. The Crimean Tatar Squadron (which was separate from the proposed voluntary Tatar civilian militia) had formed with funding from the community and was sent to defend Kronstadt. Wealthy Tatar nobility gave over their homes for officers' quarters. Crimean Tatars of all estates provided food from their gardens and baked bread. They delivered their animals for work details and consumption. They drove carts and wagons, portaging the army and its supplies throughout the peninsula. Poorer Tatars, particularly state peasants, were conscripted as day laborers for building roads and trenches. Tatars were essential to the Russian army's war effort. Russia could not have held on to Sevastopol as long as it did without Tatars' support. Nevertheless, some Russian officials remained suspicious of the population upon which the military so heavily relied. As fighting resumed with the warming winds of spring, suspicion of Tatars burned with greater intensity.

Russians in Crimea began to fear Islam, that Tatars' faith predisposed them toward alliance with the Ottoman Empire. Equally, soldiers accused Tatars of hoarding food, convinced that they sat upon hidden stashes of grain. Some eighty years before the Soviets accused Ukrainians of hoarding grain, starving Russians felt themselves to be victims of *kulachnichestvo*.

In reflecting upon Russian attitudes toward Tatars during the war, the intendant Zatler drew an analogy between accusations of *kulachnichestvo* and witch-hunts. Just as people once blamed poor harvests upon supernatural, diabolical activity, moderns attributed hunger and inflation to *kulaks*, a term Russia imported from Germany in 1846. It was easier for hungry people, in this case soldiers, to understand food shortages as the peculation of greedy individuals (depicted variously as military intendants, Jews, or Tatars) than to grapple intellectually with larger systemic complexities of war and market forces.[39] In Crimea, panic about food manifested in anxiety that Tatars were selling, trading, or simply giving food to the enemy. Pestel's replacement in Simferopol, Count N. V. Adlerberg, typified the panic.

St. Petersburg recalled Pestel from his position on November 11 and replaced him with Adlerberg.[40] The move reflected controversy over Pestel's evacuation of Simferopol following the Battle of Alma, on one hand, and belated appreciation of Crimea as a war zone on the other. Before arriving in Crimea in 1854, Adlerberg had had a long career in Russian service. He had fought in the Caucasus and had led Russian troops into Hungary in 1849. An Orthodox Christian, he had also written a memoir of his travel through holy places in Rome and Jerusalem that was published in 1853.[41] Upon arriving in his post in Crimea, Adlerberg conducted a campaign of oppression against Crimean Tatars, intent to squash a Tatar resistance that existed in the dark corners of his imagination.

His annual report for Tauride submitted in the beginning of 1855 reflects an abiding, bitter sentiment toward Tatars. In a section titled "*narodnaia nravstvennost'*," or "people's morals," Adlerberg noted that the murder rate in Crimea had substantially increased, which he attributed to the "rude morals, or what might be more accurately called—character—belonging to the majority of the population of the province, Tatars." Adlerberg iterated a growing belief among Christians that the Islamic faith did not view murder of non-Muslims as a crime, "but the opposite, in many cases advantageous." In contrast to Pestel's relatively frequent intercession on behalf of Tatars who had been plundered by Cossacks, or Crimea's Greeks and Russians, Adlerberg's report attributed the mass robberies and looting in Evpatoria and Perekop exclusively to Tatars.[42]

Adlerberg also accelerated observation of Tatars. His increased dependence upon informants often resulted in punishment without trial. In a typical example, a woman identified in the documents as "Aisha" approached the

Commander of the Greek Battalion in March 1855 with incriminating information against the Tatars of her village. At first, she informed the Greek Commander that the Tatars of the villages near Alushta gather in crowds in the middle of the night to plan for the arrival of the French ships. Aisha supplied the Greek Commander with names, and met with his superiors. Based on her accusation, with no other supporting evidence, ten Tatar men were arrested.

On July 15, Aisha made another accusation against some of her relatives in a nearby small village.[43] She claimed that four Tatars visited them from Yalta, who had said the French planned to disembark in fifteen to twenty days. These same four Tatars (whose names she also gave) hid in the forest with their families, and visited Alushta every few days to gather supplies for themselves, and to learn about Russian military operations.[44] Aisha's denunciations reached the ears and desks of Crimea's highest authorities.

Although officials had no tangible proof to support her claims, they arrested the men she identified anyway. Unfortunately, we know nothing about Aisha but her name. Was she such a loyal Russian patriot that she would denounce her kinsmen? Did she receive financial or other kind of reward for making a denunciation? Was she coerced? Or did her relatives scorn and abuse her? Whatever the case, Aisha was not the only Tatar informant for the Russian military. In December 1854, a Third Guild Tatar merchant in Bakhchisarai reported another Tatar for "having a relation with the enemy."[45]

Reports of Tatars collaborating with the Allies multiplied. Even after the fall of Sevastopol, a district official reported that Crimean Tatars visited the Allies, "congratulated them, gave gifts, and kissed their hands." He complained that villagers gave the invaders cattle, sheep, chickens, tobacco, fruit, and other goods. The Tatars allegedly showed French soldiers the locations of the Yalta treasury and provisions, churches, and important district buildings. The official reported rumors of a potential Tatar insurgency against the Russians, but the whisper "Now is still not the time," floated through the countryside.[46]

Toward the war's conclusion, accusations against Crimean Tatars continued unabated.[47] Another set of allegations, reported on February 6, 1856, involved supposed spies. Tatars from Miskhor, Markur, Simferopol, and Toktar were accused of hiding out in the Baidar foothills near Foros and reporting to the French about the Russian position. However, the evidence of their having spied appears only to have been that these Tatars visited the Russian camps, which they could have done for trade or labor.[48]

The chief complaints against the Tatars were that they supplied the enemy with food, informed the enemy of the whereabouts of Russian forces and, apparently, Orthodox churches, which the Allies repeatedly robbed. Adlerberg himself believed that the Tatars constructed a vast spy network that stretched from Berdiansk to Evpatoria and spread information along secret channels. His anxieties were fanned by knowledge of a British spy who had at least one Tatar in his employ.

Charles Cattley was a Russian-born Englishman who served as a consul in Kerch until May of 1854. Cattley left for England at the beginning of the war and became a chief advisor to Lord Raglan, supplying valuable information about Crimean geography. He landed with the English in Evpatoria in September 1854 and built a small network of spies from Polish deserters, including Chodasiewicz, and a few discontented Tatars. But for Adlerberg and many Russians losing the war, the number of traitors seemed infinite, and Tatars were an easy target for blame.[49]

After Tsar's Nicholas I's death, his son Alexander II immediately altered decades of Islamic policy. He eliminated the Tatar courts and required accusations of treason to move through military tribunals. Those found guilty were to be quickly exiled to Kursk. Tatars denounced by Aisha, for example, were sent to Kursk. Shortly after that episode, more than one hundred Tatars were exiled to Kursk, and another forty-nine were sent to Ekaterinoslav.[50] For the most part, however, the only evidence of Adlerberg's policy that survives is a few atypical or precedent-setting cases that warranted a significant amount of paperwork. One such story involved four young boys.

In June 1855, four boys under the age of sixteen were sent to military headquarters for questioning because they purportedly visited an Allied ship. The boys pressed their innocence, claiming they left their homes only to sell a horse to a Cossack. Despite their testimony, Russian authorities detained them.

Subsequently, the investigator of this particular case received letters of reference from important Tatars in the village, including a high-ranking bureaucrat and a Tatar princess. Given the elite witnesses, the case was sent to Gorchakov, who commanded they be released due to lack of evidence. In January 1856, the case was still open, for between the initiation of the investigation and Gorchakov's order, a space of approximately three months, the boys had been sent to Kursk. On January 16 the Military Governor of Kursk reported that two of the boys had already been dispatched to Simferopol in September 1855. The third he promised to send back immediately, but the fourth, he noted, had died long before while under arrest in Perekop.[51]

Consistently, Tatars protested their innocence and the innocence of their family members. In April 1855, Adlerberg received a petition from Ahmed Menshid requesting the release of his father and brother from prison. He acknowledged that a few Tatars in Evpatoria had collaborated or looted property.

Seeing the chaos in Evpatoria he, along with his father and brother, fled to a nearby village in the Russian zone. Shortly after, Cossacks seized his family and sent them to prison in Ekaterinoslav. Despite having letters of support from a number of witnesses, including the landlord whose estate had been pillaged, Menshid's father and brother remained under arrest.[52]

Spurred on by his suspicion of Tatars, Adlerberg pressed authorities to reopen the matter of Tatar deportation. He wrote to von Bradke asking for information about the last efforts to relocate Tatars. Von Bradke described in detail multiple obstacles to relocating Tatars. Mainly he emphasized the illegality of deportation. "The few orders about resettling Tatars did not have consequence," von Bradke stated, and "the proposed project did not come into being."[53] Von Bradke refused to assist Adlerberg, but by then he had left his post in New Russia on grounds of ill health during the winter and was writing from St. Petersburg. He could do little to stop a plan that Adlerberg had already put into motion.

Despite von Bradke's caution and the protests of innocent Tatars, Gorchakov ordered the relocation of all Tatars living within 25 kilometers of the western Crimean coast, between the Tarkankhut Bay and the River Alma. Issued on May Day, his order was repeated on May 3 by Count Adlerberg.[54] Tatars were to be sent "to more remote villages, primarily in the Perekop district," a land by then riddled with disease and scorched by drought.[55] Military authorities made no plans for transporting or provisioning the population, only demanded they move. Gorchakov left it to the Governor of Tauride, Adlerberg, to make arrangements, who in turn passed direct responsibility for relocation to the local authorities in Evpatoria and the Cossacks. The ensuing relocation unfolded in chaos and met resistance as local authorities considered the logistics and contested the legalities of the move.

The general of the Cossack cavalry tasked with relocating Tatars reported on May 11 that the "removal of Tatars 25 kilometers from the shore" had been fulfilled. After all the descriptions of Tatar encounters with Cossacks, one can imagine how this was done: Cossack horsemen pounding into village after village, sabers flashing through clouds of dust as women hid their children behind the folds of their skirts, bold young men swearing at the indignity and resisting as they could.

Cossacks tasked with driving Tatars from their villages resisted orders to transport people to their new location. They could not spare the soldiers, their commander wrote, nor did they have transportation capability. Managing the population's needs was the responsibility of the civilian authority, not the military.[56] His words reflected the chronic breakdown between civilian and

military chains of command that worsened conditions for the civilian population throughout the war. Tatars thus lost their shelter and subsistence, with
no way to get to their new, temporary homes.

By this point in the war (perhaps as a result of changing leadership styles
between Tsar Nicholas I and his son), orders of the Commander in Chief
in Crimea took priority over the wishes of the Ministry of State Domains,
which had been tasked with finding living space. Nevertheless, on May 23,
Kiselev wrote to Adlerberg demanding that the treasury release funds for Tatars'
food and accommodation.[57] No reply from Adlerberg is contained in the
documents, but given the general shortage of food in Crimea as well as from
the mass migration of Tatars that began in 1855 and continued until after the
war, we might assume they received nothing. All Kiselev could do was release
state peasants from taxes, land duties, and society collections. He further ordered that relocated Tatars should receive provisions for their families until the
next harvest, and he set aside a specific store of grain for that purpose.

Who fell under the relocation order was a constant question. At the beginning of May, the Evpatoria Court presented a letter to Adlerberg asking for
clarification. The local police tasked with pushing people out of their homes
did not have complete authority over nobility, merchants, and townspeople.
The court expressed concern that forcibly moving ranked subjects might generate substantial resistance. Finally, the court raised questions about the *Russian*
state peasants. Were they also to be relocated?[58] Their question about relocation of Russians was an important one, for it struck at the heart of the forced
migration: was it a punishment of Tatars and reflection of perceived loyalties,
or was it an emergency evacuation measure, the sort outlined by Gorchakov
in his earlier discussion of population management on the Bessarabian front?

Questions about who to relocate, whether the migration was aimed specifically at Tatars or also included Russians, and whether district police had the
legal right to move those civilians who held various ranks took weeks to reach
Gorchakov for a response. Eventually Gorchakov clarified to Adlerberg that *all*
residents were to be removed: "townspeople, merchants, nobility and clergy,
and equally the Russian peasants in the villages."[59] For Gorchakov, the relocation was an emergency evacuation measure—Tatars were not to be singled
out, but all residents were to be moved. The bombardment of Sevastopol had
gained new momentum at the end of March; Russian commanders reported
more than 700 casualties in one day on March 31. The possibility of retreat was
not far from Gorchakov's mind.[60] Despite Gorchakov's orders, local authorities
remained reluctant to forcibly relocate ranked subjects, regardless of ethnicity,
while many Russian bureaucrats proved reluctant to remove other Russians.

Requests poured in from villages and individual residents to be excluded from the relocation. In one example, a Tatar nobleman from a village in the Simferopol district directly approached Gorchakov about the relocation of his family. First, he opposed relocation on the grounds that his family lived beyond the 25-kilometer mark. But after looking on a detailed map with military leaders, he conceded that his estate indeed fell within the catchment zone. After further debate, Gorchakov allowed the man and his family to stay, due to their demonstrated service to the military.[61] Similarly, the marshal of the local nobility refused to evacuate his estates. Instead, he made a formal complaint that the Cossacks attacked his property with intentions of stealing his livestock. Rather than taking the responsibility of evicting a man whose rank was probably higher than his own, the regimental commander requested that Adlerberg handle the matter.[62]

As the forced relocation was underway, delegations of Tatar peasants similarly approached Gorchakov. They did not have the rank of nobility to resist their exile, but they did negotiate their destination. Rather than being moved toward Perekop, they asked to go to Karasubazar or near the Chongarskii Bridge, a request Gorchakov granted.[63] In another case, Gorchakov ordered a few *auls* in the valley of the Alma River not to be evacuated. The documents do not give a reason. One can only imagine either the residents were located at a strategic point for the Russian military, they sat close to the border of the specified 25 kilometers, or they had a highly ranked patron.[64]

Only two weeks after he issued the order to evacuate Tatars, Gorchakov issued an order to cease the relocation, evidently persuaded to stop by the Ministry of State Domains. On May 16, he wrote to Adlerberg that according to "the Tauride Department of State Domains, I must inform you that now is not the time for the relocation of Crimean Tatars."[65] More than a week later, Gorchakov repeated the order to Adlerberg: "The recommendation to resettle those Crimean Tatars living up to 25 kilometers from the coast between Perekop and Sevastopol, to the interior of the region, now is not to be followed."[66]

Even in June, local leaders were still asking whether the Tatar relocation was taking place, for although Gorchakov had issued an order to desist, Adlerberg had not passed it on to his agents. One local commander complained that his office had received nothing about Gorchakov's order in writing. In any case, he acknowledged, the relocation had not been completed because his office did not have the staff.[67]

At the end of July, the official in Evpatoria who had originally posed the question about whether highly ranked subjects as well as Russian settlers were to be moved wrote to the Evpatoria court again, stating that he still had not received any answer to his question.[68] He wrote his superiors on four separate occasions between May and July, but, he complained, he had received neither a clear instruction about how to carry out the deportation nor about who exactly should be deported. He did receive a report in mid-June that Gorchakov had ordered an end to the relocation, but from his own superiors he had heard nothing. Meanwhile, he reported that Don and Ural Cossacks, without officers or civil agents, forced their way through villages. They raided salt stores and stole grain, and livestock.[69]

The Ministry of State Domains calculated altogether that the Russian military had forcibly relocated 4,279 men and 3,090 women to Simferopol and Perekop, a number that does not include children or those thousands pushed out of their homes into the wilderness. Tatars whose names reached the Ministry of State Domains were given strips of land and remained there until the war's conclusion.[70] Removed from their sources of food and livelihood, others starved during the war and lost their homes afterward as landlords seized their estates. Others returned to their property in the summer to gather up their harvests, and were arrested for their trouble.

In August 1855, authorities once again considered deporting Evpatoria and Perekop Tatars. Adlerberg and Wrangel were driving forces behind this proposal.[71] Adlerberg held among the most hostile views toward the Tatars, and perceived them as a major threat to Crimean military operations. Wrangel, whose wartime command covered western Crimea, from the salt lake in Saki, Evpatoria, and Perekop, had already pressed for the deportation of all Tatars who were under his surveillance. To be clearer, Wrangel advocated that whether guilt had been established or not, Tatars who might be considered "suspicious" should be deported.

Adlerberg agreed with Wrangel: "There is no doubting Tatars give the enemy information about our military, and experience shows everywhere any enemy appears, there are traitors from the Tatars." Exiling those under suspicion was not enough. Any Tatar, he said, "who finds himself in a forbidden zone, should be treated as a traitor, given the death sentence, and should be shot." He continued, "As concerns the Tatars on the southern coast, I consider it absolutely necessary to deport all Tatars, without exception." The place to send them, he argued, is Kursk, for several had already been exiled there. To maintain productivity of Crimean estates held by elite landowners, he concluded that Russian peasants should be settled in their place.[72] Authorities again contemplated a much wider mass relocation of all those Tatars living within 25 kilometers from the sea in February 1856. Fortunately, the war came to a conclusion before this larger resettlement came to pass.[73] Still, the relocation of thousands of people and the persistence of similar proposals left lasting impressions on the Tatar population.

Just as General Gorchakov ultimately slowed the pace of relocation after reading reports from the Ministry of State Domains, he condemned Adlerberg's oppressive treatment of Tatars. Repeatedly, he commanded Adlerberg and others to cease anti-Tatar activities. After reviewing a few cases that had escalated to his attention, Gorchakov wrote to Adlerberg asking him to "let go all the surveillance and arresting of Tatars, as well as similar orders on baseless denunciations," for, he continued, they "might produce more harm than good."[74] When the authorities in Perekop decided to establish a Military judicial committee to try Tatars for collaboration, Gorchakov insisted upon sending a representative to monitor the proceedings. After the monitor's first reports, the judicial committee was quickly disbanded. On May 7, 1856, Gorchakov ordered all districts in Tauride that "the activities of the Military Commission about the Tatar collaboration, be closed and that all Tatars be quickly released from custody."[75]

Gorchakov consistently advocated freeing Tatar prisoners. One of the most well documented cases in the archives follows that of Seid Assan-Chilibi [sic], a translator in the court.[76] Chilibi was believed to be a spy known to the authorities under the name of Osman Tselebii [sic], accused of meeting the enemy in Yalta. In Yalta, this Tselebii/Chilibi allegedly showed the enemy where the Russians kept their provisions, and "advised the enemy of all that might harm [Russia]." The translator was also accused of "meeting the enemy in Odessa, helping them receive 700 cattle, and promising 300 cattle and 1,000 sheep from the villagers of Iskut, Tuak and Sudak."

This case began in September 1854 and went through several levels before it reached Gorchakov soon after his appointment. Gorchakov resolved to hand over the case to the Muslim Spiritual Assembly. He retained faith in Tatar institutions, and believed that they would handle the matter justly. The Tatar assembly tried Chilibi and found him not guilty. Adlerberg, however, refused to adhere to their decision, and kept the accused in custody. Finally, hearing of this case again in April 1855, Gorchakov commanded Adlerberg to release the prisoner, "because there is not enough evidence against him."[77]

Another case in which Gorchakov secured the release of Tatar prisoners involved those accused by Aisha. Following Aisha's accusations, ten Tatars were arrested and sent to Kursk in May of 1855. These prisoners included two district heads and other important village members. Gorchakov received a petition from the nephew of one of the prisoners, Abduri Manchikov, who was a captain in the Crimean Tatar Squadron. The petition asserted that the accused Tatars were innocent, and one of the arrestees was a seventy-year-old man whose health would quickly deteriorate in prison.

Gorchakov intervened on their behalf and arranged for the release of at least five people. He wrote to Adlerberg, arguing that the petitioner Manchikov was in Russian service and so should be respected and trusted. The men in question were released. After the war, the Russian government officially recognized that they had been falsely charged. They returned home by July 1858 only to find that they had nowhere to go because the Yalta district authorities had reallocated their lands.[78]

The conflicts between Kiselev and Menshikov, and Gorchakov and Adlerberg, illustrate significant disagreement over how to handle the question of Tatar loyalty. While some Russian officials, notably those who had served in the Caucasus, advocated a punitive deportation, many Russians at the highest levels of authority, including Kiselev and Gorchakov, opposed Tatar oppression. It is not clear, however, why Gorchakov did not act further to protect the Tatars. To be sure, he was preoccupied with the Sevastopol siege and no one could have predicted the mass migration of Tatars at the war's end. By the end of August 1855, Gorchakov remained caught between Alexander II's desire to continue the war, and his own private correspondence with the French that contained overtures of peace.[79] Additionally, as head of the southern forces, he had little control over the chaotic daily affairs of the district officials. The chain of command vested Adlerberg with extraordinary powers of civil administration, and consequently Gorchakov heard only a few exceptional cases.

Kerch Strait and the towns of the Azov Sea. *Collin's Complete Map of the Crimea, H. G. Collins, 1854, detail of the eastern peninsula and the Sea of Azov. Courtesy Harvard Map Collection.*

7

The Kerch Strait and the Azov Sea

As GORCHAKOV CALLED AN END to the Tatar deportation, the Allies entered the Kerch Strait and laid siege to shore towns on the Azov Sea: Kerch-Enikale, Genichesk, Berdiansk, and Taganrog.[1] The American merchant John Codman described Kerch before the Allied invasion as "a thriving city, its harbor filled with peaceful traders, its magazines full of grain and merchandise, its 18,000 inhabitants thronging in the streets or domesticated in their often splendid homes or kneeling at the altars of their magnificent churches."

Overnight, war desolated the town. Charred mastheads and blackened stumps littered the once-sparkling bay. Smoke spiraled from burnt grain storehouses. The city had been ruthlessly ransacked from top to bottom in bald violation of the Allies' promise to protect life and property in exchange for surrender. Kerch's treasured museum of artifacts dating to the era of Mithridates had been plundered, the city's ancient history vandalized by "the same drunken frenzy that perpetrated murder and rape scarcely surpassed by the hell-hounds of Delhi and Cawnpore." Codman attributed blame for this wonton destruction equally to the British and the French: "What a comment upon the idea advanced by the Western powers that Russia required lessons in civilization from them!"[2]

The Allies had contemplated the attack on Kerch Strait and the Azov Sea for months. Command of the strait meant command of the Azov Sea, from where the enemy could threaten the mouth of the Don, a critical supply route and waterway to Russia's interior. On the north shore of the Azov Sea, Berdiansk

functioned as the chief depot for army provisions, while a central communication artery through the recently constructed postal road on the Arabat spit
linked news of the Crimea peninsula with the Russian heartland.

The Allies attacked Kerch and towns along the Azov Sea in the spirit
of *guerre de course*, or economic warfare. British, French, and Russian
governments had each debated whether to pursue economic warfare from
the opening of hostilities. Russian and American officials, for example,
considered issuing letters of marque to privateers in the Pacific. A holdover
from the age of sail, letters of marque granted ship captains license to seize
merchant cargo. Ultimately, however, Grand Duke Constantine discouraged the plan, citing difficulties of organizing crews and safe harbors for
privateers in San Francisco or Baltimore.

British and French navies, however, blockaded Russian harbors, set fire to
Russian merchant ships, and razed coastal industries. A British paddle steamer
caused an international uproar in May 1854 after it annihilated dozens of
Finnish merchant ships and incinerated tar and timber stores in the Gulf
of Bothnia.[3] The destructive Baltic campaign foreshadowed a much more
terrifying campaign in Crimea, in which the British targeted food stores as
well as industry. Admiral Lyons of the British navy argued, for example, that
destroying Russian provisions in Kerch would hasten the collapse of defenses
in Sevastopol.[4]

The Allied siege of Kerch and towns along the Azov Sea proved an unmiti-
gated disaster for Russian forces and for civilians. Gorchakov abandoned these
cities to the Allies, much as Menshikov had done with Evpatoria some eight
months before. The devastation on Crimea's eastern shores, however, was even
worse than in Evpatoria, for local commanders sank their own vessels before
the Allies could seize them. The Allies finished the job, setting fire to merchant
houses and city buildings. Those civilians who had the means fled in panic,
and those who could not travel endured or committed terrible violence. Fear
of uncertain Tatar loyalties swept through Christian populations living in the
eastern peninsula with the same intensity as it had gripped Evpatoria. Wrangel,
whose authority extended to Kerch in March 1854, fanned anti-Tatar anxieties
at the highest levels and proposed another forced relocation of Tatars.[5]

Kerch

Allied ships sailed along the eastern shores of the Crimean peninsula in
September 1854. From January 1855, ships appeared more frequently, and more
boldly approached shore. Khomutov, the Hetman who initially commanded

Cossacks in the districts surrounding the Azov Sea, knew his small forces could not repel an attack on Kerch. He repeatedly sent requests to the war ministry in St. Petersburg for more men and more artillery, but received little response.

In February 1855, after enemy ships sailed along Kerch strait and exchanged fire with a scouting expedition, he sent a particularly impassioned appeal for supplies, writing without necessary support that he "with shame and without giving battle must retreat, abandoning Kerch with all its batteries, hospitals, offices, and provisions." If Genichesk fell next, he warned, the large army gathered around Sevastopol would lose its supply of food. He ended with another note of caution, arguing that the 40,000 Tatars who lived in eastern Crimea and around the shores of the Azov Sea might join the Allies. Once the Allies entered the Azov Sea, Khomutov insisted, the war in Crimea was over.[6]

By the time Khomutov's letter reached its destination in St. Petersburg, however, he had already been transferred to the eastern shore of the Black Sea in Temriuk. Wrangel took Khomutov's command of nearly 7,000 men dispersed between Feodosia and Kerch. Gorchakov tasked Wrangel with preventing the enemy from gaining access to the Azov Sea or spreading to the interior. Given delays in communication through Crimea, Gorchakov gave Wrangel authority to take immediate action, without waiting for higher permission.[7]

In April, Admiral Lyons presented the case for the attack on Kerch to the Secretary of the Admiralty, who was then embroiled in debates about how to break the back of Russian resistance in Sevastopol. Mastery of the Azov Sea, in Lyons's view, was critical. He argued:

> Never was an army more in want of some success than the allied armies now before Sebastopol, and considerable success is at hand, for we have only to send 8,000 French and 5,000 Turkish troops and as many as could be spared from our small army, and in a fortnight we should be masters of the Straits of Kertch and the Sea of Azoff, thus cutting off the principal route by which the enemy receives his supplies and reinforcements, and producing, in all probably, a desirable effect on the negotiations at Vienna . . . [T]his expedition to Kertch appears to me to be a measure of self-preservation infinitely greater than that of crowding the heights of Sebastopol with troops.[8]

Lyons's feelings about the importance of the Kerch Strait and the Azov Sea met resistance from the French, who favored an overland attack on Simferopol.[9] "The indecision of General Canrobert," Lyons wrote, "is notorious."[10]

At the end of April, the Allied fleet moved toward the Kerch Strait. En route, a few ships fired upon Novorossiisk, a small town on the eastern shore of the Black Sea. With the exception of the hospital, Novorossiisk escaped severe damage. Fortunately, hospital patients had been relocated before the building caught on fire. On April 23, Khomutov noted that forty-eight ships traveled the space between Kerch and Novorossiisk. He had received intelligence that some 10,000 soldiers had left Sevastopol to lay siege to Novorossiisk and Anapa or the Caucasus. Khomutov was nervous. More than 700 Cossacks at the fort had fallen ill with contagion, and fortifications were in terrible need of reinforcement.

Khomutov and Wrangel (who was then already in charge of the opposite side of the strait) discussed plans for a united defense only to conclude they had too few men in their respective posts to help each other. "We are both located," Khomutov wrote to Gorchakov, "in a critical situation."[11] Much to Wrangel and Khomutov's relief, the enemy aborted their April expedition after disagreement between French and British forces over strategy.[12]

The British renewed their attack upon Kerch approximately two weeks later. On May 22, Lyons led a force from Sevastopol consisting of 15,000 men (3,000 British, 7,000 French, and 5,000 Ottoman).[13] Khomutov reported signs of a land and sea attack on his post in Novorossiisk: "Our military here," he wrote, "is threatened by combined forces of Turks and mountaineers on the dry road, and from the sea, the British and French navies." Under these circumstances the Allies had clear the advantage. And without reinforcement from the Russian military, Khomutov feared that the futile battle ahead would not only lose the fort, but meaninglessly sacrifice his men.[14]

Hoped-for help from Gorchakov never came as British and French forces had accelerated the bombardment of Sevastopol. On May 7 and 8, Gorchakov's men were frantically fortifying the trench around the 5th bastion. Days later, 6,000 Russian soldiers met twice as many Frenchmen in a bloody battle. Russians held onto the bastion but suffered 2,500 casualties.[15] When a mass flotilla of Allied ships set sail for Kerch in mid-May, Gorchakov's attention and resources were focused solely on Sevastopol. Simferopol, meanwhile, had been hit with another wave of cholera. Medical staff recorded more than one hundred civilians with the illness at the end of May with only a 50 percent survival rate. The epidemic continued to grow and with it, alarm.[16] With no reinforcement from Sevastopol or support from Simferopol, Wrangel ordered evacuation of town treasuries and set a scorched earth policy in motion as seventy enemy warships threatened the strait.

In the village of Sultanovka (on the north edge of the Kerch peninsula, bordering the Azov Sea), local leaders destroyed anything that could help the

Allies. This included blowing up ammunition and guns at the battery that could not be dragged away, and spoiling or burning food. Officials in Kerch decided to save the treasury but to destroy everything else. Food reserves were spoiled, and ships were either burned or sunk.[17] Blazing fires from burning ships and factories illuminated the night; smoke impregnated the atmosphere for miles.[18] Lyons recorded the scene:

> The enemy, apparently taken by surprise at the celerity of [our] movements, and at the imposing appearance of the expedition, blew up his fortifications on both sides of the straits, and retired after destroying three steamers and other armed vessels, as well as large quantities of provisions and stores, thus leaving us masters of the entrance to the Sea of Azoff.[19]

After driving off the Cossacks, Allied troops descended into Kerch and other coastal cities they had conquered.

Receiving official confirmation that the Allies had approached Kerch to lay siege to the city, Gorchakov sent orders to destroy grain and evacuate treasuries and archives from coastal towns. Worried that the Allies would move southward toward Feodosia, and from there invade the interior of the peninsula, he also ordered the evacuation of Karasubazar, the closest city to Feodosia.[20] As the second-most important interior base of the Russian army after Simferopol, Karasubazar had huge stores of grain and other supplies for the army, which Gorchakov ordered destroyed as well.

His orders met swift challenge. Karasubazar contained a military hospital with 1,000 wounded soldiers. When asked how to transport patients, Gorchakov reiterated his order to remove state treasuries and property to Melitopol, and to destroy the grain. As for the hospitals and wounded men, relocation was "not possible, because there are insufficient means."[21]

Many residents in Kerch and surrounding villages fled at the sight of Allied warships and the destruction of property by Russian forces. The Allies bombarded Kerch, setting fire to more homes and buildings. Allied soldiers roamed the streets committing acts of violence and robbery. Women were accosted and children, murdered.[22] The following days filled with chaos as Allied ships rounded the Kerch peninsula en route toward Arabat. They fired upon Cossacks and civilians protecting grain stores and set ships ablaze. Reports also surfaced, however, of deserters from the Allied camps who hid among Kerch refugees.[23]

N. F. Dubrovin and other historians following his example blame Tatars for the looting and worse: murder and rape.[24] The record is not so clear, however, as looting occurred *after* the evacuation—that is, after most Tatars and Russians had removed themselves from the path of the invasion. Admiral Mends, whose men laid siege on the town, laid blame for destruction first upon the French and then upon the Tatars, writing, "Much havoc has been committed, in part by the French troops when they first passed through [the city] but much more afterwards by the Tartar population, who, on being freed from the iron rule of their harsh taskmasters, have committed every possible depredation."[25] Yet, at a different point in his narrative, Mends acknowledges the wonton destruction committed by British forces. Other reports show Cossacks being taken under arrest for violence or looting during the invasion of Kerch, and Tatars risking their lives to protect grain stores and working for the Russian military under enemy fire.[26]

The idea of Tatar participation in Kerch's violence is further complicated by a British war strategy that intentionally targeted civilians with the aim of making "all parties feel the evils of war as much as possible."[27] By blocking trade in Russia's major ports from Odessa to the White Sea, British military and civil leaders hoped impoverished and hungry civilians might rebel against Russian authority. In the same vein of making civilians "feel" war, British warships fired upon coastal towns. Describing the destruction wrought on the Finnish coastline, one European observer noted "the strange mania [the] French & English have for burning & destroying wherever they set foot . . . bringing suffering & distress on the poor harmless inhabitants."[28] Not every British officer supported the targeting of civilians; however, the practice was common enough to elicit debates in European newspapers and to lead some military officers to deflect blame for destruction onto others.

Unlike Evpatoria, where the civilian bureaucracy left first, civil servants in Kerch stayed behind to pack boxes and to settle office affairs. Wrangel appointed two warships to transfer government accounts and papers to Berdiansk, a location that proved unfortunate.[29] Only one of the ships reached its destination. The other lost secret state documents and a vast store of local wealth to British plunder. Mends described the looting with undisguised glee:

The ship proves to be laden with all the public documents; books from every description at the public offices of Kertch; peculiar ornamented gilded little Russian cabinets surmounted with a gilded Russian eagle; several enameled heads of our Saviour encased in silver and gilded frames enclosed in cases with glazed fronts; ladies' dresses; abundance of petticoats, chemises, etc.; two cases of champagne—in fact, almost any and everything you can think

of, packed to carry off. Great is the fun while they are unpacking them all
on the quarter-deck. We find charts, plans, etc., and a whole Russian mail,
among which is a letter from Sebastopol, only six days ago to prepare for
15,000 sick coming from Sebastopol.[30]

Mend's comments offer an interesting depiction of the mercenary aspect of
Allied campaigns as well as Russian priorities of evacuation. Having spent
their time organizing evacuation of documents that ultimately fell into British
hands, the civil servants departed last, joining some 12,000 Kerch residents
clogging the lower roads out of the city.[31] In the rush to leave, people took only
themselves, leaving behind all household property and valuables.[32]

Despite hysteria surrounding the evacuation, many Kerch civil servants
fared better than their counterparts in Evpatoria. The appearance of Allied
ships off the shores of the Kerch peninsula in February had prompted a quick
flurry of exchanges about establishing benefits for evacuees. In March, the
Ministry of Internal Affairs agreed to distribute an advance of three months'
salary for evacuation.[33] Still, the advance did not stretch very far. People spent
much of the money in the first week on transportation.[34]

Refugees from Kerch found themselves in a desperate situation. Officials
were at odds over where to place them, and the subsequent delays placed undue
stress on families. At the end of May, the New Russian Governor General
wrote to the Kherson Treasury requesting an emergency release of 15,000 silver
rubles to the Tauride treasury immediately. He proposed placing refugees in the
northern Ekaterinoslav province near the Dnieper so they had easier access to
provisions moving through military supply routes, and so they could return to
their homes more quickly through the river system should the Allies depart.[35]

By June, Kerch civil servants and their offices had made their way to
Orekhov, a small town north of Berdiansk and Melitopol. Critical personnel
were to be dispersed among surrounding villages to prevent crowding. Those
whose jobs had been destroyed by the invasion, such as officials attached to
the quarantine, could settle where they wished provided they remained on
call for potential duty. People identified as "foreign residents" of Kerch were
also allowed to settle in the Orekhov district, primarily "Greeks occupied with
trade and industry."[36]

Sources surrounding the Kerch evacuation provide a rare glimpse into
Russian efforts to alleviate the strain of war upon the civilian population. In
addition to caring for its own civil servants, the New Russia General Governor's
office presented plans for refugees organized according to the social estate and
legal status of the subjects. Thus, for example, of the 15,000 rubles disbursed

from Kherson, 9,000 rubles went to pay two months' salaries for the civil servants. The remaining 6,000 rubles were allocated for the poor. The New Russian Governor also tasked Kerch city officials with finding employment for Kerch's poor, insisting that refugee settlement areas must be in need of hands to help with the war effort. "I am sure in this regard," he wrote to his agent, "you will be an attentive protector of the poor refugees from oppression and injustice."[37]

Residents who fell outside traditional Russian estates, such as the German and Mennonite colonists, or Bulgarian settlers who arrived in New Russia in the late eighteenth and nineteenth centuries, received special documentation allowing free passage to unspecified "places to which they have been assigned." In order to claim benefits, all refugees had to apply with the Kerch government in exile. The New Russian General Governor gave the exiled bureaucrats an additional 3,600 rubles from his own treasury for benefits, and charged his agent with making sure no one was taking advantage of the system by double-dipping into funds provided by Adlerberg or other government offices.[38]

The effort to support Kerch refugees was well-intentioned but had come too late for most. In June, a 100-gun ship docked in Feodosia with 256 residents from Kerch. One can imagine the cramped, crowded, and unhygienic conditions aboard the ship and the shortages of food these refugees must have endured since the Allied invasion two weeks earlier. Told they needed to wait still longer before disembarking to go through the quarantine, the residents mutinied. They took their fates in their own hands along with the ship and sailed on to Turkey.[39]

Evacuation from Kerch to Orekhov took weeks, as did the distribution of benefits. Civil servants who had stayed behind to pack up and dispatch city documents and treasuries were still in Kerch when the Allies disembarked. Many had to bribe bands of Allied soldiers and sailors for the right to leave and gave away everything they possessed. Several civil servants mourned wives and children who fell victim to hunger, deprivation, and contagion.[40]

In September 1855, the official in Kerch reported he had distributed the salaries to the state servants as specified, but the money was "far from protecting the *chinovniki* from extreme needs, particularly those with large families." Having left everything behind, Kerch's civil servants needed to start over. The disbursement, he wrote, "was hardly enough to buy underclothing and some kind of outer dress." Many families could not afford the basics of establishing a new household and had no way to heat their quarters or preserve food for the coming winter. "In short," he concluded, "without the means for existence, they underwent extreme need and loss which still increases continuously with the higher prices for food and, in general, rising costs for all the of necessities of life."[41] Although the numbers were much smaller, the movement of refugees during the Crimean War anticipated the crisis of displaced populations of later modern wars.[42]

Many of the poorer residents did not evacuate but attempted to stay in Kerch or as close to Kerch as Cossack and Allied forces permitted. Policies crafted on the ground sharply distinguished Christian from Muslim populations. At the end of May, staff officers allowed Kerch evacuees to return to the city temporarily to retrieve family members left behind and to collect necessary household items. Wrangel, however, modified the order received from his superiors, telling the field commander holding the line around Kerch not to let everyone pass the Cossack patrol. He required all people wishing to go into Kerch to be given particular passes (*propuski*) and all Christians to "be given documents according to their needs." Tatars in contrast, were only to receive passes into the city if they were "trustworthy, or were hired drivers."[43]

Such policies created a climate of oppression and corruption among military personnel, and granted tremendous powers to the Cossacks over lives of Tatars. At the same time, the local commander ordered the disarming of all Tatars, specifically "to take from them private and army guns, and to carefully check their carriages, not only for some kind of weapon, but for other monies or private things" which appear to have been stolen. Any Tatars found with stolen items were to be presented to Wrangel.[44]

Leontiev was among those who fled Kerch. A Cossack with a spare horse helped him out of the city and he quickly found a post in the Cossack regiment. Of this period, he writes only that he "sat continuously upon a horse, traveled with the regiment from place to place, from *aul* to *aul*; drank wine with the officers, and took part in small expeditions and reconnoitering. Here were many impressions and meetings, very curious, but about this I will remain silent. . . ."[45] Given his position with the Cossacks, the group who policed Tatar villages and organized the flow of refugees, Leontiev was uniquely positioned to leave a detailed account for posterity. But like Tolstoy, who remained mostly mute on the war's effect on the local population, Leontiev elected to keep quiet.

Berdiansk

The day after the Allies set fire to Kerch, they steamed into Berdiansk. Russia's four ships were no match for the Allies' fourteen. Upon seeing warships on the horizon, Russians set fire to their own vessels as they had in Kerch. Not to be outdone by their Russian counterparts, the Allies set fire to the fish factories and merchant ships in the harbor as soon as they arrived.[46] Seeing the fires in the harbor, city residents fled to Orlov and Kursk. Only the Berdiansk harbormaster remained alongside a few police officers and two chancellery workers. Even postal agents had evacuated early, taking all of their horses with them.[47] City officials and remaining civilians wishing to communicate with Simferopol, Sevastopol, Odessa, and elsewhere took their chances with postal stations 25 kilometers away.[48]

Approximately forty British and French soldiers disembarked alongside the French commander who attempted to engage the harbormaster, G. N. Chernaev, in negotiation. Chernaev explained, as did his counterparts many months prior in Evpatoria, that all persons of rank had left the city and he did not have any authority to sign official agreements. Meanwhile, the Allied soldiers looted the city. They stole what they could carry and set fire to government buildings.[49]

From Berdiansk, the ships sailed back to Kerch. Several days later, the Allies returned for herds of cattle they had spotted grazing on hills surrounding the shore. If they could buy food in an orderly fashion, the French commander guaranteed Chernaev no soldier would leave the ships. If, however, Chernaev refused cooperation, the Allies would allow their men to roam the city to take what they needed. Under these circumstances, the commander told Chernaev, he could not guarantee peaceful behavior.[50] Again as in Evpatoria, Chernaev explained the city was completely empty, and the residents had taken all of their property with them. When questioned about cattle seen atop a hill from the Sea, Chernaev responded that they were oxen transporting the residents' property. Subsequently, the French commander asked whether a few hens or greens might be purchased. Chernaev again refused, reiterating that residents had fled with all of their property, including animals and food.

In a last-ditch effort to procure meat from Berdiansk, the French commander invoked an agreement he had made with a Russian merchant V. Anopov. Through the translation of a German doctor attached to the Poltava regiment in a small hospital in Berdiansk, Anopov had agreed to sell one hundred cattle to the French commander. Upon interrogation by Russian authorities, Anopov confessed he had been "frightened to his bones" and had made the arrangement "in haste."[51] Throughout the affair, Chernaev steadfastly refused to provision the Allies, stating that he was "very sorry if the city was to suffer, but there was nothing he could do."[52]

In addition to Anopov and the German doctor, other Berdiansk residents had fallen under suspicion for collaborating with the Allies. Chernaev and the Cossacks reported rumors that a few foreigners provided the Allies with maps and books about Berdiansk, while "many Jews and Tatars" provided the Allies with food.[53] By now, rumors about Cattley had spread to Berdiansk, and they attributed the Allies' success to his intelligence. Reports of collaboration combined with the Allies' constant pressure upon Berdiansk civilians to supply provisions prompted a hastily composed policy.

As opposed to Kerch, in which a civilian evacuation to some degree had been anticipated, no arrangements had been made for residents of Berdiansk. Gorchakov therefore allowed the poor to return home after the Allied ships had gone. Yet he ordered temporary evacuations should the Allies return to Berdiansk's harbor. Anyone found treating with the enemy, whether they be "ranked or common, Russian or foreign," was to be dispatched to the military court.[54] Evidently, Russian military authorities had concerns about all populations collaborating with the Allies, not only Tatars. Naturally, even temporary evacuation proved challenging. Impoverished civilians of the lower social estates often slept outside in the open air, and many suffered the diseases rampaging through the armies.[55]

Hearing rumors about collaboration in Berdiansk, arrests, and orders for evacuation, the New Russian Governor General sent his own agent to research accusations and to organize a policing force in the Azov Sea. The agent was to base himself in Berdiansk, so he could travel between Melitopol, Mariupol, Genichesk, and Taganrog. The Governor General tasked the agent to report upon residents' relations with the enemy, if any. "You are charged," he wrote, "to settle the minds of the region, to ensure the residents return to their usual occupations, and follow without question all orders of the Authorities, and similarly to vigilantly observe the activities of the local civil servants." Additionally, the agent was to inquire about corruption in local military detachments and civilian administration. Finally, the agent was to "learn the nature of the thoughts and behavior of the Nogai Tatars," who so far had demonstrated loyalty to Russia.[56]

The agent returned a detailed report describing a few isolated cases of European merchants in Berdiansk—of British and Maltese extraction— selling the Allies cattle and oxen.[57] In addition to Cattley, the British picked up a certain Mr. Platt in Kerch, a British engineer who had worked in Russia for twelve years and who became stuck in Crimea when the war opened. Platt's sister-in-law was married to a Russian naval commander; still, he became a translator for the British during the Azov invasion and supplied a good deal of intelligence on the Russian position.[58] Although the agent in Berdiansk had discovered European residents like Mr. Platt responding to the Allies, he failed to uncover any evidence of

Tatar transgression. Instead, he reported that the Nogai Tatars feared "the enemies' destruction," and so "zealously fulfill all the demands of their [wartime] obligations."[59]

At the end of June, Gorchakov rescinded the order of temporary evacuation for the nearby Arabat spit. Despite the possibility of a few people trading or approaching the Allies for other purposes, the residents inhabited a small stretch of land, which did not in any case have "the means to provision a large military army."[60]

Of significant concern, however, was Berdiansk's vast grain stores. The fate of food reserves in Kerch peninsula and the towns along the Azov Sea embroiled the military, civilian authorities, and the residents in endless conflict. En route to Berdiansk the Allies threatened large grain reserves in a small village on the Kitiansk bay. The local field commander employed his Cossack forces to oversee the removal of the grain and in hours had 120 wagons in motion.

Bombardment of the stores brought the operation to a halt in the late afternoon. The field commander wrote to Wrangel for orders, asking whether he should destroy the reserve or attempt further removal of the grain should the Allies leave the harbor. He also confessed to Wrangel that his operation drew complaint from civilian authorities, for his men requisitioned all wagons from the *auls* without going through the proper channels of documentation.[61] Wrangel soothed his man, stating, "Don't pay those complaints any attention as they are completely untimely and in the present circumstances, irrelevant."[62] Such a harsh attitude made sense to an army commander charged with saving or spoiling the grain, but caused civilians who depended on wagons for safe evacuation tremendous anxiety.

Removal of the grain was a dangerous affair for the Cossacks and their Tatar workers, for Allies rained a constant stream of shells on the harbor and more than one Tatar cart had been upturned by a shell.[63] The operation to remove the grain from the quay continued through the end of May.[64] By June, however, the operation was aborted after several Cossacks and workers died during another bombardment.[65]

Berdiansk was the main depot for the Army's grain on the eastern peninsula; its magazines contained more than 1.2 million bushels of grain, enough to supply the army in Sevastopol for several months. When Gorchakov first heard reports of Allied ships in the Azov Sea (May 16) he was reluctant to destroy the grain, lest Russians might make a "sacrifice in vain." Still, he ordered that Berdiansk remove grain 7 kilometers (a bit over 4 miles) to the interior and then destroy means of transport so the Allies could not remove the grain if they succeeded in getting on shore.[66] Chernaev considered multiple ways of removing or destroying the grain, but could do nothing due to the shortage of workers. He even considered burning the stores. Fear of catching the entire city on fire stopped him.[67]

Through June, the question of Berdiansk's grain remained unresolved, and desperately needed provisions remained stuck in a besieged city. In mid-July, citizens of Berdiansk who had temporarily relocated to Novospasskaia (Novospas'ke), a small village some 87 kilometers (54 miles) away by modern highway, pushed Adlerberg to transfer the grain to a safer place. They emphasized that saving the grain would save their own community from hunger and could also benefit residents in surrounding districts who were unable to sow or harvest due to war conditions. The petitioners expressed their frustration with the Russian army that firstly forced residents to sell grain reserves to the military and then, when people went hungry, prevented them from rescuing grain from Allied and Russian fire.[68] Berdiansk merchants and "foreign guests" signed the petition; individual names were composed in Cyrillic as well as *kirimtatar*.

The spirit of interethnic cooperation was absent in Melitopol, where Christian communities and refugees descended into hysteria fearing Nogai Tatars would "use the present confusing circumstances" to enter Christian areas for "killing and for murder."[69] To engender peace of mind and to preserve order in the region, Gorchakov encouraged Adlerberg to go to Melitopol and Berdiansk to direct affairs personally and to bolster the spirits of local authorities. Further, Gorchakov posted the Sixty-Second Cossack regiment in Melitopol, and another one hundred men at the Chongar Bridge. He distributed Cossack regiments in Genichesk and Berdiansk under Chernaev's orders. Other bands of Cossacks were appointed to the small towns and around Nogaisk. In addition to preserving order among the urban and rural residents, the Cossacks were to harass enemy parties attempting to move inland.[70]

Damage Assessment

As Admiral Lyons predicted, the Allies' seizure of Kerch-Enikale and towns along the Azov Sea marked a terrible defeat for Russia. In the words of the European dispatch to the *New York Times*:

> The allied fleets have taken uncontested possession of Kertch. They bombarded the forts of Arabat on the southwest corner of the Sea of Azoff, which sea contains now but a single Russian steamer, the other having been destroyed by the Allies and partly by the Russians themselves. More

than one hundred merchantmen shared the same fate. The Allies conquer, in fact, nothing but ruins and wrecks,—the Russians, true to their ancient tactics, destroying whatever they cannot save. The progress of the Allies is, however, not the less real. By the possession of Arabat, which lies at the foot of the road that runs along the putrid sea to the Crimea, they will have restricted the Russian communications between the Peninsula and the Empire to the only outlet in their hands—the neckland of Perekop. If this should fall into the hands of Omar Pacha, they will be shut up as effectively as any rat in a trap.[71]

The seizure of Kerch, the unidentified author of this *New York Times* dispatch argues, left Russia with only one line of access to Sevastopol through Perekop, an avenue notorious for bottlenecks, and vulnerable to Allied raids staged from Evpatoria.

Beyond the strategic value of the Kerch victory, the attack upon Kerch and the Azov Sea devastated once-thriving communities. Although Russians sank their own ships to prevent vessels from falling into Allied hands, they did not set fire to their own buildings as the author of the dispatch intimated. Instead, the British were responsible for much of the damage. British commanders boasted about the destruction they wrought. At the end of May, Lyons wrote, "In four days the squadron has deprived the enemy of at least 6 million rations of corn and flour, and destroyed four war-steamers."[72] Lyons reported more destruction two days later: "[T]he squadrons forced the enemy to run on shore, burn to the water's edge, and abandon four steamers of war . . . they bombarded Arabat, and blew up the powder magazine, and they destroyed 246 merchant vessels, which were employed in the conveyance of supplies to the Russian army in the Crimea, as well as immense magazines of corn and flour at Berdiansk and Genitchi, containing at least two months' rations for an army of 100,000 men."[73]

Mends recorded the destruction of the city in great detail, blaming a good bit on the French, whom he described as "lawless . . . they destroy for the mere love of destruction; everything they could get hold of they broke."[74] Yet, his account of British havoc and plunder was quite damning: "Today we intend to blow up a foundry near the quay, and as soon as the stores are completely cleared out we intend to burn all the public buildings. It is very exciting work." To that, Mends added a long list of loot he and his colleagues carried away in the few hours spent in Kerch, including: "a beautiful fire-engine worth 300 pounds," plants, furniture, phaeton, and so on.[75]

Table 7.1 Damage in Towns along the Azov Sea

City	Estimated Value in Rubles
Taganrog	
325 homes and other buildings	245,449
19 vessels	59,698
Miscellaneous trade and goods	610,601
Grain and fodder	88,356
Total	1,004,106
Mariupol	
102 houses and other buildings	118,022
14 vessels	39,107
Various trade and things	36,524
Grain and fodder	434,862
Total	628,517
Berdiansk	
364 buildings	128,777
63 vessels	130,471
Various trade and things	22,927
Grain and fodder	134,645
Total	416,821
Genichesk	
203 buildings	34,050
46 vessels	155,950
Various trade and things	10,324
Grain and fodder	9,945
Total	210,270
Other towns	
55 vessels	162,958
Miscellaneous trade and goods	5,272
Grain and fodder	31,639
Total	199,869
Total for all Azov	
994 homes	526,299
197 vessels	548,186
Various trade and things	685,650
Grain and fodder	699,449
Total	2,459,585

Source: Table translated from MVD, 22 Dec. 1856, no. 1518, RGIA, f. 560, op. 12, d. 346, l. 159. The total values are rounded up to reflect small differences in kopeeks.

At the end of the war, the Russian government calculated losses to the cities on the Azov Sea following the enemy bombardment. From the point of view of total destruction, these cities ranked among the hardest hit of the war. Table 7.1, a table produced for the Ministry of Internal Affairs in December 1856, presents a preliminary effort at quantifying damages.

The total loss of 2.5 million rubles does not even include values for Kerch, the largest city in the region. Allied destruction of Russian provisions used by both military and civilians was terrible, but was perhaps rivaled by the devastation caused by the Russians' own scorched earth policy that preceded the invasion. Enacting orders issued from the center and practiced through out the war, Russians sank their own ships, blew up their own fortification, and burnt or spoiled their own food supplies.

Refugees gather at the harbor to meet ferries as flames engulf government buildings in Kerch on June 9, 1855. In the distance, archaeological ruins dating to the ancient Mithridates Kingdom remind viewers of Crimea's unique past. Burning of the Government Buildings at Kertch. *W. Simpson and E. Walker, artists; Paul & Dominic Colnaghi & co., 1855.*

8

Between War and Peace

THE ALLIES' MASTERY OF THE Azov Sea cut Russian supply lines, as Admiral Lyons had anticipated.[1] Subsequently, the clogged road through Perekop became the sole supply route. Near immediately, food and artillery shortages affected Sevastopol. Russian soldiers wearied of the war; dozens deserted per day as the bombardment continued through June. Feeling hopeless about saving Sevastopol, Gorchakov and Osten-Sacken advocated a retreat from the bombed-out city. To Gorchakov's dismay, the tsar ordered him to continue holding Sevastopol *and* to go on the offensive. After receiving reinforcements in July and consulting with Osten-Sacken, Kotzebue, Totleben, and others, Gorchakov chose to attack the enemy at Fedukhin Heights on the Chernaya (Black) River. Victory would have dislodged the Allies from their source of fresh water and arrested their advance on the rear of Sevastopol. Despite his misgivings, Gorchakov had come to believe the attack was necessary, writing to the War Minister on the eve of battle, "I go against the enemy because if I did not, Sevastopol will assuredly fall."[2]

Still, he remained pessimistic about the chances of success, perceiving the Allied forces as better positioned, better reinforced, and better equipped. On August 4, 1855, more than 47,000 Russian soldiers and 10,000 cavalry met nearly 60,000 French, Ottomans, and Sardinians at the battle of the Chernaya River. As Gorchakov anticipated, Allies carried the day. Russia retreated with 8,000 casualties; the Allies suffered 1,800 casualties by comparison.[3]

When the Allies launched a full assault on Sevastopol ten days later, Gorchakov's men blew up the last Russian canon, setting the city alight. Russians exited on a long pontoon bridge hastily constructed over the Sevastopol Bay after the Chernaya River battle. Most of Sevastopol's civilians had already left in June. Those who had remained scrambled over one another to escape.[4]

The capitulation of Sevastopol did not bring an immediate end to the war, however. Its fall was not even decisive. Sevastopol, as Winfried Baumgart has pointed out, was a fortress "on the periphery of a peripheral province of the Russian empire." Only a small portion of the Russian army defended it. The rest of the army was deployed in the Caucasus, on the western border, in the Baltic, and on the Pacific.[5] Sevastopol's fall left Russian defenses in the heartland still intact. Tsar Alexander II's often-quoted remark, "Sevastopol is not Moscow, the Crimea is not Russia," was no idle reflection.[6] When the city fell, the tsar pressed forward with the war and Russian soldiers hunkered down in Crimea's interior. The new front shifted to the Caucasus, where Russia launched an attack on Kars.[7] Russia's position in the interior of the Crimean peninsula was well fortified and, in the words of one British officer, "too strong to be attacked."[8]

Tsar Alexander II traveled to New Russia after the collapse of Sevastopol. He spent six weeks in Nikolaev, visiting the nearby cities of Odessa and Kherson. He came to Crimea at the end of October 1855, touring the major sites of battle still in the hands of the Russian military at the MacKenzie foothills, Alma, and the north side of Sevastopol. He greeted officers, sailors, and soldiers outside the church in Bakhchisarai, many of whom had defended Sevastopol. The tsar announced the creation of special silver medals for Sevastopol's warriors, proclaiming, "I thank you from the depth of my soul for your service, your feats," and sacrifices for the "faith, the Tsar and the Fatherland."[9] He also granted new relief measures for civilians "suffering from the circumstances of war," and established an extraordinary sum to support refugees.[10]

Relief measures did little to stave off the tide of local hunger and desperation as war continued. Tsar Alexander II did not settle upon an armistice until March of 1856, and until that time, the Russian army in Crimea retrenched around Bakhchisarai, the Belbek River, and Simferopol.[11] Gorchakov had ordered another forced evacuation from towns along the Azov Sea after Sevastopol's collapse, while Russian and Allied forces skirmished around Evpatoria and made small raids upon each other's positions.[12] Local populations remained dislocated, while the land suffered shock anew as more trees were felled for the construction of barracks, more fields given over to the grazing of horses, new earth overturned for dugouts and cemeteries. And while the declaration of peace in March enabled some Russian soldiers to trickle back toward their homes, civilians still waited months, and in some cases years, to return.

For civilians, peace did not come with an official armistice. Rather, they endured the long period between war and peace, as Russian and Allied militaries disarmed and demobilized, medical police sanitized spaces, and officials regulated civilian reintegration. Demobilization, as Adam Seipp argues, "bridges the chasm between 'wartime' and 'postwar,' effectively extending the lived experience of war beyond the conclusion of hostilities and the diplomatic agreements."[13] Transitioning to peace was a fraught process of deepening economic and cultural crises. Unable to cope with war-induced deprivation, many people began to leave their homeland for a new life outside of Crimea or beyond Russian borders.

The Fall of Sevastopol and the Attack on the Kinburn Fortress

In a letter to Tsar Alexander II after the battle of the Chernaya River, Gorchakov lamented the deaths of so many men: "I did not count on success, but neither did I envision such loss." He also expressed his concern that "the massive bombardment threatening Sevastopol will force us soon to abandon the city." Only continued construction on the pontoon bridge across the bay delayed his retreat. Tsar Alexander II urged Gorchakov to hold out for a few more days, but he conceded, "if circumstances require you to leave the southern part of Sevastopol and sacrifice the last of our flotilla, the cause *is still far from lost.* . . ."[14]

In dawn's light on August 5/17, the Allies renewed their bombardment. Merchants closed the last surviving shops. Streets emptied of traffic, and civilians fled toward Bakhchisarai. The next day Sevastopol's cathedral, which had maintained regular liturgy through many months of war, conducted its final procession. Priests and believers murmured solemn prayers as they carried the Gospels, chalice, icons, and crosses out of the city under heavy fire. Gorchakov toured crumbling fortifications on August 8/20, and determined Russia could hold out one more week for the engineers to finish the bridge. "With the bridge," he wrote to the War Minister later that evening, "we will have far fewer casualties" than were they to leave Sevastopol immediately. It was a troubling equation; 500 to 700 men died or were severely wounded every day.[15]

Engineers and laborers had completed the bridge ahead of schedule, yet Gorchakov decided to defend as long as he could, partly to lead the Allies into another costly bombardment and partly to divert them from making an attack elsewhere in Crimea. When the French stormed the Malakhov Kurgan following the sixth and final bombardment begun on August 24/ September 5, Gorchakov prepared his retreat. The highest point in the city, Malakhov Kurgan connected the Russian position between the north and south side of the bay.

From sunset through the night, Russian soldiers, their families, and civilian stragglers evacuated the south side of Sevastopol on the pontoon bridge. The Russian army relocated hospitals and wounded men; about 500 soldiers who would not recover were left behind with medics bearing letters from Gorchakov to the French commander on their behalf.[16] The last soldiers to cross pulled the bridge behind them, leaving no pathway to the south side. As they retreated to the north side of the city, the army exploded remaining bastions and scuttled the last of the Black Sea Fleet. Fires raged for two days and two nights; thick black smoke filled the air for miles. More than 170,000 men had died at Sevastopol: 102,000 Russian and 71,000 Allies.[17]

Fires raged so terribly the Allies could not enter the city for several days. They found upon their arrival a desolate scene of destruction, and worse, the wounded men who had not been evacuated with the retreating army. William Russell recorded the scene for readers of the *Times*, noting he had never witnessed anything so heartbreaking: "the rotten and festering corpses of the soldiers, who were left to die in extreme agony, unattended, uncared for, packed as close as they could be stowed. . . . Many lay, yet alive, with maggots crawling about in their wounds."[18]

Six kilometers away to the north, Pirogov had been transferred to treat patients in the overflowing hospitals near the Belbek River. Fields had been turned into pools of viscous, clingy mud; the vineyards' scraggly branches had been completely stripped by soldiers. Wounded soldiers from Sevastopol crowded floors of barracks and hospitals, or spread outside in the open damp air, directly on the ground with no mattresses, pillows, or blankets. The doctor was incensed to discover much-needed supplies just a few yards away: "I did not know how to make things better, and I went more by instinct than intention to have a look at the armory; to my surprise I found a few well-built tents and unopened crates; it seems there were more than 400 blankets, which the virtuous hospital commissariat had not unpacked, dissuaded by the extra bookkeeping."[19]

In the wake of Sevastopol's capitulation, the British Naval Command decided to wage one last major naval campaign against the Kinburn fortress. Located on a long, narrow spit of land at the westernmost end of Tauride, the Kinburn fortress was founded by the Ottomans and stood opposite the once-formidable Ochakov fortress. Historically, the fortress at Kinburn and Ochakov protected the mouth of the Bug and Dnieper estuaries. Although the Ochakov fortress had been destroyed by Russian forces some seventy years earlier, Kinburn had survived, and had become the base of Russian operations on the Black Sea in the era of Catherine the Great.[20] Its capture during the Crimean War opened a possible attack on the naval city of Nikolaev or the eponymous capital of the Kherson province.[21] Kinburn had been bombarded in September 1854 but abandoned as a point of attack once the Allied forces settled upon Sevastopol.[22]

The British led an attack on October 3/15, 1855, with a force of thirty-five British and thirty-five French ships.[23] State servitors in Dneprovsk reported a light bombardment on October 3 and 4 followed by a heavier bombardment on the 5th. Residents immediately fled and remained without any place to live. Local officials who received news of the attack from harried refugees estimated the enemy force at a few thousand to 25,000.[24] In reality, the Allies sent a force of seventy ships evenly divided between the French and British and landed approximately 8,000 men evenly divided between the Allies.[25] They easily overwhelmed the small Russian contingent posted there and took 1,200 Russian prisoners of war. The Allied victory released thousands of new civilians to the growing refugee population from Crimea.

Refugees

When Allies threatened Genichesk, a small town on the shores of the Azov Sea in September, Gorchakov issued another order to evacuate Kerch. This forced evacuation produced an unprecedented refugee crisis in the region. Civilians who had already lost everything had no means to leave again. Extreme overcrowding followed the soldiers' retreat, and so residents competed with the army for space. Cities in Ekaterinoslav, which had taken refugees in May, refused to do so a second time. Either their spare supplies had been exhausted feeding and housing refugees, or space and resources had been committed to tens of thousands of departing Russian soldiers.[26]

As 1855 turned to 1856, the problem of Kerch refugees had not been solved. The city of Orekhov reported that Kerch refugees had applied for help, some with appropriate documentation and passes, and many without papers. These people traveled 200 to 300 kilometers (125 to nearly 200 miles) looking for shelter and arrived in a state of "dire extreme, not having necessary clothing or means to feed themselves."[27] By December, evacuees from Kerch had no place to live, no support from government, and no means of providing for their families in the approaching winter.

Residents of Berdiansk petitioned Chernaev to allow their return:

> You already know very well that merchants have suffered huge losses during the French invasion of the Azov Sea, so now that there are no merchants left, but we still have other residents located in shanties and earthen dugouts with their families on city lands . . . above all [we] have been focused on preparing preserves for the winter for ourselves and our animals, but now we receive this order to leave our places and go somewhere else.

Leaving their homes, the petitioners argued, would "deprive us of all possibility to provision ourselves and our animals, as well as prevent the [albeit small] sowing of grain for the coming year." In a letter containing two pages of signatures, the petitioners asked to remain in their uncomfortable, decimated homes, with the understanding that should the Allies appear, they would flee to an outlying area.[28]

Their petition was denied, and by the end of September, Count A. S. Stroganov, who replaced Annenkov as the Governor General of New Russia, wrote to Gorchakov asking for a repeal of the decision. Multiple reports depict the plight of Berdiansk refugees, he wrote, who "live in the steppe sleeping under the sky; [they] endure hardships, are vulnerable to illness, especially the children who have been terribly struck with small pox. All they ask for is the city. . . . With the approaching cold, the poverty of these people will become even worse if they are not allowed to return."[29]

On October 9, Gorchakov allowed refugees to return to the city, stipulating that they were to evacuate again if Allies reappeared. This order applied only to the merchants and Christian residents, however.[30] The Nogai Tatars were not allowed to return to their homes until November 22, an order that filtered down to local authorities two or three weeks later.[31]

Although civilians near the war zone who managed to stay in their homes through the fall of 1855 may have had a more secure existence than refugees, everyone lived at the edge of subsistence and remained uncertain whether the violence would resume. On October 2, Feodosians panicked when Allied ships appeared in the harbor.[32] Rather than opening fire, however, the British surprised everyone by releasing prisoners of war: 300 Greek residents from Balaklava taken captive a year earlier.[33] Flying a white flag, Allied naval officers helped the city police transport the civilians to shore. Hampered by the wind, it took nearly twelve hours for everyone to disembark with all of their belongings.[34]

The prisoners' return immediately ignited controversy. Like other Crimean towns, Feodosia was overcrowded and under-resourced; it had no place to put the Balaklava prisoners or extra bread to feed them. Adlerberg, meanwhile, complained to Feodosia city officials that the captives had not spent enough time in quarantine and might spread new contagions into Simferopol.[35] Gorchakov's chief of staff Kotzebue questioned whether the Allies used the prisoner release as a pretense for inspecting the Feodosia battery.[36] The British never did attack Feodosia; it is equally likely that they did not want the burden of feeding and clothing an entire village through another Crimean winter. In the end, the Balaklava refugees added to the crowd in Simferopol and Karasubazar.

While Adlerberg and Kotzebue fretted about various dangers associated with having the Allies ashore, local officials in Feodosia confronted their inability to evacuate the city in the case of a real siege. As ordered by Adlerberg, city officials had packed and prepared all the archival, treasury, police, and court affairs it had accumulated over the last two years of war. But, as the police chief wrote to Adlerberg, the recommendation to requisition wagons by warrant was decidedly impossible, for Tatar state peasants and districts' colony populations were continuously occupied with military transport.

Moreover, he called attention to the destitution of local civil servants who had not received any pay since the surrender of Sevastopol. They lived in extreme poverty and continuous alarm. Frustrated, the Feodosia official insisted, "If you leave all state servitors and their affairs in such a condition until the very last minute, then countless archives must perish. Therefore, would it not be better to provide the means to purchase two pairs of oxen for the police and the court to transfer all remaining affairs in an emergency?"[37] Despite his well-reasoned argument, no help came.

Fortifying the Interior

Apart from the attack on Kinburn fortress in October and a few small skirmishes, the Allies refrained from penetrating Crimea's interior; they had control over the sea and the coast, but did not have an army large or healthy enough to wage battle on dry land.[38] Nevertheless, Gorchakov spent the remainder of 1855 fortifying the Russian line and resettling the army in the space between Sevastopol, Simferopol, and Karasubazar. More than 100,000 men lived in the barracks, trenches, and dugouts in and around Sevastopol.

When the city capitulated, soldiers flowed toward the interior looking for places to eat and sleep. Army headquarters, hospitals, and provision depots already occupied the interior Crimean cities. Simferopol alone housed the medical department, the pharmacy, hospitals, army intendancy, the engineering brigade, all their offices, personnel, commanders, couriers, and their horses. Provisions were stuffed into every available space, so that bread often molded in open courtyards and thousands of pairs of boots overflowed dirty rooms. When the Fourth Artillery Division relocated to Simferopol, they could not even find two tables and two stools for their offices.[39]

Gorchakov ordered Adlerberg to requisition more homes from civilians, and many peasants in surrounding villages were relocated to make space for the army. In November 1855, for example, the military relocated a Simferopol suburb of seven Russian families and five Tatar families in order to accommodate the ammunition factory relocated from northern Sevastopol.[40] Sevastopol engineers who had spent nearly a year continuously rebuilding batteries now raced against the weather to complete their next hopeless task: building barracks and hospitals in Crimea's wasteland before the winter.

Sensing crisis, General Sukhozanet, commander of the Third Infantry, raised the alarm about accommodation. He had turned first to Simferopol and Bakhchisarai looking for land in state forests to make a new base camp. Both cities refused him. Forest timber belonging to state lands had already been cut and all available ground occupied. The cost of private lands was just too high for Sukhozanet's budget.[41]

To resolve the problem, Gorchakov (at Sukhozanet's recommendation) organized a committee of local bureaucrats and civilians to identify suitable locations for his men along the Belbek River, and the Tash-Basty ravine. He required the landowners to set reasonable prices, that is to say prices that reflected prewar values.[42] Understanding that the trees composed a chief source of income for the people, Gorchakov implemented the plan in Tash-Basty to build trust among the local community. Their effort to form a price commission with civilians was a good idea that quickly failed.

In Tash-Basty (now Bolshoe Sadovoe), the deputation of citizens and officers estimated village losses at 30,550 rubles. As rumors of the proposal for Tash-Basty spread, other individuals and villages came forward demanding compensation for requisitioned property.[43] A local landowner, for example, had complained to Menshikov the previous September about the destruction of his estate near the river Belbek. The military had razed vineyards and orchards to make camp and a supply store. Continuous traffic had turned his property into a mud pit, which hitherto had provided him an annual income of 12,000 rubles. With the construction of the barracks in the fall of 1855, he sent in a new petition protesting the military's destruction of his forest, an asset he had held in reserve for emergencies. Knowing he had no choice of refusing Gorchakov's demands, the landlord pressed for immediate payment at a more attractive rate.[44]

As similar queries and petitions came in from the residents around the Belbek River, Gorchakov concluded if the measures for Tash-Basty were to be followed, the minimum compensation would be a huge expense for the treasury. Subsequently, he rescinded his initial offer and gave the residents from Tash-Basty only 3,000 rubles toward the full value of the sum. He promised further compensation only if their "behavior demonstrated sincere respectful attention to their Government."[45] In practice, this meant that in the best of circumstances, the army compensated Crimean civilians (most but not all of whom were Tatars) one-tenth of the estimated value of their losses. In the worst of circumstances, such a policy implied that civilians who attempted even the mildest of resistance to army requisitioning would receive nothing during, or at the end of, the war.

Beyond the challenge of payment, the army struggled to find building material for the barracks. Crimean forests in the area between Sevastopol had either already been decimated or had been earmarked for other military projects. In the bone-chilling damp of fall rains, army engineers scrambled to find material and raced to finish construction. Meanwhile, tensions on the peninsula grew as thousands of soldiers endured the "ridiculous quarters" of open air, flimsy tents and muddy dugouts, or crowded into hungry Tatar villages already over-full of coastal evacuees.[46] In November, the exasperated official in charge of the operation asked to be removed from his duties.[47] At last, by December 25, 1855, the engineers reported that more than thirty barracks were either fully completed or near completion.[48]

As Gorchakov's engineers built barracks in Simferopol, civil servants in Crimean towns and cities compiled statistics on damage. In his end-of-year report for 1855, Adlerberg indicated seven Tatar villages destroyed in the Yalta district; eleven completely destroyed in Simferopol district and an additional seventeen in ruins; and sixty-nine Tatar villages demolished in Evpatoria district. Official statistics of razed estates numbered twenty-four in Yalta; seventy-two in Simferopol; twenty-six in Evpatoria; and ten in Feodosia. This quantity does not reflect those estates that had fallen into ruin through abandonment or plundering. Fisheries, a lucrative pre-war industry for Crimea, had been completely annihilated, particularly in Feodosia, Evpatoria, and Berdiansk.[49] Agriculture in Crimea had come to a halt. Authorities did not expect a harvest in 1856 and feared famine.[50] The degree of damage in territory captured by the Allies', including the towns of Evpatoria, Sevastopol, Balaklava, and Kerch, was still unknown.

One of the biggest issues addressed in Adlerberg's report was the migration of Crimean Tatars. Crimean Tatars first began to leave their homes during the war, in a slow trickle from the fall of 1854 through the spring of 1855.[51] On June 30, 1855, a Simferopol administrator reported to Adlerberg that a local aristocrat together with thirteen members of his family had gathered at their property and "went to the enemy [Ottoman Empire]."[52] Later, in December of 1855, forty-six men and fifty women abandoned their homes in the village of Kuchuk-koi. Only one male elder and four women remained. When questioned by Yalta authorities, they explained that they "did not know what happened, for the residents left in the middle of the night."[53]

These early departures caused concern among local officials yet were overshadowed by the continuing battle waged against the enemy along the Crimean coast. This migration, along with spreading disease and hunger among the refugee population, caused Tauride's population to drop by another 20,000. At about 650,000 before the war, the province's population had fallen below the 600,000 mark.[54] This number dropped further as the Tauride administration gathered more data on civilian villages and populations after the declaration of peace.

The Problem of Peace

The destruction of Crimea continued unabated as the Great Powers turned toward peace talks, while the dislocation of coastal peoples, Russians, Greeks, Tatars, and Jews turned into an unprecedented humanitarian disaster for the region. Some of these people were kicked out of their homes by the enemy; others by the Russian army. In both cases few people had the money to leave. Nor did they know where to go. Provisions that had been set aside for refugees rarely made it to the right destination, while refugees at any moment could be pushed out of their camps by soldiers needing space.

As soldiers in Crimea's interior held the peninsula against an Allied advance, their compatriots in the Caucasus led a several-month siege on the city of Kars. Diseased and hungry Ottoman forces proved unable to resist, and surrendered Kars on November 26, 1855. Victory at Kars meant that the Russians had captured more territory than had the Allied forces and gave Tsar Alexander II substantial leverage for peace talks. Britain cared less about Kars than the possibility of a Russian march upon Istanbul, which, with the help of disgruntled Anatolian Greeks, suddenly appeared more possible than at the war's beginning. [55] Peace talks took place from December through February, until all sides agreed upon an armistice in March.

Former foes in Crimea met the armistice with great fanfare; crowds who attended the signing of the peace treaty at the Traktir Bridge drank champagne and exchanged small gifts. The Chernaya River set the demarcation line between the two camps, and in the spirit of peace, Russian, English, and French soldiers threw crosses, coins, and trinkets balled up in clay across the river at one another.[56] Shortly after the armistice, the Russian government increased size of the local police in New Russia and Bessarabia, a temporary measure to ease the transition between from war to peace.[57]

A few local Crimean bureaucrats received medals at the conclusion of peace along with soldiers for their bravery in defending Sevastopol.[58] Postal agents and city police in Perekop and Simferopol won recognition for managing transportation needs of the military on the northern side of the Sevastopol. Most of the awardees were of Russian or Greek heritage, but a few were Tatars. A Tatar translator for the Simferopol court received a medal for working "without absence" from October 1854 through January 1855 for the Commander in Chief.[59] One of the more unusual medals involved a Tatar driver who helped to evacuate the treasury and archive connected to the salt trade at Saki. This man also protected the supervisor and his family, and helped them to evacuate during the Allied invasion. Shortly after, the Russian authorities falsely arrested him during the chaos of September 1854. When released he returned to work for the treasury in Evpatoria. The Ministry of Finance, rather than the Commander in Chief, proposed this particular medal in 1859. It was silver and inscribed "for diligence." A St. Stanislavskii ribbon attached the medal to his chest.[60]

Crimean refugees rushed back to their homes only to be refused entry into their villages and cities.[61] The peace brought no immediate release for civilians. While many soldiers returned to their homes and families (the state was financially unprepared to maintain the swollen army and so did not mandate full-term service for everyone), the civilian populations who had been evacuated from Crimea had to wait until their villages and cities had gone through sanitization. Others were forced to continue military obligation, working transportation duty until the very last soldier had ridden or marched out of the peninsula.

Civilians in the province of Tauride were so tied up in war obligations that local landowners petitioned the Ministry of State Domains to import workers to gather up the hay. Rather than forcing workers to come to Crimea, the Committee of Ministers proposed allowing volunteers from the interior to work as paid laborers in New Russia.[62] The idea reflected Kiselev's antipathy to forced relocation and set the foreground for serf emancipation. Yet, the proposal also revealed how out of touch St. Petersburg was with the realities of the front, as no one in Crimea (neither local bureaucrats, nor local landowners, not even the military) had money with which to *hire* laborers at normal wages, much less at the inflated prices of the war zone.

Beyond the dearth of laborers, Crimea was still very much riddled with disease and sanitation problems. In the fall of 1855 the Medical Department called Leontiev to serve the hospitals in Karasubazar. He recalled "people by the hundreds dying of typhus, fevers and gangrene; every half hour the church bells rang for the deceased; from fourteen doctors, only two remained standing, others were either in their grave or in a sickbed." Leontiev himself nearly died there, and he left for Feodosia at his first chance.[63]

French bases in Chersoneses and Evpatoria were particularly rampant with disease. Some 42,000 Frenchmen (nearly one-third of total French forces in Crimea) took sick leave in the spring of 1856, with a death rate of 250 men per day. Hired by the French army to transport sick soldiers, Codman noted that the 13,000-strong garrison in Evpatoria "had been reduced to six thousand without a battle."[64] Britain fared considerably better, reporting only 5,000 men suffering scurvy, typhus, cholera, and tuberculosis.[65] According to Codman, however, British (as well as French) officers and medical staff under-reported death rates. He and his crew stationed in Crimea read with incredulity reports in French and British papers celebrating the excellent sanitary standards of the camps. The reports, he wrote, "had their effect in deceiving their countrymen at home and encouraging perseverance in the war, while everyone on the ground knew they were stupendous falsehoods."[66]

Peace introduced rigorous measures to cleanse the disease from the war zone. The standard set by the Russian Medical Regulation drew from recent years of research and experience combating epidemics. Instructions for typhus, for example, required firstly, airing of all houses, so that "all windows, doors and (home chimneys) be opened" for eight days. Next, all walls were to be scrubbed with bleach and water, with workers moving in two different teams (one bleach, one water). Water-based paint was to be ground down from the walls, which were next whitewashed with oil-based paint, and then cleaned again with bleach. Any wallpaper was ordered stripped off and burned, along with all straw or thatch. Everything else remaining in the house, whether doors, shutters, windows, or utensils was similarly to be cleaned with bleach and rinsed with water. All of this was to take place under the supervision of the medical authority, with enforcement from local police.[67]

Medical authorities also combatted the spread of sexually transmitted diseases associated with camp brothels. Prostitutes had long traveled with European armies, leading Duke Wellington to describe his Spanish campaign in 1812 as "a marching brothel."[68] In the Crimean War, prostitutes could be found housed both comfortably and miserably within or on the outskirts of all army camps. Many women working as prostitutes among the Allies were recent widows who had traveled from their homes to support their husbands in combat. Others were Tatar women, many of whom had been captured, raped, and forced into prostitution.[69] In the Russian camp, prostitutes similarly derived from the military population, widows and daughters of soldiers. Prompted by destitution, perhaps, other women traveled from Crimean cities or surrounding provinces.

When the military abandoned northern Sevastopol in September 1855, Gorchakov ordered Adlerberg to make space in an already overcrowded Simferopol for the many prostitutes who had been attached to the military base.[70] The concentration of soldiers and brothels in Simferopol quickly led to an outbreak of sexually transmitted diseases that spread to the civilian population. From February 1856 through the beginning of 1858, doctors struggled to treat a syphilis epidemic that affected all ranks and ethnicities in the local populations, including children.

Following public health procedures outlined in the 1840s, doctors worked with police to prevent epidemics through regulating prostitution.[71] Records show that police registered thirty-one prostitutes in Simferopol working in seven brothels in the month of June 1856. A sampling of documents belonging to fifteen women shows an age range between sixteen and twenty-two. Only one was indicated as having a Jewish background; six were described as soldiers' daughters, and four were described as Simferopol townswomen; all the others came from nearby provinces such as Kherson or from other Crimean villages.

These women led precarious lives. They reported rape and abuse to local authorities. Few had chosen to work in the brothels. Women brought complaints against brothels for forcing them into prostitution and preventing them from leaving. Despite repeated allegations made to city police and even the governor of Simferopol, Russian authorities did nothing to help them. Only the outbreak of sexual diseases at the end of the war brought attention to their plight and influenced subsequent reform.[72]

Crimea was the first war in which sanitizing followed as a condition of peace. By war's end, most in the medical community still believed miasmas carried contagion. Nonetheless, medical scientists like Snow and Pirogov, and nurses like Nightingale and Bakunina, had begun to draw connections between filth and disease. Military medical departments understood that sanitizing prevented the spread of sickness among soldiers and the civilian population, and so demanded sanitization of the war zone.

Postwar sanitization proved quite labor-intensive and difficult for local officials to carry out, and so delayed the return of civilians to their homes. Stuck in refugee camps and shantytowns, the civilians nevertheless caught diseases endemic to crowded areas. Many local officials questioned the orders preventing refugees' return, believing that the cities posed less danger to civilians than their temporary homes. In April, the New Russian General Governor requested Adlerberg to allow Kerch-Enikale residents to return immediately due to their impoverished conditions. He also ordered Adlerberg to award benefits to civilians, particularly women and children, to fund their return.[73]

Gorchakov ordered the local bureaucrats and police to return home to begin the process of sanitizing Simferopol, surrounding villages, and the spaces formerly occupied by the Allies.[74] When local civil servants returned to Evpatoria following the evacuation of French forces on May 18, they found "healthy people living in a pleasing condition," that is, without illness. The city, however, had been utterly destroyed. Few houses remained intact, having no furniture, glass, or other interior contents.[75] The filth, more than the destruction, most horrified local officials. More than 100,000 people and 20,000 horses had crowded into a city built for fewer than 10,000 people. Human and animal waste was everywhere: in the streets, in the houses, on the walls.[76] The smell was as bad as the sight.

Despite the tremendous mess, Evpatoria received funds for only forty workers and twenty wheelbarrows. The leader of the local nobility wrote to Adlerberg requesting more support, namely 200 workers and fifty wheelbarrows, which would make the cleanup "go much more quickly" and defeat the spread of contagion threatening to develop with the hot weather.[77] His request remained unanswered and Evpatoria workers labored through the month.

The Odessa agent sent to approve Evpatoria's resettlement was amazed that the medical police had pronounced the city habitable. The agent wrote at the beginning of July: "I did not find evidence that authorities made any effort to put [the town] into any kind of order." Five months after the conclusion of the war, corpses remained half buried: bones stuck out from the earth, skulls lay on top of the ground. He complained that in the Quarantine buildings, traps, fur, bone, "even entire corpses of dead animals" lay strewn about. Nevertheless the Quarantine conducted business in the mess; local officials had resumed their duties logging passengers and checking in merchants. The agent issued strong orders that included "Remind[ing] the committee based in Simferopol about their responsibility to protect from infectious disease and to clean the city and to do so as soon as possible."[78]

The criticism stung Evpatoria administrators who had been tasked with cleaning the city without real support. "We have restored everything as best we could," wrote one official, and "if something is amiss, or needs further attention," then the responsibility belonged upon the shoulders of higher officials. It became apparent to people in Evpatoria that neither the government in Odessa nor that in St. Petersburg had any concept of Crimea's utter ruin. "To suggest that the city is the same as when the enemy left, I have to say [you] are mistaken . . . in Evpatoria miasmas have been cleaned from 895 homes, while 475 homes suspected of typhus have been sanitized according to the demands of the medical office. Another 426 homes have been destroyed, which gives the city is pitiful appearance."[79]

All Crimean towns and cities held by Russian and occupying forces went through sanitization by the occupying powers. The French worked on cleaning the southern side of Sevastopol until May 23 and the British finished sanitizing Balaklava a few days later.[80] When Russians took over those cities, they found the spaces far from sanitary and continued the process of cleaning through July. Quite often the Medical-Police, as they were called in Russian sources, found certain hospitals and buildings beyond redemption, and so burned entire structures. The medical department had sufficient sway that it was at least able to persuade the Russian state to compensate local individuals and institutions for buildings it condemned, while the military intendancy was ordered to reimburse civilians for all hospital space requisitioned.[81]

Even then, residents who wanted to return could not. Crimean buildings still served as hospitals. Simferopol wards held 5,000 men as late as May 1856; many were too ill or wounded to be moved.[82] And as the Governor General wrote to the War Minister, "Balaklava was occupied by the enemy around 22 months. The invasion suddenly put in the hands of the enemy not only immovable property of the residents but also all movable property, and many people were even taken captive. Now only the land remains." Houses that still stood were half in ruins. Orchards and gardens, which once constituted the basis of Balaklava's income, had been destroyed. No trace of movable property remained in the entire city. As Stroganov, the Governor General, wrote, "In a word, Balaklava residents . . . do not have even shelter or the means of subsistence." Moreover, because they were not allowed to enter the city until after the sanitizing, the *Balaklavtsy* could not even "earn a living through the labor of their own hands."[83]

Because the Balaklava Greek battalion fell into a special status, they received a small number of benefits from the military during the war. Upon peace, Balaklava families transitioned under civilian authority and became among the first recipients of state aid following the war. Stroganov apportioned 70,000 rubles for the Balaklava returnees: 400 rubles for staff officers, 200 for lesser officers, and 100 rubles for the lower ranks in every family, for a total estimate of 60,000 rubles.[84] However, local authorities provisionally estimated that the damage to Balaklava alone came to more than half a million rubles. The disbursement of 70,000 rubles was thus considered an extreme measure for resettling Balaklava.

People out of Place

As Russians took over Crimean towns from the enemy, they discovered hundreds of undocumented migrants left behind.[85] Some were illegal traders who had made an illicit living off the war; others had deserted Allied armies. In the space between war and peace, the departure of foreign occupiers and the establishment of Russian authority, these groups mixed poorly with returning refugees. Drunkenness and thievery abounded, and murder rates soared. In an effort to establish control, Stroganov ordered Adlerberg's replacement, the incoming governor of Tauride G. V. Zhukovskii, to gather information on all foreign citizens. Zhukovskii was to distinguish between those with passports and legitimate reasons for being in Crimea, and those without documents and clear assignments. Every foreign subject was to be expelled from Crimea. Those with established credentials had until mid-August to sell their belongings and leave voluntarily; everyone else was to be taken under arrest and dispatched to their country of origin without ceremony. For this task, Stroganov assigned a Cossack regiment and the Greek Battalion.[86]

In June, local authorities composed a list of people who had no proof of citizenship, and needed help returning to their homes. This list included four Turks, twelve Greeks and Bulgarians (undifferentiated), eight Armenians, and eight Frenchmen. Russian authorities gave them 3 rubles each and sent them on to Istanbul.[87] Other foreigners were less fortunate. In Kerch, authorities found a group of Sardinians, including a nineteen-year-old who had left the French foreign legion. The young man found asylum in the home of local Karaim in July of 1855, and after making a short trip to Istanbul, returned to Kerch-Enikale to engage in small trade.

Another Sardinian had deserted the army also in July of 1855, and then had made his way to Kerch, where he had served a British officer. When the British left, the young Sardinian stayed for work at a hotel. To Gorchakov's chagrin, these Sardinians were arrested as war prisoners and sent to Kostroma. "Were not clear instructions about such foreigners established in the conclusion of peace?" he asked.[88]

Here, Gorchakov was referring to a clause in the Paris Peace Treaty that required all powers to grant amnesty and safe passage to enemy combatants. As in previous conflicts with the Ottoman Empire, conquered peoples of both empires sided with the enemy. In the Crimean War, regiments of Ottoman Bulgarians and Greeks fought for Russia, just as Evpatorian Tatars formed a militia unit to fight for the Ottomans. To prevent Russia and the Ottoman Empire from taking retributive measures against these groups, the Treaty of Paris provided for their asylum.

According to point five of this treaty, all warring nations had to "give full pardon to those of their subjects who appeared guilty of actively participating in the military affairs of the enemy." The treaty further required "each of the warring powers give full pardon to those who served for another warring power during the war."[89] The clause produced a religiously inflected population exchange as Muslim Tatars fled Russia and Christian Bulgarians fled the Ottoman Empire, taking up new residence in the state of their co-religionists. Thus, some arrested foreigners petitioned to obtain Russian citizenship, such as Nikola Bezeo, a Greek national from the Ottoman Empire.[90] At the end of 1856, hundreds of Greek volunteers followed suit.

In addition to the hundreds of foreigners left behind, thousands of deserters and displaced peoples wandered New Russia. Many were Russians and Ukrainians who had escaped serfdom from the northern provinces and had found employment in Simferopol, Sevastopol, and Karasubazar during the war. Labor shortages in Crimea and resettlement schemes generated rumors of serf-emancipation for peasants willing to relocate to Tauride. Thousands of undocumented Russian serfs from Ekaterinoslav worried local officials as they streamed through Perekop in 1856.[91] Women who worked as prostitutes along the war zone also remained.

In April of 1856, the Committee of Ministers published instructions meant to reduce itinerancy in the war zones. These instructions cautioned landowners to check the passports of their workers and police to check vagrants' documents. Those who did not have appropriate passports were to be sent immediately back to their places of origin.[92] But local police, at least in Crimea, were too busy assisting with the sanitation of cities and suppressing major crimes to check vagrants for their papers, while many landlords were not willing to hand over their workers.[93]

Peace did little to improve circumstances for Tatars and unfair policies continued. With no end in sight, Tatars must have seen little future for themselves in Crimea. Many Russians blamed Tatars for defeats in Crimea, and others sought to gain from Tatar misfortune. Crimean landlords of Russian and European heritage moved quickly to absorb Tatar property into their estates, including the property of Tatars who had been forced into the interior of the province. In the village of Chorgun, for example, more than forty Tatars protested the seizure of their land by the Mavromikhaili sisters during the war. Three years after the war's conclusion, the women (who had been Sisters of Mercy in Sevastopol) still had not returned their land. Instead, they had settled it with Russian families.[94]

On April 22, 1856, 4,500 Tatars left Balaklava for Istanbul, their right to leave guaranteed in the Treaty of Paris.[95] Despite the provisions in the treaty, alarmed local officials brought the matter to the tsar, asking whether they should prevent the future departure of Tatars. Alexander II responded that there was no reason to prevent Tatar outmigration, stating, "It would be advantageous to rid the peninsula of this harmful population."[96] Subsequently, the tsar's statement was forwarded to all of Crimea's districts, including those most affected by the war: Perekop, Yalta, Theodosia, and Evpatoria.[97] Stroganov interpreted the tsar's words strictly and communicated to provincial officials in Crimea that "His Imperial Majesty ordered that it was *necessary* [my emphasis] to free the region of this harmful population."[98]

Settling vacated or confiscated Tatar lands around the war zones with German and Russian colonists quickly evolved into a de facto policy supported by authorities in Tauride. In his annual report for 1855, Military Governor of Simferopol and Tauride Adlerberg (who had not yet been replaced by Zhukovskii) argued, "experience has shown [Tatars] as incapable of being successful agriculturalists." In their place, he recommended settling German and Mennonite colonists on half of this territory "due to the real advantage they bring to agriculture in the northern districts." On the other half, he proposed settling veterans of the war, who showed "particular zeal and devotion to the Government."[99]

The marshal of the nobility in Evpatoria shared Adlerberg's sentiment. In a proposal discussing how to reestablish agricultural production after the war, the marshal suggested that agricultural estates could achieve their former value, and might actually increase in price following the departure of Tatars. "The transfer of land from Tatars to Russian owners will strengthen grain harvesting," he wrote, as well as "improving agriculture and the raising of livestock."[100]

Such racialized notions of labor dated to the era of Catherine II, when the state fixed upon German colonists and Christian refugees of the Ottoman Empire as a solution to settling the sparsely populated regions conquered during the Russo-Turkish Wars.[101] Russian administrators from the era of Catherine II compared the agricultural practices of Germans and Mennonites favorably with Russian serfs and other ethnic groups. Alexander I and Nicholas I expanded the racialized approach to labor by including Russian Old Believers and sectarian groups deemed more productive and skilled than natives in colonized areas.[102] The Crimean War had the effect of calling into action the most cynical of racialist settlement schemes.

Stroganov supported Adlerberg's desire to replace the native Tatar population with foreign settlers, and in April of 1856 he forwarded a proposal to St. Petersburg. He took this plan to the Ministry of State Domains. Despite its rich natural gifts, Stroganov wrote in his proposal that Crimea "remained for seventy years in the same state of wilderness, due in large part to the inability of the Muslim population to work hard." Stroganov emphasized the recent concerns about Tatar mutinies, arguing that Tatars demonstrated readiness to harm Russia. Pointing to Crimea's significant salt industry, and the importance of the Azov Sea to accessing Russia's interior and the Caucasus, Stroganov asserted that the peninsula was too strategically important to leave to a non-Russian population and advocated populating Crimea with "pure Russian tribes, even without taking German colonists." The plan needed to be "attentively thought out, founded upon sensitive study of the details of practical accomplishment."[103]

Tsar Alexander II had changed ministerial appointments by the time Stroganov's proposal reached St. Petersburg. He appointed Kiselev as Ambassador to Paris and selected M. N. Muraviev to replace him. Muraviev represented a large victory for conservative elements of the government who had long opposed expanding rights to the serfs. A distressed Kiselev wrote to his brother, "My poor ministry, which I left to the blowing of an arbitrary wind, without compass and without sustenance! Twenty years of uninterrupted and conscientious service, will probably be devoured and wasted."[104] Muraviev's appointment, as Kiselev predicted, resulted in a drastic change in the Ministry's philosophy. Muraviev attempted to slow the pace of freedoms granted to peasants from the moment he assumed his appointment in April of 1857. Thus, one historian argues, peasant emancipation in 1861 occurred in spite of Muraviev; Kiselev's reforms had already raised peasant expectations and put the process in motion.[105]

Under Muraviev, the Ministry approved Stroganov's proposal to settle Crimea with Russian populations in July of 1856, with strong reservations. It recommended limiting settlement to those territories from which Tatars had already been expelled, or whose land was confiscated by the state following proven mutiny. Most likely the ministry exercised this limited caution because Gorchakov had intervened in earlier exchanges among local officials about land Tatars vacated during wartime. When Yalta and Evpatoria district officials recommended reassigning vacant Tatar land to the state in 1855, for example, Gorchakov warned officials first to determine whether the "empty lands" belonged to mutinous Tatars, Tatars who had been forcibly evacuated, or Tatars who had been taken captive.[106]

Under Muraviev, the Ministry suggested that the state acquire Tatars' private property as it came up for sale along the shore for resale exclusively to Russian peasants. Stroganov responded that the "ability to clean (*ochistit'*) Crimea of Tatars by degrees through the state acquiring private lands for Russian settlers could be successful," but such would "require significant capital." Purchasing lands, Stroganov complained, would not happen quickly because "the lazy and useless Tatars would not leave Crimea voluntarily." Instead, one would have to "forcibly evict them."[107]

Stroganov's plan anticipates the mass deportation of Tatars during the Second World War.[108] Although Stroganov did not succeed, some local officials took quick steps to claim Tatar property and resettle with Russian populations. As early as May 1856, before residents fully returned to the city, Evpatoria officials compiled a list of homes belonging to Tatars believed to have left for the Ottoman Empire. The city valued the homes with an eye toward selling and using the profit for restoring public buildings. Alternatively, residents in the city who were actively rebuilding were permitted to strip wood from empty Tatar homes for their own use without pay.[109] A new Crimea was emerging from the rubble.

Russians make a panicked retreat across the pontoon bridge connecting the north and
south sides of Sevastopol Bay. Ships explode in the harbor, the city is in flame, and, pushed
by the crowd, men and horses fall from the bridge into the sea. Retreat of the Russians
from the South of Sevastopol. *J. Hine, artist G. Price, The London Printing and Publishing
Company, 1855.*

9

Reconstruction

BEFORE THE WAR, THE UNDULATING road between Sevastopol and Yalta was a beautiful stretch of highway. Craggy mountain cliffs studded with cypress trees trailed north toward Bakhchisarai. To the south, steep hills dropped to the sparkling seawaters below. Forests and vineyards dotted the vista. Around the near-hidden bends of steep mountain passes, careful observers might glimpse graceful Tatar *sarai* blending into the rugged landscape. But two years of war had given the once-stunning region a funereal cast.

Now, decaying corpses littered roadsides. Barracks and cemeteries replaced verdant orchards. Barren hills of blackened stumps had replaced forests. Smoke and smells from cannons hovered over the seashore for months; soot blackened the earth years later. Sevastopol and Kerch had been blasted into virtual non-existence. Other villages and towns had been plundered, vandalized beyond recognition. Herds of sheep and cattle disappeared, consumed by the great belly of war. Productive farms had become scorched fields. Hungry people with wild eyes flowed along the major thoroughfares moving in the opposite direction of weary soldiers marching out. The continual tread of hundreds of thousands of feet, hooves, and wheels reduced the postal roads to long mud pits that mired horse and man in knee-level muck.

St. Petersburg's lavish preparation for Alexander II's coronation contrasted sharply with the picture of local despair. Held eighteen months after he had ascended the throne, Alexander's coronation presented the most opu-lent Romanov spectacle to date. Festivities began August 17, 1856, and lasted a month. Sumptuous palaces hosted epic parties across St. Petersburg and Moscow. More than eighty colorfully dressed peasant delegations bearing traditional gifts of bread and salt represented provinces of the empire. Emissaries arrived from across the globe to watch the imperial family parade in gilded carriages.[1]

On the day of the coronation, imperial proclamations expressed the tsar's love for his subjects and granted clemency to political prisoners, including the Decembrists. Manifestos awarded medals to commemorate brave sailors, soldiers, and civilians, and granted special relief to veterans. The tsar and his cabinet announced sweeping programs of debt deferment and forgiveness, a reward for Russian subjects' war donations, and an implicit recognition of a postwar economic slump. One of many manifestos issued on August 26, 1856, the day of coronation, granted freedom from recruitment for four years; cancellation, reduction, or deferment of state tax, whether in money or in kind; relief in repayment of agricultural loans and loans given for war reconstruction. The manifesto also granted widows and orphans special privileges, abolished cantonist schools, and granted soldiers and sailors early release from their terms of service.[2]

The tsar also announced a new census. Provinces across the empire had lost men in Sevastopol, while near the war zone all populations had suffered higher death rates due to epidemics, starvation, homelessness, and general impoverishment. The new census also assessed mass migrations produced by war. Separate proclamations praised residents of Bessarabia, Kherson, Ekaterinoslav, and Tauride for their sacrifices in the war.[3] The proclamation devoted to the Tauride province was among the most grandiloquent. It praised civilians for their sacrifice, which the tsar compared to that of the soldiers:

> In the life of a people there are inevitably periods of hard trial. . . . The last conflict, in which you shared the danger, belongs to such an epoch. Glory and suffering were your burden. From the beginning of the violent struggle you gave significant donations to Our valiant military as they strove to defend of our native borders; but that did not end your participation in the salvation of our Fatherland. The war burned you more and more with the hard destiny of the enemy invasion.[4]

Beyond addressing the loss of house and home, the tsar invoked the image of Crimea as the Cradle of Christianity, arguing that war and suffering had made Crimea more holy. Referring to the cannonjzed viking prince of ancient Kyiv, Vladimir (Volodymyr), he noted that to "this same place nine centuries ago, the great Enlightener of Russia [Vladimir] brought the holy font of Christianity, and from there the light of love and enlightenment spilled out in the immense space of our North."[5] With these words, Tsar Alexander II recast Crimean identity from a Muslim region to a Christian one.

In the same vein of transformation, the tsar praised Crimeans, who he described as "native Russians" (*korennye Russkie*) and "young settlers." These people, he said, had "made significant donations; assisting transportation of the military, sharing sustenance free of charge, and anticipating, in accordance with the size of their forces, their smallest needs and wishes. In your homes, in your families, you gave shelter to the wounded and the suffering, comforted the dying and gave helping hands to your brothers, pulled from the yoke of invasion."[6]

To be sure, the population of Tauride, Crimea included, did give everything they had to the war effort. One can only imagine, however, that the characterization of the region's population as "native Russians" (*korennye Russkie*), and "the young settlers of other tribes" must have sat uncomfortably with the Crimean Tatars. The "young settlers" referred to foreign colonists, while *korennye Russkie* could only have meant those with Russian roots. Tatars, not Russians, were the majority population who carried the most burdensome war service, yet the tsar had written them out of history.

While Russians living in the imperial capital may have been awed by the splendor attached to the coronation, tsarist luminescence reflected dim light in the former war zones. With the conclusion of peace and the cleaning of the cities, new reports of devastation poured in. In addition to the complete destruction of Sevastopol, Balaklava, Evpatoria, and Kerch-Enikale, officials estimated that another 132 landed estates and 105 Tatar villages in the surrounding environs lay in ruins. The once beautiful palace of the Crimean Khans, depicted by Pushkin in his 1823 poem "The Fountain of Bakhchisarai," had served as a military hospital. "The walls were open to all kinds of damp; the magnificent reception hall—torn to the studs, the fountain, empty. Everything poetic about it," wrote Russian nurse Bakunina, "had fallen, to be replaced with a sad, hard reality."[7]

In Sevastopol, Allied and Russian forces created 187 cemeteries in civilian green spaces for the bodies of more than 120,000 men.[8] Only fourteen houses remained intact in the city. American observers visiting the area in October 1855 described Sevastopol as "a mass of ruins"; the city had disappeared into the earth. Trenches plowed over boulevards and shot and shell had reduced buildings to broken bricks.[9] On the opposite side of the peninsula, only 380 of 1,940 homes still stood in Kerch. Officials estimated that only one-fourth of the peninsula's work animals survived, a number that seems optimistic, and further noted a complete collapse of agricultural production. Because war prevented peasants from sowing new crop in the fall of 1855, wheat and rye did not sprout from the ground in the spring of 1856.[10] Starvation was imminent.

The devastation evident in Crimea stretched through all of southern Ukraine. Mobilization had begun in 1852. For a year the military remained in Bessarabia and the southern districts of the Kherson Province. Residents in these regions transferred, quartered, and provisioned the military for thirty months. Before war prompted relocation of Russian troops toward Varna and later Crimea, civilians built highways, bridges, and rafts. They fortified dams on the Prut, the Danube, the Bug, and the Dnepr. All of these areas had low populations, poor roads, and often scarce fresh water, which made work particularly dangerous and exhausting for people and animals.

Although certain towns along postal roads bore the brunt of maintaining the military, even the most remote village of the region had been tapped for food, wagons, timber, or animals. Civilians donated more than 100,000 carriages along with the beasts of burden. Compensation, if given at all, rarely filtered down to the peasants who were the most in need. Animals never returned and carriages, if they came back, often did so broken and without wheels. The toll on local populations was very heavy, particularly in the winter of 1855, when residents began transporting the hospitals out of Sevastopol. Many involved in this obligation contracted diseases and died.[11]

The Memory of 1812

As the tsar received his crown in the Dormition cathedral in Moscow, a humanitarian crisis was building in the south, and particularly in Crimea. "In such difficult circumstances," Adlerberg had written before he relinquished his post to Zhukovskii in May of 1856, "it pays to settle the region as much as possible and to relieve the condition of the rural population." Fearing the possibility of social collapse and uprising, Adlerberg recommended that the government take immediate measures to "change the activity of extraction" and "grant a few benefits."[12]

Stroganov, the recently appointed Governor General of the region called New Russia, followed through upon Adlerberg's recommendation. In the fall of 1855, Stroganov presented the tsar with a list of steps to alleviate pressures on the New Russian population who had been most affected by the war. These measures ranged from long-term relief to immediate distribution of food and clothing. For Kerch, Sevastopol, Yalta, and the other places occupied or attacked directly by the enemy, he proposed complete cessation of all taxes and duties. Similarly, he suggested prohibiting courts and other state institutions, banks, and private lenders from seeking debt repayment until circumstances improved.

In areas of those southern districts called upon to feed and transfer soldiers, he recommended similarly deferring poll taxes on peasants and land taxes on nobility as well as ending extractions of capital and interest from landowners. The list of cities recommended for relief reveals how far the war had reached into the empire: Kagul, Akkerman, Benderskol, Tiraspol, Odessa, Kherson, Dneprov, Aleksandrov, and Rostov. Stroganov proposed that peasants in remaining districts of New Russia and Bessarabia be granted two years' deferral of land and poll taxes. He suggested releasing Tauride residents from the salt excise and freeing the merchants from paying guild fees.

More immediately, Stroganov advocated expanding the emergency fund, which had been created in Kerch and Simferopol for war refugees. This fund would provide clothing and food for those in need, and would help establish grain reserves for the poorest of residents, whether for free or for loan. In April, the tsar passed along Stroganov's list of recommendations to the Committee of Ministers. He asked them to consider which measures could be taken.[13]

The Committee of Ministers turned to Russia's last major example of public war-time relief following the Napoleonic invasion of 1812. The war had had a catastrophic effect on Russian treasury; on top of damages produced from the violence, sixteen provinces had failed to meet their regular tax debt. One member of the finance department recalled the situation during and after the war:

> Every day, millions were needed to meet the unforeseeable military costs; cash was sent from one province to another to protect it from looters; crowds of unfortunate citizens came running from the enemy masses, needing shelter and bread; it was necessary to arm the people, since in terms of numbers, the Russian forces were far from equal to those of Napoleon. [. . .] Various unforeseeable costs were incurred; indeed costs could not even have been imagined: provisions and supplies for hundreds of thousands of prisoners of war, arrangements for those who had been living in areas taken by the enemy, warm clothing and footwear for Russian troops pursuing the French in freezing conditions, the need to burn corpses of men and horses blocking the road from Moscow to the border in order to prevent infectious diseases.[14]

The invasion of 1812, as well as the extraordinary toll it took on everyday life, left a lasting impression. It was only natural that the ministers turned to the recovery program following 1812 as model for Crimea. They asked Stroganov whether the 1812 aid package, which consisted of ten-year, interest free loans, and 1,400,000 rubles in immediate aid for Moscow, would work for his region.[15] The ministers further asked Stroganov to estimate how many animals had died from exhaustion in transporting the military.

Stroganov had begun his military career in 1812. He was thus a first-hand witness to Napoleon's devastation and the postwar rebuilding. Unlike many ministers in St. Petersburg who shared his experience of 1812, however, Stroganov also viewed the damages caused by the Crimean War first-hand. It is therefore significant that he believed not only that the recovery package for the Napoleonic invasion was inadequate at the time, but that the Crimean War had been far more destructive.

In Stroganov's view, the 1812 recovery package had dramatically failed civilians in the regions it had intended to help. By mid-century, industry and agriculture in Smolensk, Mogilev, and Vitebsk still had not reached pre-1812 expectations, while many inhabitants there remained in debt or in arrears. If the package was insufficient for 1812, it certainly would not meet the need in 1856, he argued, for the damage in Crimea was much more severe.

Only Moscow had burned in 1812. In contrast, Sevastopol, Kerch, Berdiansk, Genichesk, Yalta, and Balaklava went up in flames in 1855.[16] Further, he reiterated an argument also made by Zatler, that whereas armies in 1812 were constantly on the move for only a few months, the prolonged concentration of combatant militaries in Crimea for more than a year had drained the peninsula to a point of exhaustion hitherto never seen. More research on both wars would be necessary to determine whether his impressions are accurate.[17]

As Stroganov debated the details of postwar reconstruction, animals moved to the top of the recovery package.[18] Upon the declaration of peace, it quickly became apparent the large part of the work-animal population in Tauride, Kherson, and Ekaterinoslav had perished, and civilians had no means of transporting the army out of the peninsula, much less plowing their lands to salvage a harvest for 1857. Therefore, before Kiselev left his ministerial position, he proposed distributing 3,000 pair of oxen immediately to the residents of Crimea. Within weeks, the tsar consented to raise the number of oxen to 8,000. By June 1856, imperial authorities in St. Petersburg had agreed upon a minimum distribution of 10,000 pairs of oxen.[19]

Distributing the oxen was a large operation, complicated by the distance oxen had to travel before coming to Crimea. Kiselev stipulated that the animals should come from areas north of Poltava and Kharkov, as war had depleted animal stock anywhere further south.[20] The military intendancy was to pay for the oxen, which were physically to be purchased and transported to Crimea by trusted local bureaucrats. Local agents for the Ministry of State Domains then were to determine places of greatest need and apportion the oxen accordingly.[21] He instructed local bureaucrats to keep strict accounting and ensure the oxen were in good health and younger than eight years. Given the high value of these animals in a war-torn region, he also demanded an escort of well-armed Don Cossacks as the oxen traveled to Crimea.[22]

In some villages, the distribution of work animals went smoothly; oxen and horses (which were later added to the relief) reached the poorest of villagers as intended. Frequently, however, village elders either kept oxen for themselves or sold them to the highest bidders. Often refugees had not yet returned to their homes and were absent for distribution of these animals. Less commonly, village elders were simply corrupt. More than one local official lost a position for selling animals to the highest bidder.[23]

In addition to purchasing oxen for Crimean residents, the military released animals and carriages from local depots upon the final evacuation of soldiers and supplies. Thus, in July of 1856, Karasubazar received sixty horses and thirty carriages for disbursement among "people with real needs, who lost their working livestock." The city council (*duma*) of Karasubazar, however, decided to sell rather than distribute the livestock and carriages. When questioned, the council argued that the war burdened the "prosperous" population more than the poor, as merchants and others donated money as well as goods.[24] In such ways, local leaders subverted or redirected the imperial recovery program. Sometimes modification better suited community needs, and sometimes modification merely benefited greedy and corrupt individuals.

Beyond animals and tax relief, local officials demanded salaries either they had not received, or which fell well short of the inflation in Crimea. Months after peace, many state servitors remained stuck in those places to which they had evacuated. Unable to afford the journey home, officials from Kerch, Yalta, and Feodosia petitioned provincial and central offices for assistance returning home.

The Ministry of the Interior approved a salary disbursement for Kerch civil servants in November 1856 based on a sliding scale. Those who stayed in the city until the occupation, for example, received more than those who managed "to relocate with their families into a decent place."[25] Following the example of

Kerch, eight Yalta officials who had stayed to secure the city through 1855 were awarded 500 rubles in June to spread between them to cover lost property. The highest portion (100 rubles) went to the city's police chief.[26]

This amount may have covered a few emergency costs but not an extended evacuation. In January 1857, the chief's family remained in Kursk; his wife petitioned the Tauride governor for a disbursement of 200 rubles so that she might return home. She pointed out that her request matched the same amount given to peasants for their return after evacuation, although how she came to that figure is unclear as most peasants were lucky to receive 10 rubles.[27]

In October 1856 the governor of Tauride applied for special benefits for Evpatoria bureaucrats to ameliorate the impoverishment caused "by the former military circumstances in Crimea and the inflation of the necessities of life."[28] One civil servant, Rakov, went fourteen months without pay during an era of exponentially increasing inflation and scarcity of goods. When Gorchakov called him back for the medical-policing of Simferopol, Rakov could not afford transportation. Nor could he afford accommodation in the extraordinarily expensive city.[29]

When the Ministry of the Interior finally released compensation for Crimean civil servants, it upset those in Evpatoria by placing the city's benefits on a rate commensurate with Ekaterinoslav. Subsequently, Evpatoria petitioned for compensation at the same level as their counterparts in Bakhchisarai and Simferopol. With Stroganov's help, they managed to raise their allotment from 2,057 rubles to be distributed among thirty-five bureaucrats to 3,086 rubles.[30]

Rakov's experience was fairly typical. A customs agent from Feodosia evacuated with his twelve-member family to Melitopol at the orders of the military. He applied to the Tauride governor for assistance in May of 1855, who in turn ordered administrators in Melitopol to disburse 100 rubles that had been set aside for bureaucrats "suffering from the invasion." In January, however, he learned the customs office had deducted the award from his annual salary. He wrote to the Tauride governor again, this time protesting the deduction. He argued that his evacuation from Feodosia was not his decision but was court-mandated. Leaving in a hurry, he had had no time to take "necessary things from the house."

His family lived in dire circumstances, having to reestablish a household from scratch when "basic domestic necessities have gone up in price." He asked the governor to press the Feodosia customs office to restore the money to his salary. After receiving no response, he repeated his request a second time in

June 1856. By then, the Feodosia customs office had moved again to a village near Nikopolia, while he had relocated to Luhansk.[31]

Imperial Program for Relief

In October 1856, Stroganov presented another report to the Committee of Ministers for a larger plan of relief. Drawing from multiple sets of data, he calculated losses for Bessarabia at about 10 rubles per male; in southern districts of Kherson and Ekaterinoslav at 15 rubles; and in the three northern districts of Tauride, up to 25 rubles per male, with a total for all three provinces approaching 12,600,000 rubles.[32] Stroganov did not yet have a figure for Crimea, which he estimated was far greater than the other provinces combined. He further emphasized that the figure did not include decimation of animals or industry for any part of the region.

Until his agents could compile a reasonable figure, he reiterated that Crimea had not suffered only from the enemy invasion but also from activities of the Russian military, which destroyed villages surrounding Evpatoria, Sevastopol, and Kerch. Throughout Crimea, he argued, the high concentration of the military wore down the land and overconsumed resources. Stroganov again addressed the high death rate of animals from exhaustion, starvation, sickness, and slaughter for food. Particularly toward the end of the war, peasants were rarely paid for their animals. Civilians in the mountains escaped the worst of the destruction, but even so, "many localities inland were destroyed, gardens and vineyards neglected [due to civilian diversion to military obligation], which has led to the ruin and disrepair of all property."[33] The epidemics that affected the military also ravaged civilians, he noted, who experienced a high and hard-to-calculate rate of death.[34]

After months of research and allowing policy to develop ad hoc, the tsar formally announced the relief plan for the region called New Russia on February 5, 1857. The plan consisted of three main parts. The first part of the plan aimed to compensate individuals in New Russia who had lost property due to the war. The second part involved drawing upon charity to supplement government measures. Third, the Ministry of Finance provided a series of tax relief and other concessions for New Russian residents.

Under the oversight of the Governor General of New Russia, a series of committees formed to document damages. The steering committee was based in Odessa and staffed by agents of the Governor General, local representatives of every social estate, as well as officials appointed by the Ministries of War, Interior, Finance, and State Domains. Its mission was to establish and supervise committees at the local level. Each local committee, similarly staffed with representatives of each estate, compiled a list of everyone in the community who lost property during the war, and (after research) attached a real value of the lost property. Each local committee forwarded their registers to the Odessa Committee for Stroganov's approval, who then submitted the master list to the Ministry of the Interior. Acknowledging that damage assessment would be time-consuming, the relief plan called for a temporary aid committee with a budget of 500,000 rubles for people in dire circumstances.[35]

In many ways, the plan merely standardized relief efforts already underway. In April 1855, Stroganov's predecessor, Annenkov, had established an extraordinary committee, invested with tens of thousands of rubles from the Kherson chancellery, in the town of Orekhov to help displaced civil servants and residents from Kerch-Enikale. The committee evolved to oversee emergency relief for displaced peoples from Berdiansk and Melitopol as well. Another committee had emerged in Simferopol to manage the districts of Simferopol, Perekop, Yalta, Feodosia, and Dneprovsk. The Simferopol and Kerch committees had been announced in August and officially opened in September 1855.[36]

In June 1856, the Kerch committee had reconvened to assist the refugees' return and was staffed by city notables, including court counselor Ivan Ivanovich Zmacha, Kerch Police-Major Ivan Matveevich Trushevskii, the Kerch postmaster Piotr Vasilievich Mistrov, and a designated "Foreign Guest," Andrei Dmitrievich Vlastari.[37] On the first day, the committee heard fifteen petitions from a diverse body of civilians whose circumstances were shared by many across the peninsula.

One Kerch resident, Feodor Metelino, found his home "ruined to the foundation." He petitioned the Committee for emergency assistance to feed his family of six (four daughters, his wife, and his elderly father) and provided eyewitness testimony from Kerch police in March documenting damage. The committee allocated Metelino 10 rubles. A sailor returned to Kerch similarly to find his home in ruins. He received 8 rubles to support himself, his wife, and two small daughters. A "Greek townsman" received 9 rubles to feed himself, his wife, and his son. A widow received 10 rubles to feed herself and her son. Her husband was a sailor, and had died over the winter in Melitopol. Together they had a house in the Old Quarantine district of Kerch, which she found "ruined to the foundation."

Henceforth, the Kerch Committee heard from dozens of people per day; on July 14, 1856, the Committee met with fifty people, including widows. Each petitioner presented evidence of their property's destruction, and received 3 to 10 rubles, often based on the family's number of children.[38] Widows tended to receive more than families with a working-age male. As time wore on and lines grew longer, the committee stopped writing down details. By 1857, it recorded only names and disbursements. In the spring, the committee finally began to reach the end of Kerch petitioners. Lines shrank from forty or fifty per day to about five or ten per day. The Kerch committee closed on July 26, 1857.

The Simferopol committee operated on a similar basis. Residents presented documentation of damages and received a handful of rubles to cover immediate food and shelter. While most petitioners received between 5 and 10 rubles, those of noble birth and connections with the Russian elite could walk away with thousands. The Mavromikhaili sisters (who spent the war in Sevastopol as Sisters of Mercy and were locked in battle with Tatars they tried forcing off their estate) requested several thousand rubles each for emergency compensation. After having been refused in Simferopol, the sisters enlisted their benefactor to intervene with Stroganov on their behalf. A prince from the powerful Golitsyn family, their benefactor wrote to Stroganov that the sisters were in extreme need as "one of them, due to illness, must quickly go abroad for treatment." He asked that these sisters each be given 5,000 rubles from Stroganov's emergency fund of 500,000. They each received 3,000 rubles.[39]

In contrast to the emergency committee, the commission for property compensation founded on February 5, 1857, required much more extensive documentation and research. The committees operated in all districts of Tauride and major cities of Crimea, as well as other places in New Russia. Many, like the Kerch Commission, had predated the official order of February 5, 1857.

Typically, residents presented commissioners with detailed petitions stating the nature of their losses, a full list of damaged, destroyed, or stolen property, and estimated value. Commission members visited the property when possible, and collected evidence from neighbors. Then, the commission filled in a form for each petition that described the nature of the property and the level of damage (see Table 9.1). As the form indicates, the commission aimed for a precise record of movable and immovable property, livestock, furniture, buildings, and so on.

Thousands of surviving forms in Crimean archives attest to the tremendous material losses civilians experienced during the war. They also give insight into the lives people led before the war. All estates and all ethnic and religious backgrounds are represented. For example a *soldatka*, or soldier's wife, widowed during the war included in her account the destruction of two stone houses and theft of all of her household equipment. She calculated damages at 723 rubles and 50 kopeks (320 rubles for the buildings, and 400 for the movable property). The list of movable property she compiled included icons,

Table 9.1 War Damages Form, Simferopol Committee

Name	Quantity of Losses												Insured Property	
	Immovable Property				Movable Property									
	Number of destroyed or harmed				Miscellaneous things, such as: furniture, linens	Animals				Other			Immovable	Movable
	Houses	Work-shops and Factories	Other buildings	Total		Large	Small	Chickens	Total	Grain	Hay and Salt	Total		

dishware, a table and stool, her bridal chest, a cow, its calf, 10,800 lbs. of hay, fertilizer, a bucket, and a bed.[40] The committee weighed her petition against a larger a batch of 146 applications, and allocated 155 rubles for her movable property.[41]

Seid Ibraim Osmanov's estate near Belbek had been taken over by the Russian military. He submitted for 3,000 rubles, which broke down as follows: eight hundred liters of wine estimated at 700 rubles; 350 rubles for a destroyed fruit garden; 20 rubles' worth of hay; cattle for 60 rubles; furniture and various agricultural equipment for 300 rubles; a ruined house at 1,500 rubles.

The commission's agent interviewed two neighbors. They swore under oath that Osmanov's estate earned up to 400 rubles a year from the vineyard; the military took 1,080 pounds of hay; he had had two heads of cattle, and the house had been full of furniture, dishes, and vessels for winemaking. The commission conceded the estate earned an income of 150 rubles a year, and the military requisitioned hay and cattle. They admitted being convinced that the military destroyed or used all moveable property, but in its absence "could neither determine the quantity nor the value." Further, the commission could see "by looking at it" that the house had been ruined by the military and needed total rebuilding, which they valued at 1,000 rubles. In all, the commission granted Osmanov 1,643 rubles restitution.[42]

The Simferopol nobleman Selimish Murza Dzhankichev, who had evacuated along with all his family upon the military's orders, asked for an award of 3,000 rubles "for losses incurred during the war."[43] In the same way as with the Bakhchisarai merchant, the commission sent representatives to his property and took depositions from neighboring residents who estimated losses at an even greater value than the Tatar nobleman originally proposed. In response, the commission awarded him 2,292 rubles and 50 kopeks. By February 7, 1858, however, still no disbursement had been made apart from the initial emergency distribution of 20 rubles (5 rubles per family member).[44]

As these cases show, not everyone received compensation for their property. At the minimum, people waited one or two years for disbursements. The poorest people lived in lean-tos through the summer and winter of 1857. They struggled to feed themselves on inadequate budgets and in weakened conditions were susceptible to the contagions that circulated Crimea in the months after peace. Long waits for compensation dropped the wealthy into middling status and the middling to the poor.

Sometimes local committees proved less willing, or less able, to compensate the elite. Thus, for example, the Simferopol committee dragged its feet in reimbursing the Mavromikhaili sisters. After multiple petitions from the sisters, the Simferopol committee explained that it refused their request for 132,000 rubles compensation because there was not enough evidence regarding the nature of the destruction and, further, compensation was capped at 100,000 rubles. Another three years went by and then finally, the sisters' petition traveled to the tsar, who ordered the War Ministry to respond. In May of 1862, some six years after the peace declaration, the sisters received 64,000 rubles.[45]

Although Odessa closed the window for petitions in 1857, late appeals poured in well through the 1860s. A Sevastopol widow with five children had lost her husband during the war. Probably like many in similar circumstances, she did not know how or to whom to apply for compensation, or even that aid was available. By the time she understood her options she had missed the opportunity. Subsequently, she applied to the Odessa Committee directly and to the Ministry of the Interior. In June 1860, she sent in a petition composed with help from a local nobleman who was the son of a well-respected Vice Admiral.[46] The benefactor had asked the commission for 920 rubles on the widow's behalf to compensate her for the Russian army's destruction of her wine cellar.

Imperial Charity

In addition to the government commissions opened for the immediate relief and longer term compensation, the tsar opened a charity fund for the benefit of civilians made destitute by the war. Philanthropy was essential to the duties and public image of the Imperial Family. The Dowager Empress Maria Feodorovna operated several charities before her death in 1828, while the Grand Duchess Elena Pavlovna had been particularly active raising attention to the needs of soldiers, veterans, orphans, and widows during the Crimean War.[47] A circular published on June 28, 1857, states:

> All of Russia knows how much personal sacrifice and loss, inevitable in any war, was endured by the population of our southern provinces. . . . The cities of Sevastopol, Evpatoria and Kerch, the town Balaklava, various other seaside places and more than 100 villages in Crimea—suffered more or less significant ruin. [We] recall with pride and respect, Sevastopol citizens did not despair even seeing their homes destroyed by degrees, and they shared with the military the work and danger of the selfless commitment to defend the motherland.[48]

The circular went on to describe measures the government had already taken to revive agriculture and to support orphans. It also referenced the 1.5 million rubles that had been given for emergency relief and a separate relief program for sailors and other military personnel. This fund, the circular clarified, was to provide additional support for the poor. It invited donors to give according to "means and desire," and expressly asked merchants to support the "lost seafaring and fishing industry, which was so useful for a region."[49]

Children of the tsar became the board of trustees, which was managed by the Empress. Other members included Baron Korf, Menshikov, and the empress's privy councilor. Tsar Alexander II opened the fund with a donation of 10,000 rubles. Members of the imperial family filled the coffers to 25,000 rubles by January 1, 1858. Small donations trickled in from the provinces. Vladimir contributed 2 rubles, 30 kopeks; Arkhangelsk, 11 rubles 6 kopeks; Kazan, 6 rubles 41 kopeks; Poltava, 1 ruble, 48.5 kopeks; and so on. By 1860, the fund held 47,989 rubles.[50]

There are many reasons why the fund was not robust. The fund could have been poorly advertised, or provinces might have been already financially exhausted from supporting the war. Just as likely, concerns about voluntary donations streamed together with perceptions of corruption in the military intendancy. A donation of 16,000 rubles, for example, was sent to the intendancy to assist with the care and transport of disabled veterans to hospitals or homes. Books showed the money arriving, but not leaving. Earlier, the empress had opened a voluntary fund for widows and orphans that had disappeared. Begun in May of 1855, it started under good management, but the original director in Simferopol had died, as did the three other account managers who succeeded him. What happened to the fund subsequently, no one knew.[51] Other rumors suggested that "out of selfish pride" certain individuals, seeking imperial recognition, recorded a much higher sum than they actually gave.[52]

After peace, accounting became more reliable and donations were much more likely to reach the place for which they were intended. Most local commissions earnestly tried to assess damage and help residents in need. Actual compensation depended upon the Ministry of the Interior, however, and disbursement could take years, if it occurred at all.

Tax Relief

The last major element of the tsar's plan announced on February 5, 1857, involved a structured tax relief for areas affected by the war. This relief evolved from tax breaks granted during the war as well as recommendations from Stroganov, who wrote to the Minister of Finance on behalf of Crimean residents:

> You are completely aware of the ruin and deprivation residents of Tauride province experienced during almost two years war. This devastation primarily affected the residents in the enemy-occupied coastal cities: Evpatoria, Sevastopol, and Kerch and those places that were invaded such as Yalta, Feodosia, and Berdiansk. Much more time is demanded for these cities, particularly the first group, to return to their former status. Evpatoria might serve as an example, which according to my information, the foreign military completely desolated. Beyond that . . . the city must be cleaned of terrible filth. Under such conditions, I would think trade cannot quickly be restored. Apart from that, trade in the cities in general and primarily in Southern Russia, goes hand in hand with the status of agriculture and commerce in surrounding localities. How can trade can be carried out in Crimean Ports at the present? The surrounding environment has turned into a desert: the gardens and vineyards are destroyed, the fields [lie fallow] as military obligations diverted residents from their agricultural work and they could not complete the sowing. The most important means of transport in agriculture and industry—the working animals—are almost all destroyed.[53]

Stroganov asserted that the war completely devastated trade in Crimea, and it would take years to recover. Particularly in light of rampant inflation, he predicted even ten years might not be enough time for merchants to restore their businesses and turn even a small profit.

Stroganov's petition for tax relief arrived in St. Petersburg amid a crisis in imperial finances. Before the war, the Russian government owed 166 million rubles. During war, inflation soared, while the costs of an expanding military generated a deficit of 772.5 million rubles between 1852, when Russia began to mobilize, and 1857, when the peace process had run its course.[54] In 1855, the Russian finance ministry committed to a policy of issuing credit to cover war expenses. The Allied blockade had also taken its toll; custom revenue from exports fell from a high of 31 million rubles in 1852 to 16 million rubles in 1855. Further, diversion of farm labor and animals to the battlefield caused a catastrophic rupture in harvest across the empire. By the end of the war, grain production had collapsed. Even if merchants ships could leave the harbors, Russian merchants had very little to put in them.[55]

The Finance Minister considered a ten-year extension of tax relief for Crimea but met opposition from the Minister of the Interior, S. S. Lanskoi. As Lanskoi wrote, guilds "have a direct obligation to local residents and are responsible exclusively to their communities."[56] In imperial Russia, taxes gathered from the guilds supported crucial local services, including hospitals, orphanages, and care for indigents.[57] The revenue was particularly necessary in the wake of war.

Eventually, the Ministry of Finance crafted a plan of deferred taxes and suspended fees based on the three-tiered system proposed by Stroganov but for shorter time scales. The first tier included Kherson, Ekaterinoslav, and other places that fed and transported the military at the expense of local industry and agriculture. The second tier included Simferopol, Bakhchisarai, and Melitopol, places that similarly neglected local industry and agriculture for war duties, but at a more serious level and with greater cost to local production.

Sevastopol, Kerch, Yalta, and Balaklava, places directly altered by violence, composed the third tier. These cities were granted full tax relief through 1858. The second series had tax benefits through 1857, and the first only through 1856. Local petitions to the Ministry of Finance in 1856 (in addition to Stroganov's advocacy) helped secure these privileges. Thus, for example, a petition signed by Russian, Tatar, and Greek merchants from Evpatoria asked for continued suspension of dues, stating that they were "completely unable to fulfill the demands of the Tauride Treasury."

Ultimately, the Ministry of Finance released Sevastopol merchants from paying their duties for ten years. Kerch, Evpatoria, and Balaklava guilds received five years' relief.[58] The clock for these privileges started in 1854, however, not 1856, which meant that most Crimean merchants would need to begin paying their guild fees by 1859. [59]

Finally, the Ministry of the Interior granted tax and guild relief to foreign and native Crimeans alike.[60] The special inclusion of "foreigners" was stipulated in part to protect asylum seekers from the Ottoman Empire. Many Greeks, Serbs, and Bulgarians who volunteered to fight for the Russian Empire (in the Greek Legion of Tsar Nicholas I) remained in Crimea after the war; others returned to Russia after encountering resistance from Ottoman officials. The Russian government granted these people financial support in return for service. Dissatisfied former volunteers wandered southern Russia, approaching local officials in towns like Mariupol insisting that they were owed financial benefits and land.[61]

In addition to offering tax relief for the guilds, the Ministry of Finance and Ministry of the Interior worked together to offer a package of low-interest and no-interest loans to Crimean landowners to renew agriculture on their estates. In order to assess values of estates devastated by the Allies or the Russian army, the Ministry created a general committee comprised of Tauride nobility under the oversight of marshals from each district. The Ministry of the Interior stipulated that "the value must be calculated not on the property's present condition, but its potential, which would include costs of restoration to its former condition."[62]

Not all noblemen embraced the plan. The Yalta marshal of the nobility, for example, could not find anyone willing to participate from his district because all estates were ruined. No one was willing to take time from rebuilding; nor could any of the newly impoverished nobility pay for inflated accommodations in Simferopol for undetermined length of time. The marshal expressed skepticism about the entire project, asking, in essence, how anyone could pay back a loan when it would take a lifetime to restore what had been lost?[63] The chief produce in Yalta was wine and fruit; their razed vineyards and orchards would require decades to plant, mature, and bear fruit.

The Evpatoria nobles, in contrast, expressed concerns about managing vacant Tatar lands, as the majority of the 15,000 Tatars who left Crimea in 1855–1856 had come from their district. The Evpatoria representative used the discussion about land prices to advocate replacing Tatars with Russians: "The transfer of land from Tatars to Russian owners will strengthen grain production," he wrote, as well as "improving agriculture and the raising of livestock."[64]

Results

Following the peace, Russian authorities embarked on a recovery program for Crimea. It was the largest state-sponsored social project ever undertaken by the Romanovs before the Great Reforms, and in many ways it might be seen as a prototype for a new civil society. The government released millions of rubles for the immediate feeding and clothing of refugees, while the Imperial Family founded multiple charities dedicated to compensating civilians who lost property during the war. Further, the state established a complex code of tax relief and benefits. Modeled after the measures undertaken following the war of 1812, the plan attempted to help peoples of all social estates.

In the 1840s, the civil engineer and future head of Russian transportation, P. P. Melnikov, had proposed linking the Black and Baltic Seas with rail. Reflecting the abiding concern of tying Warsaw more closely to Moscow, Nicholas I had chosen to expand rail construction in a westerly rather than a southerly direction. The outbreak of war in 1853, however, refocused the tsar's attention, and surveyors projected a network of nearly 2,500 miles between Moscow, Kharkov, and Feodosia with links to Sevastopol, the Donbas, and other areas. The defense of Sevastopol had consumed too many resources, however, and construction of an imperial railroad line fell to the bottom of a long list.[65]

Viewing a new railway as a boon for local industry, residents of Feodosia embraced the concept of a new line after the war. Cash-strapped Tatars, Greeks, and Russians alike pooled their limited resources to raise nearly 8,000 rubles toward the project in 1856. The vast majority of supporters for this project were in fact local Tatars who still composed the majority population in the city.[66]

Simultaneously, the Russian government formed a merchant marine, which became the Russian Society of Steamship and Trade.[67] Under the leadership of Admiral N. A. Arkas, the Society was Russia's clever answer to the clause in the Paris Peace Treaty prohibiting Russia from keeping a navy in the Black Sea.[68] Before the treaty had even been signed, Grand Duke Constantine proposed to Alexander II "upon the conclusion of peace, it would be altogether advantageous to establish a large steamship society in the Black Sea from capital investment . . . [built so that] . . . the government might hire or buy them for military transferring, disembarkment or turning into war ships."[69]

The Society of Steamship and Trade built capital on publically traded stock and employed many of the 4,000 surviving Sevastopol sailors. It also supplied the fleet that defeated the Ottoman Empire in the Russian–Ottoman War of 1877–1878. Beyond military applications, the merchant marine was planned as part of the recovery program; Stroganov hoped that it might be able to attract volunteer sailors to Crimean port cities.[70]

Perhaps in preparation for this merchant marine, the tsar commissioned an American engineering company to raise or remove the more than seventy ships that had been sunk at Sevastopol. The ships blocked the harbor, which made redeveloping Sevastopol as a sea or navy center impossible until they were removed. Moreover, the ships were worth millions of rubles, even after having been waterlogged for more than a year.

Before the navy sank the ships, crews had protected them by kyanatizing the engines with tar, tallow, and zinc, which meant Russian leaders had sunk the ships with intentions of salvaging them.[71] To accomplish this gargantuan task the tsar hired an American team managed by John Gowen, who cleared seventy-four ships from the shipping channel. Gowen's crew raised twenty-two ships whole; the others were blasted and left on the sea floor.[72] The clearing of Sevastopol's harbor marked a milestone on the path of the recovery, and on the surface, a testament to Russian resiliency.

Despite these efforts, relief fell vastly short of the need. Plans for the railroad were delayed as the state transitioned rail construction to private investors with different priorities. Thus, the St. Petersburg–Warsaw line opened in 1862, but rail did not extend into Crimea until the 1870s, and then the terminus had shifted from Feodosia to Sevastopol.[73] The merchant marine had trouble attracting sailors to Crimean port cities because the conditions remained too primitive.[74]

Plans to renew Sevastopol in 1856 amounted to empty promises. International scandal erupted nearly immediately over desecration of graves pillaged by hungry residents who fed themselves from selling medals pulled from dead bodies.[75] Traveling through Crimea in the 1860s, ethnographer Evgeny Markov pointedly stated, "Sevastopol is now dead—this is above all doubt—its beautiful buildings and wide boulevards [have] been replaced with a corpse."[76]

Grand palaces with colonnades crumbled to the ground; glass and charred material littered the fundaments. A deathly pall had settled over the silent city. Only a small and miserable population lived among the undemolished corners of old state buildings, or partially standing wings of bombed-out houses. No one had work, and nature had begun to overtake civilization. Fresh grass sprouted in unkempt boulevards; weedy trees poked through tumbled down bricks.[77] Sevastopol native A. S. Lukomskii echoed Markov: "After the Crimean War, Sevastopol completely died." He grew up playing in abandoned ruins and war torn streets. Criminals ran the city of his youth. Roving gangs committed robbery without ceasing; murder was common.[78]

Similarly, Evpatoria "remained half destroyed." Writing in 1904, Rakov noted, "streets until recently remained empty, half in ruins."[79] By the turn of the twentieth century, the Kinburn fortress and village remained a derelict shell. The British had used the fortress as a hospital; before they handed the fortress back to Russia, they had stripped it and the church of all its guns, cannons, metals, and valuables. Only a cemetery with the bones of Allied soldiers remained.[80]

Impoverished local landowners struggled to keep their estates and often could not compete with wealthy Russian investors from Moscow and St. Petersburg who speculated on land prices in the peninsula.[81] Merchants endeavored to renew business; year after year, they petitioned to extend dues forgiveness. They paid their first postwar dues in 1867.[82] The biggest evidence of the failure to renew the peninsula, however, was the exodus of nearly 200,000 Crimean Tatars from 1859 to 1864.

The Tatar Migration

Tatars trickled out of Crimea each year after the war. Suddenly, however, in the fall of 1859, a new, much larger wave of migration gathered momentum. Stunned Russian officials attributed their migration to religious motivations, writing to the central government in St. Petersburg about Turkish emissaries who circulated a proclamation encouraging migration of Crimean Tatars to the Ottoman Empire.[83] A translation of the document attached to official correspondence and preserved in Russian archives offers a rare glimpse of religious aspects of the migration. It states:

> God said: "my land is wide: one can live where one wants." And the Prophet said: "yes, be with them in peace!" If you cannot freely fulfill the Sharia (the Muslim law and all its religious-civil practices and religious civil rituals) then settle in another (Muslim) country, be careful doing this, don't waste time resettling to our country. Those who do not move, will be shamed, and will not receive help in the future life [material in parenthesis from the Russian original].[84]

Whether or not religion inspired the Tatar migration remains an important historical question. In reviewing the causes of the migration of more than 400,000 mountaineers from the Caucasus between 1861 and 1864, one scholar suggests that policies of "forced exile complemented the Muslim tradition of *hijra (makhadzhirstvo)*, or voluntary migration in times of trouble."[85] Another has similarly seen the possibility of *hijra* behind Crimean Tatar exodus, suggesting that a different emigration of Nogai Tatars, begun in 1858, prompted Crimean Tatars to leave.[86] According to Ottoman specialist Kemal Karpat, the Ottoman government did invite Tatars to settle in the Ottoman Empire, and published an official invitation in March of 1857 offering would-be immigrants land and tax incentives in the eastern portions of the southern Balkan peninsula. Karpat notes, however, that Ottoman officials intended foreign settlement to resolve labor shortages, and did not aim this offer specifically at Muslim populations.[87]

The role of religion in motivating behavior is extremely difficult to assess, and is particularly so in Crimea when religious language penetrated all sides of the conflict. Although historians have recently turned their attention to religion in the Crimean War, they have yet to sift fully through the rhetoric to separate nationalist discourse from authentic belief. Moreover, as scholars of religion and violence have noted, separating materialist conditions from spiritual ones can be challenging.[88] Still, religion should not be dismissed out of hand.

It is indeed quite possible that a desire to live under a Muslim government held attraction for Tatars, and it is also quite possible that living under a state infused with Orthodox nationalism had grown too burdensome.

Russian officials like Stroganov, who already agitated for pushing Tatars out of Crimea, seized the opportunity to encourage Tatar migration. Stroganov wrote to officials in St. Petersburg that Ottoman agents attended religious meetings and night prayers to persuade Tatars to leave Russia. These agitators, according to Stroganov, warned Tatars they would not find salvation in Christian lands and explained clauses in the treaty that allowed emigration.

Stroganov insisted that these Turkish emissaries promised money and livestock upon resettling in Turkey but first demanded 1,000 rubles per person to "sign up those desiring to settle, to find a seat on the ship, and necessary shelter in Constantinople." He argued that the emissaries did everything they could to incite Tatar emigration, including spreading rumors that a recently proposed Orthodox diocese for Crimea was an attempt to Christianize all the Tatars, and that the government planned to resettle all Tatars in the northern provinces. [89] Here he depicted the rumors of government relocation to the interior as if such were the fantasy, rather than a real product of his own ambition. With his prodding Russian officials decided to permit Tatar emigration to Turkey on the foundation established by Tsar Alexander II three years earlier. [90]

By August 1860, officials recorded 89,190 people of both sexes who had either left for the Ottoman Empire or applied for passports. [91] By mid-November 1860, reports indicated that 28,000 Nogai Tatars and 57,000 Tatars from the steppe and mountains had already left. Of this latter group, 13,500 Tatars lived on state lands, 43,500 lived on estates and private lands (i.e., were not state peasants), 12,000 came from the steppe, 23,000 from the mountains, and 8,800 from the shore. [92] The departure of nearly 90,000 people in just a few months dramatically changed Crimean landscapes. Already severely damaged from war, with an economy in tatters, the sudden population loss sent Crimea deeper into shock. Those left behind feared for Crimea's total collapse.

Pessimists anticipated total ruin of Crimean agriculture without the experienced labor of the Tatars and an end to Crimean crafts and industry, including wool and silk trades, Turkish-style carpets, and other handiwork. Collapse of Crimean cities and postwar urban recovery seemed immanent without Tatar tax revenues and labor for reconstruction. "There is no sadder vision than in the steppe part of Crimea," wrote one observer, "in which now, entire empty villages and fields remain without workers and [the land goes] unsown. Deeper in the country, the more remote roads and the surrounding view is completely empty, where one hears only the howls of despondent packs of Tatar dogs left behind."[93] It remains to be determined, he continued, "From grain harvest or sowing, from crafts to factories what in Crimea will be touched in consequence of this exodus. How various interests will be defeated by this sudden event— what will fall into disrepair and what will be lost—is much more significant than is evident at a glance."[94]

Life continues in Crimea after the fall of Sevastopol. On a hill with a view of the Simferopol cityscape visited by Tsar Alexander II on October 27, 1855, Tatars build a new structure. F. Gross, artist. Published by A. Munster, 1856. *Courtesy Harvard Map Collection.*

10

Transformation

NOT LONG AFTER THE WAR'S conclusion, the Ministry of the Interior ordered Tauride noblemen to establish a committee to improve the lives of *pomeshchik* (seigniorial) peasants. Delegates from every district in Tauride joined the group headed by Aristide Reveliotti, a landowner who had brought charges against both Cossacks and Tatars during the war.

Most noblemen responded pro forma to Reveliotti's queries about the status of their peasants. Their message was often the same: as conscientious serf-owners, they always strove to make their peasants happy and agreed with the Ministry of the Interior that peasant welfare was important. One landlord added that his peasants "did not suffer the hunger many people endured in recent years."[1] Engaged in recovery efforts, several Crimean local landowners found participating in the committee to be a burden on time and resources.[2] Yet another expressed his willingness to "present [his] peasants with personal freedom . . . to transfer them from serf into free status."[3] These men, whether they realized it or not, were responding to a survey later used in the structuring of serf emancipation. Russia's Great Reforms were about to begin.

Conditions in Crimea, meanwhile, deteriorated. Industry and agriculture had not recovered from the war. Perhaps debate over coming reform distracted the tsar from his promise "to remember forever the sacrifice Crimean civilians had made for Russia during the war." Largely unaided or deliberately bypassed in the war recovery program, Crimean Tatars had been emigrating from the peninsula for three years before news of their departure reached the Ministry of Interior. Kiselev had been reappointed as the ambassador to Paris and the conservative M. N. Muraviev replaced him as Minister of State Domains. Following Kiselev's departure, Muraviev had approved Stroganov's plan to replace emigrating Tatars with Russian settlers.[4]

News of the mass Tatar migration caught Russian administrators in the Ministry of the Interior by sharp surprise. "In the more than three and one-half years [of Tatar emigration], the Ministry of Internal Affairs has not received any kind of information or recommendations about the exodus of the Crimean Tatars from the Crimean peninsula," wrote Lanskoi in December 1859. News of the Crimean Tatar exodus had spread widely, prompting the leader of the Tatar community in Lithuania to ask the Tauride Muslim Spiritual Assembly about the emigration. Unfortunately, the archives do not preserve the answer.[5]

The Committee of Ministers initiated an official inquiry into the Tatar emigration, which it assigned to Prince Vasilchikov, who had researched corruption in the Military Intendancy.[6] Vasilchikov was a logical choice for this new investigation: he had successfully concluded a major corruption case and had first-hand experience with Crimean affairs. His inquiry into the Tatar migration resulted in hundreds of pages of government reports between local and imperial officials, different ministries, and Tatar petitions, the latter of which, unfortunately, have not survived.[7]

In addition to building an archive of significant local and central correspondence on the question, he canvassed Crimean landowners, and sent Totleben to Tauride to research the migration personally. One of the most widely celebrated heroes of the siege of Sevastopol, Totleben held the respect of the Committee of Ministers and the tsar himself. His damning exposé of the disgraceful treatment of Tatars during the war, the peculation of local landowners, and complicity of Russian bureaucrats caused a terrible sensation when it circulated among St. Petersburg ministers and became a cornerstone of Vasilchikov's report.

Totleben linked the Tatar exodus to religious rhetoric of the Crimean War, military civilian policy, and greed. The mutiny of a few Tatars during the war, he argued, led local authorities to become convinced that "Tatars as peoples of a non-Orthodox faith [inovertsy] were harmful for Russia." Many Russians began to believe Tatars would endanger the success of Russian forces and because of fanatical religious beliefs would forever inhibit Crimean development. Such views, Totleben maintained, were a fantasy, as the Tatars had "altogether only weak influence on our lack of success, which as is known, stemmed from many other better known existing causes." Harsh wartime abuse from Cossacks, and the relocation of Tatars into the interior of the province, left many Tatars to fear their own government.[8] The war only accelerated this process as neighboring landowners seized Tatar land during their exile.

The marshal of the nobility in Perekop shared Totleben's bleak assessment of the Tatars' position on the peninsula. He suggested that no simple explanation for emigration existed, but rather, many complex ones. Only a people in despair would leave the land of their ancestors for a distant, unknown destination in an unfamiliar country. The Perekop marshal emphasized the harsh conditions of war, particularly the dangerous belief in Tatar disloyalty, and the subsequent plans to remove Tatars from the shore. It must have been terribly difficult, he wrote, for Tatars during the war to see members of their faith deported to distant provinces, from where many had not yet returned.[9]

The Perekop marshal shared many of Totleben's criticisms of landlord abuses. He emphasized that labor obligations had increased after the war and that Russian administrators like Stroganov had continued to agitate for Tatars' removal. He further attributed Tatar outmigration to the pillaging of grain reserves, and abuse of villages during the war by the police and local officials. In the postwar recovery program, Tatars lost in the redistribution of land and livestock. He certified that although the program had intended to help the poorest of Crimean villagers, aid often went to the wealthiest. The tax burden had increased for the lowest estates, and Tatars bore the brunt of the peninsula's rebuilding. Finally, the marshal pointed to pervasive corruption in local government during and after the war.[10]

After studying these and many other similar statements, Vasilchikov concluded that oppressive wartime conditions, and not religious motivation, had pushed Tatars from Crimea. He further underscored the erosion of Tatar access to land. Before the war, estate owners had encroached upon Tatar lands. After the war the Ministry of State Domains took over of Tatar property, while simultaneously increasing land-labor requirements and state taxes.

"Taking into account [that] this version of events corresponds with the report submitted by Totleben on the affair of resettlement of the Crimean Tatars," the Ministers concluded that the policies of the Ministry of State Domains under Muraviev and Stroganov contributed to the causes of Tatar migration.[11] The Committee professed that it would have liked to order an official review of Stroganov's office, which would typically result in the dismissal or disciplining of provincial governors.[12] Due to the war and its many terrible consequences, however, the Committee of Ministers agreed that such a formal review would serve little benefit. In bypassing the standard procedure of the Senatorial review, the Committee proposed several changes and encouraged Stroganov to resign his post. He left Odessa by 1862.

Moving forward, the Committee of Ministers required the Tauride Governor Zhukovskii to usher Tatar land disputes more quickly through Russian courts. Quite often, Tatar petitions against landlord encroachment went through procedures at the district level, the provincial level in Simferopol, and then escalated to the regional high court in Odessa, only to be sent back again to the district, with the process repeating again. Such a lengthy trial process, the Committee noted, served the interests of wealthy landlords who better knew Russian laws and had the money and time to wait out poor Tatar peasants who gave up on cases before decisions had been reached.[13]

The Committee next advocated compensating Tatars who had suffered during the war, and established a three-member committee to formally research abuses of authority in the Ministry of State Domains. Such a committee would develop a plan for improving Tatar conditions and guard against future exploitation.[14] It assigned still another committee consisting of the Tauride provincial authority, a local representative from the Ministry of State Domains, Crimean noblemen, and Tatar representatives to re-establish reasonable working obligations for Tatars, with particular attention to reducing the labor debt for spring planting and transportation obligation for government officials. Finally, the Committee of Ministers threw obstacles in the path of Tatars wishing to migrate, such as making it difficult to obtain passports and requiring a lengthy waiting period between receiving passports and actual departure.[15]

The Ministers' plan made a difference for a few individuals. For example, a Tatar court case against a landlord building on *vakif* land, which opened August 1854 and had been postponed by the Allied invasion, was reopened in 1863. After nine years, the court ruled in favor of the Tatar petitioner.[16] However, efforts to rectify conditions for Tatars came too late to stop Crimea's transformation. Tatars continued to migrate, albeit with a few more obstacles, through the mid-1860s. Many settled in Ottoman territory in Bulgaria and Romania.[17] By 1867, the Tauride Statistical Committee concluded that, in all, 104,211 men and 88,149 women immigrated to the Ottoman Empire.[18] They left hundreds of villages completely vacant, including 68 villages in Berdiansk, 9 villages in Melitopol, 278 villages in Perekop, 24 villages in Simferopol, 67 villages in Feodosia, and 196 villages in Evpatoria.

To resolve population crisis, the local government with the imperial government's permission continued the foreign and internal settlement program. Russian peasants settled vacated lands. More than 1,600 families had been called from Chernigov, Poltava, Voronezh, Kursk, and Tambov provinces even before the Committee of Ministers finished its review.[19] By 1864, local

officials allocated approximately 440,000 hectares of land for settlement by
Montenegrans, Greeks, Mennonites, and Bulgarians, who could settle in the
Russian Empire in accordance with the Paris Peace Treaty.[20] The dreams of those
officials who wished to repopulate Crimea with Christian populations came
true, and Russians, Armenians, Greeks, and Bulgarians soon overwhelmed the
Tatar population that remained.[21]

As ink dried on the Treaty of Paris, Crimean laity signed a petition requesting
a bishopric. The petition reveals the degree to which Crimean Christians had
internalized the voluminous prewar writings about the holiness of Crimea's
Christian antiquities, as well as anti-Islamic rhetoric of the war. "The Tauride
Peninsula, since the Christianizing of our great Prince Vladimir," began the
petition, "has served as the cradle of Orthodox faith for all of Russia, from the
first centuries of Christianity." The petition provided a list of saints identified
with Crimea and summarized what it described as shameful "persecution [of
Christians] under the cruel rule of the Mongols, Tatars, and Turks."[22]

Without an active bishop, believers maintained, Islam remained the governing faith in Crimea. They pointed to the mufti writing, "Crimean Islam,
in the person of its mufti, has its own highly-ranked spiritual authority, but
the Orthodox Church is represented before the Tatars only in the persons of
its lowly ranked servitors." Petitioners circled back to Crimea's historic legacy
for the Russian empire, emphasizing the "unnatural position of Orthodoxy,
in . . . Russia's cradle of Christianity." Believers argued that a bishop would
provide a bastion against Islam and would "enable Christians to heal from the
ulcer of the harmful invasion and mutinous uprisings of the native Tatars."[23]
The military and civilian governors of Tauride signed the document, as did
officials from all of Crimea's principal districts, cities, and towns. Archbishop
Innokentii forwarded the petition to the Holy Synod in 1857.[24]

The next year, the two provinces, Kherson and Tauride, separated their diocesan hierarchies and marked a watershed event in the history of Christianity in
Crimea.[25] Crimean clergy were granted independence from Kherson, and the
Russian Orthodox Church expanded into Muslim territory. Catalyzed by the
religious fervor during the Crimean War, this diocese heralded a new era in
the political dynamic of Crimea's religious life. In fewer than fifteen years, the
diocese established the first seminary for Tauride, and within twenty years had
more than doubled the number of Crimean churches.[26] The balance between
Muslim and Christian populations had shifted.

In the short space of a decade, Crimea had undergone dramatic, rapid
change. War had ruined the landscape and decimated the population. The
mass migration of Crimean Tatars was a more meaningful a consequence of

the Crimean War than the Russian cessation of Bessarabia to the Ottoman Empire or Russia's restrictions in the Black Sea. One hundred and fifty years later, Crimean Tatar writer and activist Gulnara Abdulaeva reflected: "It is not hard to imagine what prompted the native population to abandon its homeland. Hunger and devastation ruled together. Crimean Tatars were of interest to belligerents only for the ability to supply provisions, carriages, and transport. Russian bureaucrats ran away at the beginning of the war, leaving the Tatars to their fate."[27] Although there were many reasons prompting Tatar migration, crisis of war and punitive policies rank highly among them.

Despite Vasilchikov's findings in 1861, the conviction that Tatars betrayed the tsar during the war persisted in the mainland. "We have accepted this fact without any doubt," wrote Markov, but he said, in Crimea, the perception had changed. Wise elders "despised from the depth of their souls" any aspersion cast upon Tatars and pointed out that Russia would have fallen without them. Markov reiterated the comments of many observers, that Tatars provided the military with provisions and all means of transportation. When Russian administrators fled Evpatoria and Simferopol, Tatar drivers helped them leave. When wealthy Russian landowners left for the mainland, Tatars dutifully protected the grain, or burned it as instructed.[28] Markov explicitly stated that *Tatars* were the Russian subjects who suffered and sacrificed the most for the war.

Russian resettlement schemes and recovery efforts had no quick effect. "Whoever was in Crimea, even if only for one month," according to Markov, "knows Crimea died after the departure of the Tatars." Only Tatars who had lived and worked the land for centuries understood how to cultivate the dry steppe and where to find water. They worked where the Germans and Bulgarians could not or would not. Where thirty large herds of sheep once roamed, only one group remained. Dry, dead pools replaced fountains. Deserts replaced industrious villages.[29] The Tatars' departure had changed Crimea forever.[30]

The migration of Crimean Tatars after the Crimean War constituted one of the largest internal mass migrations of nineteenth-century Europe, but is very little appreciated by scholars outside Russian-Ottoman studies.[31] The general scholarship on migration during the nineteenth century has tended to focus on western European labor movements and mass urbanization, and ascribe violence-inspired migration to the provenance of the twentieth century.[32] Yet, when we look at Europe from the perspective of those states in the east, we see a long history of violence and population exchanges along the Russian-Ottoman frontier.

With each major turn in the Eastern Question and the Russian-Ottoman Wars, waves of Tatars left Crimea for the empire of the Sultan. Christian refugees traced an opposite path, and streamed into southern Ukraine. Greeks, Bulgarians, Serbs, and Armenians who had taken arms against the Ottoman Empire sought asylum in the empire of the tsars.[33] Millions of Muslims left Russia, the Balkans, and the Caucasus. They immigrated to the Ottoman Empire during the nineteenth century through the First World War, including nearly 1,800,000 Tatars, in what some have called the Great Muslim Exodus from Europe.[34] Others have described the phenomenon as "demographic warfare." They emphasize that hostile state policies evident in the Crimean War were reflected throughout mass Muslim migrations from Balkans and the Russian Empire.

Before closing this book, a few words might be said about the relationship between the Crimean War and the Great Reforms that quickly followed in the wake of violence. The Crimean War fundamentally changed the relationship between the people and the state. Civilians mobilized for the home front began to expect concessions for their sacrifices, while new, civilian institutions and charity networks created for recovery efforts gave the government experience with new methods of community management.[35]

A closer look at the civilian and military experience during the Crimean War, from mobilization through reconstruction, suggests a much more complicated explanation for the Great Reform than a top-down reaction to "humiliating defeat."[36] The notion of Alexander II and his ministers responding to a "humiliating defeat" is an inaccurate cliché of the field at best, while the emphasis on top-down reforms dismisses iterative engagement with peasants and civil society as well as ongoing reform begun during the Nicolaevin era. The war itself was both the engine and the accelerator of social, cultural, and bureaucratic change.

Other historians have shown that Kiselev's reforms during the 1830s–1840s created a revolutionary situation on the eve of the Crimean War. His changes in the Ministry of State Domains produced a glaring imbalance in the freedoms enjoyed by state peasants as compared with serfs attached to noble estates. The creation of hospitals and schools in state villages produced a rising intelligentsia whose numbers swelled during the Crimean War. Further, wartime peasant rebellions in Kiev, Poltava, Voronezh, and Crimea motivated the government to rethink policy as the war unfolded.[37]

Russia had already begun to invest in rail and steam. During the war, even in the lifetime of Nicholas I, the state made the development of these industries a priority.[38] War with Europe did not demonstrate the need for rail; rather, war with Europe—the violence and the expense—delayed its implementation. On a different tack, the Crimean War transformed medical care for Russia as much as it did for Western Europe, and due to the enhanced demand for doctors, produced a new cadre of professionals. The war generated a new appreciation for engineers like Totleben, who along with nurses, doctors, industrialists, and bankers (many who structured recovery loans) became the new women and men of Russia. Here again, the Great Reforms did not create, but rather codified policy already in motion.[39]

In a related point, popular interest in the war led to a mini-explosion in the Russian periodical press so that, for example, readership of the provincial journal in Tambov grew from fifty-seven people in 1853 to 357 in 1854.[40] Similarly, subscriptions to *The Northern Bee* doubled as readers were eager to absorb news of the conflict. Russians perceived the war as the definitive event of their lives and by 1855 censorship standards relaxed further. *The Russian Veteran* and *The Naval Journal* published uncensored accounts of battles and saw their readership increase. Participants in the siege of Sevastopol and other battles filled Russian publications with heroic tales of bravery as well as hostile criticism of military commanders. Heated debate unfolded publicly, in print, about wartime policy.[41] Men like Totleben, who led official inquiries into allegations of corruption, published their findings. Subjects of investigation, like Zatler, defended themselves openly in the press.[42] Doctors and nurses wrote exposés about Russian war medicine.[43]

The war thus forged a new, broader readership and placed new demands upon the Russian press. In many ways, the Russian experience resembles Britain's explosion of the popular press, where the *Times* editor John Delane and journalist William Russell regularly reported on events to a reading public avid for news.[44] Although the blast in Russia was not as bright (and the latitude of expression not nearly as broad), the light nevertheless exposed the Russian government to a new level of scrutiny and criticism. There is a misperception in the field that the Great Reforms ignited literacy and *post ipso facto* permitted open reflection upon the war, when in fact the opposite might be said to be true, that is, that war itself ignited literacy and forged the Great Reforms.[45]

The crisis of violence further accelerated the rise of Russian nationalism and reinforced the relationship between Russian Orthodoxy and Russian identity. The state allowed Christians to expand into Muslim spaces and permitted Orthodox missions to flourish. Changes in Islamic policy evident during the war, such as the closing of Tatar courts, accelerated as well. The war had called Catherine the Great's vision of a multi-confessional empire into doubt, and introduced the notion of Muslims as fanatics.[46] Rather than viewing Islamic institutions as mediums through which state and subject might communicate, officials after the war argued that Islamic schools and assemblies planted anti-Russian attitudes and seeds of mutiny.[47] Russification policies aimed at assimilating Muslim institutions eliminated official acceptance of Sharia.[48]

During the war, Nicolaevin reformers like Kiselev, von Bradke, and others viewed peasants of all ethnicities as civilians with certain rights. These men cared very deeply about following due processes of law. That Kiselev lost his battle to anti-Islamic parties and the arbitrary exercise of power bode poorly for the Great Reforms ahead; the Crimean War experience demonstrated that Russia's evolving rule of law could not withstand crisis.

Nor could the rule of law and civilian rights take precedence over perceived military needs, a trend that continued through the reigns of Alexander II and his successors. By the same token, the Crimean War proffered forced migration as a tool of population management as state fears of internal enemies escalated. In so doing, the war prepared the way for what one scholar has described as a "radicalizing of military policy" which resulted most immediately in the ethnic cleansing of the Caucasus, and more persistently, a paranoid policy of "preventative ethnic cleansing" aimed at removing entire population groups before they could harm the state.[49] The larger Military Reform of the 1860s and 1870s, moreover, began with a Ministry of War proposal in 1855.[50]

The Crimean War was a landmark event of Russia's nineteenth century, perhaps more monumental even than the Great Reforms that came after. The war touched all communities in Russia to a degree that has yet to be fully understood. Violence deeply altered what is today southern Ukraine and utterly transformed Crimea. Even after the terrible violence of the twentieth century, the Crimean War's indelible mark has persisted through the present.

NOTES

Introduction

1. George Paget, *The Light Cavalry Brigade in the Crimea: Extracts from the Letters and Journals of the Late George Paget* (London: John Murray, 1881), 15.

2. Iu. A. Naumova, *Ranenie, Bolezn' i Smert': Russkaia Meditsinskaia sluzhba v Krymskuiu voinu, 1853–1856 gg.* (Moscow: Modest Kolerov, 2010), 297.

3. A. A. Skal'kovskii, *Opyt statisticheskogo opisaniia novorossiiskogo kraia, chast' 1, Geografiia, etnografiia i narodoschislenie Novorossiiskogo kraia* (Odessa: tip. L. Nichte, 1850), 272–73; B. S. El'iashevich, *Karaimskii biograficheskii slovar' (s kontsa VIII v. do 1960)* (Moscow: RAN, 1993); and S. Ia. Kozlov and L. V. Chizhova, *Tiurskie narody Kryma: Karaimy, Krymskie Tatary, Krymchaki* (Moscow: Nauka, 2003).

4. For a groundbreaking study of Crimea in the aftermath of annexation under Catherine the Great, see Kelly Ann O'Neill, *Claiming Crimea: A History of Catherine the Great's Southern Empire* (New Haven, CT: Yale University Press, 2017). A good analysis of the precarious coexistence of borderland populations can be found in Eric D. Weitz and Omer Bartov, *The Shatterzone of Empires: Coexistence and Violence in the German, Habsburg, Russian and Ottoman Borderlands* (Bloomington: Indiana University Press, 2003), 3–6.

5. A. I. Markevich, "Pereseleniia Krymskikh Tatar v Turtsiiu v sviazi s dvizheniem naseleniia v Krymu," *Izvestiia Akademii Nauk SSSR*, otd. gumanitarnykh nauk, vol. 1 (1928): 375–405, and vol. 2 (1929): 1–16; Kemal H. Karpat, *Ottoman Population, 1830–1914: Demographic and Social Characteristics* (Madison: University of Wisconsin Press, 1985), 66. See also the discussion of Russian annexation in the classic by Alan Fisher, *The Russian Annexation of Crimea, 1772–1783* (Cambridge: Cambridge University Press, 1970).

6. John R. Staples, *Cross Cultural Encounters on the Ukrainian Steppe: Settling the Molochna Basin* (Toronto: University of Toronto Press, 2003), 18–44.

7. Brian Glyn Williams, *The Crimean Tatars: From Soviet Genocide to Putin's Conquest* (London: C. Hurst and Co., 2015), 3.

8. Napoleon's invasion of Russia, in contrast, lasted from June through December 1812.

9. M. I. Bogdanovich, *Vostochnaia Voina, 1853–1856*, 4 vols. (St. Petersburg: tip. F. Sushchinko, 1876), 4: 72.

10. Scholars of British history have explored these aspects of the war in much more depth than their colleagues working in Russian history. For a review of English language and largely Anglo-centric scholarly literature of the Crimean War, see the introduction of Andrew Lambert's *The Crimean War: British Grand Strategy against Russia, 1854–1856*, 2nd ed. (Farmham: Ashgate, 2011).

11. F. K. Zatler, *Zapiski o prodovol'stvii voisk v voennoie vremia*, 3 vols. (St. Petersburg: tip. Torgovogo doma S. Strugovshikova, 1860).

12. The two major Western historical surveys on military logistics note the paucity of theoretical works on the subject, and neither appears to have been aware of Zatler. These are John A. Lynn, *Feeding Mars: Logistics in Western Warfare from the Middle Ages to the Present* (Oxford: Westview, 1993); and Martin Van Creveld, *Supplying War: Logistics from Wallenstein to Patton* (Cambridge: Cambridge University Press, 1995).

13. Anon., "Fedor Karlovich Zatler," *Rossiiskii Biograficheskii Slovar'* (Petrograd: tip. Glavnogo upravleniia udelov, 1916), 7: 270–73.

14. It is apparent that Tolstoy was aware of Zatler. See Lev Nikolaevich Tolstoi, *Polnoe Sobranie Sochinenii* (Moscow: izd. "Khudozhestvennaia literatura," 1935), 4: 282–83; 17: 360–61.

15. Anon., "The Crimean War. Section II. The Loss of Money," 117–21, *The Advocate of Peace* (1869): 120; see also Paul LeRoy Beaulieu, *Contemporary Wars (1853–1866): Statistical Researches Representing the Loss of Men and Money Involved in Them*, trans. London Peace Society (London: Harriett and Sons, 1869).

16. Andrew C. Rath, *The Crimean War in Imperial Context, 1854–1856* (New York: Palgrave Macmillan, 2015), 7–10.

17. V. Stepanov, "Krymskaia voina i ekonomika Rossii," in *The Crimean War, 1853–1856: Colonial Skirmish or Rehearsal for World War? Empires, Nations and Individuals*, ed. Jerszy W. Borejsz (Warsaw: Wydawnictwo Neriton Instytut PAN, 2011), 276.

18. Costs of Crimean War (and comparison with the Napoleonic Wars) is found in two archives in the Ministry of the Interior (henceforward MVD) and Ministry of Finance, respectively: Rossiiskii Gosudarstvennyi Istoricheskii Arkhiv (RGIA), f. 1287, op. 6, d. 1138 (O vspomozheniiakh Novorossiiskomu Kraiu i voobshche o merakh k vosstanovleniiu onogo posle voiny), ll. 1–265; and RGIA, f. 560, op. 12, d. 346 (O darovanii posobii Novorossiiskomu kraiu i Bessarabskoi oblasti, po sluchaiu nyneshnikh voennykh obstoiatel'stv), ll. 1–531. Much of this material was printed and preserved in the Russian National Library (subsequently RNB), *O vspomozheniiakh Novorossiiskomu kraiu i voobshche o merakh k vosstanovleniiu onogo posle voiny* (St. Petersburg: tip. MVD, 1856).

19. *Polnoe sobranie zakonov Rossiiskoi imperii* (PSZRI) 2nd ser., vol. 31 (St. Petersburg: 1856), no. 30881, 803–4. So ends the proclamation dated 26 Aug. 1856.

20. On the volume of Crimean wine production, see M. K. Balas, *Istoriko-statisticheskii ocherk vinodeliia v Rossii (Kavkaz i Krym)* (St. Petersburg: Obshchestvennaia Pol'za, 1877), 90–115.

21. Rumours of British and Russian aristocratic spectators arriving to witness battles spread in both empires. See Susan Layton, "Russian Military Tourism: The Crisis of the Crimean War

Period," in *Turizm: the Russian and East European Tourist under Capitalism and Socialism*, ed. Anne E. Gorsuch and Dianne P. Koenker (Ithaca, NY: Cornell University Press, 2006), 43–63; and David William Lloyd, *Battlefield Tourism: Pilgrimage and the Commemoration of the Great War in Britain, Australia and Canada, 1919–1939* (Oxford: Berg, 1998), 21–23; and for early American war tourism, which gives context for Twain's interest, see Thomas A. Chambers, *Memories of War: Visiting Battlefields and Bonegrounds in the Early American Republic* (Ithaca, NY: Cornell University Press, 2012).

22. Samuel Clemens, *Innocents Abroad* (Hartford, CT: American Publishing Company, 1869), 279–80.

23. The migration has been the focus of substantial research focusing on the postwar period. A. I. Markevich, "Pereseleniia Krymskikh Tatar v Turtsiiu"; Alan W. Fisher, "Emigration of Muslims from the Russian Empire in the Years after the Crimean War," *JGO* 35.3 (1987), 356–71; Marc Pinson, *Demographic Warfare—An Aspect of Ottoman and Russian Policy, 1854–1866* (PhD diss., Harvard University, 1970); Brian Glyn Williams, "Hijra and Forced Migration from Nineteenth-Century Russia to the Ottoman Empire," *Cahiers du monde Russe* 41/1 Janvier-Mars (2000), 79–108; James Meyer, "Immigration, Return, and the Politics of Citizenship: Russian Muslims in the Ottoman Empire, 1860–1914," *International Journal of Middle East Studies* 39.1 (2007), 9–26; and Mara Kozelsky, "The Crimean War and the Tatar Exodus," in *Russian Ottoman Borderlands*, ed. Lucien Frary and Mara Kozelsky (Madison: University of Wisconsin Press, 2014), 165–92.

24. Anon., Zapiska o vyselenii tatar iz Kryma, 20 Nov. 1860, RGIA, f. 1287, op. 6, d. 1710 (O pereselenii Krymskikh tatar za granitsu i o kolonizatsii vladelicheskikh v Krymu imenii), l. 70.

25. Exceptions include John Shelton Curtiss, *Russia's Crimean War* (Durham, NC: Duke University Press, 1979); Mara Kozelsky, "Casualties of Conflict: Crimean Tatars During the Crimean War," *SR* 67.4 (2008): 862–91; Kozelsky, *Christianizing Crimea: Shaping Sacred Space in the Russian Empire and Beyond* (DeKalb: Northern Illinois University Press, 2010); Orlando Figes, *The Crimean War: A History* (New York: Metropolitan Books, 2011).

26. Military histories have described the formation of policy before and after the Crimean War, but not the application of policy during actual combat. See John Shelton Curtiss, *The Russian Army under Nicholas I, 1825–1855* (Durham, NC: Duke University Press, 1965); John Keep, *Soldiers of the Tsar: Army and Society in Russia, 1462–1874* (Oxford: Clarendon Press, 1985), 325–26; Elise Wirtschafter, *From Serf to Russian Soldier* (Princeton, NJ: Princeton University Press, 1990); Frederick W. Kagan, *The Military Reforms of Nicholas I: The Origins of the Modern Russian Army* (New York: St. Martin's Press, 1999); Brian D. Taylor, *Politics and the Russian Army: Civil–Military Relations, 1689–2000* (Cambridge: Cambridge University Press, 2003), 52–53; and David R. Stone, *A Military History of Russia: From Ivan the Terrible to the War in Chechnya* (Westport, CT: Praeger, 2006). Similarly, little research has been devoted to activities of the Third Section during the Crimean War, and the major English language studies of the Third Section under Nicholas I end on the eve of war. P. S. Squire, *The Third Department: The Establishment and Practices of the Political Police in the Russia of Nicholas I* (Cambridge: Cambridge University Press, 1968); and Sidney Monas, *The Third Section: Police and Society under Nicholas I* (Cambridge, MA: Harvard University Press, 1961).

27. Food policy has been the subject of research for the First and Second World Wars, but until now, not for the Crimean War. See, for example, Lars Lih, *Bread and Authority in Russia, 1914–1921* (Berkeley: University of California Press, 1990); William Moskoff, *The Bread of Affliction: The Food Supply in the USSR during WWII* (Cambridge: Cambridge University Press, 2002); and the collected essays in Wendy Z. Goldman and Donald Filtzer (eds.), *Hunger and War: Food Provisioning in the Soviet Union during WWII* (Bloomington: Indiana University Press, 2015). Exceptions in the study of war-financing include the dissertation by S. V. Gavrilov which discusses the Crimean War as a topic in passing: "Razvitie material'nogo snabzheniia russkoi armii v XIX veke" (PhD diss., Voennaia akademiia tyla i transporta imeni generala armii A. V. Khruleva, St. Petersburg, 2010); David Moon, "Russian Peasant Volunteers at the Beginning of the Crimean War," *SR* 51.4 (1992): 691–704; and Stepanov, "Krymskaia voina i ekonomika Rossii," cited in note 17.

28. For a summary of the literature relating to the home front, see Joseph Bradley, "Subjects into Citizens: Societies, Civil Society, and Autocracy in Tsarist Russia," *American Historical Review* 107.4 (2002): 1094–123; and Adele Lindenmeyr, "Primordial or Gelatinous? Civil Society in Imperial Russia," *Kritika* 12.3 (2011): 705–20. For recent research on the Russian home front during the First World War, see Adele Lindenmeyr, Christopher Read, and Peter Waldron (eds.), *Russia's Home Front in War and Revolution, 1914–1922* vol. 3, book 2 (Bloomington, IN: Slavica Publishers, 2011).

29. Soviet scholarship has pursued the relationship between the Crimean War and the Great Reforms to a greater extent than Western scholarship. P. A. Zaoinchkovskii and N. M. Druzhinin persuasively argue that economic pressures of the Crimean War (including peasant rebellions and discontented peasant veterans) accelerated the pace of prewar agrarian reform. See, for example, P. A. Zaionchkovskii, *The Abolition of Serfdom in Russia*, ed. and trans. Susan Wobst, introduction by Terrence Emmons (Gulf Breeze, FL: Academic International Press, 1978); and N. M. Druzhinin, *Gosudarstvennye Krest'iane i reforma P. D. Kiseleva*, 2 vols. (Moscow: Isdatel'stvo Akademii Nauk SSSR, 1958).

30. The idea that defeat prompted Tsar Alexander II to undertake reform pre-dates Alfred Reiber's influential *Politics of Autocracy: Letters of Alexander II to Prince A. I. Bariatinskii 1857–1864* (Paris: Moulton and Co., 1966). For a discussion of the literature on the Great Reforms, see Abbott Gleason, "The Great Reforms and the Historians since Stalin," in *Russia's Great Reforms, 1855–1881*, ed. Ben Eklof, John Bushnell, and Larisa Zakharova (Bloomington: Indiana University Press, 1994), 1–16.

31. With few exceptions, the revival of Russian military history (in Anglophone literature) depicted by Bruce Menning more than a decade ago has bypassed the Crimean War. Bruce Menning, "A Decade Half Full: Post–Cold War Studies in Russian and Soviet Military History," *Kritika* 2.2 (Spring 2001): 341–62.

32. Daniel Rothbart and Karina Korostelina, *Why They Die: Civilian Devastation in Violent Conflict* (Ann Arbor: University of Michigan Press, 2011), 2.

33. In this regard, I have found Adam R. Seipp's description of demobilization following the First World War as a cultural and social process (as well as diplomatic, bureaucratic, and economic) particularly helpful. See Adam R. Seipp, *The Ordeal of Peace: Demobilization and the Urban Experience in Britain and Germany, 1917–1921* (Burlington, VT: Ashgate, 2009).

34. After the war, the poet I. S. Nikitin caricatured the term with an extended story in verse, which he titled *Kulak*: Ivan Savvich Nikitin, *Kulak* (Moscow: tip. Kakova, 1858).

35. See Pavel Polian, *Against Their Will: The History and Geography of Forced Migrations in the USSR* (Budapest: Central European University Press, 2004); Willis Brooks, "Russia's Conquest and Pacification of the Caucasus: Relocation Becomes a Pogrom in the Post-Crimean War Period," *Nationalities Papers* 23.4 (1995), 675–86; Austin Jersild, *Orientalism and Empire: North Caucasus Mountain Peoples and the Georgian Frontier* (Montreal: McGill-Queen's University Press, 2002), 22–27; Peter Holquist, *Making War, Forging Revolution: Russia's Continuum of Crisis, 1914–1921* (Cambridge, MA: Harvard University Press, 2002); David L. Hoffman, *Cultivating the Masses: Modern State Practices and Soviet Socialism* (Ithaca, NY: Cornell University Press, 2011), 242–53; and Eric Lohr, *Nationalizing the Russian Empire: The Campaign against Enemy Aliens during World War I* (Cambridge, MA: Harvard University Press, 2003).

36. Peter Gatrell, *A Whole Empire Walking: Refugees in Russia During World War I* (Bloomington: Indiana University Press, 1999); William Fuller, *The Foe Within: Fantasies and the End of Imperial Russia* (Ithaca, NY: Cornell University Press, 2006).

37. Many works address peasant relocation, particularly (but not exclusively) those dealing with religious minorities. See, for example, the literature reviews in Willard Sunderland, "Peasants on the Move: State Peasant Resettlement in Imperial Russia, 1805–1830s," *Russian Review* 52.4 (2007): 472–85; and Sunderland, *Taming the Wildfield: Colonization and Empire on the Russian Steppe* (Ithaca, NY: Cornell University Press, 2004); and also Nicholas Breyfogle, *Heretics and Colonizers: Forging Russia's Empire in the South Caucasus* (Ithaca, NY: Cornell University Press, 2005).

38. For later use of statistics, see Peter Holquist, "To Count, To Extract, To Exterminate: Population Statistics and Population Politics in Late Imperial and Soviet Russia," in *A State of Nations: Empire and Nation-Making in the Age of Lenin and Stalin*, ed. Ronald Suny and Terry Martin (New York: Oxford University Press, 2001), 111–43; as well as David Rich, "Imperialism, Reform and Strategy: Russian Military Statistics, 1840–1880," *The Slavonic and East European Review* 74.4 (1996): 621–639.

39. Irma Kreitin, "A Colonial Experiment in Cleansing: The Russian Conquest of Western Caucasus, 1856–1865," *Journal of Genocide Research* 11.2/3 (2009): 213–41. For a discussion of institutional power in Russia and changes between Nicholas I and Alexander II, see the classic English-language works (as well as other works referenced throughout the pages of this book): Richard Wortman, *The Development of a Russian Legal Consciousness* (Chicago: University of Chicago Press, 1976); Daniel T. Orlovsky, *The Ministry of Interior Affairs* (Cambridge, MA: Harvard University Press, 1981); and Don Karl Rowney and Walter Pintner, *Russian Officialdom: The Bureaucratization of Russian Society from the Seventeenth to the Twentieth Century* (Chapel Hill: University of North Carolina Press, 1980).

40. Reputations of both tsars (Nicholas as conservative, and Alexander II as progressive) have been changing as scholars develop more research into the body of their reigns. See sources referenced throughout this introduction.

41. W. E. Mosse's classic portrayal of Alexander II as "Tsar Liberator" has had an enduring impact on the field: *Alexander the II and the Modernization of Russia* (New York: Collier, 1958).

42. In the Crimean War, as Korostelina has argued for the Second World War, the demonization of Tatars served to "invigorate notions of outgroup vices and ingroup virtues": Karina

V. Korostelina, "Deportation from Crimea," in *Why They Die: Civilian Devastation in Violent Conflict*, ed. Daniel Rothbart and Karina V. Korostelina (Ann Arbor: University of Michigan Press, 2011), 44–57.

43. Robert Crews, "Empire and the Confessional State: Islam and Religious Politics in Nineteenth Century Russia," *American Historical Review* 108.1 (2003): 50–83; and Alan W. Fisher, "Enlightened Despotism and Islam under Catherine II," *SR* 27.4 (1968): 542–53.

44. Orthodox Christian nationalism also permeated Russian portrayals of the Napoleonic War. See Alexander M. Martin, *Romantics, Reformers, Reactionaries: Russian Conservative Thought and Politics in the Reign of Alexander I* (DeKalb: Northern Illinois University Press, 1997), 123–42.

45. I do not offer a study of language in this book as I am well persuaded by the arguments about the importance of language by scholars who have preceded me. Language and identity labels matter, particularly in times of war. Although officials during the Crimean War pulled upon the most negative strains of Orientalist discourse, it might be more useful to broaden the discussion to consider the use of language in exercises of state violence. Thus, the dovetailing of Orientalist discourse with enemy labels becomes a potent vehicle of violence. See the excellent treatment of dangerous elements of Bolshevik rhetoric in the chapter "Languages of Power" in *Experiencing Russia's Civil War: Politics, Society and Revolutionary Culture in Saratov*, ed. Donald Raleigh (Princeton, NJ: Princeton University Press, 2002), 43–72; see also Lars Lih, *Bread and Authority in Russia, 1914–1921* (Berkeley: University of California Press, 1990), 4–5; and Korostelina, "Deportation from Crimea" (cited in note 42). For the debate on Orientalism in the field of Russian history, see Adeeb Khalid, "Russian History and the Debate over Orientalism," *Kritika* 1.4 (2000): 691–99; and Nathaniel Knight's response in the same issue, 701–15.

46. For good bibliographic essays on spatial history in Russia, see Nick Baron, "New Spatial Histories of Twentieth Century Russia and the Soviet Union: Surveying the Landscape," *JGO* 55.3 (2007): 374–401; and Mark Bassin, Christopher Ely, and Melissa K. Stockdale, *Space, Place and Power in Modern Russia: Essays in the New Spatial History* (DeKalb: Northern Illinois University Press, 2010), 3–19.

47. Many scholars have explored Crimea's multiple uses as a national symbol. See, for example, Katya Hokanson, "Pushkin's Captive Crimea: Imperialism in the Fountain of Bakhchisarai," in *Russian Subjects: Empire, Nation, and the Culture of the Golden Age*, ed. Monika Greenleaf and Stephen Moeller-Sally (Evanston, IL: Northwestern University Press, 1998), 123–50; Kerstin S. Jobst, "The Crimea as a Russian Mythical Landscape (18th–20th Century)," in *Mythical Landscapes Then and Now: The Mythification of Landscapes in Search for National Identity*, ed. Judith Peltz and Ruth Büttner (Yerevan: Yerevan State University, 2006), 78–91; Andreas Schönle, "Garden of the Empire: Catherine's Appropriation of the Crimea," *SR* 60 (2001): 1–23; and Sarah Dickinson, "Russia's First 'Orient': Characterizing the Crimea in 1787," *Kritika* 3.1 (2002): 9–10.

48. See, for example, Metropolitan Makarii (Bulgakov), *Istoriia russkoi tserkvi*, vol. 1, *Istoriia khristianstva v Rossii do ravnoapostol'nogo kniazia Vladimira kak vvedenie v istoriiu russkoi tserkvi* (Moscow: Izdatel'stvo Spaso-Preobrazhenskogo Valaamskogo monastyria 1994), 226.

Chapter 1

1. Dolgorukov to Gorchakov, 12 Feb. 1853 (no. 78), Rossiiskii gosudarstvennyi voenno-istoricheskii archiv (RGVIA), f. 846, op. 16, d. 5392 (O naznachenii voisk 5-go pekhotnogo korpusa v sostav Odesskogo i Sevastopol'skogo desantnykh i sukhoputnogo peredovogo otriadov na Moldavskoi granitse, i o dvizheniiakh ikh na sbornye punkty), ll. 6–8; David M. Goldfrank, *The Origins of the Crimean War* (New York: Longman, 1994), 115–30.

2. Dolgorukov to Gorchakov, 11 Feb. 1853 (no. 75), RGVIA, f. 846, op. 16, d. 5392, ll. 3–4.

3. Dolgorukov to Gorchakov, 12 Feb. 1853 (no. 15), RGVIA, f. 846, op. 16, d. 5392, ll. 10, 10 ob.

4. Nicholas I, "Declaration of War," in "Sermons of the Crimean War," in *Orthodox Christianity in Imperial Russia: A Sourcebook on Lived Religion,* trans. Mara Kozelsky, ed. Heather Coleman (Bloomington: Indiana University Press, 2014), 74–75.

5. Quoted in Nicholas V. Riasanovsky, *Nicholas I and Official Nationality in Russia, 1825–1855* (Berkeley: California University Press, 1959), 265.

6. Radu Florescu, *The Struggle against Russia in the Romanian Principalities* (Iasi: The Center for Romanian Studies, 1997), 74; Candan Badem, *The Ottoman Crimean War* (1853–1856) (London: Brill, 2010), 100; David Goldfrank, "Policy Traditions and the Menshikov Mission of 1853," and V. N. Vinogradov, "The Personal Responsibility of Emperor Nicholas I for the Coming of the Crimean War: An Episode in the Diplomatic Struggle in the Eastern Question," in *Imperial Russian Foreign Policy,* ed. Hugh Ragsdale (Cambridge: Cambridge University Press, 1993), 119–58 and 159–70; John Shelton Curtiss, *Russia's Crimean War* (Durham, NC: Duke University Press, 1979), 12–34. Excellent bibliographies of diplomatic aspects of the war can be found in both Goldfrank, *The Origins of the Crimean War* (cited in note 1), as well as Winfried Baumgart, *The Crimean War: 1853–1856* (London: Bloomsbury Academic Press, 1999).

7. For a review of scholarly literature examining religious and other causes of conflict between the Russian and Ottoman Empires, see *Russian Ottoman Borderlands,* ed. Lucien Frary and Mara Kozelsky (Madison: University of Wisconsin Press, 2014), 3–34.

8. PSZRI, 2nd ser., vol. 28, no. 27707 (19 Nov. 1853): 561; PSZRI, 2nd ser., vol. 31, no. 30822 (7 Aug. 1856): 661.

9. His official title was *Komandir Otdel'nago Korpusa.* According to the Military Regulation, *Komandir Otdel'nago Korpusa* controlled multiple forces (i.e., army and navy) and possessed the authority of a commander-in-chief (*Glavnokomandiushchii*) within their territories. PSZRI, 2nd ser., vol. 21, no. 20670 clause 1072–1078 (5 Dec. 1846): 586–87.

10. PSZRI, 2nd ser., vol. 21, no. 20670 clause 20 (5 Dec. 1846): 495.

11. PSZRI, 2nd ser., vol. 29, no. 27932 (16 Feb. 1854): 183.

12. Gosudarstvennyi Arkhiv Odesskoi Oblasti (GAOO), f. 1, op. 172, d. 69 (Ob ob"iavlenii voennogo polozheniia Gubernii: Khersonskoi, Tavricheskoi i Bessarabskoi oblasti), ll. 1–12; PSZRI, 2nd ser., vol. 28, no. 27707 (19 Nov. 1853): 561.

13. M. Usov, "Chto takoe voennoe polozhenie v gubernii?" *SP* 46 (2 Mar. 1854): 193.

14. For Kagan's discussion of military reforms under Nicholas I, see "Russia's Small Wars, 1805–1861," in *The Military History of Tsarist Russia,* ed. Kagan and Robin Higham (New York: Palgrave McMillan, 2002), 123–37; the longer study, *The Military Reforms of Nicholas I: The Origins of the Modern Russian Army* (New York: St. Martin's Press, 1999); and L. G. Beskrovnyi, *The Russian Army and Fleet in the Nineteenth Century: Handbook*

of Armaments, Personnel and Policy, ed. and trans. Gordon E. Smith (Gulf Breeze, FL: Academic International Press, 1996), 133–144.

15. L. G. Beskrovnyi, *Russkoe voennoe iskustvo XIXv* (Moscow: izd. Nauka, 1974), 233–35.

16. Women also traveled with the British Army. See Christine Kelly, ed. *Mrs. Duberly's War: Journal and Letters from the Crimea, 1854–1856* (Oxford: Oxford University Press, 2007), xi–xlvii.

17. A. M. Zaionchkovskii, *Vostochnaia Voina, 1853–1856*, 2 vols. (St. Petersburg: Ekspeditsiia izgotovleniia gosudarstvennykh bumag, 1908–1913), 1: 784–90.

18. RGVIA, f. 846, op. 16, d. 5536 (O morskoi provizii, zagotovliaemoi dlia voisk Chernomorskoi beregovoi linii), ll. 1–9.

19. Zaionchkovskii, *Vostochnaia Voina*, 1: 784–90.

20. Dominic Lieven, *Russia against Napoleon: The True Story of the Campaigns of War and Peace* (New York: Penguin Books, 2009), 225–26.

21. Dolgorukov to Gorchakov, 11 Feb. 1853 (no. 74), RGVIA, f. 846, op. 16, d. 5392, ll. 1–2.

22. Lieven, *Russia against Napoleon*, 215–21.

23. Also translated as *Naval Miscellaney* and *Naval Collection*.

24. E. D. Vyzhimov, "*Tambovskie gubernskie vedomosti* kak istochnik izucheniia patrioticheskoi deiatel'nosti zhitelei gubernii v period Krymskoi voiny 1853–1856 gg." *Vestnik Tomskogo gosudarstvennogo universiteta*, 2.46 (2007): 129–31. Charles Ruud, *Fighting Words: Imperial Censorship and the Russian Press, 1804–1906* (Toronto: University of Toronto Press, 1982; reprint 2009), 65, 94. Subscription to the journal *Severnaia Pchela* doubled with an additional 5,000 subscriptions in 1855.

25. For details of this battle, see Badem, *The Ottoman Crimean War* (cited in note 6), 112–23.

26. *SP*, no. 22 (28 Jan. 1854): 85.

27. The faculty and staff of Kharkov University took up donations for orphans and widows and raised 750 rubles; similarly, students of the Moscow Practical Academy of Commerce collected 500 rubles from their peers, and pupils of the Imperial Aleksandrovskii lyceum gave 1,400 rubles for the benefit of soldiers. Their donation was forwarded to Gorchakov for distribution. *SP*, no. 37 (15 Feb., 1854); *SP*, no. 33 (10 Feb. 1854): 130; *SP*, no. 46 (26 Feb. 1854): 181.

28. *SP*, no. 37 (15 Feb. 1854).

29. *SP*, no. 25 (1 Feb. 1854): 97.

30. For a good review of the literature, see Jude C. Richter, "Philanthropy and Welfare in Russia, 1914–18," in *Russia's Home Front in War and Revolution, 1914–22*, ed. Adele Lindenmeyr, Christopher Read, and Peter Waldron (Bloomington: Slavica Publishers, 2016), 11–29.

31. Janet M. Hartley, *Russia 1762–1825: Military Power, the State, and the People* (Westport, CT: Praeger, 2008), 3–4; 69–83.

32. Lieven, *Russia against Napoleon* (cited in note 20), 227–29.

33. *SP*, no. 57 (11 Mar. 1854): 226.

34. *SP*, no. 21 (27 Jan. 1854): 82.

35. *SP*, no. 21 (Wed. 27 Jan. 1854): 82.

36. *SP*, no. 21 (Wed. 27 Jan. 1854): 82. This vignette was also published in *Russkii Invalid*.

37. Russian periodicals are full of such stories. See, for example, *SP*, no. 15 (20 Jan. 1854): 57; *SP*, no. 46 (Fri. 26 Feb. 1854): 181.

38. A. I. Markevich, *Tavricheskaia guberniia vo vremia Krymskoi Voiny po arkhivnym materialam* (1905; repr., Simferopol: Tavrida, 1994), 10–12.

39. "Kiselev, Pavel Dmitrievich," *RBS* 8 (St. Petersburg: tip. Glavnogo upravleniia udelov, 1897): 702–17. Bruce Lincoln, "Count P. D. Kiselev: A Reformer in Imperial Russia," *Australian Journal of Politics and History* 16.2 (1970): 177–86; Druzhinin, *Gosudarstvennyie Krest'iane i reforma P. D. Kiseleva.*

40. John R. Staples, *Cross Cultural Encounters on the Ukrainian Steppe: Settling the Molochna Basin* (Toronto: University of Toronto Press, 2003), 165–72.

41. von Bradke to Pestel, 4 Mar. 1854, GAARK, f. 26, op. 1, d. 19518 (O pozhertvovanii Gosudarstvennymi Krest'ianami Severnykh uezdov 20,000 chetv. khleba dlia deistvuiushchikh voisk), l. 11.

42. von Bradke to Pestel, 12 Feb. 1854, GAARK, f. 26, op. 1, d. 19518, ll. 5–6.

43. Ibid., 13.

44. The same was true for the Napoleonic Wars. See Janet M. Hartley, "Partiotism in the Provinces," in *Russia and the Napoleonic Wars*, eds. Janet M. Hartley, Paul Keenan, and Dominic Lieven (New York: Palgrave McMillan, 2015), 156.

45. F. K. Zatler, *Zapiski o prodovol'stvii voisk v voennoie vremia*, 3 vols. (St. Petersburg: tip. Torgovogo doma S. Strugovshikova, 1860), 2: 188–200.

46. Simferopol Provision Committee, to Simferopol Police, 5 April 1854, GAARK, f. 197, op. 1, d. 132 (Simferopol'skaia Gorodskaia Politsiia), ll. 77, 107 ob.

47. von Bradke to Pestel, 4 Mar. 1854, GAARK, f. 26, op. 1, d. 19518, l. 13.

48. Menshikov to Pestel, 25 Apr. 1854, GAARK, f. 26, op. 1, d. 19518, l. 28.

49. Simferopol Provision Committee to A. S. Menshikov, 26 Apr. 1854, GAARK, f. 26, op. 1, d. 19518, l. 32.

50. Simferopol Provision Committee, 24 May 1854, RGVIA, f. 846, op. 16, d. 5536, ll. 15–17; and Simferopol Provision Committee to A. S. Menshikov, 26 Apr. 1854, GAARK, f. 26, op. 1, d. 19518, ll. 33–34.

51. von Bradke to Pestel, 17 May 1854, GAARK, f. 26, op. 1, d. 19518, l. 38. For a concise treatment of Russia's enlightened bureaucrats, see W. Bruce Lincoln, "The Genesis of an 'Enlightened' Bureaucracy in Russia, 1825–1856," *JGO* (Sept. 1972): 321–30; as well as his longer study, *In the Vanguard of Reform: Russia's Enlightened Bureaucrats, 1825–1861* (DeKalb: Northern Illinois University Press, 1982).

52. Simferopol Provision Committee to Pestel, 28 May 1854, GAARK, f. 26, op. 1, d. 19518, l. 58.

53. For an analysis of "sackmen" in early twentieth-century conflicts, see Lars Lih, *Bread and Authority in Russia, 1914–1921* (Berkeley: University of California Press, 1990), 76–77.

54. John Shelton Curtiss, *The Russian Army under Nicholas I, 1825–1855* (Durham, NC: Duke University Press, 1965), 97–100.

55. Kagan, "Russia's Small Wars, 1805–1861" (cited in note 14), 130.

56. Keep, *Soldiers of the Tsar*, 336–38.

57. Dolgorukov to Menshikov, 9 Feb. 1854, RGVIA, f. 846, op. 16, d. 5536, ll. 1–2.

58. RGVIA, f. 846, op. 16, d. 5536, l. 18.

59. Menshikov to Dolgorukov, 17 June 1854, RGVIA f. 846, op. 16, d. 5579 (O summakh postupivshikh v Simferopol'skuiu proviantskuiu kommissiiu i tamoshnee uezdnoe kaznacheistvo iz raznykh mest), ll. 19, 19 ob.

60. Pestel to Menshikov, 12 Mar. 1854, RGVIA f. 846, op. 16, d. 5579, ll. 4, 4 ob.

61. Menshikov to Pestel, 25 Feb. 1854, RGVIA f. 846, op. 16, d. 5579, l. 1.
62. Menshikov, quoted in M. I. Bogdanovich, *Vostochnaia Voina, 1853–1856*, 4 vols. (St. Petersburg: tip. F. Sushchinko, 1876), 2: 262.
63. RGVIA, f. 846, op. 16, d. 5611, ll. 1–22.
64. Excerpt, Ministry of War, RGVIA, f. 846, op. 16, d. 5786, ch. 1 (Upravlenie General-Kvartirmeistera Iuzhnoi armii i voisk v Krymu nakhodiashchikhsia, o rassledovanii prichin, pokoim nepriiatel'skaia flotiliia mogla bez zatrudneniia proiti cherez Kerchenskii proliv), ll. 11–27 ob.
65. Paskevich, Instructions, 17/25 Feb. 1854, RGVIA, f. 846, op. 16, d. 5543, ll. 322, "Mneniia, rasporiazheniia i predpisaniia general-fel'dmarshala kniazia Paskevicha otnositel'no raspolozheniia i dvizehniia voisk, obshchego polozheniia politicheskikh i voennykh del, a takzhe otvety i doneseniia emu kniazia Gorchakova," ll. 1, 1 ob.
66. Predpisaniye general-fel'dmarshala 17/25 Feb. 1854, RGVIA, f. 846, op. 16, d. 5543, l. 5.
67. A. S. Khomiakov, *Stikhotvoreniia i dramy* (Leningrad: Sov. pisatel', 1969), 124–43. For interesting insight into the church's interpretation of the Eastern Question, see Filaret, Metropolitan of Moscow, *Sobraniia mnenii i otzyvov Filareta mitropolita moskovskogo i kolomenskogo po delam pravoslavnoi tserkvi na vostoke* (St. Petersburg: Synodal'naia tip., 1886); Nicholas Riasanovsky, *Russia and the West and the Teachings of the Slavophils* (Cambridge, MA: Harvard University Press, 1952), 180–82; and Peter J. S. Duncan, *Russian Messianism: Third Rome, Revolution, Communism and After* (New York: Routledge, 2000), 28–32.
68. Pogodin quoted in Curtis Hunter Porter, *Mikhail Petrovich Pogodin and the Development of Russian Nationalism, 1800–1856* (PhD diss., Vanderbilt University, 1973), 308–65.
69. F. N. Glinka, "Ura!" *SP* no. 3 (5 Jan. 1854): 7–8.
70. "Glinka, F. N.," *Russkii biograficheskii slovar'* (henceforth *RBS*), vol. 5 (Moscow: G. Lissner i D. Sobko, 1916), 297–315. N. Arbuzov was another Russian patriot whose poetry depicted the war in religious terms and who was regularly published in *SP*. See, for example, "Vragam Rossii," *SP*, no. 25 (1 Feb. 1854): 97; and "Ded ko vnukhu," *SP*, no. 32 (9 Feb. 1854): 127–28.
71. See, for example, Theophilus Prousis, "Russian PhilorthodoxRrelief during the Greek War of Independence." *Modern Greek Studies Yearbook* 1 (1985): 31–60; and Prousis, *Russian Society and the Greek Revolution* (DeKalb: Northern Illinois University Press, 1994); and L. V. Mel'nikova, *Russkaia Pravoslavnaia Tserkov' i Krymskaia Voina* (Moscow: Kuchkovo pole, 2012).
72. "Metropolitan Filaret (Drozdov), 20 Oct 1853," in *Zhizn' i trudy M. P. Pogodina*, ed. N. P. Barsukov, vol. 3 (St. Petersburg: M. M. Stasiulk, 1899), 9.
73. See Archbishop Innokentii (Borisov), "Sermons of the Crimean War: Speech Read upon the Announcement of War with the Ottoman Empire," in *Orthodox Christianity in Imperial Russia: A Sourcebook on Lived Religion*, trans. Mara Kozelsky, ed. Heather Coleman (Bloomington: Indiana University Press, 2014), 75–76.
74. Stephen M. Norris, *A War of Images: Russian Popular Prints, Wartime Culture, and National Identity, 1812–1945* (DeKalb: Northern Illinois University Press).
75. Karl Marx, "The Decay of Religious Authority," *New York Tribune*, 24 Oct. 1855, 482–88, in *The Eastern Question: A Reprint of Letters Written 1853–1856 Dealing with the Events of the Crimean War*, ed. Eleanor Marx Aveling and Edward Aveling (London: Swan Sonnenschen & Co., 1897), 483.

76. Ian Almond offers an intriguing update on Marx's interpretation in *Two Faiths, One Banner: When Muslims Marched with Christians across Europe's Battlegrounds* (Cambridge, MA: Harvard University Press, 2009).

77. Marx, "The Decay of Religious Authority," 486. Marx thus established a framework of interpretation for the Crimean War that persisted through the end of the twentieth century.

78. Violent upheavals of the early twenty-first century has made all too apparent that the secular era Marx anticipated has not in fact, materialized. Now scholars highlight the manner in which religion continues to underpin political choices and international violence. See Regina Schwartz, *The Curse of Cain: The Violent Legacy of Monotheism* (Chicago: University of Chicago Press, 1997); Mark Juergensmeyer, *Terror in the Mind of God: The Global Rise of Religious Violence* (Berkeley: University of California Press, 2000); J. Harold Ellens, ed., *The Destructive Power of Religion: Violence in Judaism, Christianity and Islam*, 4 vols. (Westport, CT: Praeger, 2004); Charles Kimball, *When Religion Becomes Evil* (New York: Harper Collins, 2008); and Charles Selengut, *Sacred Fury: Understanding Religious Violence* (Lanham, MD: Altamira, 2003). For works that hew more closely to the Crimean War, see Mel'nikova, *Russkaia Pravoslavnaia Tserkov' i Krymskaia Voina*; Jack Fairey, *The Great Powers and Orthodox Christendom: The Crisis Over the Eastern Church in the Era of the Crimean War* (New York: Palgrave Macmillan, 2015); Mara Kozelsky, *Christianizing Crimea: Shaping Sacred Space in the Russian Empire and Beyond* (DeKalb: Northern Illinois University Press, 2010), 125–129; Lucien Frary, *Russia and the Making of Modern Greek Identity, 1821–1844* (Oxford: Oxford University Press, 2015).

79. Menshikov to Nicholas I, 29 June 1854, RGVIA, f. 846, op. 16, d. 5450 (Kopii s perepiski kniazia Menshikova s Gosudarem imperatorom po delam voennym), l. 12.

80. Olga Maiorova, "Searching for a New Language of Collective Self: The Symbolism of Russian National Belonging before and after the Crimean War," *AI* 4 (2006): 187–224.

81. David M. Goldfrank, "The Holy Sepulcher and the Origin of the Crimean War," in *The Military and Society in Russia: 1450–1917,* ed. Eric Lohr and Marshal Poe (Leiden: Brill, 2002), 491–506.

82. Riasanovsky, *Nicholas I and Official Nationality in Russia* (cited in note 5), 16.

83. Cynthia H. Whittaker, "The Ideology of Sergei Uvarov: An Interpretive Essay," *RR* 37.2 (1978): 158–76, 161; see also Whittaker, *The Origins of Modern Russian Education: An Intellectual Biography of Count Sergei Uvarov, 1786–1855* (DeKalb: Northern Illinois University Press,1984); Andrei Zorin, *Kormia Dvuglavogo Orla . . . Literatura i gosudarstvennaia ideologiia v rossii v poslednei treti XVIII-pervoi treti veka* (Moscow: novoe literaturnoe obozrenie, 2001), 337–74; Riasanovsky, 84.

84. For works addressing Russia's religious policy, see Daniel R. Brower and Edward J. Lazzerini, *Russia's Orient: Imperial Borderlands and Peoples, 1700–1917* (Bloomington: Indiana University Press, 1997); Robert Geraci, *Window on the East: National and Imperial Identities in Late Tsarist Russia* (Ithaca, NY: Cornell University Press, 2001); Geraci and Michael Khodarkovsky, *Of Religion and Empire: Missions, Conversion, and Tolerance in Tsarist Russia* (Ithaca, NY: Cornell University Press, 2002); Paul W. Werth, *At the Margins of Orthodoxy: Mission, Governance and Confessional Politics in Russia's Volga-Kama Region, 1827–1905* (Ithaca, NY: Cornell University Press, 2002); Werth, *The Tsar's Foreign Faiths: Toleration and the Fate of Religious Freedom in Imperial Russia* (Oxford: Oxford University Press, 2014); Robert Crews, *For Prophet and Tsar: Islam and Empire in Russia and*

Central Asia (Harvard University Press, 2006); and Charles Steinwedel, *Threads of Empire Loyalty and Tsarist Authority in Bashkiria, 1552–1917* (Bloomington: Indiana University Press, 2016).

85. For the political consequences of Orientalism in the Caucasus, see Austin Jersild, *Orientalism and Empire: North Caucasus Mountain Peoples and the Georgian Frontier* (Montreal: McGill-Queen's University Press, 2002).

86. Fisher, "Enlightened Despotism and Islam under Catherine II," *SR* 27.4 (1968): 542–53.

87. This is one of the historical legacies reflected in the present, as the Russian state follows a similar state organization of religion. Following the annexation of 2014, Russia once again assimilated Crimean Tatars into the Russian Muslim Spiritual Society, while ties with Anatolian Islam have been officially cut.

88. Fisher, "Enlightened Despotism and Islam under Catherine II," 547.

89. Hakan Kırımlı, "O Krymskotatarskikh voiskakh v sostave Osmanskoi armii v period Krymskoi voiny," *GK* Oct. 31, 2003, 7; for Tatar's syncretic religious practices, see Kozelsky, *Christianizing Crimea*, 104, 108, 114–17.

90. "Vozzvanie Tavricheskogo muftiia Seid-Dzhelil'-Efendiia vsemu musul'manskomu dukhovenstvu i narodu, v Tavricheskoi gubernii obitaiushchim," in *Materialy dlia istorii krymskoi voiny i oborony Sevastopolia*, ed. N. F. Dubrovin, 5 vols. (St. Petersburg, 1871–1874), 1: 251.

91. "Vozzvaniie Tavricheskogo muftiia Seid-Dzhelil'-Efendiia," 250.

92. For an important analysis of Tatars' experience following Russian annexation, see Kelly Ann O'Neill, "Between Subversion and Submission: The Integration of the Crimean Khanate into the Russian Empire, 1783–1853" (PhD diss., Harvard University, 2006).

93. RGIA, f. 651, op. 1, d. 468 (O pereselenii Tatar za granitsu), ll. 112–18.

94. E. I. Totleben, "O Vyselenii Tatar iz Kryma v 1860 godu," *RS* 78 (1893): 535.

95. For a brief summary of the literature on court practices for Muslims in the Russian empire, see Stefan B. Kirmse, "Law and Empire in Late Tsarist Russia: Muslim Tatars Go to Court," *SR* 72.4 (Winter 2013): 778–801.

96. Ramil Khaÿrutdinov, "The Tatar Ratusha of Kazan: National Self Administration in Autocratic Russia, 1781–1855," *Islam and Politics in Russia and Central Asia (Early Eighteenth to Late Twentieth Centuries)*, ed. Stephane A. Dudoignon and Komatsu Hisao (New York: Routledge, 2001), 35. Khaÿrutdinov notes that the Kazan ratusha closed in 1854 due to concerns about Russian Muslims aligning with the Ottoman Empire (p.42), although a recent dissertation suggests that the ratushi closed due to overlapping jurisdiction with other bureaucratic institutions. See Rita S. Guenther, "One Local Vote at a Time: Electoral Practices of Kazan Province, 1766–1916" (PhD diss., Georgetown University, 2011), 104.

97. Izmail Muftizade, "Ocherk voennoi sluzhby krymskikh tatar, s 1783 po 1899 god (po arkhivnym materialiam)," *ITUAK* 30.20 (1899): 1–24.

98. Muftizade, "Ocherk voennoi sluzhby krymskikh tatar," 8; "Vozzvanie Tavricheskogo muftiia Said-Dzhelil'-Efendiia," 238.

99. For a concise treatment of Russia's enlightened bureaucrats, see W. Bruce Lincoln, "The Genesis of an 'Enlightened' Bureaucracy in Russia, 1825—1856," *JGO* (Sept. 1972): 321–30; as well as his longer study, *In the Vanguard of Reform: Russia's Enlightened Bureaucrats, 1825–1861* (DeKalb: Northern Illinois University Press, 1982).

100. "Bradke (von), Egor Fedorovich," *RBS* vol. 3 (St. Petersburg: tip. Glavnogo upravleniia udelov, 1897): 318–19. Unfortunately, his memoirs, published in excerpts, end with 1854. His reassignment cost the Tatars an ally.

101. Muftizade, "Ocherk voennoi sluzhby krymskikh tatar'," 9–17.

102. Gul'nara Abdullaeva, "Murzy kak soslovie v Krymskom Khanstve," *Advet* 24 (16 June 2014), http://avdet.org/node/9674, accessed May 31, 2016.

103. "Vozzvanie Tavricheskogo muftiia Seid-Dzhelil'-Efendiia," 253.

104. Norihiro Naganawa, "A Civil Society in a Confessional State? Muslim Philanthropy in the Volga-Urals Region," in *Russia's Home Front in War and Revolution, 1914–1922*: vol. 3:2, ed. Adele Lindemeyr, Christopher Read, and Peter Waldron (Bloomington, IN: Slavica Publishers, 2011), 59–78.

Chapter 2

1. RGIA, f. 1287, op. 6, d. 1174 (O posobii chinovnikam, poteriavshim imushchestvo pri vtorzhenii nepriiatelia v Evpatoriiu), ll. 1–41.

2. V. I. Charykov to N. N. Annenkov, 12 Sept. 1854, RGVIA, f. 846, op. 16, d. 5492 (Izvestiia iz Sevastopolia: ob Al'minskom srazhenii, o grabezhakh i nasiliiakh evpatoriiskikh tatar, o postydnom begstve mestnykh vlastei iz Perekopa i Simferopolia, o grabezhakh nashikh Kazakov), 52–53. Winfried Baumgart, *The Crimean War: 1853–1856* (London: Bloomsbury Academic Press, 1999), 116; E. V. Tarle, *Krymskaia voina*, 2 vols. (Moscow: Akademiia Nauk SSSR, 1944), 2: 132.

3. Tarle, *Krymskaia voina*, 2: 132.

4. Anon., "Balaklava," *NK 1846* (Odessa, 1845): 338–42. See also O. A. Gabrielian et al., *Krymskie Repatrianty: Deportatsiia, Vozvrashchenie, i Obustroistvo* (Simferopol: Amena, 1998).

5. GAARK, f. 26, op. 1, d. 14800 (O dostavlenii Tavricheskoi Kazennoi Palaty svedeniia o narodonaselenii g. Balaklava), ll. 1–2.

6. RGVIA, f. 846, op. 16, d. 5536, ll. 15–17.

7. Somerset J. Gough Calthorpe and George Cadogan (illustrator), *Cadogan's Crimea* (New York: Atheneum, 1980; text originally published as Somerset J. Gough Calthorpe, *Letters from Headquarters by a Staff Officer*, 1856), 59.

8. The literature on the siege of Sevastopol is understandably vast. For representative examples, see Leo Tolstoy, *The Sebastopol Sketches*, trans. D. McDuff (London: Penguin, 1986); Aleksandr Khrushchev, *Istoriia oborony Sevastopolia* (St. Petersburg: tip. V. V. Komarova, 1889); A. M. Zaionchkovskii, *Oborona Sevastopolia: podvigi zashchitnikov, kratkii istoricheskii ocherk* (St. Petersburg: tip. Ekspeditsii zagotovleniia gos. bumag, 1904); E. V. Tarle, *Gorod Russkoi Slavy: Sevastopol' v 1854–1855 gg.* (Moscow: Voenizdat, 1954); and, more recently, V. G. Shavshin, *Sevastopol' v istorii Krymskoi Voiny* (Sevastopol: Teleskop, 2004).

9. M. I. Bogdanovich, *Vostochnaia Voina, 1853–1856*, 4 vols. (St. Petersburg: tip. F. Sushchinko, 1876), 2: 244.

10. Despite the importance of events in Evpatoria, the occupation of the city has yet to be the focus of a monograph, and in general, Evpatoria has rarely been treated in the literature at all. One exception includes a recently published collection of primary sources with a scholarly introduction. See A. V. Sakovich and G. N. Grzhibovskaia, eds., *Evpatoria v gody Krymskoi voiny (1854–1856)* (Simferopol: AntikvA, 2007).

11. John Daly, *Russian Seapower and "the Eastern Question," 1827–1841* (Annapolis, MD: Naval Institute Press, 1991), 45.

12. Ibid., 223, fn. 84.

13. Tarle, *Krymskaia voina*, 2: 127.

14. A perspective shared by Jacob Kipp, in "The Grand Duke Konstantin Nikolaevich and the Epoch of Great Reforms, 1855–1866," (PhD diss., The Pennsylvania State University Graduate School, 1970), 56–60.

15. George B. McClellan, *The Armies of Europe: Comprising Descriptions in Detail of the Systems of England, France, Russia, Prussia, Austria, and Sardinia, Adapting Their Advantages to All Arms of the United States Service* (Philadelphia: J. B. Lippincott, 1861), 12.

16. For McClellan's tour of Europe and Crimea, see Matthew Moten, *The Delafield Commission and the American Military Profession* (College Station: Texas A&M University Press).

17. D. A. Miliutin, quoted in Tarle, *Krymskaia voina*, 2: 130.

18. Tarle, *Krymskaia voina*, 2: 131.

19. Crimean doctor N. I. Pirogov was another detractor of Menshikov's. See *Sevastopol'skiia pis'ma N. I. Pirogova 1854–1855*, ed. Iu. G. Malis (St. Petersburg: tip. M. Merkusheva, 1907).

20. Ann K. Erickson, "E. V. Tarle: The Career of a Historian under the Soviet Regime," *ASEER* 19.2 (1960): 202–16.

21. Daly, *Russian Seapower*, 191.

22. Rath, *The Crimean War in Imperial Context*, 21–22.

23. Menshikov to Tsar Nicholas, 29 June 1854, RGVIA, f. 846, op. 16, d. 5450, l. 10.

24. "Ukazatel' dostoprimechatel'neishikh predmetov vo gorodakh i mestechkakh novorossiiskogo kraia i Bessarabii," *NK 1848* (Odessa, 1847), 77.

25. Menshikov to Tsar Nicholas, 29 June 1854, RGVIA, f. 846, op. 16, d. 5450, ll. 10, 10 ob.

26. V. V. Dmitriev, "Sravnitel'naia kharakteristika razvitiia Kerch'-Enikal'skogo gradonachal'stva do i posle Krymskoi voiny," in *Vostochnaia (Krymskaia) voina, 1853–1856, Novye materialy i novoe osmyslenie*, vols. 1–2 (Simferopol: Krymskii Arkhiv, 2005), 1: 51–55.

27. Menshikov to Tsar Nicholas, 29 June 1854, RGVIA, f. 846, op. 16, d. 5450, ll. 10, 10 ob.

28. Menshikov to Tsar Nicholas, 29 June 1854, RGVIA, f. 846, op. 16, d. 5450, l. 11.

29. Ibid.

30. Menshikov to Tsar Nicholas, 29 June 1854, RGVIA, f. 846, op. 16, d. 5450, l. 12.

31. William C. Fuller, *Strategy and Power in Russia, 1600–1914* (New York: Macmillan, 1992), 239.

32. Ibid., 254.

33. See Tarle on Paskevich: E. V. Tarle, *Krymskaia voina*, 2 vols. (Moscow: Akademiia Nauk SSSR, 1944), 1: 278–309.

34. G. A. Babenko and V. P. Diulichev, *Tavricheskaia Guberniia: Istoriia v ocherkakh* (Simferopol: Tavriia, 2009), 189.

35. O. Iu. Zakharova, *Svetleishii Kniaz' M. S. Vorontsov* (Simferopol: Biznes-Inform, 2008), 234.

36. Babenko and Diulichev, *Tavricheskaia Guberniia*, 161.

37. Tarle, *Krymskaia voina*, 2:39.

38. Zakharova, *Svetleishii Kniaz' M. S. Vorontsov*, 213.

39. For a more detailed discussion of Crimean roadways, see Bogdanovich, *Vostochnaia Voina* (cited in note 9), 2: 246–50.

40. Robert Adolf Hodasevich (Chodasiewicz), *A Voice from within the Walls of Sebastopol: A Narrative of the Campaign in the Crimea and of the Events of the Siege* (London: John Murray, 1856), 59.

41. John Codman, *An American Transport in the Crimean War* (New York: Bonnell, Silver and Co., 1897), 47.

42. Quoted in Doroteia Atlas, *Staraia Odessa, ee druz'ia i nedrugi* (Odessa: tip.-lit. Tekhnik 1911), 13.

43. Patricia Herlihy, *Odessa: A History 1794–1914* (Cambridge, MA: Harvard Ukrainian Institute, 1986), 126.

44. Paskevich to Osten-Sacken, 24 Feb. 1854, RGVIA, f. 846, op. 16, d. 5500 (Doneseniia general-ad"iutanta barona Osten-Sackena i predpisaniia emu ot glavnokomanduiushchego armiei otnositel'no raspolozheniia, dvizheniia i deistviia voisk, sostoiashchikh pod ego nachal'stvom), ll. 28–36.

45. Gorchakov, Report, RGVIA, f. 846, op. 16, d. 5496 (O narodnom soprotivlenii v sluchae vtorzheniia nepriiatelia v predely Imperii), l. 1 ob.

46. Gorchakov to Liders, 7 Sept. 1854, RGVIA, f. 846, op. 16, d. 5498, ch. 1 (Sekretnye predpisaniia kniazia Gorchakova i otzyvy Glavnogo shtaba na imia generala Lidersa s 10 avgusta po 7 noiabria 1854 goda,), ll. 35–37.

47. Gorchakov to Liders, 16 Sept. 1854, RGVIA, RGVIA, f. 846, op. 16, d. 5498, ch. 1, ll. 43–44.

48. John A. Shepherd, *The Crimean Doctors: A History of the British Medical Service during the Crimean War* (Liverpool: Liverpool University Press, 1991), 64; Codman, *An American Transport in the Crimean War*, 19.

49. Shepherd, *The Crimean Doctors*, 83; Robert B. Edgerton, *Death or Glory: The Legacy of the Crimean War* (Boulder, CO: Westview Press, 1999), 72–74; Iu. A. Naumova, *Ranenie, Bolezn' i Smert': Russkaia Meditsinskaia sluzhba v Krymskuiu voinu, 1853–56 gg.* (Moscow: Modest Kolerov, 2010), 124–26.

50. Marx, *The Eastern Question: A Reprint of Letters Written 1853–1856 Dealing with the Events of the Crimean War*, ed. Eleanor Marx Aveling and Edward Aveling (London: Swan Sonnenschen & Co., 1897), 478; Geoffrey Gill, Sean Burrell, and Jody Brown, "Fear and Frustration—The Liverpool Cholera Riots of 1832," *The Lancet* 358 (2001): 233–37; Roderick E. McGrew, *Russia and the Cholera, 1823–1832* (Madison: University of Wisconsin Press, 1965).

51. Gorchakov to Osten-Sacken, 6 July 1854, RGVIA, f. 846, op. 16, d. 5500, ll. 66–69; Codman, *An American Transport in the Crimean War*, 24.

52. Menshikov to Tsar Nicholas, 20 July 1854, RGVIA, f. 846, op. 16, d. 5450, l. 44.

53. Tsar Nicholas to Menshikov, 1 Aug. 1854, RGVIA, f. 846, op. 16, d. 5450, l. 45.

54. Menshikov to Tsar Nicholas, 26 Aug. 1854, RGVIA, f. 846, op. 16, d. 5450, ll. 48, 48 ob.

55. For a vivid portrayal of the cholera and fires in Varna, see Orlando Figes, *The Crimean War: A History* (New York: Metropolitan Books, 2011), 191–92.

56. Tarle, *Krymskaia voina*, 2: 8–35.

57. "M. V. Iuzefovich to M. P. Pogodin, 22 May 1854," in *Zhizn' i Trudy M. P. Pogodina*, 13:53–54.

58. RGIA, f. 797, op. 24, d. 174 (Pis'ma o voine v Odesse), ll. 1–11.

59. César Lecat baron de Bazancourt, *The Crimean Expedition to the Capture of Sevastopol: Chronicles of the War in the East, from Its Commencement to the Signing of the*

Treaty of Peace, trans. Robert Howe Gould, 2 vols (London: Sampson Low, Son & Co, 1856), 1: 8.

60. V. S. Rakov, *Moi vospominaniia o Evpatorii v epokhu Krymskoi voiny, 1853–1856* (Evpatoria: tip. M. L. Murovanskago, 1904), 20.

61. RGIA f. 1287, op. 6, d. 1184 (O raskhodakh na unichtozhenie zapasov khleba v Evpatorii, pri vtorzhenii v onuiu nepriiatelia), ll. 6–7.

62. Markevich, *Tavricheskaia guberniia vo vremia Krymskoi Voiny*, 7–8.

63. RGIA f. 1287, op. 6, d. 1184, ll. 6–7.

64. Predpisaniia Dneprovskomu Ugolovnomu sudu o poriadke opredeleniia i uvol'neniia chinovnikov, 27 April 1854, Rossiiskaia natsional'naia biblioteka (RNB), f. 1000, op. 1, d. 1921 (Predpisaniia (2) Dneprovskomu Ugolovnomu sudu o poriadke opredeleniia i uvolneniia chinovnikov i o zablagovremennoi perevozke v bezopasnoe mesto sudebnykh del v sluchae voennykh deistvii), l. 2.

65. PSZRI, 2nd ser., no. 20670 clause 15–20 (5 Dec. 1846): 494–95.

66. For a study of the military's approach to civilians as instruments of warfare, see Peter Holquist, "Forms of Violence during the Russian Occupation of Ottoman Territory and Northern Persia: Urimia and Astrabad, Oct. 1914–Dec. 1917), in Eric D. Weitz and Omer Bartov, *The Shatterzone of Empires: Coexistence and Violence in the German, Habsburg, Russian and Ottoman Borderlands* (Bloomington: Indiana University Press, 2003), 344–61.

67. Hartley, *Russia, 1762–1825*, 134–39.

68. Rakov, *Moi vospominaniia*, 20.

69. Pestel to Menshikov, GAARK, f. 26, op. 1, d. 20004 (O pereselenii Tatar iz Kryma vnutri Rossii), l. 2.

70. Orlando Figes, *The Crimean War: A History* (New York: Metropolitan Books, 2011), 159, 194–5. Alexander Kinglake, *The Invasion of Crimea*, 9 vols. (London and Edinburgh: W. Blackwood, 1863–1887), 2:241.

71. Bazancourt, *The Crimean Expedition*, 1: 192.

72. The French population in Odessa dated to Catherine the Great's amnesty and land grant program aimed at aristocrats fleeing the guillotine during the French Revolution.

73. Karl Marx, "The Attack on Sevastopol," in *The Eastern Question: A Reprint of Letters Written 1853–1856 Dealing with the Events of the Crimean War*, ed. Eleanor Marx Aveling and Edward Aveling (London: Swan Sonnenschein & Co., 1897), 478.

74. Tarle, *Krymskaia Voina*, 1:29–35.

75. Timothy Gowing, *A Soldier's Experience, or a Voice from the Ranks Showing the Cost of War in Blood and Treasure* (Norwich: W. H. Stevens, 1884), 38. Christine Kelly, *Mrs. Duberly's War: Journal and Letters from the Crimea, 1854–1856* (Oxford: Oxford University Press, 2007), 54–60. For a thought-provoking treatment of competing sounds of the Crimean War, see: Gavin Williams (ed.), *Hearing the Crimean War: Wartime Sound and the Unmaking of Sense* (Oxford: Oxford University Press, 2019).

76. Calthorpe, *Cadogan's Crimea*, 20–23.

77. Menshikov to Tsar Nicholas, 1 Sept. 1854, RGVIA, f. 846, op. 16, d. 5450, l. 49.

78. Nekotorye obstoiatel'stva zhizni Evpatoriiskikh Khristian vo vremia i posle zaniatiia goroda Evpatorii Angliiskimi, Frantsuzskimi i Turetskimi Voiskami, RNB, f. 313, op. 1, d. 44 (lichnyi arkhivnyi fond Arkhiepiskopa Innokentiia), ll. 727–40.

79. Rakov, *Moi vospominaniia*, 22–23.

80. N. Mikhno, "Iz Zapisok Chinovnika o Krymskoi Voine," in Dubrovin, ed., *Materialy dlia istorii krymskoi voiny i oborony Sevastopolia*, 3:8.

81. RNB, f. 313, op. 1; d. 44 (Nekotorye obstoiatel'stva zhizni Evpatoriiskikh Khristian), l. 727.

82. Rakov, *Moi vospominaniia*, 24.

83. RNB, f. 313, op. 1, d. 44, l. 729.

84. Calthorpe, *Cadogan's Crimea*, 24.

85. RNB, f. 313, op. 1, d. 44, l. 727.

86. Rakov, *Moi vospominaniia*, 24.

87. New Russia Governor General to the MVD, RGIA f. 1287, op. 6, d. 1184, ll. 6–7.

88. In contrast to Russian sources, Bazancourt counted wounded soldiers at a "few hundred." Bazancourt, *The Crimean Expedition*, 1: 196.

89. RNB, f. 313, op. 1; d. 44, l. 740.

90. Markevich, *Tavricheskaia Guberniia vo Vremia Krymskoi Voiny*, 15–17.

91. RNB, f. 313, op. 1; d. 44, ll. 740–41.

92. Markevich, *Tavricheskaia Guberniia vo Vremia Krymskoi Voiny*, 15.

93. M. S. Leonidov, "Pestel', Vladimir Ivanovich," *RBS*, vol. 13 (St. Petersburg: tip. I. N. Skhorokhodova, 1902): 591–92; Markevich, *Tavricheskaia Guberniia vo Vremia Krymskoi Voiny*, 15.

94. N. N. "Desiatoe sentiabria 1854 goda v Simferopole," in Dubrovin, ed., *Materialy dlia istorii krymskoi voiny i oborony Sevastopolia*, 3: 36–41.

95. RGIA, f. 1287, op. 6, d. 1174, ll. 1–18. For Yalta, see also RGIA, f. 1287, op. 6, d. 1071 (O posobii chinovnikam, lishivshimsia imushchestva pri zaniatii nepriatelem g. Yalta), ll. 1–19.

96. For criticism of Crimean civil servants, see chapter 4.

97. Quoted in Rath, *The Crimean War in Imperial Context, 1854–1856*, 25.

98. RNB, f. 313, op. 1, d. 44, l. 731.

99. New Russia Governor General to MVD, RGIA f. 1287, op. 6, d. 1184, ll. 6–7.

100. New Russia Governor General to MVD, RGIA f. 1287, op. 6, d. 1184, ll. 6–8.

101. RGIA, f. 1263 op. 1, d. 2481 (Otchet nachalnika Tavricheskoi gubernii za 1854), ll. 17–18.

102. Calthorpe, *Cadogan's Crimea*, 24.

103. Both the priest and Rakov describe Kostiukov's role in destroying the grain and subsequent seizure by Tatars and Allies. Rakov, *Moi vospominaniia*, 25; RNB, f. 313, op. 1, d. 44, l. 733.

104. Georgii Chaplinskii, "Vospominaniia o Sevastopol'skoi oborone," in *Sbornik Rukopisei predstavlennykh ego imperatorskomu vysochestvu gosudariu nasledniku tsesarevichu o Sevastopol'skoi oborone sevastopol'stami* (St. Petersburg: tip. A Transheliia, 1872), 67.

105. RGIA f. 1287, op. 6, d. 1184, ll. 8–9.

106. GAARK, f. op. 1, d. 19778 (Ob unichtozhennii ili vyvoze v otdalennoe ot berega moria zapasov drov v Ialtinskom i Feodosiiskom uezdakh), l. 1.

107. GAARK, f. op. 1, d. 19778, ll. 9–23.

108. See, for example, GAARK, f. 26, op. 4, d. 1527, 1855–1856 (Po predlozheniiu Novorossiiskogo i Bessarabskogo General-Gubernatora, O merakh mogushchego otkryt'sia v Novorossiiskom Krae nedostatka v khlebe i ustranenenii zatrudnenii v dvizhenii voisk).

109. Markevich, *Tavricheskaia guberniia vo vremia Krymskoi Voiny*, 14.

110. Although the Allies entered Evpatoria and took over the city 1/13 September, the French depict the invasion of Crimea as happening on the anniversary of the day Napoleon entered Russia in 1812. Bazancourt, *The Crimea Expedition*, 203.

111. A. V. Sakovich, "Evpatoria v period Krymskoi Kampanii vostochnoi voiny, 1854–1856 gg.," in *Evpatoria v gody Krymskoi voiny (1854–1856)*, ed. A. V. Sakovich and G. N. Grzhibovskaia, 11.

112. Rakov, *Moi vospominaniia*, 32. According to Rakov, these prisoners received an allowance in London large enough for them to send home money to their families.

113. Calthorope, *Cadogan's Crimea*, 27.

114. RNB, f. 313, op. 1, d. 44, l. 732.

Chapter 3

1. Gorchakov to Liders, 4 Sept. 1854, RGVIA, f. 846, op. 16, d. 5498, ch. 1, l. 31.

2. George Paget, *The Light Cavalry Brigade in the Crimea: Extracts from the Letters and Journals of the Late George Paget* (London: John Murray, 1881), 25. Paget attributed the "completeness of the victory" to the "proverbial Russian fear of losing guns . . . which were prematurely withdrawn, to save being taken" (26).

3. L. G. Beskrovnyi, *Russkoe voennoe iskusstvo XIXv* (Moscow: izd. Nauka, 1974), 254.

4. E. V. Tarle, *Krymskaia voina*, 2 vols. (Moscow: Akademiia Nauk SSSR, 1944), 2: 132–37.

5. By way of comparison, Rakov earned 250 rubles per year. RGIA, f. 1287, op. 6, d. 1174, ll. 1–18.

6. Mikhno, "Iz zapisok chinovnika o Krymskoi voine," 7, 29–33.

7. Rakov, *Moi vospominaniia*, 27; RNB, f. 313, op. 1, d. 44, l. 737.

8. Quite often bands of soldiers committed robbery. On September 3rd, for example, a convoy from Podolia reported being held up at gunpoint near Mangup, en route to Sevastopol by "the enemy"—whether English, French, or Ottoman they did not say. The enemy stole the flour the *chumaki* (Ukrainian cart drivers) were transporting, the carts, and the oxen. The men survived and kept their documents, but lost their investment and means of getting back home. GAARK, f. 26, op. 1, d. 19731 (Ob ograblennykh nepriiateliami u raznykh chumakov imushchestve), ll. 1–35.

9. RGIA, f. 1263, op. 1, d. 2481, l. 502; GAARK, f. 26, op. 1, d. 20079 (Ob ubiistve bliz derevni Urkutsa dvukh karaimov), ll 1–15.

10. Charykov to Annenkov, 13 Sept. 1854 (morning), RGVIA, f. 846, op. 16, d. 5492, ll. 62, 62 ob.

11. For a general history of the Caucasus, see Charles King, *The Ghost of Freedom: A History of the Caucasus* (Oxford: Oxford University Press, 2008). For a study of Russian policy, see Firouzeh Mostashari, *On the Religious Frontier: Tsarist Russia and Islam in the Caucasus* (London: I. B. Tauris, 2006). For the role of Cossacks in expanding the Russian empire through the Caucasus, see Thomas Barrett, *At the Edge of Empire: The Terek Cossacks and the North Caucasus Frontier, 1700–1860* (Boulder, CO: Westview Press, 1999), and several articles about Shamil and Circassians by the same author.

12. A. I. Markevich, "Pereseleniia Krymskikh Tatar v Turtsiiu v sviazi s dvizheniem naseleniia v Krymu," *Izvestiia Akademii Nauk SSSR, otd. gumanitarnykh nauk*, vol. 1 (1928), 375–405, and vol. 2 (1929), 392.

13. Candan Badem, *The Ottoman Crimean War (1853–1856)* (London: Brill, 2010), 285, 91–92.

14. "Vozzvanie Tavricheskogo muftia Seid-Dzhelil'-Efendiia vsemu musul'manskomu dukhovenstvu i narodu, v Tavricheskoi gubernii obitaiushchim," in *Materialy dlia istorii*

krymskoi voiny i oborony Sevastopolia, ed. N. F. Dubrovin, 5 vols. (St. Petersburg: Tip, Departmenta udelov, 1871–1874), 252.

15. A. D. Panesh, *Zapadnaia Cherkesiia v sisteme vzaimodeistviia rossii s turtsiei, angliei, i imamatom shamiilia v XIXv (do 1864)* (Maikop: Adygeiskii respublikanskii institut gumanitarnykh issledovanii im. T. M. Kerasheva, 2007), 182–84. Bazancourt, *The Crimean Expedition*, 1: 129.

16. Hakan Kırımlı, "O Krymskotatarskikh voiskakh v sostave Osmanskoi armii v period Krymskoi voiny," *GK* Oct. 31, 2003, 7.

17. Many of these Orthodox warrior-nationalists settled in New Russia with each Russian-Ottoman War. For a discussion of the legacy of their settlement in Crimea, see Mara Kozelsky, *Christianizing Crimea: Shaping Sacred Space in the Russian Empire and Beyond* (DeKalb: Northern Illinois University Press, 2010).

18. Kırımlı, "O Krymskotatarskikh voiskakh v sostave Osmanskoi armii v period Krymskoi voiny," 7.

19. RNB, f. 313, op. 1, d. 44, l. 738.

20. RNB, f. 313, op. 1, d. 44, ll. 737–38 ob; Markevich, *Tavricheskaia guberniia vo vremiia Krymskoi Voiny*, 15.

21. Somerset J. Gough Calthorpe and George Cadogan (illustrator), *Cadogan's Crimea* (New York: Atheneum, 1980; text originally published as Somerset J. Gough Calthorpe, *Letters from Headquarters by a Staff Officer*, 1856), 23.

22. Paget, *The Light Cavalry Brigade in the Crimea*, 81.

23. Entry 21 Sept. 1854, RGVIA, f. 846, op. 16, d. 5616 (Zhurnal Voennykh deistvii voisk v Krymu), ll. 6, 6 ob.

24. RNB, f. 313, op. 1, d. 44, l. 733 ob; entry 21 Sept., 1854, RGVIA, f. 846, op. 16, d. 5616, ll. 6, 6 ob; Mikhno, "Iz zapisok chinovnika o Krymskoi voine," 37.

25. Charykov to Annenkov, 13 Sept. 1854 2:00 a.m.; and Charykov to Annenkov, 14 Sept. 1854, RGVIA, f. 846, op. 16, d. 5492, l. 54.

26. RGVIA, f. 846, op. 16, d. 5616, ll. 14–16.

27. Markevich, *Tavricheskaia guberniia vo vremiia Krymskoi Voiny*, 15–16.

28. RGIA, f. 796, op. 138, d. 647, 1857–1861 (O sostoianii krymskikh skitov posle razoreniia nepriiatel'skogo), ll. 1–20.

29. RNB, f. 313, op. 1, d. 44, l. 726.

30. RNB, f. 313, op. 1, d. 44, l. 732.

31. Rumors stressed that Tatars turned their angst toward Russian Orthodox Churches. One memoir describes a rumor in which Tatars forced an Orthodox priest to perform a Muslim service; however, archbishop Innokentii dismissed it as nonsense. For one such story, see "Tri rasskaza Odesskogo Protoiereia A. A. Solov'eva, peredal A. I. Rubanovskii," in *Khersonskie eparkhial'nye vedomosti*, Pribavlenie, 9 (1904), 265.

32. Paget, *The Light Cavalry Brigade in the Crimea*, 30.

33. For an account of Cattley's activities for the British Intelligence division, see Stephen M. Harris, *British Military Intelligence in the Crimean War* (London: Frank Cass, 1999); John Codman, *An American Transport in the Crimean War* (New York: Bonnell, Silver and Co., 1897), 45–46.

34. RGVIA, f. 846, op. 16, d. 5492, l. 50.

35. Mikhno, "Iz zapisok chinovnika o Krymskoi voine," 9, 25.

36. Kopiia s otnosheniia Ialtinskogo uezdnogo predvoditelia dvorianstva, Chinovniku Diplomaticheskoi Kantseliarii Ego Siiatel'stva Glavnokomandovavshego Voiskami v Krymu G. Kolezhskomu Sovetniku Baronu Offenbergu ot 2 Oktiabria 1855, GAARK, f. 26, op. 4, d. 1587 (O vozvrativshikhsia iz plena Murzov Biiaralanovyikh), ll. 4–5.

37. Gorchakov to Zhukovskii, 26 April 1856, GAARK, f. 26, op. 4, 1683 (O vozvrashchenii iz plena murzi), ll. 1–3; GAARK, f. 26, op. 4, d. 1587, l. 1.

38. Peter Holquist, "Information is the Alpha and Omega of Our Work: Bolshevik Surveillance in Its Pan-European Context," *JMH* 69 (1997): 415–60; here 416. Others have also made similar points about the unreliability of denunciations. In *The Third Department*, Squire notes that up to 90 percent of volunteer denunciations to the Third Section were proven false (195), while Jeffrey Burds has emphasized peasant uses of denunciation to control change in the village: Jeffrey Burds, "A Culture of Denunciation: Peasant Labor Migration and Religious Anathematization in Rural Russia, 1860–1905," *JMH* 68 (Dec. 1996): 786–818.

39. The Tatar Prince Muhammad Bey Balatukov gave asylum to Russians seeking shelter, and he spoke out against the rebellion. He built up a substantial following among Tatars and preserved many villages from raids or destruction. See Rakov, *Moi vospominaniia*, 21; and RNB, f. 313, op. 1, d. 44, l. 736.

40. Charykov to Annenkov, 12 Sept. 1854, RGVIA, f. 846, op. 16, d. 5492, l. 54.

41. Charykov to Annenkov, 13 Sept. 1854 (morning), RGVIA, f. 846, op. 16, d. 5492, ll. 62, 62 ob.

42. Charykov to Annenkov, 13 Sept. 1854, 2:00 a.m., and Charykov to Annenkov, 14 Sept. 1854, RGVIA, f. 846, op. 16, d. 5492, ll. 61–63.

43. Archbishop Innokentii to Annenkov, 13 Sept. 1854, 5:00 a.m., RGVIA, f. 846, op. 16, d. 5492, l. 57.

44. See various reports in RGVIA, f. 846, op. 16, d. 5492, ll. 106–21.

45. Knorring II to Annenkov, 13 Sept. 1854, RGVIA, f. 846, op. 16, d. 5492, ll. 50, 50 ob.

46. Badem explores the use of *bashibozuks* in detail in *The Ottoman Crimean War* (cited in note 13), particularly pp. 52, 154–55; and 377–93. British Staff Officer Calthorpe describes Zouaves looting Crimean homes. See Calthorpe, *Cardogan in Crimea*, 26.

47. Robert H. MacNeal, *Tsar and Cossack 1855–1914* (New York: St. Martin's Press, 1987), 23–42.

48. Ibid., 49.

49. A rare survey of the Don Cossack's role in the Crimean War provides important information about campaigns Cossacks partook in during the Crimean War, but does not address the controversy surrounding the treatment of Tatars. See O. V. Didukh, *Donskie kazaki v Krymskoi voine 1853–1856 gg.* (Moscow: VINITI, 2007).

50. RGVIA, f. 846, op. 16, d. 5616, ll. 2, 2 ob.

51. Report from the Tauride Gendarme to Orlov (Chief of the Third Section), 30 Sept. 1854, RGVIA, f. 846, op. 16, d. 5492, l. 79.

52. Journal entry, 8 Oct. 1854, RGVIA, f. 846, op. 16, d. 5616, ll. 19 ob, 20.

53. Journal entry, 7 Oct. 1854, RGVIA, f. 846, op. 16, d. 5616, ll. 16 ob, 17. See also entry for 21 Sept. 1854, RGVIA, f. 846, op. 16, d. 5616, ll. 6, 6 ob.

54. GAARK, f. 26, op. 1, d. 19999 (O vysylke v voennosudnuiu kommissiiu tatar, izmenivshikh Russkomu Prestolu), ll. 93–94 ob.

55. Ibid., ll. 88–93.

56. Pestel to Sukharev, 15 Sept. 1854, GAARK, f. 26, op. 1, d. 19726 (O vospreshchenii soldatam brat' pod arest Tatar bez prichiny), ll. 1–2.
57. GAARK, f. 26, op. 1, d. 19999, l. 38.
58. Nicholas Reed Ogle, *Rear Admiral Thomas MacKenzie: Life and Times with the Black Sea and Azov Sea Command, 1783–1786.* http://stephenhicks.net/genealogy/getperson. php?personID = I1436&tree = 1.
59. Testimony, GAARK, f. 26, op. 2, d. 66 (O dozvolenii Tatarinu Seliamet Memirsh Olgu vozvratit'sia v Krym na vremia prodazhi ego imushchestva), l. 16.
60. Selim Ahmed to the New Russian governor general, Mar. 1859, GAARK, f. 26, op. 2, d. 66, l. 4.
61. GAARK, f. 26, op. 2, d. 34 (Ob arestovanii i vysylke Tatar, vyslannykh v voennoe vremia iz Kryma i samovol'no siuda vozvrativshikhsia), l. 48.
62. GAARK, f. 27, op. 1, d. 6649 (Po raportu Simferopol'skogo Zemskogo Ispravnika o besporiadkakh v derevne Uppy), ll. 5–6.
63. GAARK, f. 26, op. 1, d. 20065, 27 Nov. 1854 (Po ob'iavleniiu Shtab- rotmistra Revelioti ob ograblenii ego v derevne Kontugan donskimi kazakami), ll. 3–4.
64. Report from the Tauride Gendarme, 30 Sept. 1854, RGVIA, f. 846, op. 16, d. 5492, l. 79.
65. Ibid.
66. New Russia governor general to the Ekaterinoslav Garrison Battalion Commander, 3 Oct. 1855, GAARK, f. 27, op. 1, d. 6634 (O vodvorenii na mestozhitel'stvo tatar Meshchaninom Mehmet Ahmed Oglu s tovarishchami), ll. 3–4.
67. Sentence, Aug. 1856, GAARK, f. 27, op. 1, d. 6634, l. 55 ob.
68. GAARK, f. 197, op. 1, d. 132, ll. 36–53.
69. GAARK, f. 26, op. 1, d. 19999, ll. 35–45.
70. Pestel to the Simferopol city Police Chief, 15 Sept. 1854, GAARK, f. 197, op. 1, d. 132, l. 187–88.
71. Evpatoria District Police Chief to Pestel, 3 Oct. 1854, GAARK f. 26, op. 1, d. 20024 (O sokhranenii imushchestva ostavlennogo tatarami bezhavshimi k nepriiateliu), l. 1.
72. Official of Reserve Uhlan Division to Pestel, 18 Oct. 1854, GAARK f. 26, op. 1, d. 20024, l. 2.
73. "Postanovlenie Tavricheskogo magometanskogo dukhovnogo pravleniia ot 6-go oktiabria," in *Materialy dlia istorii krymskoi voiny i oborony Sevastopolia*, ed. N. F. Dubrovin (St. Petersburg: Tip, Departmenta udelov, 1871–1874), 4: 17–18.
74. "Proshenie deputatov nogaiskogo plemeni, ot 12-go oktiabria," in *Materialy dlia istorii krymskoi voiny i oborony Sevastopolia*, ed. Dubrovin, 4:18–19.
75. Ibid., 18–19.
76. Ibid., 20.
77. The Tauride Muslim Assembly continued to try Tatars suspected of treason through the summer of 1855. See GAARK, f. 315, op. 1, d. 948 (Zhurnal Tavricheskogo Dukhovnogo Obshchestva za Ianvar', Fevral', Mart, Aprel', Mai i Iiun' mesiatsy 1855).
78. William C. Fuller, "Civilians in Russian Military Courts, 1881–1904," *The Russian Review* 41.3 (1982): 288–305.
79. Testimony, 2 Feb. 1855, GAARK, f. 315, op. 1, d. 948, ll. 48–76.
80. One Tatar statement of loyalty to the Ottoman government survives in the Ottoman archives, for example. In this document, Tatar clergy from Evpatoria expressed willingness to die for the Ottoman Empire. Yet, the document was written in October, well

after the enemy had occupied Evpatoria and choices had therefore been conscribed. See Hakan Kırımlı, "Krymskie Tatary i Osmanskaia imperiia vo vremia Krymskoi voiny," in *The Crimean War (1853–1856): Colonial Skirmish or Rehearsal for World War? Empires, Nations and Individuals,* ed. Jerszy W. Borejsz (Warsaw: Wydawnictwo Neriton Instytut PAN, 2011), 336.

81. Kırımlı, "Krymskie Tatary i Osmanskaia imperiia vo vremia Krymskoi voiny," 337, 341.
82. RNB, f. 313, op. 1, d. 44, ll. 731–32.
83. See the report filed by Eduard Totleben to Prince V. A. Dologurkov, 15 Nov. 1860, RGIA, f. 651, op. 1, d. 468, ll. 106–20.
84. Alexander Kinglake, *The Invasion of the Crimea,* 9 vols. (London and Edinburgh: W. Blackwood, 1863–1887), 2: 191.

Chapter 4

1. L. G. Beskrovnyi, *Russkoe voennoe iskusstvo XIXv* (Moscow: izd. Nauka, 1974), 227–28.
2. Charykov to Annenkov, 12 Sept. 1854, RGVIA, f. 846, op. 16, d. 5492, l. 51.
3. E. V. Tarle, *Krymskaia Voina,* 2 vols. (Moscow: Akademiia Nauk SSSR, 1944), 2: 142–43.
4. Gorchakov to Liders, 4 Sept. 1854, RGVIA, f. 846, op. 16, d. 5498 ch. 1, l. 31.
5. Gorchakov to Liders, 7 Sept. 1854, RGVIA, f. 846, op. 16, d. RGVIA, f. 846, op. 16, d. 5498, ch. 1, l. 32.
6. Tarle, *Krymskaia Voina,* 2: 275.
7. Menshikov to Annenkov, 13 Sept. 1854, RGVIA, f. 846, op. 16, d. 5492, ll. 58–59.
8. Prikaz: Po Voiskam Otriadov: Zakudanskago, Tamanskago, Kerchenskago, Feodosiiskago, Chernomorskoi Kordonnoi linii i na pravoi i levoi storone r. Dona, 13 Oct. 1854, RGVIA, f. 846, op. 16, d. 5497 (Prikazy nakaznogo atamana Voiska Donskogo po voiskam, sostoiashchim v ego vedenii), ch. 2, ll. 1–2. The hetman's description of Gorchakov's authority differs from the official order from St. Petersburg, which designated him as *Kommander Otdel'nogo Korpus.* See 2nd ser., no. 28576 (24 Sept. 1854): 785.
9. Gorchakov to Liders, 7 Sept. 1854, RGVIA, f. 846, op. 16, d. RGVIA, f. 846, op. 16, d. 5498, ch. 1, ll. 32–34.
10. Archbishop Innokentii, "Sermons of the Crimean War: Speech Read upon the Announcement of War with the Ottoman Empire," in *Orthodox Christianity in Imperial Russia: A Sourcebook on Lived Religion,* trans. Mara Kozelsky, ed. Heather Coleman (Bloomington: Indiana University Press, 2014)," 76.
11. Bariantinskii to Menshikov, 6 Nov. 1854, RGVIA, f. 846, op. 16, d. 5425 (Perepiska o dostavlenii v Sevastopol' porokha v pervyi period osady pod nabliudeniem ad"iutanta voennago ministra), l. 6 ob.
12. Ibid., ll. 6–9.
13. Records on the uprisings in the western provinces are contained in the file: RGVIA, f. 846, op. 16, d. 5496 (O narodnom soprotivlenii v sluchae vtorzheniia nepriiatelia v predely Rossii), l.61.
14. Quoted in A. Iu. Bezugol'nyi, N. F. Kovalevskii, and V. E. Kovalev, *Istoriia voenno-okruzhnoi sistemy v Rossii* (Moscow: Tsentrpoligraf, 2012), 26.
15. RGVIA, f. 846, op. 16, d. 5428 (Ob otpravlenii porokha v Sevastopol' iz ukrepleniia Enikale i Pavlovskoi batarei), ll. 1–12.

16. E. I. Totleben, *Opisanie Oborony g. Sevastopolia,* 2 vols. (St. Petersburg: tip. I. Tiblena i komp., 1863), 1:197, 200–202.

17. Beskrovnyi, *Russkoe voennoe iskusstvo,* 253–54.

18. Robert Adolf Hodasevich (Chodasiewicz), *A Voice from Within the Walls of Sebastopol: A Narrative of the Campaign in the Crimea and of the Events of the Siege* (London: John Murray, 1856), 83.

19. Totleben, *Opisanie Oborony g. Sevastopolia,* 1:225.

20. Beskrovnyi, *Russkoe voennoe iskusstvo,* 256.

21. George B. McClellan, *The Armies of Europe: Comprising Descriptions in Detail of the Systems of England, France, Russia, Prussia, Austria, and Sardinia, Adapting Their Advantages to All Arms of the United States Service* (Philadelphia: J. B. Lippincott, 1861), 12.

22. Georgii Chaplinskii, "Vospominaniia o Sevastopol'skoi oborone," in *Sbornik Rukopisei predstavlennykh ego imperatorskomu vysochestvu gosudariu nasledniku tsesarevichu o Sevastopol'skoi oborone sevastopol'stami* (St. Petersburg: tip. A Transheliia, 1872)," 72–73.

23. César Lecat baron de Bazancourt, *The Crimean Expedition to the Capture of Sevastopol: Chronicles of the War in the East, from Its Commencement to the Signing of the Treaty of Peace,* trans. Robert Howe Gould, 2 vols (London: Sampson Low, Son & Co, 1856), 360–62.

24. RGVIA, f. 846, op. 16, d. 5616, ll. 14–16; Beskrovnyi, *Russkoe voennoe iskusstvo,* 254–8.

25. N. I. Pirogov, *Sevastopol'skiia pis'ma N. I. Pirogova 1854–1855,* ed. Iu. G. Malis (St. Petersburg: tip. M. Merkusheva, 1907), 77; For an English language discussion of the Sisters of Mercy, see John Shelton Curtiss, "Russian Sisters of Mercy in the Crimea," *SR* 25, no. 1 (Mar. 1996): 84–100; and Marina Soroka and Charles A. Ruud, *Becoming a Romanov: Grand Duchess Elena and her World* (New York: Routledge, 2016), 191–218.

26. V. G. Shavshin, *Balaklava* (Simferopol: Tavria, 1994), 11–13.

27. "Balaklava," *NK 1846* (Odessa, 1845), 338–42.

28. For examples of the Greek battalion subduing or spying on Tatars, see Kelly Ann O'Neill, "Between Subversion and Submission: The Integration of the Crimean Khanate into the Russian Empire, 1783–1853" (PhD diss., Harvard University, 2006), 59.

29. Victor Amanton, *Notices sur les diverses populations du gouvernment de la Tauride et spécialement de la Crimée; moeus & usages des Tatars de la Crimée* (Besançon: Imprimerie de J. Bonvalot, 1854), 22.

30. Rev. Thomas Milner, *The Crimea, Its Ancient and Modern History: The Khans, the Sultans, and the Czars. With Notices of Its Scenery and Population* (London: Longman, Brown, Green, and Longmans, 1855), 303–4.

31. Archbishop Innokentii, "Zapiski o vosstanovlenii drevnikh sviatykh mest po goram krymskim," *ITUAK* 5 (1888): 92.

32. Christine Kelly, *Mrs. Duberly's War: Journal and Letters from the Crimea, 1854–1856* (Oxford: Oxford University Press, 2007), 73.

33. George Paget, *The Light Cavalry Brigade in the Crimea: Extracts from the Letters and Journals of the Late George Paget* (London: John Murray, 1881), 35–47.

34. Somerset J. Gough Calthorpe and George Cadogan (illustrator), *Cadogan's Crimea* (New York: Atheneum, 1980; text originally published as Somerset J. Gough Calthorpe, *Letters from Headquarters by a Staff Officer,* 1856), 43–47.

35. Ibid., 55.

36. Shavshin, *Balaklava*, 70; Totleben, *Opisanie Oborony g. Sevastopolia*, 1:230–33.

37. V. Zelenkevich, "Napadenie na Balaklavu," in *Materialy dlia istorii krymskoi voiny i oborony sevastopolia*, ed. Dubrovin, 3:128–35.

38. Zelenkevich, "Napadenie na Balaklavu," 132.

39. Steven Johnson, *The Ghost Map: the Story of London's Most Terrifying Epidemic, and How it Changed Science, Cities and the Modern World* (New York: Riverhead Books, 2006), 69–70; 130–136.

40. Zelenkevich, "Napadenie na Balaklavu," 134.

41. Ibid.

42. Calthorpe, *Cadogan's Crimea*, 48.

43. RGIA, f. 796, op. 13, d. 37, ll. 1–3.

44. RGIA, f. 797, op. 24, d. 16, ll. 39–41 ob.

45. Ibid., ll. 88–89 ob, 92, 92 ob.

46. Shavshin, *Balaklava*, 43.

47. Entry 21 Sept. 1854, RGVIA, f. 846, op. 16, d. 5616, l. 6 ob.

48. GAARK, f. 26, op. 2, d. 52 (O vospreshchenii Pomeshchitse Mavromikhaili zakhvatyvami ostavshiesia posle ushedshikh za granitsu tatar), ll. 1–5.

49. Shavshin, *Balaklava*, 71.

50. RNB, f. 313, d. 44, l. 72. For the Battle of Balaklava, see Terry Brighton, *Hell Riders: The Truth about the Charge of the Light Brigade* (London: Viking, 2004); A. J. Barker, *Vainglorious War* (London: Weidenfeld and Nicolson, 1971), 150–74; and Tarle, *Krymskaia Voina*, 2: 154–56.

51. Orlando Figes, *The Crimean War: A History* (New York: Metropolitan Books, 2011), 53.

52. Father Nikolai to Archbishop Innokentii, 16 Oct. 1854, RNB, f. 313, d. 44, l. 72.

53. Kelly, *Mrs. Duberly's War*, 115.

54. The monk Innokentii (at Inkerman) to Archibhop Innokentii, 12 Oct. 1854, RNB, f. 313, d. 44, l. 57.

55. Tarle, *Krymskaia Voina*, 2: 204, 206. Tarle gives the following numbers: 41,800 Frenchmen; 24,500 English; and 5,000 Turks.

56. Tarle, *Krymskaia Voina*, 2:226; Beskrovnyi, *Russkoe voennoe iskusstvo*, 260.

57. Tarle, *Krymskaia Voina*, 2:209.

58. The monk Innokentii (at Inkerman) to Archibhop Innokentii, 12 Oct. 1854, RNB, f. 313, d. 44, l. 57.

59. Gorchakov to Liders, 4 Nov. 1854, RGVIA, f. 846, op. 16, d. 5498, ch. 2, l. 3.

60. Gorchakov to Liders, 6 Nov. 1854, RGVIA, f. 846, op. 16, d. 5498 ch. 2, l. 1.

61. Gorchakov to Liders, 4 Nov. 1854, RGVIA, f. 846, op. 16, d. 5498, ch. 2, l. 2.

62. A. D. Komovskii, "Pod gromom Krymskoi Voiny," *RV* (1878) 134.1: 163–97, 165–66; Tarle, *Krymskaia Voina*, 2: 287.

63. Baumgart, *The Crimean War*, 137–38.

64. Archimandrite Nikolai to Archbishop Innokentii, 24 Sept. 1854, RNB, f. 313, d. 44, l. 54.

65. Friedrich Prinzing, *Epidemics Resulting from Wars* (Oxford: Clarendon Press, 1916), 170–72.

66. Iu. A. Naumova, *Ranenie, Bolezn' i Smert': Russkaia Meditsinskaia sluzhba v Krymskuiu voinu, 1853–56 gg.* (Moscow: Modest Kolerov, 2010), 13, 47.

67. Ibid., 49.

68. Pirogov, *Sevastopol'skiia pis'ma*, 67.

69. Ibid., 75.

70. Prikaza Obshchestvennogo Prizreniia, 10 Nov. 1854, GAARK, f. 197, op. 1, d. 141 (O kholere v g. Simferopole i bor'be s nei), ll. 1–2.

71. GAARK, f. 128, op. 1, d. 1 (Proshenie dvorianina Selimisha Murzyi Dzhankicheva), ll. 8–9.

72. S. A. Sapozhnikov, "Shevchenko i Blarambergi Mavromikhaili," *Nauchnye Zapiski I.T.Sh.* (Institute of Taras Shevchenko), Tetrad' 6, http://www.it-shevchenko.ru/index.php/ytsh. html.

73. Golitsyn to Stroganov (untitled report), Feb. 1858, RGIA, f. 1287, op. 6, d. 1156 (Po Pros'bam chastnykh lits, o voznograzhdenii za poteriannoe po sluchaiu voiny imushchestva), ch. 1, ll. 190, 190 ob.

74. Umer Muzhadin to the Simferopol District Commission (founded to establish the losses produced from the war circumstances), 23 Jun. 1857, GAARK, f. 128, op. 1, d. 79 (Delo o donosennoi Bakhchisaraiiskim Meshchaninom Umerom Muzhadin Oglu v minuvshchiiu voinu poter'), ll. 1–3.

75. I. Krasil'nikov (untitled report), 12 Dec. 1856, RGIA f. 20, op. 3, d. 2326, l. 50.

76. See, for example, Filipov to Lanskoi, 23 Aug. 1856, RGIA, f. 1287, op. 6, delo 1156, ch. 1, ll. 27–30.

77. GAARK, f. 197, op. 1, d. 147 (Simferopol'skaia Gorodskaia Politsiia), ll. 1–22.

78. Tolstoy, *Sevastopol Sketches*, 79.

Chapter 5

1. Somerset J. Gough Calthorpe and George Cadogan (illustrator), *Cadogan's Crimea* (New York: Atheneum, 1980; text originally published as Somerset J. Gough Calthorpe, *Letters from Headquarters by a Staff Officer*, 1856), 205–206; Edgerton, *Death or Glory*, 101–102.

2. N. I. Pirogov, *Sevastopol'skiia pis'ma N. I. Pirogova 1854–1855*, ed. Iu. G. Malis (St. Petersburg: tip. M. Merkusheva, 1907), 94.

3. "Prikazanie po Evpatoriiskomu otriadu," 9 Dec. 1854, RGVIA, f. 846, op. 16, d. 5610 (Prikazy i prikazaniia Evpatoriiskogo otriada s 20 Noiabria 1854 po Dekabr' 1855 goda), l. 8.

4. Prikaz no. 3, 5 Jan. 1855. This order, a note states at the end, was to be read to all regiments and batteries, "Prikazanie po Evpatoriiskomu otriadu," RGVIA, f. 846, op. 16, d. 5610, l. 12.

5. V. F. Vunsh was confirmed as the head of the department overseeing the chancellery on 20 Feb. 1855, and Moshinskii became his immediate report. Prikaz no. 58, 20 Feb. 1855, RGVIA, f. 846, op. 16, d. 5617 (Prikazy, prikazaniia i ob'iavleniia po Iuzhnoi i Krymskoi armii za 1855–1856 gody), l. 20.

6. Books focusing on the Military Reform offer much more nuanced analysis than the cliché of "humiliating defeat," although do not perhaps give as much attention to reform generated out of Crimea during the war itself. Instead, military histories tend to tell the story of reform through the activities of D. A. Miliutin after his appointment as war minister in 1861. See, for example, Bruce Menning, *Bayonets before Bullets: The Imperial Russian Army, 1861–1914* (Bloomington: Indiana University Press, 2000); and the classic, P. A. Zaionchkovskii, *Voennye Reformy 1860–1870* (Moscow: Moscow University Press, 1952).

7. Dominic Lieven, *Russia against Napoleon: The True Story of the Campaigns of War and Peace* (New York: Penguin Books, 2009), 18.

8. F. K. Zatler, *Zapiski o prodovol'stvii voisk v voennoe vremia*, 3 vols. (St. Petersburg: tip. Torgovogo doma S. Strugovshikova, 1860),1: vii–viii.

9. Ibid., 1: 230.

10. Iu. A. Naumova, *Ranenie, Bolezn' i Smert': Russkaia Meditsinskaia sluzhba v Krymskuiu voinu, 1853–56 gg.* (Moscow: Modest Kolerov, 2010), 151–52.

11. Ibid., 130–32.

12. Simferopol Commandant to V. F. Vunsh, 1 Oct. 1854, RGVIA, f. 846 op. 16, d. 5477 (O nariade podvod ot grazhdanskogo vedomstva na vremia peredvizheniia voisk i dlia perevozki v gospitali bol'nykh i ranenykh), l. 8.

13. Naumova, *Ranenie, Bolezn' i Smert'*, 142–44.

14. Pirogov, *Sevastopol'skiia pis'ma*, 75. See also John Shelton Curtiss, "Russian Sisters of Mercy in the Crimea," *SR* 25, no. 1 (Mar. 1996): 84–100, and E. M. Bakunina, "Vospominaniia sestry miloserdiia Krestovozdvizhenskoi obshchiny, 1854–1860," *Vestnik Evropy* 190.2 (March 1898): 132–176; here, 146.

15. Pirogov, *Sevastopol'skiia pis'ma*, 79.

16. K. N. Leontiev, "Sdacha Kerchi v 55 godu (vospominaniia voennogo vracha)," in *Sobranie sochinenii K. Leontieva* (St. Petersburg: Rus. kn. t-vo, 1912), 9: 187.

17. Nikolai Ogarev, "Monologi: Chego khochu," *Stikhotvoreniia N. Ogareva* (Moskva: tip. Aleksandra Semenova, 1856), 83–84.

18. Leontiev, "Sdacha Kerchi," 9: 192.

19. Leontiev, "Pis'ma k materi iz Kryma, 1854–57," 25 Nov. 1854, in *Sobranie sochinenii K. Leontieva* (St. Petersburg: Rus. kn. t-vo "Deiatel'," 1912), 9: 155.

20. Leontiev, "Moi dela s Turgenevym i t.d." in *Sobraniie sochinenii K. Leontieva* (St. Petersburg: Rus. kn. t-vo "Deiatel'," 1912), 9: 146.

21. Leontiev, "Sdacha Kerchi," 9: 187–41.

22. Bakunina, "Vospominaniia," 190.2, 165.

23. Ibid., 511.

24. For a good treatment of Americans in Crimea during the war (including the doctors), see Arthur Thomas, "The U.S. Military Commission to the Crimean War and its influence on the U.S. Army before the American Civil War," (PhD diss., University of Kansas, 1993).

25. Naumova, *Ranenie, Bolezn' i Smert'*, 145–52.

26. Simferopol Quartering Commission, Report 31 Aug. 1855, GAARK, f. 26, op. 1, d. 20194 (O raznykh pozhertvovaniiakh v pol'zu deistvuiushchikh voisk), ch. 5, ll. 109–10 ob.

27. Naumova, *Ranenie, Bolezn' i Smert'*, 145–46.

28. M. Usov, "Chto takoe voennoe polozhenie v gubernii?" *SP*, no. 46 (2 Mar. 1854): 193.

29. Ibid., 194.

30. Pestel to Vunsh, 17 Sept. 1854, RGVIA, f. 846 op. 16, d. 5477, ll. 1–4.

31. Bakhchisarai city head Arslan bei Tashchi Oglu to the Head of Tauride Province and Cavalry, 14 Aug. 1854, GAARK, f. 26, op. 1, d. 19518, ll. 80–81.

32. A. D. Komovskii, "Pod gromom Krymskoi Voiny," *RV* part 1, vol. 134 (1878): 163–97, here 187.

33. Simferopol Provisions Committee to Petrov, Sept. 1854, GAARK, f. 197, op. 1, d. 132, ll. 190–92.

34. Ministry of War to Simferopol Provisions Committee, Sept. 1854, GAARK, f. 197, op. 1, d. 132, l. 190–192.

35. Karasubazar city head to the Authority of the Tauride Province, 18 Sept. 1854, GAARK, f. 26, op. 1, d. 19518, l. 113.

36. "Ukazatel' dostoprimechatel'neishikh predmetov vo gorodakh i mestechkakh Novorossiiskogo kraia i Bessarabii," *NK 1848* (Odessa, 1847), 68; Pirogov, *Sevastopol'skiia pis'ma*, 89.

37. Karasubazar city head to Pestel, 18 Sept. 1854, GAARK, f. 26, op. 1, d. 19518, ll. 113, 113 ob.

38. Simferopol Merchant Bolat Konzh Ali Oglu to Zhukovskii, 29 Nov. 1856, GAARK, f. 26, op. 1, d. 21447 (Po zhalobe Simferopol'skogo meshchanina Bolata Konzeh Avi Oglu za razorenie pekarni ego nizhnimi chinami Minskogo Pekhotnogo Polka), ll. 1–2.

39. Orlov (untitled report), 30 Sept. 1854, RGVIA, f. 846, op. 16, d. 5492, l. 79.

40. Prikaz no. 4, 5 Jan. 1855, 9 Dec. 1854, RGVIA, f. 846, op. 16, d. 5610, l. 12.

41. Prikaz no. 1, 26 Feb. 1855, RGVIA, f. 846, op. 16, d. 5610, l. 114.

42. Pirogov, *Sevastopol'skiia pis'ma*, 65.

43. Ibid., 79.

44. Pestel to Vunsh, RGVIA, f. 846 op. 16, d. 5477, ll. 1–2; MVD agent in Tauride to Simferopol city police chief, 16 Sept. 1854, GAARK, f. 197, op. 1, d. 132, l. 188.

45. "Pravil," GAARK, f. 26, op. 1, d. 19798 (Ob otobranii ot Tatar loshadei dlia ukomplektovaniia podvizhnykh kazennykh magazinov i formirovanii v'iuchnogo konnogo transporta), l. 16.

46. Gorchakov to the Acting Tauride Governor, 17 Mar. 1855, GAARK, f. 26, op. 1, d. 19798, l. 31.

47. Markevich devotes a rather large chapter to the amount of hay demanded by the military and the amount Crimea ultimately delivered. See Markevich, *Tavricheskaia guberniia vo vremiia Krymskoi voiny*, 148–72.

48. Zatler, *Zapiski o prodovol'stvii voisk v voennoe vremia*, 3: 191.

49. von Bradke to Pestel, 30 Oct. 1854, GAARK f. 26, op. 1, d. 20024 (O sokhranenii imushchestva ostavlennogo tatarami bezhavshimi k nepriiateliu), ll. 7–8.

50. Zatler, *Zapiski o prodovol'stvii voisk v voennoe vremia*, 3: 191.

51. Osten-Sacken, Prikaz no. 75, 6 Mar. 1855, RGVIA, f. 846, op. 16, d. 5617, ch. 1, l. 45.

52. On the dangers of Crimean roads, see Zatler, 3:194.

53. Prikaz no. 118, 20 July 1855, RGVIA, f. 846, op. 16, d. 5610, l. 146.

54. Calthorpe, *Cadogan's Crimea*, 172.

55. See, for example, Pirogov, *Sevastopol'skiia pis'ma*, 79.

56. Edgerton, *Death or Glory*, 105; Christine Kelly, ed., *Mrs. Duberly's War: Journal and Letters from the Crimea, 1854–1856* (Oxford: Oxford University Press, 2007), 109.

57. Zatler, *Zapiski o prodovol'stvii voisk v voennoe vremia*, 3:193–96.

58. Menshikov to Vunsh, 13 Dec. 1854, RGVIA, f. 846, op. 16, d. 5576 (O snabzhenii voisk Krymskoi armii prodovol'stviem i boevymi pripasami v 1854 godu), ll. 4–7.

59. Menshikov to Osten-Sacken, 8 Jan. 1855, RGIVA. f. 846. op. 16, d. 5609, ll. 1–2. Menshikov attempted to solve the problem by appointing a single receiver for the northern side of Sevastopol.

60. von Bradke to Pestel, 12 Feb. 1854, GAARK, f. 26, op. 1, d. 19518, ll. 175–76.

61. Ibid., l. 177.

62. Prikaz no. 32, 4 Mar. 1855, RGVIA, f. 846, op. 16, d. 5610, ll. 31–32.

63. RGIA, f. 1263, op. 1, d. 2481, ll. 2–3.

64. Ibid., l. 37.

65. Calthorpe, *Cadogan's Crimea*, 115.

66. RGIA, f. 1263, op. 1, d. 2481, l. 11.

67. GAARK, f. 26, op. 1, d. 20938 (O dostavlenii svedenii o pogibshem rabochem skote obyvatelei pri ispolnenii imi perevozok dlia voisk sobstvenno po nariadu s 1-go maia 1854 goda), l. 75.

68. RGIA, f. 1263 op. 1, d. 2481, l. 2.

69. Ibid., ll. 17–21.

70. Ibid., ll. 21–23.

71. The Department of Manufacturing and Internal Trade/MF to the Department of Taxes and Collections, 1 Jan. 1855, RGIA, f. 20, op. 3, d. 2326 (Dela departamenta torgovli i manufactur o predstavlenii kuptsov gorodov Simferopolia, Sevastopolia, Kerchi), ll. 1–2.

72. From the Tauride Treasury to the Department of Taxes and Collections, 21 June 1855, RGIA, f. 20, op. 3, g. 1855–170, d. 2326, l. 4.

73. From the MF to the Department of Taxes and Collections, 11 Aug. 1855, RGIA, f. 20, op. 3, g. 1855–170, d. 2326, l. 6.

74. Alison K. Smith, *For the Common Good and Their Own Well-Being: Social Estates in Imperial Russia* (New York and Oxford: Oxford University Press, 2014), 113, 123–125.

75. Francis William Wcislo, *Reforming Rural Russia: State, Local Society, and National Politics, 1855–1914* (Princeton, NJ: Princeton University Press, 1990), 4.

76. Peter Holquist, "To Count, to Extract, and to Exterminate: Population Statistics and Population Politics in Late Imperial and Soviet Russia," in *A State of Nations: Empire and Nation-Making in the Age of Lenin and Stalin*, ed. Ronald Suny and Terry Martin (New York: Oxford University Press, 2001), 113–16; and Holquist, "Forms of Violence during the Russian Occupation of Ottoman Territory and Northern Persia: Urimia and Astrabad, Oct. 1914–Dec. 1917), in Eric D. Weitz and Omer Bartov, *The Shatterzone of Empires: Coexistence and Violence in the German, Habsburg, Russian and Ottoman Borderlands* (Bloomington: Indiana University Press, 2003)," 344–61.

77. Unsigned letter to Vasil'chikov, RGIA, f. 651, op. 1, d. 416 (Perepiska po delu o zloupotrebleniia v intendantstve iuzhnoi armii), ll. 57–60, here 57 ob.

78. Pirogov, *Sevastopol'skiia pis'ma*, 112–15.

79. Menshikov, Prikaz no. 56, 18 Feb. 1855, RGVIA, f. 846, op. 16, d. 5617, l. 18.

80. Menshikov, Prikaz no. 72, 28 Feb. 1855, RGVIA, f. 846, op. 16, d. 5617, l. 42. Figes points out that in his last days Tsar Nicholas asked his son and imminent successor Alexander to replace Prince Menshikov. Orlando Figes, *The Crimean War: A History* (New York: Metropolitan Books, 2011), 322.

81. Notes from the General Quartermaster Butirlin to Prince Kherkheulidze, 7 Sept. 1855 RGVIA, f. 846, op. 16, d. 5786, ch. 1, l. 26.

82. Gorchakov, Prikaz no. 83, 10 Mar. 1855, RGVIA, f. 846, op. 16, d. 5617, l. 49.

83. Menshikov received the official rescript announcing his release from duty on February 15 while he was in Simferopol. Pirogov also expressed relief at Menshikov's departure. Hearing unfounded rumors that Menshikov had died in Perekop, the doctor exclaimed, "and Thank God! [he had died]." A. S. Menshikov to Tsar Alexander II, 24 Feb. 1855 RGVIA, f. 846, op. 16, d. 5450, ll. 65, 65 ob; Pirogov, *Sevastopol'skiia pis'ma*, 118.

84. Zatler, *Zapiski o prodovol'stvii voisk v voennoe vremia*, 1:253.

85. Gorchakov, Prikaz no. 82, 10 Mar. 1855, RGVIA, f. 846, op. 16, d. 5617, l. 49.

86. Gorchakov, Prikaz no. 87, 17 Mar. 1855, RGVIA, f. 846, op. 16, d. 5617, l. 52. On March 17, for example, Gorchakov reprimanded a commander of the Thirteenth Army infantry in Sevastopol for failing to provide provisions for the reserve brigade.

87. Kopii s zapisok za podpisam general-ad"iutanta kniazia Gorchakova, RGVIA, f. 846, op. 16, d. 5946 (O narodnom soprotivlenii v sluchae vtorzheniia nepriiatelia v predely Imperii), l. 3.

88. Liders, Prikaz no. 86, 14 Mar. 1855 RGVIA, f. 846, op. 16, d. 5617, l. 73.

89. "Fedor Karlovich Zatler," *RBS*, 270–73.

90. Zatler, *Zapiski o prodovol'stvii voisk v voennoe vremia*, 1: 254.

91. Prikaz no. 102, 28 Mar. 1855, RGVIA, f. 846, op. 16, d. 5617, l. 60.

92. Zatler, *Zapiski o prodovol'stvii voisk v voennoe vremia*, 1: 240–41.

93. Gorchakov, Prikaz no. 99, 25 Mar. 1855, RGVIA, f. 846, op. 16, d. 5617, l. 59.

94. Ibid.

95. Gorchakov, Prikaz no. 102, 28 Mar. 1855, RGVIA, f. 846, op. 16, d. 5617, l. 60.

96. Ibid, ll. 60–62.

97. Gorchakov, Prikaz no. 86, 14 Mar. 1855, RGVIA, f. 846, op. 16, d. 5617, l. 51.

98. Gorchakov, Prikaz no. 88, 18 Mar. 1855, RGVIA, f. 846, op. 16, d. 5617, l. 53.

99. V. Stepanov, "Krymskaia voina i ekonomika Rossii," in *The Crimean War, 1853–1856: Colonial Skirmish or Rehearsal for World War? Empires, Nations and Individuals*, ed. Jerszy W. Borejsz (Warsaw: Wydawnictwo Neriton Instytut PAN, 2011), 277–78.

100. The Vasil'chikov family collection in RGIA contains multiple files about Vasil'chikov's inquiry into the Intendancy. See, for example, RGIA, f. 651, op. 1, d. 416 (perepiska po delu o zloupotreblenie v intendantstve iuzhnoi armii).

101. Zatler, *Zapiski o prodovol'stvii voisk v voennoe vremia*, 2:293.

102. Zatler, *Zapiski o prodovol'stvii voisk v voennoe vremia*, 2:293.

103. MVD, Department of the Economy, 22 Dec. 1856, no. 1518, "O vspomozheniiakh Novorossiiskomu kraiu i voobshche o merakh k vosstanovleniu onogo posle voiny," Printed collection of documents published by the Ministry of Interior and preserved in the Russian National Library, 16.

104. MVD, Department of the Economy, 22 Dec. 1856, no. 1518, 21.

105. Ina Zweiniger-Bargielowska, Rachel Duffett, and Alain Drouard (eds.), *Food and War in Twentieth Century Europe* (Farnham, England: Ashgate, 2011), 1.

106. For a brief review of reforms related to provisioning, see S. V. Gavrilov, "Reformirovanie sistemy material'nogo snabzheniia russkoi armii vo vtoroi polovine XIX veka," *Izvestiia Rossiiskogo gosudarstvennogo pedagogicheskogo universiteta im. A. I. Gertsena*, no. 115 (2009): 22–31; and for a discussion of the war itself, Gavrilov, "Problemy razvitiia intendantskogo snabzheniia russkoi armii nakanune Vostochnoi (Krymskoi) voiny 1853–1856 goda," *Sbornik voenno-nauchnykh statei voennoi akademii*, no. 49.61 (2008): 437–45.

Chapter 6

1. The Tsar called upon peasant volunteers from April of 1854. Rumors quickly spread that volunteers would receive their freedom after a brief period of service. David Moon, "Russian Peasant Volunteers at the Beginning of the Crimean War," *SR* 51.4 (1992): 691–704.

2. Adlerberg to MVD, 6 Mar. 1855, RGVIA, f. 846, op. 16, d. 5673 (Po otnosheniiu s Simferopol'skim Gubernatorom), ll. 12–13.

3. Mufti Seid Efendi Dzhelil, Call to the Faithful Muslim People!, Feb. 1855, RGVIA, f. 846, op. 16, d. 5673, ll. 10–11.

4. Adlerberg to Kotzebue, Mar. 1855, RGVIA, f. 846, op. 16, d. 5673, l. 6; Kotzebue to Adlerberg, 30 Apr. 1855, RGVIA, f. 846, op. 16, d. 5673, l. 17.

5. Tarle, *Krymskaia voina*, 2: 418.

6. E. V. Tarle, *Napoleon's Invasion of Russia, 1812* (New York: Oxford University Press, 1942), 256–71, 345–56.

7. Victor Taki, "From Partisan War to the Ethnography of European Turkey: The Balkan Career of Ivan Liprandi, 1790–1880," *CSP* 58.3 (September 2016): 257–285.

8. Gorchakov to Dolgorukov, 12 Mar. 1855, no. 1, RGVIA, f. 846, op. 16, d. 5496, ll. 12–14.

9. Gorchakov to Dolgorukov, 12 Mar. 1855, no. 1, RGVIA, f. 846, op. 16, d. 5496, ll. 14, 14 ob.

10. Hundreds of pages of clerical correspondences during the war survive in the personal papers of Archbishop Innokentii located in the Russian national library. See RNB, f. 313, op. 1, d. 44.

11. See Mara Kozelsky, *Christianizing Crimea: Shaping Sacred Space in the Russian Empire and Beyond* (DeKalb: Northern Illinois University Press, 2010), 141–46. For a full list of priests, monks, and clerics awarded for their service during the war, see L. V. Mel'nikova, *Russkaia Pravoslavnaia Tserkov' i Krymskaia Voina* (Moscow: Kuchkovo pole, 2012), 243–64.

12. Roy R. Robson, *The Story of Russia Told through Its Most Remarkable Islands* (New Haven, CT: Yale University Press, 2004), 155–69; Andrew C. Rath, *The Crimean War in Imperial Context, 1854–1856* (New York: Palgrave Macmillan, 2015), 26.

13. P. A. Zaionchkovskii, *The Abolition of Serfdom in Russia*, ed. and trans. Susan Wobst, introduction by Terrence Emmons (Gulf Breeze, FL: Academic International Press, 1978), 42.

14. Mel'nikova, *Russkaia Pravoslavnaia Tserkov' i Krymskaia Voina*, 186–91.

15. Military Governor of Kiev to Liders, 6 April 1855, RGVIA, f. 846, op. 16, d. 5496, ll. 23, 23 ob; and 7 April 1855, RGVIA, f. 846, op. 16, d. 5496, ll. 25–32.

16. Military Governor of Kiev to Liders, 20 April 1855, RGVIA, f. 846, op. 16, d. 5496, l. 45 ob. There has been some debate in the literature over whether the uprising was economic or nationalist in nature. Mel'nikova suggests the former. See Mel'nikova, *Russkaia Pravoslavnaia Tserkov' i Krymskaia Voina*, 212.

17. Gorchakov, Report, RGVIA, f. 846, op. 16, d. 5496, ll. 1, 1 ob.

18. Ibid., l. 4.

19. Ibid., ll. 3–4.

20. Gorchakov to Adlerberg, 30 April 1855, RGVIA, f. 846, op. 16, d. 5673 (Po otnosheniiu s Simferopol'skim Gubernatorom), l. 17.

21. David R. Stone, *A Military History of Russia: From Ivan the Terrible to the War in Chechnya* (Westport, CT: Praeger, 2006)127–129.

22. A. Iu. Bezugol'nyi, N. F. Kovalevskii, and V. E. Kovalev, *Istoriia voenno-okruzhnoi sistemy v Rossii* (Moscow: Tsentrpoligraf, 2012), 1–13.

23. These instructions were initially composed for Bessarabia, but were later passed on to Menshikov. Annenkov to Gorchakov, 7 Oct. 1854, RGVIA, f. 846, op. 16, d. 5492, l. 95.

24. Annenkov to Menshikov, 7 Oct. 1854, RGVIA, f. 846, op. 16, d. 5492, l. 92.

25. A. F. Geirot, *Opisanie vostochnoi Voiny* (St. Petersburg: Eduard Gonik, 1872), 226; L. G. Beskrovnyi, *Russkoe voennoe iskusstvo XIXv* (Moscow: izd. Nauka, 1974), 247. K. N. Leontiev, "Sdacha Kerchi v 55 godu (vospominaniia voennogo vracha)," in *Sobranie*

sochinenii K. Leontieva (St. Petersburg: Rus. kn. t-vo, 1912), 9: 193. "Wrangel (Aleksandr Evstaf'evich)" in *Entsiklopedicheskii slovar'*, ed. F. A. Brokgauz and I. A. Efron (St. Petersburg, tip. I. A. Efrona, 1892), 7: 335–36.

26. Annenkov to Menshikov, 7 Oct. 1854, RGVIA, f. 846, op. 16, d. 5492, ll. 95–97.

27. Hartley, *Russia, 1762–1825*, 109–19.

28. Willard Sunderland, "Peasants on the Move: State Peasant Resettlement in Imperial Russia, 1805–1830s," *Russian Review* 52.4 (2007): 472–85; and Sunderland, *Taming the Wildfield: Colonization and Empire on the Russian Steppe* (Ithaca, NY: Cornell University Press, 2004), 73–95, 137–43, 150–52.

29. Pestel to Menshikov, 28 Sept. 1854, GAARK, f. 26, op. 1, d. 20004, l. 2.

30. Catherine II departed from the traditional Russian estate system to apply physiocrat economic doctrines to the new southern frontier. For an extended discussion of these policies, see James A. Duran, Jr., "Catherine II, Potemkin and Colonization Policy in Southern Russia," *RR* 28.1 (1969): 23–36.

31. Alan W. Fisher, *Crimean Tatars* (Stanford, CA: Stanford University Press, 1986), 90–91. In the words of Alan Fisher, "Catherine had determined that imperial interests would be best served if the peasants' free status were preserved, yet she found that she had to incorporate them into the Russian class of state peasants to do it."

32. Menshikov to Pestel, GAARK, f. 26, op. 1, d. 20004, l. 1. Menshikov had in mind Kerkemeiskii Bay, not Kherkezhenskii Bay (which did not exist), one of many mistakes Russian military leaders made about local geography.

33. Pestel to Menshikov, 28 Sept. 1854, GAARK, f. 26, op. 1, d. 20004, ll. 4–5.

34. Menshikov to Pestel, 30 Sept. 1854, GAARK, f. 26, op. 1, d. 20004, l. 5.

35. Kiselev to Pestel, 9 Oct. 1854, GAARK, f. 26, op. 1, d. 20004, l. 27.

36. Ibid., l. 28.

37. Ibid., l. 29.

38. Von Bradke, Report no. 82, 14 Oct. 1854, GAARK, f. 26, op. 1, d. 20004, ll. 18–20 ob.

39. Zatler, *Zapiski o prodovol'stvii voisk v voennoe vremia*, 2:1–22. Conceptualization of the *kulak* as an enemy class is often attributed to the Bolsheviks. However, the term pre-dated the Stolypin reform and in Russia, gained its negative association during the Crimean War. For a discussion of the term in relation to Stolypin, see Donald W. Treadgold, "Was Stolypin in Favor of Kulaks?" *ASEER* 14.1 (1955): 1–14; for a discussion of the term in relation to the Bolsheviks, see Lars Lih, *Bread and Authority in Russia, 1914–1921* (Berkeley: University of California Press, 1990).

40. M. S. Leonidov, "Pestel', Vladimir Ivanovich," *RBS* (St. Petersburg: tip. I. N. Skhorokhodova, 1902), 13: 591–92.

41. "Adlerberg, Count Nikolai Vladimirovich," *RBS* (New York: Kraus Reprint Corporation, 1962): 1:78.

42. RGIA, f. 1263, op. 1, d. 2481, l. ll. 38–40.

43. Report from the Greek Battalion Commander, 26 Mar. 1855, GAARK, f. 26, op. 4, d. 1472 (Po donosu tatarki Aishe o neblagonamerennykh budto by zamyslakh nekotorykh tatar s mest Alushty), l. 1.

44. Pribytkov to Adlerberg, GAARK, f. 26, op. 4, d. 1472, ll. 2–3.

45. See, for example, GAARK, f. 26, op. 4, d. 1456 (O Tatarine Abdullaeve Selidzhate i ego otnosheniiakh s nepriiatelem), l. 1.

46. Yalta Police Chief to Adlerberg, GAARK, f. 26, op. 4, d. 1449 (O zaderzhanii tatar Zh. Osmana, Musdina, Bengli-Adzhi i Seid Asana Cheleben), ll. 13–14.

47. GAARK, f. 26, op. 4, d. 1685 (Ob osvobozhdenii iz pod aresta i ot suda lits, zamechannykh v snoshenii s nepriiatelem), ll. 1–65; GAARK, f. 26, op. 4, d. 1673 (O komandirovanii deputata s grazhdanskoi storony sledstvenniiu kommissiiu uchrezhdenno v Perekope nad tatarami) ll. 1–7.

48. Gorchakov to Adlerberg, GAARK, f. 26, op. 4, d. 1644 (O nabliudenii za poiavleniem v Krymu raspolozheniia nashikh voisk shpionov iz Tatar, sluzhashchikh nepriiateliu) ll. 1–2.

49. Russians had spies among the British as well, including a Balaklava Greek who dressed as a Tatar and spoke Kirimtatar, and so attempted to infiltrate British intelligence. He was recognized and caught by one of Cattley's Tatar agents. See Harris, *British Military Intelligence in the Crimean War* (London: Frank Cass, 1999), 79–85.

50. A. B. Shirokorod, *Russko-Turetskie Voiny: 1676–1918* (Moscow: AST, 2000), 353–56.

51. Governor of Kursk to the Governor of Tauride, 16 Jan. 1856, GAARK, f. 26, op. 4, d. 1493 (O Tatarakh Akhmulla Ibraim Oglu, Khalim-Selim Oglu), l. 29.

52. Borasan Amed Menshid Oglu "Proshenie," Apr. 1855, GAARK, f. 26, op. 1, d. 20004, l. 74.

53. von Bradke to Adlerberg 30 Apr. 1855, GAARK, f. 26, op. 1, d. 20004, l. 61.

54. Evpatoria District Commander to Adlerberg, 11 May 1855, GAARK, f. 26, op. 1, d. 20004, l. 99.

55. MGI to N. V. Adlerberg, 23 May 1855, GAARK, f. 26, op. 1, d. 20004, ll. 113, 113 ob.

56. Evpatoria District Commander to Adlerberg, 11 May 1855, GAARK, f. 26, op. 1, d. 20004, l. 99.

57. Kiselev to Adlerberg, GAARK, f. 26, op. 1, d. 20004, l. 113.

58. Evpatoria District Court to Adlerberg, 3 May 1855, GAARK, f. 26, op. 1, d. 20004, l. 71.

59. Gorchakov to Adlerberg, 10 June 1855, GAARK, f. 26, op. 1, d. 20004, l. 127.

60. RGVIA, f. 846, op. 16, d. 5694 (Zhurnal Voennykh deistvii), l. 53. Of this number, 92 men had died, 384 men were wounded, and 255 were concussed.

61. Gorchakov to Adlerberg, June or July 1855, GAARK, f. 26, op. 1, d. 20004, l. 173.

62. Evpatoria District Commander to Adlerberg, 20 June 1855, GAARK, f. 26, op. 1, d. 20004, l. 142.

63. Gorchakov to Adlerberg, GAARK, May 1855, f. 26, op. 1, d. 20004, l. 83.

64. Evpatoria District Commander to Adlerberg, 13 May 1855, GAARK, f. 26, op. 1, d. 20004, l. 79.

65. Gorchakov to Adlerberg, 16 May 1855, GAARK, f. 26, op. 1, d. 20004, l. 87.

66. Gorchakov to Adlerberg, 24 May 1855, GAARK, f. 26, op. 1, d. 20004, l. 103.

67. Evpatoria District Commander to Adlerberg, 14 June 1855, GAARK, f. 26, op. 1, d. 20004, l. 135.

68. Evpatoria police chief to the Evpatoria Court, 27 July 1855, GAARK, f. 26, op. 1, d. 20004, l. 202.

69. Ibid., l. 209.

70. Muraviev, untitled MGI report, no. 2292, 21 Nov. 1860, RGIA, f. 651, op. 1, d. 468, l. 145.

71. Adlerberg to Gorchakov, Aug. 1855, GAARK, f. 26, op. 4, d. 1522 (O merakh k preduprezhdeniiu vozmozhnosti dlia tatar imet' snosheniia s nepriiatelem), l. 12.

72. Adlerberg to Gorchakov GAARK, f. 26, op. 4, d. 1522, ll. 12–14.

73. RGIA, f. 651, op. 1, d. 468, ll. 44–46.

74. Gorchakov to Adlerberg, 2 July 1855, GAARK, f. 26, op. 4, d. 1495 (O tatarakh kotorie i bezhali k nepriatliu), ll. 4–5.

75. GAARK, f. 26, op. 4, d. 1673, ll. 1–7; GAARK, f. 26, op. 4, d. 1685, l. 1.

76. The most likely spelling of this suspect's last name was Chelebi, not Chilibi. However, "Chilibi" was most commonly used in official reports.

77. Governor General of New Russia to the Tauride Governor, 25 Nov. 1854 GAARK, f. 26, op. 4, d. 1449, ll. 6–29. This letter was one of many sent during the transition between Pestel and Adlerberg.

78. GAARK, f. 26, op. 4, d. 1472, ll. 1–28.

79. W. E. Mosse, "How Russia Made Peace September 1855 to April 1856," *Cambridge Historical Journal* 11, no. 3 (1955): 297–316; here 300–304.

Chapter 7

1. Gorchakov to Adlerberg, 21 May 1855, RGVIA, f. 846, op. 16, d. 5673, l. 23. Dubrovin describes the enemy occupation of Kerch in detail, but gives less attention to Berdiansk and Genichesk. See N. F. Dubrovin, *Vostochnaia Voina: 1853–1856* (St. Petersburg: tip. Imperatorskoi akademii nauk, 1878), 453–69. See also Trevor Royle, *Crimea: The Great Crimean War, 1854–1856* (New York: St. Martin's Press, 2000), 372–76.

2. John Codman, *An American Transport in the Crimean War* (New York: Bonnell, Silver and Co., 1897), 76–77.

3. Rath, *The Crimean War in Imperial Context*, 28–30, 47–51.

4. Captain A. C. Dewar, ed., introduction to *Russian War, 1855: Black Sea Official Correspondence* (London: Navy Records Society, 1965), 3–24, here 11–12.

5. General Quartermaster Butirlin to Prince Kherkheulidze, 7 Sept. 1855, RGVIA, f. 846, op. 16, d. 5786, ch. 1, ll. 26–27.

6. Captain Gifford to Lyons, 1/13 Feb. 1855, in *Russian War, 1855: Black Sea Official Correspondence*, ed. A. C. Dewar (London: Navy Records Society, 1965), 78–79; and Dubrovin, *Vostochnaia Voina*, 443.

7. Dubrovin, *Vostochnaia Voina*, 444–48.

8. Lyons to the Secretary to the Admiralty, 5/17 April 1855, in *Russian War*, 119–20.

9. Field Marshal Lord Raglan to Lyons, 23 April/4 May 1855; and Lyons to the Secretary to the Admiralty, 5/17 April 1855, in *Russian War*, 145–46.

10. Lyons to the Secretary to the Admiralty, 26 April/7 May 1855, in *Russian War*, 144.

11. Khomutov to Gorchakov, 24 April 1855, RGVIA f. 846, op. 16, d. 5691 (Po chasti General'nago shtaba: Zhurnaly voennykh deistvii v Krymu), l. 11.

12. Lyons to the Secretary to the Admiralty, 25 April/6 May 1855, in *Russian War*, 143.

13. Lyons to the Secretary to the Admiralty 22 May 1855, in *Russian War*, 156–57.

14. Khomutov to Gorchakov, 7 May 1855, RGVIA, f. 846, op. 16, d. 5691, ll. 14–15 ob.; Dubrovin, *Vostochnaia Voina*, 453.

15. Excerpt, official journal of military activities, 1–18 May 1855, RGVIA, f. 846, op. 16, d. 5691, l. 23.

16. Untitled Table, 20 May through 7 June 1855, GAARK, f. 197, op. 1, d. 141 (O kholere v g. Simferopol i bor'be s nei), l. 52.

17. Dubrovin, *Vostochnaia Voina*, 454–57.

18. Bowen Stilton Mends, journal entry for 26 May 1855, in *Life of Sir Admiral Mends G. C. B. Late Director of Transport* (London: John Murray, 1899), 272.

19. Lyons to the Secretary to the Admiralty, 25 May 1855, in *Russian War*, 158.

20. Gorchakov to Adlerberg, May 1855, GAARK, f. 26, op. 4, d. 1482 (Raznye rasporiazheniia, posledovavshie vsledstvie vysadki desanta anglo-frantsuzov v Krymu, ykazy v podgotovke evakuatsii raznykh gorodov), l. 1.

21. Voinovich to Adlerberg, 16 May 1855; and Gorchakov to Adlerberg, 17 May 1855, GAARK, f. 26, op. 4, d. 1482, ll. 19, 24.

22. Mends, *Life of Sir Admiral Mends*, 275.

23. Unsigned letter to Sukhotin, 20 May 1855, RGVIA, f. 846, op. 16, d. 5740, l. 20.

24. Dubrovin, *Vostochnaia Voina*, 462. Figes also attributes the wreckage in Kerch to Tatars, and adds that they committed the crimes out of "revenge." See Orlando Figes, *The Crimean War: A History* (New York: Metropolitan Books, 2011), 344.

25. Mends, *Life of Sir Admiral Mends*, 274–75.

26. See, for example, the note to Sukhotin about the arrest of a Don Cossack from the Sixty-fifth Regiment following complaints of local residents: 21 May 1855, RGVIA, f. 846, op. 16, d. 5740 (Bumagi Shtaba Komanduiushchego Avangardom Vostochnoi chasti Kryma), l. 22; Popov to Sukhotin, RGVIA, f. 846, op. 16, d. 5740, l. 36.

27. Rath, *The Crimean War in Imperial Context*, 169.

28. Francis Pullen quoted in Rath, *The Crimean War in Imperial Context*, 175.

29. Antonovich to the New Russian Governor General, 21 Sept. 1855, RGIA, f. 1287, op. 6, d. 1089 (O posobii chinovnikam Kerchenskogo Gradonachal'stva, poterpevshim ot napadeniia nepriiatelei), l. 28.

30. Mends, *Life of Sir Admiral Mends*, 274.

31. Unsigned letter to Sukhotin, 13 May 1855, RGVIA, f. 846, op. 16, d. 5740, l. 1.

32. Antonovich to the New Russian Governor General, 21 Sept. 1855, RGIA, f. 1287, op. 6, d. 1089, ll. 28–29. Dubrovin, *Vostochnaia Voina*, 463. Annenkov was officially removed from his position at the end of March 1855, eventually to be replaced by A. S. Stroganov, and it is not clear who received Antonovich's correspondence in the interim. See PSZRI, 2nd ser., vol. 30, no. 29173 (29 Mar. 1855): 232.

33. The Ministry of Finance to MVD, 19 Mar. 1855, RGIA, f. 1287, op. 6, d. 1089, l. 16.

34. Antonovich to the New Russian Governor General, 21 Sept. 1855, RGIA, f. 1287, op. 6, d. 1089, l. 28.

35. New Russian Governor General to Antonovich, 24 May 1855, GAARK, f. 26, op. 4, d. 1482, ll. 71–72.

36. New Russian Governor General to Antonovich, 1 June 1855, RGIA, f. 1287, op. 6, d. 1089, l. 23.

37. New Russian Governor General to Antonovich, 1 June 1855, RGIA, f. 1287, op. 6, d. 1089, l. 24.

38. New Russian Governor General to Antonovich, 1 June 1855, RGIA, f. 1287, op. 6, d. 1089, l. 24–25.

39. Gagarin to Stroganov, 2 Nov., 1855, RGVIA, f. 846, op. 16, d. 5674, (O vozvrashchennykh nam nepriiatelem plennykh), ll. 12–13.

40. Antonovich to New Russian Governor General, 21 Sept. 1855, RGIA, f. 1287, op. 6, d. 1089, l. 29 ob.

41. Antonovich to New Russian Governor General, 21 Sept. 1855, RGIA, f. 1287, op. 6, d. 1089, ll. 29, 29 ob.

42. Peter Gatrell, *A Whole Empire Walking: Refugees in Russia During World War I* (Bloomington: Indiana University Press, 1999), 2.

43. Wrangel to Sukhotin, 28 May 1855, RGVIA, f. 846, op. 16, d. 5740, ll. 39, 39 ob.

44. Wrangel to Sukhotin, 29 May 1855, RGVIA, f. 846, op. 16, d. 5740, l. l51.

45. Leontiev, "Moi dela s Turgenevym i t.d." 9:148.

46. Dubrovin, *Vostochnaia Voina*, 460; Chernaev to Adlerberg, 17 May 1855, GAARK, f. 26, op. 4, d. 1483 (Raporty zemskogo ispravnika o dvizhenii nepriiatelei flota y beregov Chernogo i Azovskogo morei. Bombardirovka Genicheska, vysadka desanta v Alupke), l. 10.

47. Chernaev to Adlerberg, 17 May 1855, GAARK, f. 26, op. 4, d. 1483, l. 9.

48. Berdiansk Parish Priest to Archbishop Innokentii, RNB, f. 313, op. 1, d. 44, l. 300.

49. Chernaev to Adlerberg, 17 May 1855, GAARK, f. 26, op. 4, d. 1483, ll. 10–11.

50. Chernaev to Adlerberg, 1 June 1855, RGVIA, f. 846, op. 16, d. 5678 (O prestupnykh snosheniiakh s nepriatelem nekotorykh zhitelei g. Berdiansk), ll. 3–5.

51. Chernaev to Adlerberg, 8 June 1855, RGVIA, f. 846, op. 16, d. 5678, l. 9.

52. Pribytkov to Adlerberg, RGVIA, f. 846, op. 16, d. 5678, ll. 5–6.

53. Annenkov to Gorchakov, RGVIA, f. 846, op. 16, d. 5673, l. 18.

54. Gorchakov to Adlerberg, 4 June 1855, GAARK, f. 26, op. 4, d. 1482, ll. 96–98; "Publication," 7 June 1855, signed by Chernaev, RGVIA, f. 846, op. 16, d. 5678, ll. 11, 11 ob.

55. Gorchakov to Adlerberg, 9 Oct. 1855, GAARK, f. 26, op. 4, d. 1482, l. 326.

56. Assignment of New Russia Governor General to Ponse, 26 May 1855, GAARK, f. 26, op. 4, d. 1482, ll. 81–83.

57. Stroganov to Gorchakov, 21 June 1855, RGVIA, 846, op. 16, d. 5678, l. 19.

58. Mends, *Life of Sir Admiral Mends*, 278.

59. Stroganov to Gorchakov, 21 June 1855, RGVIA, 846, op. 16, d. 5678, l. 20 ob.

60. Gorchakov to Adlerberg, 29 June 1855, RGVIA, f. 846, op. 16, d. 5673, ll. 27–28.

61. Sukhotin to Wrangel, 20 May 1855, RGVIA, f. 846, op. 16, d. 5675 (Zakliuchaiushchee v sebe svedeniia ob uspekhakh perevozki iz nakhodiashchegosia bliz seleniia Kiteni na beregu moria sklada provianta Morskogo Vedomstva), ll. 1–2.

62. Wrangel to Sukhotin, RGVIA, f. 846, op. 16, d. 5740, l. 24; also RGVIA, f. 846, op. 16, d. 5675, ll. 3, 3 ob.

63. Sukhotin to Wrangel, 25 May 1855, RGVIA, f. 846, op. 16, d. 5675, l. 20.

64. Sukhotin to Wrangel, 20 May 1855, RGVIA, f. 846, op. 16, d. 5675, l. 24.

65. Sukhotin to Wrangel, May 1855, RGVIA, f. 846, op. 16, d. 5675, l. 32.

66. Gorchakov to unnamed recipient, 16 May 1855, GAARK, f. 26, op. 4, d. 1482, l. 23.

67. Chernaev to Adlerberg, 17 May 1855, RGVIA, f. 846, op. 16, d. 5673, l. 22; Berdiansk Parish Priest to Archbishop Innokentii, RNB, f. 313, op. 1, d. 44, l. 300.

68. Petition from Berdiansk 1st Guild Merchants, 14 July 1855, GAARK, f. 26, op. 4, d. 1482, ll. 237–238.

69. Gorchakov to Adlerberg, May 21 1855, RGVIA, f. 846, op. 16, d. 5673, l. 23.

70. Gorchakov to Adlerberg, 21 May 1855, RGVIA, f. 846, op. 16, d. 5673, l. 25.

71. Anon., "The News by the Atlantic," *The New York Times*, June 14, 1855: 4.

72. Lyons to the Secretary of the Admiralty, 31 May 1855, in *Russian War*, 168–69.

73. Lyons to the Secretary of the Admiralty, 2 June 1855, in *Russian War*, 170–71.

74. Mends, *Life of Sir Admiral Mends*, 272.

75. Ibid., 275–76.

Chapter 8

1. In the words of Andrew Lambert, "As military operations, the capture of Kertch and the subsequent control of the Azov Sea rank among the finest achievements of the war. The combination of considered planning, irresistible force and initiative completely destroyed a position the Russians knew to be vital, and which they had eight months to defend. It was the decisive blow of 1855, leading to the battle of Tchernaya and the fall of Sevastopol." Andrew Lambert, *The Crimean War: British Grand Strategy against Russia, 1854–1856*, 2nd ed. (Farmham: Ashgate, 2011), 249.

2. M. I. Bogdanovich, *Vostochnaia Voina, 1853–1856*, 4 vols. (St. Petersburg: tip. F. Sushchinko, 1876), 4: 12–13.

3. L. G. Beskrovnyi, *Russkoe voennoe iskusstvo XIXv* (Moscow: izd. Nauka, 1974), 278; Bogdanovich, *Vostochnaia Voina*, 3:45–46.

4. Orlando Figes, *The Crimean War: A History* (New York: Metropolitan Books, 2011), 373–87.

5. Winfried Baumgart, trans. Ann Pottinger Saab, *The Peace of Paris 1856: Studies in War, Diplomacy, and Peacemaking* (Oxford: ABC-Clio, 1981), 1–2.

6. See, for example, Baumgart, *The Peace of Paris 1856*, 58; Trevor Royle, *Crimea: The Great Crimean War, 1854–1856* (New York: St. Martin's Press, 2000), 435; Figes, *The Crimean War*, 397.

7. Candan Badem offers the only English-language treatment of the Battle of Kars from the Ottoman perspective in *The Ottoman Crimean War (1853–1856)* (London: Brill, 2010), 243–55. For classic accounts of the Caucasian campaign, see W. E. D. Allen and Paul Muratoff, *Caucasian Battlefields: A History of the Wars on the Turco-Caucasian Border, 1828–1921* (Cambridge: Cambridge University Press, 1953), 57–102, and the bibliography, 539–43. General Murav'ev, who led the siege of Kars, wrote memoirs of the war: N. N. Muraviev, *Voina za Kavkazom v 1855 godu* (St. Petersburg, 1863).

8. General Sir Richard Denis Kelly, *An Officer's Letters to His Wife during the Crimean War* (London: Elliot Stock, 1902), 378.

9. Dubrovin, *Istoriia Krymskoi Voiny i oborony Sevastopolia*, 3: 445.

10. MVD, Department of the Economy, 22 Dec. 1856, no. 1518, 17.

11. Baumgart describes a three-stage peace process, which included "soundings during the war itself"; "a preliminary treaty indicating the bases of the final peace settlement"; and "an armistice marking the third state" opening extended negotiations through the conclusion of formal treaty. Baumgart, *The Peace of Paris 1856*, 105.

12. Royle, *Crimea*, 433–42; Lambert, *The Crimean War*, 267–70.

13. Adam R. Seipp, *The Ordeal of Peace: Demobilization and the Urban Experience in Britain and Germany, 1917–1921* (Burlington, VT: Ashgate, 2009), 6.

14. Bogdanovich, *Vostochnaia Voina* (cited in note 2), 4: 52.

15. Ibid., 4: 58.

16. Totleben, *Opisanie Oborony g. Sevastopolia*, 2: 244.

17. Bogdanovich, *Vostochnaia Voina*, 4: 87–94; Beskrovnyi, *Russkoe voennoe iskusstvo*, 278–80.

18. Quoted in Figes, *The Crimean War*, 394.

19. N. I. Pirogov, *Sevastopol'skiia pis'ma N. I. Pirogova 1854–1855*, ed. Iu. G. Malis (St. Petersburg: tip. M. Merkusheva, 1907), 145.

20. A. Ivanov, "Kinburn," *ITUAK* 31 (1901): 27–29.

21. Peter Druckers, *The Crimean War at Sea: Naval Campaigns against Russia, 1854–56* (Barnsley, Yorkshire: Pen and Sword Books, 2011), 135.

22. Report from the Tauride Gendarme to Orlov, 30 Sept. 1854, RGVIA, f. 846, op. 16, d. 5492, l. 79.

23. Lambert, *The Crimean War*, 148–50.

24. Dneprovsk district court to Adlerberg, 7 Oct. 1855, GAARK, f. 26, op. 4, d. 1550, ll. 7, 7 ob.

25. Lambert, *The Crimean War*, 148–50; Druckers gives the number of 9,000 men, 4,000 of whom were British. Druckers, *The Crimean War at Sea*, 135–36.

26. Adlerberg to Antonovich, 13 Oct. 1855, GAARK, f. 26, op. 4, d. 1482, l. 331.

27. Zapiski o gorode Orekhovo, unsigned, 31 Dec. 1855, GAARK, f. 26, op. 4, d. 1482, l. 369.

28. Civilians of Berdiansk to Chernaev, 15 Sept. 1855, GAARK, f. 26, op. 4, d. 1482, ll. 306–307.

29. Stroganov to Gorchakov, 26 Sept. 1855, GAARK, f. 26, op. 4, d. 1482, l. 318.

30. Gorchakov to Adlerberg, 9 Oct. 1855, GAARK, f. 26, op. 4, d. 1482, l. 326.

31. Gorchakov to Adlerberg, 7 Dec. 1855, GAARK, f. 26, op. 4, d. 1482, l. 355.

32. Feodosia police chief to Adlerberg, 8 Oct. 1855, GAARK, f. 26, op. 4, d. 1550 (O Vyvoze prisutsvennykh mest iz gg. Aleshki, Feodosii i drug.), ll. 4–5 ob.

33. Kotzebue to Wrangel, 30 Sept. 1855, RGVIA 846, op. 16, d. 5674 (O vozvrashchennykh nam nepriiatelem plennykh), l. 4.

34. Gagarin to Wrangel, 2 Oct. 1855, RGVIA 846, op. 16, d. 5674, l. 7.

35. Department of Quarantine/New Russia Governor General to Gagarin, 21 Oct. 1855, RGVIA 846, op. 16, d. 5674, ll. 11–12.

36. Gagarin to Stroganov, 2 Nov. 1855, RGVIA 846, op. 16, d. 5674, ll. 12–13.

37. Feodosia police chief to Adlerberg, 8 Oct. 1855, GAARK, f. 26, op. 4, d. 1550, ll. 4–5 ob.

38. Bogdanovich, *Vostochnaia Voina* (cited in note 2), 4: 180.

39. Markevich, *Tavricheskaia Guberniia vo vremia Krymskoi voiny*, 192.

40. Ibid., 196–97.

41. Sukhozanet to Gorchakov, 7 Sept. 1855, RGVIA, f. 846, op. 16, d. 5679, ll. 1–3.

42. Trigoni to Sukhozanet, 3 Oct. 1855, RGVIA, f. 846, op. 16, d. 5679, ll. 12–13.

43. MVD, no. 1518, l. 13.

44. Trigoni to Wrangel, 28 Sept. 1855, RGVIA, f. 846, op. 16, d. 5679, ll. 8–9.

45. MVD, no. 1518, ll. 13–14.

46. Unsigned Report, 18 Nov. 1855, RGVIA, f. 846, op. 16, d. 5679, l. 23.

47. Unsigned Report, 16 Nov. 1855, RGVIA, f. 846, op. 16, d. 5679, l. 22.

48. Bukhmeyer to Gorchakov, 25 Dec. 1855 f. 846, op. 16, d. 5679, l. 37.

49. RGIA, f. 1263 op. 1, d. 2552 (Otchet gubernatora Simferopolia i Tavricheskogo Grazhdanskogo Gubernatora, o sostoianii Tavricheskoi gubernii za 1855), ll. 693–96; This file is an excerpt from the longer document in RGIA, f. 1281, op. 6, d. 97, ll. 1–53.

50. Adlergerg, RGIA, f. 1263 op. 1, d. 2552, ll. 693–96

51. This paragraph about Tatar migration consists of modified material from Mara Kozelsky, "Casualties of Conflict: Crimean Tatars During the Crimean War," *SR* 67.4 (2008).

52. GAARK, f. 26, op. 4, d. 1495, ll. 1, 11.

53. GAARK, f. 26, op. 4, d. 1579, l. 4.

54. RGIA, f. 1281, op. 6, d. 97, ll. 1–3.

55. Baumgart, *The Peace of Paris*, 5–10.

56. Kelly, *An Officer's Letters to His Wife*, 17 and 24 Mar., 429–32.

57. PSZRI, 2nd ser., no. 30238, vol. 31, (5 Mar. 1856): 111.

58. GAARK, f. 27, op. 1, d. 6628 (Chinovniki, nagrazhdennye serebrianoi medal'iu dlia sluzhby v Sevastopole), l. 1. Gorchakov specified those eligible for the awards would have served from 13 Sept. 1854 through 27 Aug. 1855.

59. GAARK, f. 27, op. 1, d. 6628, l. 50.

60. Ministry of Finance Report, 20 Feb. 1859, RGIA, f. 560, op. 38, d. 146 (O nagrazhdenii serebrianoi medal'iu), l. 1.

61. New Russian Governor General to Adlerberg, 13 Apr. 1856, GAARK, f. 26, op.1, d. 20997 (Rasporiazhenniia glavnokomanduiushchego Iuzhnoi Armii i voiskom v Krymu, o merakh vodvoreniia poriadka v gorodakh Kryma, po ostavlenii ikh nepriiatel'skimi voiskami), l. 71.

62. MVD, no. 1518, l. 20.

63. Leontiev, "Moi dela s Turgenevym," 9:148.

64. John Codman, *An American Transport in the Crimean War* (New York: Bonnell, Silver and Co., 1897), 90.

65. Baumgart, *Peace of Paris*, 106.

66. Codman, *An American Transport in the Crimean War*, 90.

67. "Instruktsia," 24 Mar. 1856, GAARK, f. 26, op. 1, d. 20997, l. 21.

68. Quoted in David Bell, *The First Total War: Napoleon's Europe and the Birth of Warfare as We Know It* (Boston: Mariner Books, 2007), 25.

69. Edgerton, *Death or Glory*, 137–41.

70. Markevich, *Tavricheskaia Guberniia vo vremia Krymskoi voiny*, 192.

71. Laurie Bernstein, *Sonia's Daughters: Prostitutes and Their Regulation in Imperial Russia* (Berkeley, CA: University of California Press, 1995), 20–29.

72. GAARK, f. 197, op. 1, d. 193 (Obshchee o publichnykh zhenshchinakh), l. 301.

73. New Russian Governor to N. V. Adlerberg, 11 April 1856, GAARK, f. 26, op. 1, d. 20997, l. 66.

74. Gorchakov to Zhukovskii, 7 Mar. 1856, GAARK, f. 26, op.4, d. 1596 (O voennykh dezertirakh, ostavshikhsia v Kerchi posle ukhoda soiuznykh voisk, Karlo Menardi, P'ere Sharl' Berar, i drug), ll. 1–4.

75. Evpatoria city police chief to Adlerberg, 20 May 1856, GAARK, f. 26, op. 1, d. 20997, ll. 136–37.

76. Evpatoria police chief to Adlerberg, 12 July 1856, GAARK, f. 26, op. 1, d. 20997, l. 332.

77. Evpatoria Marshal of the Nobility to Adlerberg, 12 June 1856, GAARK, f. 26, op. 1, d. 20997, l. 179.

78. New Russian Governor General to the Governor of Tauride, 4 July 1856, GAARK, f. 26, op. 1, d. 20997, l. 269.

79. Evpatoria police chief to Adlerberg, 12 July 1856 GAARK, f. 26, op. 1, d. 20997, l. 331.

80. GAARK, f. 26, op. 1, d. 20997, ll. 205–210, l. 353. The English also left behind 2400 barraks in Balaklava.

81. MVD, no. 1518, 21.

82. E. M. Bakunina, "Vospominaniia sestry miloserdiia Krestovozdvizhenskoi obshchiny, 1854–1860," *Vestnik Evropy* 191.3 (May 1898): 55–105, 71.

83. Outside material in the archives, it is difficult to reconstruct reasons behind the migration as Tatars left few personal accounts of their experience during the war and migration. See Maria Sonevytsky, "Overhearing Indigenous Silence: Crimean Tatars during the Crimean War," in *Hearing the Crimean War: Wartime Sound and the Unmaking of Sense*, ed. Gavin Williams (Oxford: Oxford University Press, 2019). New Russian Governor General to Dolgorukov, 25 June1856, RGIA, f. 1287, op. 6, d. 1143 (O Posobiii poselentsam mestechka Balaklavy, pri vodvorenii ikh na prezhnikh mestakh zhitel'stva), ll. 8–9.

84. MVD Report, 10 June 1856, RGIA, f. 1287, op. 6, d. 1143, l. 6.

85. Stroganov to Zhukovskii, 7 July 1856, GAARK, f. 64, op. 1, d. 20968 (O vysylke iz Kamysha, Balaklava i drugikh mest inostrantsev, ostavshchikhsia v gubernii po vykhode inostrannykh voisk), l. 1.

86. Stroganov to Zhukovskii, 7 July 1856, GAARK, f. 64, op. 1, d. 20968, ll. 2–3.

87. Gendarme officer Shcherbechev (first name and patronymic unknown) to Zhukovskii, 18 Jun. 1855, GAARK, f. 64, op. 1, d. 20968, l. 6.

88. GAARK, f. 26, op.4, d. 1596 (O voennykh dezertirakh, ostavshikhsia v Kerchi posle ukhoda soiuznykh voisk, Karlo Menardi, P'ere Sharl' Berar i drug), ll. 3, 3 ob.

89. "Traktat zakluchennyi v Parizhe 18 (30) Marta 1856," in Tarle, *Krymskaia voina*, (unpaginated appendix).

90. GAARK, f. 64, op. 1, d. 20968, ll. 105–107.

91. Druzhinin, *Gosudarstvennyie Krest'iane i reforma P. D. Kiseleva*, 531.

92. PSZRI, 2nd ser., vol. 31, no. 30426 (24 April, 1856): 242.

93. Simferopol police files contain many, many cases of vagrants and wanderers after the war. See, for example, GAARK, f. 197, op. 1, d. 181, ll. 73, 118, 160, 242, 270–271, 316–318, 399, 431.

94. GAARK, f. 26, op. 2, d. 52, ll. 1–5.

95. Winfried Baumgart's monograph on the Peace of Paris does not discuss the refugees from the war, a question that was in fact very important in the peace process and the war's aftermath. See Winfried Baumgart, *The Peace of Paris*, cited in note 5.

96. GAARK, f. 26, op. 4, d. 1605, l. 1.

97. Ibid., l. 3.

98. GAARK, f. 26, op. 4, d. 1685 (Ob osvobozhdenii iz pod aresta i ot suda lits, zamechennnykh v snoshenii s nepriiatelem), l. 65.

99. RGIA, f. 1263 op. 1, delo 2552, l. 51.

100. Report about establishing property prices in Evpatoria District for mortgage transfers from the Treasury, GAARK, f. 327 op. 1, d. 999 (Ob uchrezhdenii komiteta po sozdaniiu zakonov stoimosti zemli, razrushennoi nepriiatelem), l. 13.

101. For a good synopsis of Russian attitudes toward German settlers, see Detlef Brandes, "A Success Story: The German Colonists in New Russia and Bessarabia: 1787–1914," *Acta Slavica Iaponica* 9 (1991): 32–46; and Willard Sunderland, *Taming the Wildfield: Colonization and Empire on the Russian Steppe* (Ithaca, NY: Cornell University Press, 2004), 82–83.

102. Nicholas Breyfogle, *Heretics and Colonizers: Forging Russia's Empire in the South Caucasus* (Ithaca, NY: Cornell University Press, 2005).

103. Muraviev, Untitled report to MGI, RGIA, f. 651, op. 1, d. 468, ll. 146–47 ob.

104. Druzhinin, *Gosudarstvennye Krest'iane i reforma P. D. Kiseleva*, 536–37.

105. Ibid., 571–76.

106. RGIA, f. 1263 op. 1, d. 2552, l. 51.
107. Muraviev, untitled MGI report, RGIA, f. 651, op. 1, d. 468, ll. 148, 148 ob.
108. Peter Holquist describes a similar settlement scheme for moving Cossacks into the Caucasus after the war, and relocating "hostile mountain tribes to the Kuban plains." Holquist argues that "Russian forces were not to clear land in order to settle Cossacks; rather, they were to settle Cossacks so as to clear the land of the native population"; Peter Holquist, "To Count, to Extract, and to Exterminate: Population Statistics and Population Politics in Late Imperial and Soviet Russia," in *A State of Nations: Empire and Nation-Making in the Age of Lenin and Stalin*, ed. Ronald Suny and Terry Martin (New York: Oxford University Press, 2001)," 117.
109. Evpatoria city chief to the Tauride Governor, 20 May 1856, GAARK, f. 26, op. 1, d. 20997, 136–137.

Chapter 9

1. Richard Wortman, *Scenarios of Power: Myth and Ceremony in Russian Monarchy* (Princeton, NJ: Princeton University Press, 2000), 2: 29–48.
2. See especially PSZRI, 2nd ser., vol. 31, no. 30877 (26 Aug. 1855), 785–99; and for changes to cantonist education, Yohanan Petrovsky-Shtern, *Jews in the Russian Army, 1827–1917* (Cambridge, UK: Cambridge University Press, 2009), 124–27.
3. PSZRI, 2nd ser., vol. 31 (for the military) nos: 30884, 30891, 30892, 30893, 30854, 30895 (26 Aug. 1856): 803, 809–13; and for the New Russian relief, nos. 30877; 30879; 30881; and 30882 (26 Aug.1856): 785–99, 802–4.
4. PSZRI, 2nd ser., vol. 31, no. 30881 (26 Aug. 1856): 803–4.
5. Ibid.
6. Ibid.
7. Bakunina, "Vospominaniia sestry miloserdiia Krestovozdvizhenskoi obshchiny," 75.
8. MVD meeting minutes, 22 Dec. 1856, RGIA, f. 560, op. 12, d. 346, l. 159.
9. Matthew Moten, *The Delafield Commission and the American Military Profession* (College Station: Texas A&M University Press), 148–49.
10. RGIA, f. 560, op. 12, d. 346, l. 159.
11. Stroganov to Alexander II, 17 June 1856, RGIA, f. 560, op. 12, d. 346, ll. 54–55.
12. RGIA, f. 560, op. 12, d. 346, 1860, l. 4.
13. Ibid., ll. 3–4.
14. Liudmila P. Marnei, "The Finances of the Russian Empire in the Period of the Patriotic War of 1812 and the Foreign Campaigns of the Russian Army," in *Russia and the Napoleonic Wars,* ed. Janet M. Hartley, Paul Keenan, and Dominic Lieven, 136–47 (New York: Palgrave McMillan, 2015), 137.
15. Alexander Martin, *Enlightened Metropolis: Constructing Imperial Moscow, 1762–1855* (Oxford: Oxford University Press, 2013), 211–12.
16. Stroganov to Alexander II, 17 June 1856, RGIA, f. 560, op. 12, d. 346, 1860, ll. 53–57.
17. B. Ts. Urlanis's important comparative study of the costs of war focuses on the armed forces, and not larger damages to civilian life property, industry, agriculture, etc. See B. Ts. Urlanis, *Istoriia voennykh poter'* (St. Petersburg: Izd. Poligon, 1994).
18. RGIA, f. 1263, op. 1, d. 2619 (Otchet gubernatora za 1856), l. 8 [pagination for the report begins on l. 578 of the larger delo].

19. MGI to Governor of Tauride, 3 Mar. 1856, GAARK, f. 26, op. 1, d. 20982 (O vspomoshchestvovanii obyvateliam Tavricheskoi gubernii ot kazny 3,000 pary volov), l. 3; and MGI to Governor of Tauride, "Instruktsiia" undated, GAARK, f. 26, op. 1, d. 20982, l. 36; MVD no. 1518, 21.

20. MGI to Governor of Tauride, 3 Mar. 1856, GAARK, f. 26, op. 1, d. 20982, l. 3

21. Ibid., l. 4.

22. Ibid., l. 3; and MGI to Governor of Tauride, "Instruktsiia" undated, GAARK, f. 26, op. 1, d. 20982, l. 37.

23. Tauride Department of the MGI to the Governor of Tauride, 20 Dec. 1856, GAARK, f. 26, op. 1, d. 20982, ll. 68, 155.

24. Karasubazar Village Duma Report to the Tauride Governor, 23 Feb. 1857, GAARK, f. 26, op. 1, d. 20982, l. 168.

25. MVD, no. 1518, "O vspomozheniiakh Novorossiiskomu kraiu," 19.

26. RGIA, f. 1287, op. 6, d. 1071 (O posobii chinovnikam, lishivshimsia imushchestva pri zaniatii nepriiatelem g. Ialta), l. 7.

27. RGIA, f. 1287, op. 6, d. 1071, l. 16.

28. MVD, 25 Oct. 1856, RGIA, f. 1287, op. 6, d. 1174, l. 12.

29. V. S. Rakov, *Moi vospominaniia o Evpatorii v epokhu Krymskoi voiny, 1853–1856* (Evpatoria: tip. M. L. Murovanskago, 1904), 49–51.

30. MVD, 25 Oct. 1856, RGIA, f. 1287, op. 6, d. 1174, l. 12.

31. Feodosia Customs agent, the Councilor Demovbrovskago to the Tauride Governor, 19 Jan. 1856, GAARK, f. 26, op. 4, d. 1634 (Raznie bumagi 1856 goda, po koim osobykh del nezavedeno), ll. 13, 22–23.

32. RGIA, f. 560, op. 12, d. 346, l. 55.

33. Stroganov to Alexander II, 17 June 1856, RGIA, f. 560, op. 12, d. 346, l. 55 ob.

34. Stroganov to Alexander II, 17 June 1856, "Doklad," RGIA, f. 560, op. 12, d. 346, l. 56.

35. PSZRI, 2nd ser., vol. 32, no. 31486 (5 Feb. 1857): 123.

36. "Doklad'" 14 Mar. 1856, RGIA, f. 651, op. 1, d. 416, ll. 16, 16 ob.

37. GAARK, f. 165, op. 1, d. 1 (Zhurnal Kerch-Enikal'skogo Komiteta), l. 1.

38. Ibid., ll. 24–27.

39. Golitsyn to Stroganov, 23 Apr. 1857, RGIA, f. 1287, op. 6, d. 1156, ch. 1, l. 106.

40. GAARK, f. 165, op. 1, d. 2 (Delo Kerchenskogo komiteta o poteriakh soldatki Stepanidy Afanas'evoi i ob okazanii ei posobiia za pogibshee imushchestvo g. Kerchi), ll. 1–3.

41. Ibid., ll. 4–5.

42. GAARK, f. 128, op. 1, d. 3 (O poteriakh ponesennykh Bakhchisaraiiskim meshchaninom Seid Ibraimom Osmanovom), ll. 1–14.

43. See chapter 4.

44. GAARK, f. 128, op. 1, d. 1 (Proshenie dvorianina Selimisha Murzyi Dzhankicheva), ll. 1–8.

45. Multiple reports regarding the Mavromikhailii property exist in MVD files, the last dated May 1862. See RGIA, f. 1287, op. 6, d. 1156, chast' 1, ll. 171; 189; 194–5.

46. "Proshenie," 23 June 1860, RGIA, f. 1287, op. 6, d. 1156, l. 296.

47. Marina Soroka and Charles A. Ruud, *Becoming a Romanov: Grand Duchess Elena and her World* (New York: Routledge, 2016), 118. Jude C. Richter, "Philanthropy and Welfare in Russia, 1914–18," in *Russia's Home Front in War and Revolution, 1914–22*, ed. Adele

Lindenmeyr, Christopher Read, and Peter Waldron (Bloomington: Slavica Publishers, 2016), 19–20.

48. RGIA, f. 1287, op. 6, d. 1272 (O podpiske v pol'zu razorennym zhiteliam Novorossiiskogo kraia), l. 5.

49. Ibid.

50. RGIA, f. 1287, op. 6, d. 1272, 367.

51. RGIA, f. 651, op. 1, d. 416, ll. 17, 17 ob.

52. Ibid., ll. 19, 19 ob.

53. PSZRI, 2nd ser., vol. 32, no. 31486 (5 Feb. 1857): 123–24; Stroganov to the Minister of Finance, 2 June 1856, f. 20, op. 3, d. 2326, l. 28. For a history of postwar tax reform, see Yanni Kotsonis, *States of Obligation: Taxes and Citizenship in the Russian Empire and Early Soviet Republic* (Toronto: University of Toronto Press, 2014).

54. V. Stepanov, "Krymskaia voina i ekonomika Rossii," *The Crimean War, 1853–1856: Colonial Skirmish or Rehearsal for World War? Empires, Nations and Individuals*, ed. Jerszy W. Borejsz (Warsaw: Wydawnictwo Neriton Instytut PAN, 2011), 280.

55. Peter Waldron, "State Finances," in *The Cambridge History of Russia: vol. II. Imperial Russia, 1689–1917*, ed. Dominic Lieven (Cambridge: Cambridge University Press), 468–87; Anon. "Finansovaia politika v period 1861–1880," *OZ* 11 (1882): 33; PSZRI, 2nd ser., vol. 29, no. 27934 (12 Feb. 1854) and no. 28530 (7 Sept. 1854): 758.

56. MVD to the Ministry of Finance, 20 Dec. 1856, f. 20, op. 3, d. 2326, l. 48.

57. Alison K. Smith, *For the Common Good and Their Own Well-Being: Social Estates in Imperial Russia* (New York and Oxford: Oxford University Press, 2014), 150–56.

58. "Proshenie," Evpatoria Merchants to the Minister of Finance, 6 Nov. 1862, f. 20, op. 3, d. 2326, l. 279.

59. MVD to the Minister of Finance, 20 Dec. 1856, f. 20, op. 3, d. 2326, ll. 51–52.

60. PSZRI, 2nd ser., vol. 32, no. 31486 (5 Feb. 1857): 124.

61. GAARK, f. 197, op. 1, d. 207 (Predpisaniia gubernatora o vyiasnenii kolichestva volonterov, byvshego grecheskogo legiona prozhivavshego v Simferopole, ne priniavshikh poddanstva Rossii), ll. 1–32.

62. Stroganov to Governor of Tauride, 10 Aug. 1856, GAARK, f. 327, op. 1, d. 999 (Ob uchrezhdenii komiteta po sozdaniiu zakonov stoimosti zemli, razrushen nepriiatelia), ll. 1–3.

63. Yalta Marshall of Nobility to the Minister of the Interior, 19 Sept. 1856, GAARK, f. 327, op. 1, d. 999, ll. 9–10.

64. Report about establishing property prices in Evpatoria District for mortgage transfers from the Treasury, GAARK, f. 327, op. 1, d. 999, l. 13.

65. M. I. Voronin and M. M. Voronina, *Pavel Melnikov and the Creation of the Railway System in Russia, 1804–1880*, trans. John C. Decker (Danville, PA: Languages of Montour Press, 1995), 43–45.

66. "Mirskoi Prigovor," 26 Feb. 1856, GAARK f. 27, op. 1, d. 6784 (Po raportu Feodosiiskoi Gorodovoi dumy gorodskikh zemel' obshchestvu zheleznykh dorog), l. 61.

67. The idea had origins in a government-backed merchant trading company established by Nichoas I. See W. E. Mosse, "Russia and the Levant, 1856–1862: Grand Duke Constantine and the Russian Steam Navigation Company," *JMH* 26.1 (Mar. 1954): 39–48.

68. Russkoe Obshchestvo parakhodstva i torgovli, *Putevoditel' Russkogo obshchestva parakhodstva i torgovli na 1912* (Moscow: tip. skoropechatnia A. A. Levenson, 1912), 1–21.

69. Grand Duke Constantine to Alexander II, quoted in D. A. Stepanov, "Uchrezhdenie Russkogo obshchestva parakhodstva i torgovli (1856–1857 gody)," *Vestnik Cheliabinskogo gosudarstvennogo universiteta*, no. 22 (2011): 31.

70. GAARK, f. 26, op. 1, d. 21224 (O soobshchennii Novorossiiskomu i Bessarabskomu General-gubernatoru svedenii o merakh k pooshchreniiu torgovogo morekhodstva i sudostroeniia), ll. 1–42; the archbishop in Odessa was an early investor in the Steamship company, and applied earned capital to support postwar renewal of the monasteries in Crimea. See Mara Kozelsky, *Christianizing Crimea: Shaping Sacred Space in the Russian Empire and Beyond* (DeKalb: Northern Illinois University Press, 2010), 68–69, 159.

71. Chuck Veit, *The Yankee Expedition to Sebastopol: John Gowen and the Raising of the Black Sea Fleet, 1857–1862* (Attleboro, MA: Lulu.com, 2014), 29. Veit's important work is the only book to examine the raising of the Black Sea fleet in detail.

72. Veit, *The Yankee Expedition to Sebastopol*, 219.

73. Voronin and Voronina, *Pavel Melnikov and the Creation of the Railway System in Russia*, 48–49; Richard Mowbray Haywood, *Russia Enters the Railway Age, 1842–1855* (Boulder, CO: East European Monographs, 1998), 577–92; G. M. Agofin, ed., *Kratkie svedeniia o razvitii otechestvennykh zheleznykh dorog s 1838 po 1990* (Moscow: MPS RF, 1995), 21.

74. The Military Governor of Simferopol and Tauride to Stroganov, GAARK, f. 26, op. 1, d. 21224, ll. 36–42.

75. A. A. Orlov, "Anglo-Rossiiskii 'Krymskii' diplomaticheskii konflikt, 1856–1868," *Novaia i noveishaia istoriia*, no. 3 (2002). http://vivovoco.astronet.ru/VV/PAPERS/HISTORY/CRIME_A.HTM#4.

76. Evgeny Markov, *Ocherki Kryma: Kartiny Krymskoi Zhizni, istorii i prirody* (1872; repr., St. Petersburg: M. O. Vol'f, 1902), 74–75.

77. Ibid., 74–76.

78. A. S. Lukomskii, "Ocherki iz moei zhizni," *VI* 1 (2001): 94–95, 112. Lukomskii attributes regeneration of the city to the 1877–1878 war and the Lozovo-Sevastopol railway.

79. Rakov, *Moi vospominaniia*, 54.

80. A. Ivanov, "Kinburn," *ITUAK*, 31 (1901): 27–29.

81. Untitled report signed by a committee of Crimean nobility, 19 Sept. 1856, GAARK, f. 327, op. 1, d. 999, ll. 57–58.

82. "Proshenie," 6 Nov. 1862, The Tauride Treasury to the Department of Collections/Ministry of Finance, RGIA, f. 20, op. 3, d. 2326, ll. 279, 368.

83. Murav'ev, untitled MGI report, RGIA, f. 651, op. 1, d. 468, l. 150.

84. Ibid., l. 3.

85. Austin Jersild, *Orientalism and Empire: North Caucasus Mountain Peoples and the Georgian Frontier* (Montreal: McGill-Queen's University Press, 2002), 23.

86. Brian Glyn Williams, "Hijra and Forced Migration from Nineteenth Century Russia to the Ottoman Empire," *Cahiers du monde Russe* 41/1 Janvier-Mars (2000): 79–108.

87. Kemal H. Karpat, *Ottoman Population, 1830–1914: Demographic and Social Characteristics* (Madison: University of Wisconsin Press, 1985), 62. See also James Meyer, *Turks across Empires: Marketing Identity in the Russian-Ottoman Borderlands, 1856–1914* (Oxford: Oxford University Press, 2014), 9–11.

88. See discussions of religion and violence in the literature cited chapter 1, n. 80.

89. Stroganov to Lanskoi, 10 Aug. 1859, RGIA f. 651, op. 1, d. 468, l. 235.

90. Murav'ev, untitled MGI report, RGIA, f. 651, op. 1, d. 468, ll. 9–10.

91. Stroganov to Lanskoi, 9 Sept. 1860, f. 1287, op. 6, d. 1710, l. 4.

92. Anonymous report to Lanskoi, RGIA, f. 651, op. 1, d. 468, l. 161 ob.

93. "Zapiska o vyselenii Tatar iz Kryma," unsigned and undated, RGIA, f. 1287, op. 6, d. 1710, l. 70.

94. Ibid.

Chapter 10

1. GAARK, f. 52, op. 1, d. 1, l. 46.

2. Ibid., l. 15.

3. Ibid., l. 34.

4. Muraviev, untitled MGI report, RGIA f. 651, op. 1, d. 468, ll. 9–11.

5. RGIA, f. 651, op. 1, d. 470 (Raport musul'manskogo sviashchenosluzhitelia Aleksandr Usmanov Bagdanovich v Tavricheskoe Magometanskoe Dukhovnoe Pravlenie s zaprosom o prichinakh pereseleniia tatar Krymskogo poluostrova v Turtsuiu), l. 1.

6. MVD, "O vyselenii Tatar iz Kryma," 22 Nov. 1860, RGIA, f. 1287, op. 6, d. 1710, ll. 83, 83 ob.

7. The Committee of Ministers ordered the Tatar petitions gathered by Vasilchikov be transferred to MGI. These reports appear to have been stored in RGIA f. 383, op. 17, d. 21728, which according to RGIA records, no longer exists.

8. Totleben to Dolgorukov, 15 Nov. 1860, RGIA, f. 651, op. 1, d. 468, ll. 106, 112.

9. Lampsei to Vasilchikov, "O prichinakh pereseleniia Krymskikh tatar v Turstiiu (1861)," Feb. 1861, RGIA, f. 651, op.1, d. 471 (Zapiska perekopskogo uezdnogo predvoditelia dvorianstva Simferopolia), l. 2.

10. Lampsei to Vasilchikov, Feb. 1861, RGIA, f. 651, op.1, d. 471, l. 3.

11. Journal of the Committee of Ministers, 30th May, 6 and 20th of June 1861," RGIA, f. 1287, op. 6, d. 1710, ll. 104–105 ob.

12. For analysis of the importance of Senatorial Reviews for calling provinces back to order, see A. N. Biktasheva's *Kazanskie gubernatory v dialogakh vlastei: pervaia polovina XIX veka* (Kazan: Natsional'nyi muzei respubliki Tatarstan, 2008).

13. RGIA, f. 1287, op. 6, d. 1710, ll. 107–108.

14. Ibid., l. 110.

15. Ibid., ll. 113–23.

16. See GAARK, f. 315, op. 1, d. 947 (O postroike na vakif zemle doma nadvornyi sovetnika Raiiskim," 1854–1869) ll. 1–33.

17. See Hakan Kırımlı, "Emigrations from the Crimea to the Ottoman Empire during the Crimean War," *Middle Eastern Studies*, 44.5 (2008): 751–73; and Catalina Hunt, "Changing Identities at the Fringes of the Late Ottoman Empire: The Muslims of Dobruca, 1839–1914," (PhD diss. Ohio State University, 2015).

18. Kozelsky, "Casualties of Conflict," 889.

19. Letter from Councilor Gengros to Muraviev, 15 Sept. 1860, GAARK, f. 1287, op. 6, d. 1710, ll. 8–10.

20. GAARK, f. 26, op. 1, d. 24129 (Vysochaishe utverzhdennye pravila o zaselenii Kryma i Tavricheskoi Gubernii Russkimi i inostrannymi pereselentsami 1860), ll. 63–64.

21. Kozelsky, *Christianizing Crimea*, 152–55.

22. GAOO, f. 37, op. 1, d. 1790 (Ob uchrezhdenii eparkhii v Tavride), l. 4.

23. Ibid., l. 5–7.

24. Ibid., l. 13–14.

25. Aleksandr Nakropin, "Iz vospominanii o preosviashchennom Innokentii Arkhiepiskope Khersonskom i Tavricheskom," *Tavricheskie eparkhial'nye vedomosti* 2 (1880): 68–90.

26. A. V. Ishin, "Deiatel'nost' Arkhiepiskopa Tavricheskogo Turiia (G. P. Karpova)," *Novosti/Zhurnaly "Istoricheskoe nasledie Kryma,* 5 (2005), http://www.commonuments.crimea-portal.gov.ua/rus/index.php?v = 1&tek = 89&par = 74&l = &art = 350.

27. Gul'nara Abdulaeva, "Krymskie Tatary v Vostochnoi (Krymskoi) Voine," *Advet* (22 Jan. 2007): 11.

28. Markov, *Ocherki Kryma*, 104–5.

29. Ibid., 103.

30. A few Tatars returned, but not in significant enough numbers to offset Crimea's larger demographic change. See Tavricheskii Gubernskii Statisticheskii Komitet, "Vyselenie Tatar iz Tavricheskoi gubernii," ed. K. V. Khanatskii, *Pamiatnaia Kniga Tavricheskoi Gubernii* (Simferopol: tip. Tavr. Gub. Pravlenii, 1867), 416–33; Gul'nara Bekirova, *Krym i Krymskie Tatary* (Moscow: tip. Moskovskii Izd. Dom, 2005), 11–29; B. M. Vol'fson, "Emigratsiia Krymskikh Tatar v 1860 g.," *Istoricheskie zapiski* 9 (1940), 186–97.

31. Specifically here I am referring to migration within Europe, not the mass out migration from Europe to the United States, Africa and Asia.

32. See for example the classic migration study by Leslie Page Moch, *Moving Europeans: Migration in Western Europe since 1650*, 2nd edition (Bloomington: Indiana University Press, 1992).

33. For a summary of this literature see *Russian Ottoman Borderlands*, ed. Lucien Frary and Mara Kozelsky (Madison: University of Wisconsin Press, 2014), 3–34.

34. Kemal H. Karpat, *Ottoman Population, 1830–1914: Demographic and Social Characteristics* (Madison: University of Wisconsin Press, 1985), 66.

35. Seipp, *Ordeal of Peace*, 1–18.

36. For Anglophone works addressing a more complex origin of the Great Reforms, see Terrence Emmons, *The Russian Landed Gentry and the Peasant Emancipation of 1861* (Cambridge: Cambridge University Press, 1968); W. Bruce Lincoln, *The Great Reforms: Autocracy, Bureaucracy, and the Politics of Change in Imperial Russia* (DeKalb: Northern Illinois University Press, 1990); Ben Eklof, John Bushnell, and Larissa Zakharova, eds., *Russia's Great Reforms, 1855–1881* (Bloomington: Indiana University Press, 1994); and *Filosofskii vek al'manakh* (6) produced for the 200th anniversary of Nicholas I: *Rossiia v nikolaevskoe vremia: nauka, politika, prosveshchenie* (St. Petersburg: Sankt-peterburgskii tsentr istorii idei, 1998).

37. Druzhinin, *Gosudarstvennyie Krest'iane i reforma P. D. Kiseleva*; P. A. Zaionchkovskii, *The Abolition of Serfdom in Russia*, ed. and trans. Susan Wobst, introduction by Terrence Emmons (Gulf Breeze, FL: Academic International Press, 1978).

38. Jacob Kipp, "The Grand Duke Konstantin Nikolaevich and the Epoch of Great Reforms, 1855–1866" (PhD diss., The Pennsylvania State University Graduate School, 1970); and Richard Mowbray Haywood, *Russia Enters the Railway Age, 1842–1855* (Boulder, CO: East

European Monographs, 1998). Telegraph lines also were laid to connect cities at the front with the imperial center.

39. For more on local self-government, see Rita S. Guenther, "One Local Vote at a Time: Electoral Practices of Kazan Province, 1766–1916" (PhD diss., Georgetown University, 2011), 90–143.

40. Vyzhimov, "Tambovskie gubernskie vedomosti" kak istochnik izucheniia patrioticheskoi deiatel'nosti zhitelei gubernii v period Krymskoi voiny 1853–1856 gg." *Vestnik Tomskogo gosudarstvennogo universiteta,* 2.46 (2007): 129–31.

41. Alexis Peri, "Heroes, Cowards and Traitors: The Crimean War and Its Challenge to Russian Autocracy," *Berkeley Program in Soviet and Post-Soviet Working Papers Series* (Institute of East European and Eurasian Studies, University of California, Berkeley, Summer, 2008); Serhii Plokhy, "The City of Glory: Sevastopol in Russian Historical Mythology," *Journal of Contemporary History,* 35.3 (July 2000): 369–83; and Olga Maiorova, *From the Shadow of Empire: Defining the Russian Nation through Cultural Mythology, 1855–1870* (Madison: University of Wisconsin Press, 2010).

42. See Totleben's report to Dolgorukov, 15 Nov. 1860, RGIA, f. 651, op. 1, d. 468, ll. 106–20. Excerpts of Totleben's notes were published nearly immediately by A. I. Herzen and N. P. Ogarev, in *Kolokol* no. 117 (1861): 973–77 under the title "Gonenie na Krymskikh Tatar." Three decades later, more detailed publication appeared in *Russkaia Starina* as "O vyselenii tatar iz Kryma v 1860 gody," *Russkaia Starina,* vol. 78 (1893): 531–50; F. K. Zatler, *Zapiski o prodovol'stvii voisk v voennoe vremia,* 3 vols. (St. Petersburg: tip. Torgovogo doma S. Strugovshikova, 1860).

43. N. I. Pirogov, *Sevastopol'skiia pis'ma N. I. Pirogova 1854–1855,* ed. Iu. G. Malis (St. Petersburg: tip. M. Merkusheva, 1907); E. M. Bakunina, "Vospominaniia sestry miloserdiia Krestovozdvizhenskoi obshchiny, 1854–1860," *Vestnik Evropy* 191.3 (May 1898).

44. For details, see Tim Coates, *Delane's War: How Front-Line Reports from the Crimean War Brought Down the British Government* (London: Biteback Books, 2009).

45. See, for example, Jeffrey Brooks, *When Russia Learned to Read: Literacy and Popular Culture, 1861–1917* (Princeton, NJ: Princeton University Press, 1985). To be fair, however, Brooks does note that Russian military schools introduced literacy into curriculum in 1855, and he describes a "surge of books and print" during the war (19; 96). Louise Reynolds, in contrast, skips over the Crimean War in her survey of the origins of the press to credit Alexander II. See Louise McReynolds, *The News under Russia's Old Regime: The Development of a Mass Circulation Press* (Princeton, NJ: Princeton University Press, 1991), 21–24.

46. Elena Campbell, *The Muslim Question and Russian Imperial Governance* (Bloomington: Indiana University Press, 2015), 21–32.

47. Robert Crews, *For Prophet and Tsar: Islam and Empire in Russia and Central Asia* (Harvard University Press, 2006), 300–16, 205–6.

48. James Meyer, *Turks across Empires: Marketing Identity in the Russian-Ottoman Borderlands, 1856–1914* (Oxford: Oxford University Press, 2014), 66–80.

49. Irma Kreitin, "A Colonial Experiment in Cleansing: the Russian Conquest of Western Caucasus, 1856–1865," *Journal of Genocide Research* 11.2/3 (2009): 213–41; Pavel Polian, *Against Their Will: The History and Geography of Forced Migrations in the USSR* (Budapest: Central European University Press, 2004), 22.

50. L. G. Beskrovnyi, *The Russian Army and Fleet in the Nineteenth Century: Handbook of Armaments, Personnel and Policy,* ed. and trans. Gordon E. Smith (Gulf Breeze, FL: Academic International Press, 1996), 23.

SELECTED BIBLIOGRAPHY

Abbreviations

Archives

RGIA   Rossiiskii gosudarstvennyi istoricheskii arkhiv
RGVIA   Rossiiskii gosudarstvennyi voenno-istoricheskii arkhiv
RNB   Otdel rukopisei. Rossiiskii Natsional'naia Biblioteka
GAOO   Gosudarstvennyi Arkhiv Odesskoi Oblasti
GAARK   Gosudarstvennyi Arkhiv v Avtonomnoi Respublike Krym

Journals, Newspapers, Reference Works

AI   *Ab Imperio*
ASI   *Acta Slavica Iaponica*
AHR   *American Historical Review*
ASEER   *American Slavic and East European Review*
CSP   *Canadian Slavonic Papers/Revue canadienne des slavistes*
GK   *Golos Kryma*
ITUAK   *Izvestiia Tavricheskoi Uchenoi Arkhivnoi Kommissii*
JGO   *Jahrbücher für Geschichte Osteuropas*
JMH   *Journal of Modern History*
Kritika: *Explorations in Russian and Eurasian History*
NK   *Novorossiiskii Kalendar'*
OZ   *Otechestvennye zapiski*
PSZRI   *Polnoe sobranie zakonov Rossiiskoi imperii*
RR   *Russian Review*
RS   *Russkaia Starina*
RBS   *Russkii biograficheskii slovar'*

RV   *Russkii Vestnik*
SP   *Severnaia Pchela*
SR   *Slavic Review*
SEER   *Slavonic and East European Review*
VI   *Voprosy Istorii*

Archival Notation

f.   *fond* (collection)
op.   *opis* (inventory)
d.   *delo* (file)
l., ll.   *list listy* (folio, folios)

Archives

Rossiiskii gosudarstvennyi istoricheskii arkhiv (RGIA)

Fond 20: Department torgovli i manufaktur/MF
Fond 383: Pervyi Department Ministerstva Gosudarstvennykh Imushchestv
Fond 560: Obshchaia kantseliariia ministra finansov
Fond 651: Vasil'chikovi
Fond 796: Kantseliaria sinoda
Fond 797: Kantseliaria ober-prokurora sinoda
Fond 1263: Komitet Ministrov (1802–1906)
Fond 1287: Khoziaistvennyii department MVD
Fond 821: Department Dukhovnykh Del Inostrannykh Ispovedanii MVD

Rossiiskii gosudarstvennyi voenno-istoricheskii arkhiv (RGVIA)

Fond 846: Voenno-uchenyi Arkhiv

Otdel rukopisei. Rossiiskii Natsional'naia Biblioteka (RNB)

Fond 313: Lichnyi arkhivnyi fond Arkhiepiskopa Innokentiia

Gosudarstvennyi Arkhiv Odesskoi Oblasti (GAOO)

Fond 1: Kantseliarii Novorossii i Bessarabii
Fond 37: Khersonskaia Dukhovnaia Konsistoriia

Gosudarstvennyi Arkhiv v Avtonomnoi Respublike Krym (GAARK)

Fond 26: Kantseliariia Tavriskogo gubernatora
Fond 27: Tavriskoe gubernskoe pravlenie
Fond 52: Tavricheskii gubernskii komitet po uluchsheniiu byta pomeshchich'ikh krest'ian
Fond 64: Bakhchisaraiskii gorodskaia uprava
Fond 128: Simferopol'skii uezdnyi komitet, uchrezhdennyi dlia predostavleniia pomoshchi zhiteliam uezda postradavshim ot voiny 1853–56
Fond 165: Kerchenskii gorodskoi komitet o privedenii vedomosti ubytkov i okazaniia pomoshchii zhiteliam Kerch-Enikal'skogo gradonachal'stva, g. Feodosiia i Feodoskogo uezda

Fond 197: Simferopol'skaia Gorodskaia Politsiia
Fond 315: Tavricheskoe Magometanskoe dukhovnie sobranie
Fond 327: Kantseliariia Tavricheskogo gubernskogo predvoditelia dvorianstva

Books and articles

Abdulaeva, Gul'nara. "Krymskie Tatary v Vostochnoi (Krymskoi) Voine." *Advet* (22 Jan. 2007): 11.

Abdulaeva, Gul'nara. "Murzy kak soslovie v Krymskom Khanstve." *Advet* (16 June 2014). http://avdet.org/node/9674. Accessed May 31, 2016.

Abdullaev, Ibraim. "Mechet Kryma." *GK*, Aug. 1, 1997: 5.

Agofin, G. M. ed., *Kratkie svedeniia o razvitii otechestvennykh zheleznykh dorog s 1838 po 1990*. Moscow: MPS RF, 1995.

Allen, W. E. D., and Paul Muratoff. *Caucasian Battlefields: A History of the Wars on the Turco-Caucasian Border, 1828–1921*. Cambridge: Cambridge University Press, 1953.

Almond, Ian. *Two Faiths, One Banner: When Muslims Marched with Christians across Europe's Battlegrounds*. Cambridge, MA: Harvard University Press, 2009.

Amanton, Victor. *Notices sur les diverses populations du gouvernment de la Tauride et spécialement de la Crimée; moeus & usages des Tatars de la Crimée*. Besançon: Imprimerie de J. Bonvalot, 1854.

Anon. "Fedor Karlovich Zatler." *Rossiiskii Biograficheskii Slovar'*. Petrograd: tip. Glavnogo upravleniia udelov, 1916, 7: 270–73.

Anon. "Balaklava." *NK 1846* (Odessa, 1845): 338–42.

Anon. "The Crimean War. Section II. The Loss of Money." *The Advocate of Peace* (1869): 117–21.

Anon. "Finansovaia politika v period 1861–1880." *OZ* 11 (1882): 1–35.

Anon. "Narodno-naselenie Novorossiiskogo Kraia i Bessarabii." *NK 1856* (Odessa, 1855): 104.

Babenko, G. A., and V. P. Diulichev. *Tavricheskaia Guberniia: Istoriia v ocherkakh*. Simferopol: Tavriia, 2009.

Badem, Candan. *The Ottoman Crimean War* (1853–1856). London: Brill, 2010.

Bakunina, E. M. "Vospominaniia sestry miloserdiia Krestovozdvizhenskoi obshchiny, 1854–1860." *Vestnik Evropy* 190.2 (March–April 1898): 132–76; 515–56; and 191.3 (May 1898): 55–105.

Balas, M. K. *Istoriko-statisticheskii ocherk vinodeliia v Rossii (Kavkaz i Krym)*. St. Petersburg: Obshchestvennaia Pol'za, 1877.

Barker, A. J. *Vainglorious War*. London: Weidenfeld and Nicolson, 1971.

Baron, Nick. "New Spatial Histories of Twentieth-Century Russia and the Soviet Union: Surveying the Landscape." *JGO* 55.3 (2007): 374–401.

Barrett, Thomas. *At the Edge of Empire: The Terek Cossacks and the North Caucasus Frontier, 1700–1860*. Boulder, CO: Westview Press, 1999.

Barsukov, N. P., ed. *Zhizn' i trudy M. P. Pogodina*, 3 vols. St. Petersburg: M. M. Stasiulk, 1899.

Bassin, Mark, Christopher Ely, and Melissa K. Stockdale. *Space, Place and Power in Modern Russia: Essays in the New Spatial History*. DeKalb: Northern Illinois University Press, 2010.

Baumgart, Winfried. *The Crimean War: 1853–1856*. London: Bloomsbury Academic Press, 1999.

Baumgart, Winfried. *The Peace of Paris 1856: Studies in War, Diplomacy, and Peacemaking*, translated by Ann Pottinger Saab. Oxford: ABC-Clio, 1981.

Bazancourt, César Lecat, baron de. *The Crimean Expedition to the Capture of Sevastopol: Chronicles of the War in the East, from Its Commencement to the Signing of the Treaty of Peace*, translated by Robert Howe Gould, 2 vols. London: Sampson Low, Son & Co, 1856.

Beaulieu, Paul LeRoy. *Contemporary Wars (1853–1866): Statistical Researches Representing the Loss of Men and Money Involved in Them*, translated by the London Peace Society. London: Harriett and Sons, 1869.

Bekirova, Gul'nara. *Krym i Krymskie Tatary*. Moscow: tip. Moskovskii Izd. Dom, 2005.

Bell, David. *The First Total War: Napoleon's Europe and the Birth of Warfare as We Know It*. Boston: Mariner Books, 2007.

Bernstein, Laurie. *Sonia's Daughters: Prostitutes and Their Regulation in Imperial Russia*. Berkeley, CA: University of California Press, 1995.

Beskrovnyi, L. G. *The Russian Army and Fleet in the Nineteenth Century: Handbook of Armaments, Personnel and Policy*, edited and translated by Gordon E. Smith. Gulf Breeze, FL: Academic International Press, 1996.

Beskrovnyi, L. G. *Russkoe voennoe iskustvo XIXv*. Moscow: izd. Nauka, 1974.

Bezugol'nyi, A. Iu., N.F. Kovalevskii, and V. E. Kovalev. *Istoriia voenno-okruzhnoi sistemy v Rossii*. Moscow: Tsentrpoligraf, 2012.

Biktasheva, A. N. *Kazanskie gubernatory v dialogakh vlastei: pervaia polovina XIX veka*. Kazan: Natsional'nyi muzei respubliki Tatarstan, 2008.

Bogdanovich, M. I. *Vostochnaia Voina, 1853–1856*, 4 vols. St. Petersburg: tip. F. Sushchinko, 1876.

Bradley, Joseph. "Subjects into Citizens: Societies, Civil Society, and Autocracy in Tsarist Russia." *AHR* 107.4 (2002): 1094–123.

Brandes, Detlef. "A Success Story: The German Colonists in New Russia and Bessarabia: 1787–1914." *ASI* 9 (1991): 32–46.

Breyfogle, Nicholas. *Heretics and Colonizers: Forging Russia's Empire in the South Caucasus*. Ithaca, NY: Cornell University Press, 2005.

Brighton, Terry. *Hell Riders: The Truth about the Charge of the Light Brigade*. London: Viking, 2004.

Brooks, Jeffrey. *When Russia Learned to Read: Literacy and Popular Culture, 1861–1917*. Princeton, NJ: Princeton University Press, 1985.

Brooks, Willis. "Russia's Conquest and Pacification of the Caucasus: Relocation becomes a Pogrom in the Post-Crimean War Period." *Nationalities Papers* 23.4 (1995): 675–86.

Brower, Daniel R., and Edward J. Lazzerini. *Russia's Orient: Imperial Borderlands and Peoples, 1700–1917*. Bloomington: Indiana University Press, 1997.

Burds, Jeffrey. "A Culture of Denunciation: Peasant Labor Migration and Religious Anathematization in Rural Russia, 1860–1905." *JMH* 68 (Dec. 1996): 786–818.

Calthorpe, Somerset J. Gough, and George Cadogan, illustrator. *Cadogan's Crimea*. New York: Atheneum, 1980; text originally published as Somerset J. Gough Calthorpe, *Letters from Headquarters by a Staff Officer*, 1856.

Campbell, Elena. *The Muslim Question and Russian Imperial Governance*. Bloomington: Indiana University Press, 2015.

Chambers, Thomas A. *Memories of War: Visiting Battlefields and Bonegrounds in the Early American Republic*. Ithaca, NY: Cornell University Press, 2012.

Chaplinskii, Georgii. "Vospominaniia o Sevastopol'skoi oborone." In *Sbornik Rukopisei predstavlennykh ego imperatorskomu vysochestvu gosudariu nasledniku tsesarevichu o Sevastopol'skoi oborone sevastopol'stami*. St. Petersburg: tip. A Transheliia, 1872.

Clemens, Samuel. *Innocents Abroad*. Hartford, CT: American Publishing Company, 1869.

Coates, Tim. *Delane's War: How Front-Line Reports from the Crimean War Brought Down the British Government*. London: Biteback Books, 2009.

Codman, John. *An American Transport in the Crimean War*. New York: Bonnell, Silver and Co., 1897.

Coleman, Heather. *Orthodox Christianity in Imperial Russia: A Sourcebook on Lived Religion*. Bloomington: Indiana University Press, 2014.

Crews, Robert. "Empire and the Confessional State: Islam and Religious Politics in Nineteenth Century Russia." *AHR* 108.1 (2003): 50–83.

Crews, Robert. *For Prophet and Tsar: Islam and Empire in Russia and Central Asia*. Harvard University Press, 2006.

Curtiss, John Shelton. *The Russian Army under Nicholas I, 1825–1855*. Durham, NC: Duke University Press, 1965.

Curtiss, John Shelton. *Russia's Crimean War*. Durham, NC: Duke University Press, 1979.

Curtiss, John Shelton. "Russian Sisters of Mercy in the Crimea," *SR* 25, no. 1 (Mar. 1996): 84–100.

Daly, John. *Russian Seapower and "the Eastern Question," 1827–1841*. Annapolis, MD: Naval Institute Press, 1991.

Demidov, Anatoly. *Travels in the Crimea: Through Hungary, Wallachia, and Moldavia, During the Year 1837*. London: John Mitchell, 1853.

Dewar, Captain A. C., ed., *Russian War, 1855: Black Sea Official Correspondence*. London: Navy Records Society, 1965.

Dickinson, Sarah. "Russia's first 'Orient': Characterizing the Crimea in 1787." *Kritika* 3.1 (2002): 3–25.

Didukh, O. V. *Donskie kazaki v Krymskoi voine 1853–1856 gg*. Moscow: VINITI, 2007.

Dmitriev, V. V. "Sravnitel'naia kharakteristika razvitiia Kerch'-Enikal'skogo gradonachal'stva do i posle Krymskoi voiny." In *Vostochnaia (Krymskaia) voina, 1853–1856, Novye materialy i novoe osmyslenie*, edited by E. A. Popova, Vol. 1, 51–55. Simferopol: Krymskii Arkhiv, 2005.

Druckers, Peter. *The Crimean War at Sea: Naval Campaigns Against Russia, 1854–56*. Barnsley, Yorkshire: Pen and Sword Books, 2011.

Druzhinin, N. M. *Gosudarstvennye Krest'iane i reforma P. D. Kiseleva*, 2 vols. Moscow: Isdatel'stvo Akademii Nauk SSSR, 1958.

Dubrovin, N. F., ed. *Materialy dlia istorii krymskoi voiny i oborony Sevastopolia*, 5 vols. St. Petersburg: Tip. Departmenta Udelov, 1871–1874.

Dubrovin, N. F. *Vostochnaia Voina: 1853–1856*. St. Petersburg: tip. Imperatorskoi akademii nauk, 1878.

Duncan, Peter J. S. *Russian Messianism: Third Rome, Revolution, Communism and After*. New York: Routledge, 2000.

Duran, James A., Jr. "Catherine II, Potemkin and Colonization Policy in Southern Russia." *RR* 28.1 (1969): 23–36.

Dzhelil, Seid Efendi. "Vozzvanie Tavricheskogo muftiia Seid-Dzhelil'-Efendiia vsemu musul'manskomu dukhovenstvu i narodu, v Tavricheskoi gubernii obitaiushchim." In *Materialy dlia istorii krymskoi voiny i oborony Sevastopolia*, edited by N. F. Dubrovin, Vol. 1, 249–51. St. Petersburg: tip. Departmenta Udelov, 1871–1874.

Easley, Roxanne. *The Emancipation of the Serfs in Russia: Peace Arbitrators and the Development of Civil Society*. New York: Routledge, 2011.

Edgerton, Robert B. *Death or Glory: The Legacy of the Crimean War*. Boulder, CO: Westview Press, 1999.

Eklof, Ben, John Bushnell, and Larissa Zakharova, eds. *Russia's Great Reforms, 1855–1881.* Bloomington: Indiana University Press, 1994.

El'iashevich, B. S. *Karaimskii biograficheskii slovar' (s kontsa VIII v. do 1960).* Moscow: RAN, 1993.

Ellens, J. Harold, ed. *The Destructive Power of Religion: Violence in Judaism, Christianity and Islam,* 4 vols. Westport, CT: Praeger, 2004.

Emmons, Terrence. *The Russian Landed Gentry and the Peasant Emancipation of 1861.* Cambridge: Cambridge University Press, 1968.

Erickson, Ann K. "E. V. Tarle: The Career of a Historian under the Soviet Regime." *ASEER* 19.2 (1960): 202–16.

Fairey, Jack. *The Great Powers and Orthodox Christendom: The Crisis over the Eastern Church in the Era of the Crimean War.* New York: Palgrave MacMillan, 2015.

Field, Daniel. *End of Serfdom: Nobility and Bureaucracy in Russia, 1855–61.* Cambridge, MA: Harvard University Press, 1976.

Figes, Orlando. *The Crimean War: A History.* Metropolitan Books, 2011.

Filaret (Drozdov), Metropolitan of Moscow. *Sobraniia mnenii i otzyvov Filareta mitropolita moskovskogo i kolomenskogo po delam pravoslavnoi tserkvi na vostoke.* St. Petersburg: Synodal'naia tip., 1886.

Filosofskii vek almanakh: Rossiia v nikolaevskoe vremia: nauka, politika, prosveshchenie, 6. St. Petersburg: Sankt-peterburgskii tsentr istorii idei, 1998.

Fisher, Alan W. *Crimean Tatars.* Stanford, CA: Stanford University Press, 1986.

Fisher, Alan W. "Emigration of Muslims from the Russian Empire in the Years after the Crimean War." *JGO* 35.3 (1987): 356–71.

Fisher, Alan W. "Enlightened Despotism and Islam Under Catherine II." *SR* 27.4 (1968): 542–53.

Fisher, Alan. *The Russian Annexation of Crimea, 1772–1783.* Cambridge: University Press, 1970.

Florescu, Radu. *The Struggle against Russia in the Romanian Principalities.* Iaşi: The Center for Romanian Studies, 1997.

Frary, Lucien. *Russia and the Making of Modern Greek Identity, 1821–1844.* Oxford: Oxford University Press, 2015.

Frary, Lucien, and Mara Kozelsky. *Russian Ottoman Borderlands: The Eastern Question Reconsidered.* Madison: University of Wisconsin Press, 2014.

Fuller, William. "Civilians in Russian Military Courts, 1881–1904." *RR* 41.3 (1982): 288–305.

Fuller, William. *The Foe Within: Fantasies and the End of Imperial Russia.* Ithaca, NY: Cornell University Press, 2006.

Fuller, William. *Strategy and Power in Russia, 1600–1914.* New York: Macmillan, 1992.

Gabrielian, O. A., ed. *Krymskie Repatrianty: Deportatsiia, Vozvrashchenie, i Obustroistvo.* Simferopol: Amena, 1998.

Gatrell, Peter. *A Whole Empire Walking: Refugees in Russia During World War I.* Bloomington: Indiana University Press, 1999.

Gavrilov, S. V. "Problemy razvitiia intendantskogo snabzheniia russkoi armii nakanune Vostochnoi (Krymskoi) voiny 1853–1856 goda." *Sbornik voenno-nauchnykh statei voennoi akademii,* no. 49.61 (2008): 437–45.

Gavrilov, S. V. "Razvitie material'nogo snabzheniia russkoi armii v XIX veke." PhD diss., Voennaia akademiia tyla i transporta imeni generala armii A. V. Khruleva, St. Petersburg, 2010.

Gavrilov, S. V. "Reformirovanie sistemy material'nogo snabzheniia russkoi armii vo vtoroi polovine XIX veka." *Izvestiia Rossiiskogo gosudarstvennogo pedagogicheskogo universiteta im. A. I. Gertsena,* no. 115 (2009): 22–31.

Geirot, A. F. *Opisanie vostochnoi voiny.* St. Petersburg: Eduard Gonik, 1872.

Geraci, Robert P., and Michael Khodarkovsky, eds. *Of Religion and Empire: Missions, Conversion, and Tolerance in Tsarist Russia.* Ithaca, NY: Cornell University Press, 2002.

Geraci, Robert P. *Window on the East: National and Imperial Identities in Late Tsarist Russia.* Ithaca, NY: Cornell University Press, 2001.

Gill, Geoffrey, Sean Burrell, and Jody Brown. "Fear and Frustration—The Liverpool Cholera Riots of 1832." *The Lancet* 358 (2001): 233–37.

Gleason, Abbott. "The Great Reforms and the Historians since Stalin." In *Russia's Great Reforms, 1855–1881,* edited by Ben Eklof, John Bushnell, and Larissa Zakharova, 1–16. Bloomington: Indiana University Press, 1994.

Goldfrank, David M. "The Holy Sepulcher and the Origin of the Crimean War." In *The Military and Society in Russia: 1450–1917,* edited by Eric Lohr and Marshal Poe, 491–505. Leiden: Brill, 2002.

Goldfrank, David M. "Introduction." In *The Crimean (Eastern War): 1853–1856 Filmed from the Holdings of the Military Science Archive at the Russian State Archive of Military History in Moscow,* v–vii. Reading, England: Thomson Gale, 2004.

Goldfrank, David M. *The Origins of the Crimean War.* New York: Longman, 1994.

Goldfrank, David M. "Policy Traditions and the Menshikov Mission of 1853." In *Imperial Russian Foreign Policy,* edited by Hugh Ragsdale, 119–58. Cambridge: Cambridge University Press, 1993.

Goldman, Wendy Z., and Donald Filtzer, eds. *Hunger and War: Food Provisioning in the Soviet Union during WWII.* Bloomington: Indiana University Press, 2015.

Gowing, Timothy. *A Soldier's Experience, or A Voice from the Ranks Showing the Cost of War in Blood and Treasure.* Norwich: W. H. Stevens, 1884.

Guenther, Rita S. "One Local Vote at a Time: Electoral Practices of Kazan Province, 1766–1916." PhD diss., Georgetown University, 2011.

Harris, Stephen M. *British Military Intelligence in the Crimean War.* London: Frank Cass, 1999.

Hartley, Janet M. "Partiotism in the Provinces." In *Russia and the Napoleonic Wars,* edited by Janet M. Hartley, Paul Keenan, and Dominic Lieven, 148–162. New York: Palgrave McMillan, 2015.

Hartley, Janet M. *Russia 1762–1825: Military Power, the State, and the People.* Westport, CT: Praeger Publishers, 2008.

Haywood, Richard Mowbray. *Russia Enters the Railway Age, 1842–1855.* Boulder: East European Monographs, 1998.

Herlihy, Patricia. *Odessa: A History 1794–1914.* Cambridge, MA: Harvard Ukrainian Institute, 1986.

Hodasevich (Chodasiewicz), Robert Adolf. *A Voice from Within The Walls of Sebastopol: a Narrative of the Campaign in the Crimea and of the Events of the Siege.* London: John Murray, 1856.

Hoffman, David L. *Cultivating the Masses: Modern State Practices and Soviet Socialism.* Ithaca, NY: Cornell University Press, 2011.

Hokanson, Katya. "Pushkin's Captive Crimea: Imperialism in the Fountain of Bakhchisarai." In *Russian Subjects: Empire, Nation, and the Culture of the Golden Age,* edited by Monika

Greenleaf and Stephen Moeller-Sally, 123–150. Evanston, IL: Northwestern University Press, 1998.

Holquist, Peter. "Forms of Violence during the Russian Occupation of Ottoman Territory and Northern Persia: Urimia and Astrabad, Oct. 1914–Dec. 1917." In *The Shatterzone of Empires: Coexistence and Violence in the German, Habsburg, Russian and Ottoman Borderlands*, edited by Eric D. Weitz and Omer Bartov, 344–61. Bloomington: Indiana University Press, 2003.

Holquist, Peter. "Information Is the Alpha and Omega of Our Work: Bolshevik Surveillance in Its Pan-European Context." *Journal of Modern History* 69 (1997): 415–60.

Holquist, Peter. *Making War, Forging Revolution: Russia's Continuum of Crisis, 1914–1921.* Cambridge, MA: Harvard University Press, 2002.

Holquist, Peter. "To Count, to Extract, to Exterminate: Population Statistics and Population Politics in Late Imperial and Soviet Russia." In *A State of Nations: Empire and Nation-Making in the Age of Lenin and Stalin*, edited by Ronald Suny and Terry Martin, 111–43. New York: Oxford University Press, 2001.

Hunt, Catalina. "Changing Identities at the Fringes of the Late Ottoman Empire: The Muslims of Dobruca, 1839–1914." PhD diss., Ohio State University, 2015.

Innokentii (Borisov), Archbishop. "Zapiski o vosstanovlenii drevnikh sviatykh mest po goram krymskim." *ITUAK* 5 (1888): 81–105.

Ishin, A. V. "Deiatel'nost' Arkhiepiskopa Tavricheskogo Turiia (G. P. Karpova)." *Novosti/Zhurnaly Istoricheskoe nasledie Kryma*, 5 (2005). http://www.commonuments.crimea-portal.gov.ua/rus/index.php?v = 1&tek = 89&par = 74&l = &art = 350.

Ivanov, A. "Kinburn." *ITUAK*, no. 31 (1901): 27–29.

Jersild, Austin. *Orientalism and Empire: North Caucasus Mountain Peoples and the Georgian Frontier.* Montreal: McGill-Queen's University Press, 2002.

Jobst, Kerstin S. "The Crimea as a Russian Mythical Landscape (18th–20th Century)." In *Mythical Landscapes Then and Now: The Mythification of Landscapes in Search for National Identity*, edited by Judith Peltz and Ruth Büttner, 78–91. Yerevan: Yerevan State University, 2006.

Johnson, Steven. *The Ghost Map: The Story of London's Most Terrifying Epidemic, and How It Changed Science, Cities and the Modern World.* New York: Riverhead Books, 2006.

Juergensmeyer, Mark. *Terror in the Mind of God: The Global Rise of Religious Violence.* Berkeley: University of California Press, 2000.

Kagan, Frederick W. *The Military Reforms of Nicholas I: The Origins of the Modern Russian Army.* New York: St. Martin's Press, 1999.

Kagan, Frederick W. "Russia's Small Wars, 1805–1861." In *The Military History of Tsarist Russia*, edited by Kagan and Robin Higham, 123–37. New York: Palgrave McMillan, 2002.

Karpat, Kemal H. *Ottoman Population, 1830–1914: Demographic and Social Characteristics.* Madison: University of Wisconsin Press, 1985.

Keep, John. *Soldiers of the Tsar: Army and Society in Russia, 1462–1874.* Oxford: Clarendon Press, 1985.

Kelly, Christine, ed. *Mrs. Duberly's War: Journal and Letters from the Crimea, 1854–1856.* Oxford: Oxford University Press, 2007.

Kelly, General Sir Richard Denis. *An Officer's Letters to His Wife during the Crimean War.* London: Elliot Stock, 1902.

Kent, Neil. *Crimea: A History.* London: C. Hurst and Co., 2016.

Khalid, Adeeb. "Russian History and the Debate over Orientalism." *Kritika* 1.4 (2000): 691–99.

Khaÿrutdinov, Ramil. "The Tatar Ratusha of Kazan: National Self Administration in Autocratic Russia, 1781–1855." In *Islam and Politics in Russia and Central Asia (Early Eighteenth to Late Twentieth Centuries)*, edited by Stephane A. Dudoignon and Komatsu Hisao, 27–42. New York: Routledge, 2001.

Khomiakov, A. S. *Stikhotvoreniia i dramy.* Leningrad: Sov. pisatel', 1969.

Khrushchev, Aleksandr. *Istoriia oborony Sevastopolia.* St. Petersburg: tip. V. V. Komarova, 1889.

Kimball, Charles. *When Religion Becomes Evil.* New York: Harper Collins, 2008.

King, Charles. *The Ghost of Freedom: A History of the Caucasus.* Oxford: Oxford University Press, 2008.

Kinglake, Alexander. *The Invasion of Crimea,* 9 vols. London and Edinburgh: W. Blackwood and Sons, 1863–1887.

Kırımlı, Hakan. "Emigrations from the Crimea to the Ottoman Empire during the Crimean War." *Middle Eastern Studies,* 44.5 (2008): 751–73.

Kırımlı, Hakan. "Krymskie Tatary i Osmanskaia imperiia vo vremia Krymskoi voiny." In *The Crimean War (1853–1856): Colonial Skirmish or Rehearsal for World War,* edited by Jerszy W. Borejsza, 333–50. Warsaw: Wydawnictwo Neriton Instytut PAN, 2011.

Kırımlı, Hakan. "O Krymskotatarskikh voiskakh v sostave Osmanskoi armii v period Krymskoi voiny." *GK,* Oct. 31, 2003: 7.

Kirmse, Stefan B. "Law and Empire in Late Tsarist Russia: Muslim Tatars Go to Court." *SR* 72.4 (Winter 2013): 778–801.

Kipp, Jacob. "The Grand Duke Konstantin Nikolaevich and the Epoch of Great Reforms, 1855–1866." PhD diss., Pennsylvania State University Graduate School, 1970.

Komovskii, A. D. "Pod gromom Krymskoi Voiny," *RV* (1878), 134.1: 163–97, 165–66.

Korostelina, Karina. "Deportation from Crimea." In *Why They Die: Civilian Devastation in Violent Conflict,* edited by Daniel Rothbart and Karina Korostelina, 44–57. Ann Arbor: University of Michigan Press, 2011.

Kozelsky, Mara. "Casualties of Conflict: Crimean Tatars During the Crimean War." *SR* 67.4 (2008): 862–91.

Kozelsky, Mara. *Christianizing Crimea: Shaping Sacred Space in the Russian Empire and Beyond.* DeKalb: Northern Illinois University Press, 2010.

Kozelsky, Mara. "The Crimean War and the Tatar Exodus." In *Russian Ottoman Borderlands,* edited by Lucien Frary and Mara Kozelsky, 165–92. Madison: Wisconsin University Press, 2014.

Kozelsky, Mara. "Religion and the Crisis in Ukraine." *International Journal for the Study of the Christian Church* 14.3 (2014): 219–41.

Kozlov, S. Ia., and L. V. Chizhova. *Tiurskie narody Kryma: Karaimy, Krymskie Tatary, Krymchaki.* Moscow: Nauka, 2003.

Kreitin, Irma. "A Colonial Experiment in Cleansing: The Russian Conquest of Western Caucasus, 1856–1865." *Journal of Genocide Research* 11.2–3 (2009): 213–41.

Lambert, Andrew. *The Crimean War: British Grand Strategy against Russia, 1854–1856,* 2nd ed. Farnham, England: Ashgate, 2011.

Layton, Susan. "Russian Military Tourism: The Crisis of the Crimean War Period." In *Turizm: the Russian and East European Tourist under Capitalism and Socialism,* edited by Anne E. Gorsuch and Dianne P. Koenker, 43–63. Ithaca, NY: Cornell University Press, 2006.

Lazzerini, Edward James. "Ismail Bey Gasprinskii and Muslim Modernism in Russia, 1878–1914." PhD diss., University of Washington, 1973.

Lazzerini, Edward James. "Ismail Bey Gasprinskii (Gaspirali): The Discourse of Modernism and the Russians." In *The Tatars of Crimea: Return to the Homeland*, edited by E. A. Allworth, 48–70. Durham: Duke University Press, 1998.

Leont'ev, K. N. *Sobrianie sochinenii K. Leont'eva.* Edited V. M. Sablin. St. Petersburg: Rus. kn. t-vo, 1912.

Lieven, Dominic. *Russia against Napoleon: The True Story of the Campaigns of War and Peace.* New York: Penguin Books, 2009.

Lih, Lars. *Bread and Authority in Russia, 1914–1921.* Berkeley: University of California Press, 1990.

Lincoln, W. Bruce. "Count P. D. Kiselev: A Reformer in Imperial Russia." *Australian Journal of Politics and History* 16.2 (1970): 177–86.

Lincoln, W. Bruce. "The Genesis of an 'Enlightened' Bureaucracy in Russia, 1825–1856." *JGO* (Sept. 1972): 321–30.

Lincoln, W. Bruce. *The Great Reforms: Autocracy, Bureaucracy, and the Politics of Change in Imperial Russia.* DeKalb: Northern Illinois University Press, 1990.

Lincoln, W. Bruce. *In the Vanguard of Reform: Russia's Enlightened Bureaucrats, 1825–1861.* DeKalb: Northern Illinois University Press, 1982.

Lindenmyr, Adele. *Poverty Is Not a Vice: Charity, Society, and the State in Imperial Russia.* Princeton, NJ: Princeton University Press, 1996.

Lindenmyr, Adele. "Primordial or Gelatinous? Civil Society in Imperial Russia." *Kritika* 12.3 (2011): 705–20.

Lindenmyr, Adele, Christopher Read, and Peter Waldron, eds. *Russia's Home Front in War and Revolution, 1914–1922*, Vol. 3, Book 2. Bloomington, IN: Slavica Publishers, 2011.

Lloyd, David William. *Battlefield Tourism: Pilgrimage and the Commemoration of the Great War in Britain, Australia and Canada, 1919–1939.* Oxford: Berg Publishers, 1998.

Lohr, Eric. *Nationalizing the Russian Empire: The Campaign against Enemy Aliens during World War I.* Cambridge, MA: Harvard University Press, 2003.

Lynn, John A. *Feeding Mars: Logistics in Western Warfare from the Middle Ages to the Present.* Boulder, CO: Westview, 1993.

Lukomskii, A. S. "Ocherki iz moei zhizni," *VI* 1 (2001): 89–113.

MacNeal, Robert H. *Tsar and Cossack 1855–1914.* New York: St. Martin's Press, 1987.

Maiorova, Olga. *From the Shadow of Empire: Defining the Russian Nation through Cultural Mythology, 1855–1870.* Madison: University of Wisconsin Press, 2010.

Maiorova, Olga. "Searching for a New Language of Collective Self: The Symbolism of Russian National Belonging before and after the Crimean War." *AI* 4 (2006): 187–224.

Makarii (Bulgakov), Metropolitan. *Istoriia russkoi tserkvi: Istoriia khristianstva v Rossii do ravnoapostol'nogo kniazia Vladimira kak vvedenie v istoriiu russkoi tserkvi*, Vol. 1. Moscow: izd. Spaso-Preobrazhenskogo Valaamskogo monastyria, 1994.

Markevich, A. I. "Pereseleniia Krymskikh Tatar v Turtsiiu v sviazi s dvizheniem naseleniia v Krymu." *Izvestiia Akademii Nauk SSSR*, otd. gumanitarnykh nauk, Vol. 1 (1928): 375–405; and Vol. 2 (1929): 1–16.

Markevich, A. I. *Tavricheskaia guberniia vo vremia Krymskoi Voiny po arkhivnym materialam.* 1905; repr., Simferopol: Tavrida, 1994.

Markov, Evgeny. *Ocherki Kryma: Kartiny Krymskoi Zhizni, istorii i prirody*. 1872; repr., St. Petersburg: M. O. Vol'f, 1902.

Marnei, Liudmila P. "The Finances of the Russian Empire in the Period of the Patriotic War of 1812 and the Foreign Campaigns of the Russian Army." In *Russia and the Napoleonic Wars*, edited by Janet M. Hartley, Paul Keenan, and Dominic Lieven, 136–147. New York: Palgrave Macmillan, 2015.

Martin, Alexander M. *Enlightened Metropolis: Constructing Imperial Moscow, 1762–1855*. Oxford: Oxford University Press, 2013.

Martin, Alexander M. *Romantics, Reformers, Reactionaries: Russian Conservative Thought and Politics in the Reign of Alexander I*. DeKalb: Northern Illinois University Press, 1997.

Marx, Karl. *The Eastern Question: A Reprint of Letters written 1853–1856 Dealing with the Events of the Crimean War*, edited by Eleanor Marx Aveling and Edward Aveling. London: Swan Sonnenschein & Co., 1897.

McClellan, George B. *The Armies of Europe: Comprising Descriptions in Detail of the Systems of England, France, Russia, Prussia, Austria, and Sardinia, Adapting Their Advantages to All Arms of the United States Service*. Philadelphia: J. B. Lippincott, 1861.

McGrew, Roderick E. *Russia and the Cholera, 1823–1832*. Madison: University of Wisconsin Press, 1965.

McReynolds, Louise. *The News Under Russia's Old Regime: The Development of a Mass Circulation Press*. Princeton, NJ: Princeton University Press, 1991.

Mel'nikova, L. V. *Russkaia Pravoslavnaia Tserkov' i Krymskaia Voina*. Moscow: Kuchkovo pole, 2012.

Mends, Bowen Stilton. *Life of Sir Admiral Mends G. C. B. Late Director of Transport*. London: John Murray, 1899.

Menning, Bruce. *Bayonets before Bullets: The Imperial Russian Army, 1861–1914*. Bloomington: Indiana University Press, 2000.

Menning, Bruce. "A Decade Half Full: Post–Cold War Studies in Russian and Soviet Military History." *Kritika* 2.2 (Spring 2001): 341–62.

Meyer, James. "Immigration, Return, and the Politics of Citizenship: Russian Muslims in the Ottoman Empire, 1860–1914." *International Journal of Middle East Studies* 39.1 (2007): 9–26.

Meyer, James. *Turks across Empires: Marketing Identity in the Russian-Ottoman Borderlands, 1856–1914*. Oxford: Oxford University Press, 2014.

Mikhno, Nikolai. "Iz Zapisok Chinovnika o Krymskoi Voine." In *Materialy dlia istorii krymskoi voiny i oborony Sevastopolia*, edited by N. F. Dubrovin, 5 vols. St. Petersburg: tip. Departmenta Udelov, 1871–1874, 3:1–35.

Milner, Rev. Thomas. *The Crimea, Its Ancient and Modern History: The Khans, the Sultans, and the Czars. With Notices of Its Scenery andPpopulation*. London: Longman, Brown, Green, and Longmans, 1855.

Moch, Leslie Page. *Moving Europeans: Migration in Western Europe since 1650*, 2nd ed. Bloomington: Indiana University Press, 1992.

Moon, David. "Russian Peasant Volunteers at the Beginning of the Crimean War." *SR* 51.4 (1992): 691–704.

Monas, Sidney. *The Third Section: Police and Society Under Nicholas I*. Cambridge, MA: Harvard University Press, 1961.

Mosse, W. E. "How Russia Made Peace September 1855 to April 1856." *Cambridge Historical Journal* 11, no. 3 (1955): 297–316.

Mosse, W. E. "Russia and the Levant, 1856–1862: Grand Duke Constantine Nicolaevich and the Russian Steam Navigation Company." *JMH* 26.1 (Mar. 1954): 39–48.

Mosse, W. E. *Alexander the II and the Modernization of Russia*. New York: Collier Press, 1958.

Moskoff, William. *The Bread of Affliction: The Food Supply in the USSR during WWII*. Cambridge: Cambridge University Press, 2002.

Mostashari, Firouzeh. *On the Religious Frontier: Tsarist Russia and Islam in the Caucasus*. London: I. B. Tauris, 2006.

Moten, Matthew. *The Delafield Commission and the American Military Profession*. College Station: Texas A&M University Press.

Muftizade, Izmail. "Ocherk voennoi sluzhby krymskikh tatar, s 1783 po 1899 god (po arkhivnym materialiam)." *ITUAK* 30.20 (1899): 1–24.

Muraviev, N. N. *Voina za Kavkazom v 1855*. St. Petersburg, 1863.

N. N. "Desiatoe sentiabria 1854 goda v Simferopole." In *Materialy dlia istorii krymskoi voiny i oborony Sevastopolia*, edited by N. F. Dubrovin, 3: 37–40. St. Petersburg: tip. Departmenta Udelov, 1872.

Naganawa, Norihiro. "A Civil Society in a Confessional State? Muslim Philanthropy in the Volga-Urals Region." In *Russia's Home Front in War and Revolution, 1914–1922*: Vol. 3, Book 2, edited by Adele Lindemeyr, Christopher Read, and Peter Waldron, 59–78. Bloomington, IN: Slavica Publishers, 2011.

Nakropin, Aleksandr. "Iz vospominanii o preosviashchennom Innokentii Arkhiepiskope Khersonskom i Tavricheskom." *Tavricheskie eparkhial'nye vedomosti* 2 (1880): 68–90.

Naumova, Iu. A. *Ranenie, Bolezn' i Smert': Russkaia Meditsinskaia sluzhba v Krymskuiu voinu, 1853–56 gg*. Moscow: Modest Kolerov, 2010.

Nikitin, Ivan Savvich. *Kulak*. Moscow: tip. Kakova, 1858.

Norris, Stephen M. *A War of Images: Russian Popular Prints, Wartime Culture, and National Identity, 1812–1945*. DeKalb: Northern Illinois University Press.

Ogarev, Nikolai. "Monologi: Chego khochu." *Stikhotvoreniia N. Ogareva*. Moskva: tip. Aleksandra Semenova, 1856.

Ogle, Nicholas Reed. *Rear Admiral Thomas MacKenzie: Life and Times with the Black Sea and Azov Sea Command, 1783–1786*. http://stephenhicks.net/genealogy/getperson. php?personID = I1436&tree = 1. Accessed May 17, 2015.

O'Neill, Kelly. "Between Subversion and Submission: The Integration of the Crimean Khanate into the Russian Empire, 1783–1853." PhD diss., Harvard University, 2006.

O'Neill, Kelly. *Claiming Crimea: A History of Catherine the Great's Southern Empire*. New Haven, CT: Yale University Press, 2017.

O'Neill, Kelly. "Constructing Imperial Identity in the Borderland: Architecture, Islam, and the Renovation of the Crimean Landscape." *AI* 2 (2006): 163–191.

Orlov, A. A. "Anglo-Rossiiskii 'Krymskii' diplomaticheskii konflikt, 1856–1868." *Novaia i noveishaia istoriia*, no. 3 (2002). http://vivovoco.astronet.ru/VV/PAPERS/HISTORY/ CRIME_A.HTM#4.

Orlovsky, Daniel T. *The Ministry of Interior Affairs*. Cambridge, MA: Harvard University Press, 1981.

Paget, George. *The Light Cavalry Brigade in the Crimea: Extracts from the Letters and Journals of the Late George Paget*. London: John Murray, 1881.

Panesh, A. D. *Zapadnaia Cherkesiia v sisteme vzaimodeistviia rossii s turtsiei, angliei, i imamatom shamiilia v XIXv (do 1864)*. Maikop: Adygeiskii respublikanskii institut gumanitarnykh issledovanii im. T. M. Kerasheva, 2007.

Peri, Alexis. "Heroes, Cowards and Traitors: The Crimean War and Its Challenge to Russian Autocracy." *Berkeley Program in Soviet and post-Soviet Working Papers Series*. Institute of East European and Eurasian Studies, University of California, Berkeley, Summer 2008.

Petrovsky-Shtern, Yohanan. *Jews in the Russian Army, 1827–1917*. Cambridge, UK: Cambridge University Press, 2009.

Pinson, Marc. "Demographic Warfare—An Aspect of Ottoman and Russian Policy, 1854–1866." PhD diss., Harvard University, 1970.

Rowney, Don Karl, and Walter Pintner. *Russian Officialdom: The Bureaucratization of Russian Society from the Seventeenth to the Twentieth Century*. Chapel Hill: University of North Carolina Press, 1980.

Pirogov, N. I. *Sevastopol'skiia pis'ma N. I. Pirogova 1854–1855*, edited by Iu. G. Malis. St. Petersburg: tip. M. Merkusheva, 1907.

Plokhy, Serhii. "The City of Glory: Sevastopol in Russian Historical Mythology." *Journal of Contemporary History* 35.3 (July 2000): 369–83.

Polian, Pavel. *Against Their Will: The History and Geography of Forced Migrations in the USSR*. Budapest: Central European University Press, 2004.

Porter, Curtis Hunter. *Mikhail Petrovich Pogodin and the Development of Russian Nationalism, 1800–1856*. PhD diss., Vanderbilt University, 1973.

"Postanovlenie Tavricheskogo magometanskogo dukhovnogo pravleniia ot 6-go oktiabria." In *Materialy dlia istorii krymskoi voiny i oborony Sevastopolia*, edited by N. F. Dubrovin, 4:17–18. St. Petersburg: tip. Departmenta Udelov, 1872.

Prinzing, Friedrich. *Epidemics Resulting from Wars*. Oxford: Clarendon Press, 1916.

"Proshenie deputatov nogaiskogo plemeni, ot 12-go oktiabria." In *Materialy dlia istorii krymskoi voiny i oborony Sevastopolia*, edited by N. F. Dubrovin, 4:18–19. St. Petersburg: tip. Departmenta Udelov, 1872.

Prousis, Theophilus. "Russian Philorthodox Relief during the Greek War of Independence." *Modern Greek Studies Yearbook* 1 (1985): 31–60.

Prousis, Theophilus. *Russian Society and the Greek Revolution*. DeKalb: Northern Illinois University Press, 1994.

Rakov, V. S. *Moi vospominaniia o Evpatorii v epokhu Krymskoi voiny, 1853–1856*. Evpatoria: tip. M. L. Murovanskago, 1904.

Raleigh, Donald. *Experiencing Russia's Civil War: Politics, Society and Revolutionary Culture in Saratov*. Princeton, NJ: Princeton University Press, 2002.

Rath, Andrew C. *The Crimean War in Imperial Context, 1854–1856*. New York: Palgrave Macmillan, 2015.

Reiber, Alfred. *Politics of Autocracy: Letters of Alexander II to Prince A. I. Bariatinskii 1857–1864*. Paris: Moulton and Co., 1966.

Riasanovsky, Nicholas V. *Nicholas I and Official Nationality in Russia, 1825–1855*. Berkeley: California University Press, 1959.

Riasanovsky, Nicholas V. *Russia and the West and the Teachings of the Slavophils*. Cambridge, MA: Harvard University Press, 1952.

Rich, David. "Imperialism, Reform and Strategy: Russian Military Statistics, 1840–1880." *SEER* 74.4 (1996): 621–39.

Richter, Jude C. "Philanthropy and Welfare in Russia, 1914–1918." In *Russia's Home Front in War and Revolution, 1914–1922* Vol. 3, Book 2, edited by Adele Lindemeyr, Christopher Read, and Peter Waldron, 11–29. Bloomington, IN: Slavica Publishers, 2011.

Robson, Roy R. *The Story of Russia Told through Its Most Remarkable Islands*. New Haven, CT: Yale University Press, 2004.

Rothbart, Daniel, and Karina Korostelina, eds. *Why They Die: Civilian Devastation in Violent Conflict*. Ann Arbor: University of Michigan Press, 2011.

Royle, Trevor. *Crimea: The Great Crimean War, 1854–1856*. New York: St. Martin's Press, 2000.

Russkoe Obshchestvo parakhodstva i torgovli. *Putevoditel' Russkogo obshchestva parakhodstva i torgovli na 1912*. Moscow: tip. skoropechatnia A. A. Levenson, 1912.

Ruud, Charles. *Fighting Words: Imperial Censorship and the Russian Press, 1804–1906*. Toronto: University of Toronto Press, 1982; reprint 2009.

Sakovich, A. V., and G. N. Grzhibovskaia, eds., *Evpatoria v gody Krymskoi voiny (1854–1856)*. Simferopol: AntikvA, 2007.

Sapozhnikov, S. A. "Shevchenko i Blarambergi Mavromikhaili," *Nauchnye Zapiski I. T.Sh.* (Institute of Taras Shevchenko), Tetrad' 6, http://www.it-shevchenko.ru/index.php/ytsh.html. Accessed May 17, 2015.

Schönle, Andreas. "Garden of the Empire. Catherine's Appropriation of the Crimea." *SR* 60 (2001): 1–23.

Schwartz, Regina. *The Curse of Cain: The Violent Legacy of Monotheism*. Chicago: University of Chicago Press, 1997.

Seipp, Adam R. *The Ordeal of Peace: Demobilization and the Urban Experience in Britain and Germany, 1917–1921*. Burlington, VT: Ashgate, 2009.

Shavshin, V. G. *Balaklava*. Simferopol: Tavria, 1994.

Shavshin, V. G. *Sevastopol' v istorii Krymskoi Voiny*. Sevastopol: Teleskop, 2004.

Shepherd, John A. *The Crimean Doctors: A History of the British Medical Service during the Crimean War*. Liverpool, UK: Liverpool University Press, 1991.

Seacole, Mary. *Wonderful Adventures of Mary Seacole in Many Lands*. London: James Blackwood Paternaster Row, 1857.

Selegnut, Charles. *Sacred Fury: Understanding Religious Violence*. Lanham, MD: Altamira, 2003.

Shirokorod, A. B. *Russko-Turetskie Voiny: 1676–1918*. Moscow: AST, 2000.

Skal'kovskii, A. A. *Opyt' statisticheskogo opisaniia novorossiiskogo kraia, chast' 1, Geografiia, etnografiia, i narodoschislenie Novorossiiskogo kraia*. Odessa: tip. L. Nichte, 1850.

Smith, Alison K. *For the Common Good and Their Own Well-Being: Social Estates in Imperial Russia*. New York: Oxford University Press, 2014.

Soroka, Marina, and Charles A. Ruud. *Becoming a Romanov: Grand Duchess Elena and Her World*. New York: Routledge, 2016.

Squire, P. S. *The Third Department: The Establishment and Practices of the Political Police in the Russia of Nicholas I*. Cambridge: Cambridge University Press, 1968.

Staples, John R. *Cross Cultural Encounters on the Ukrainian Steppe: Settling the Molochna Basin*. Toronto: University of Toronto Press, 2003.

Steinwedel, Charles. *Threads of Empire Loyalty and Tsarist Authority in Bashkiria, 1552–1917*. Bloomington: Indiana University Press, 2016.

Stepanov, D. A. "Uchrezhdenie Russkogo obshchestva parakhodstva i torgovli, 1856–1857 gody." *Vestnik Cheliabinskogo gosudarstvennogo universiteta* 22 (2011): 30–38.

Stepanov, V. "Krymskaia voina i ekonomika Rossii." In *The Crimean War, 1853–1856: Colonial Skirmish or Rehearsal for World War? Empires, Nations and Individuals*, edited by Jerszy W. Borejsza, 275–89. Warsaw: Wydawnictwo Neriton Instytut PAN, 2011.

Stone, David R. *A Military History of Russia: From Ivan the Terrible to the War in Chechnya*. London: Westport, 2006.

Sunderland, Willard. "Peasants on the Move: State Peasant Resettlement in Imperial Russia, 1805–1830s." *RR* 52.4 (2007): 472–85.

Sunderland, Willard. *Taming the Wildfield: Colonization and Empire on the Russian steppe.* Ithaca, NY: Cornell University Press, 2004.

Taki, Victor. "From Partisan War to the Ethnography of European Turkey: The Balkan Career of Ivan Liprandi, 1790–1880." *CSP* 58.3 (September 2016): 257–285.

Tarle, E. V. *Gorod Russkoi Slavy: Sevastopol' v 1854–1855 gg.* Moscow: Voenizdat, 1954.

Tarle, E. V. *Krymskaia voina*, 2 vols. Moscow: Akademiia Nauk SSSR, 1944.

Tarle, E. V. *Napoleon's Invasion of Russia, 1812.* New York: Oxford University Press, 1942.

Tatishchev, S. S. *Imperator Aleksandr II, ego zhizn' i tsarstvovanie*, 2 vols. St. Petersburg: A. S. Suvorin, 1911.

Tavricheskii Gubernskii Statisticheskii Komitet. "Vyselenie Tatar iz Tavricheskoi gubernii." In *Pamiatnaia Kniga Tavricheskoi Gubenii*, edited by K. V. Khanatskii, 416–33. Simferopol: tip. Tavr. Gub. Pravlenii, 1867.

Taylor, Brian D. *Politics and the Russian Army: Civil-Military Relations, 1689–2000.* Cambridge, UK: Cambridge University Press, 2003.

Thomas, Arthur. "The U.S. Military Commission to the Crimean War and Its Influence on the U.S. Army before the American Civil War." PhD diss., University of Kansas, 1993.

Tolstoi, Lev Nikolaevich. *Polnoe Sobranie Sochinenii.* 90 vols. Moscow: izd. Khudozhestvennaia literatura, 1935.

Tolstoy (Tolstoi), Leo. *The Sebastopol Sketches*, translated by D. McDuff. London: Penguin, 1986.

Totleben, E. I. "Gonenie na Krymskikh Tatar." *Kolokol* 117 (1861): 973–77.

Totleben, E. I. *Opisanie Oborony g. Sevastopolia*, 2 vols. St. Petersburg: tip. I. Tiblena i komp., 1863.

Totleben, E. I. "O vyselenii tatar iz Kryma v 1860 gody." *RS* 78 (1893): 531–50.

Treadgold, Donald W. "Was Stolypin in Favor of Kulaks?" *ASEER* 14.1 (1955): 1–14.

Urlanis, B. Ts. *Istoriia voennykh poter'.* St. Petersburg: Izd. Poligon, 1994.

Van Creveld, Martin. *Supplying War: Logistics from Wallenstein to Patton.* Cambridge University Press, Cambridge, 1995.

Veit, Chuck. *The Yankee Expedition to Sebastopol: John Gowen and the Raising of the Black Sea Fleet, 1857–1862.* Attleboro, MA: Lulu.com, 2014.

Vinogradov, V. N. "The Personal Responsibility of Emperor Nicholas I for the Coming of the Crimean War: An Episode in the Diplomatic Struggle in the Eastern Question." In *Imperial Russian Foreign Policy*, edited by Hugh Ragsdale, 159–70. Cambridge: Cambridge University Press, 1993.

Vol'fson, B. M. "Emigratsiia Krymskikh Tatar v 1860 g." *Istoricheskie zapiski* 9 (1940): 186–97.

Voronin, M. I., and M. M. Voronina. *Pavel Melnikov and the Creation of the Railway System in Russia, 1804–1880*, translated by John C. Decker. Danville, PA: Languages of Montour Press, 1995.

Vozgrin, V. E. *Istoricheskie sud'by krymskikh tatar.* Moscow: Mysl', 1992.

Vyzhimov, E. D. "'Tambovskie gubernskie vedomosti" kak istochnik izucheniia patrioticheskoi deiatel'nosti zhitelei gubernii v period Krymskoi voiny 1853–1856 gg." *Vestnik Tomskogo gosudarstvennogo universiteta* 2.46 (2007): 129–31.

Waldron, Peter. "State finances." In *The Cambridge History of Russia, Vol. II. Imperial Russia, 1689–1917.* edited by Dominic Lieven. Cambridge: Cambridge University Press.

Wcislo, Francis William. *Reforming Rural Russia: State, Local Society, and National Politics, 1855–1914.* Princeton, NJ: Princeton University Press, 1990.

Weitz Eric D., and Omer Bartov, eds. *The Shatterzone of Empires: Coexistence and Violence in the German, Habsburg, Russian and Ottoman Borderlands.* Bloomington: Indiana University Press, 2003.

Werth, Paul W. *At the Margins of Orthodoxy: Mission, Governance and Confessional Politics in Russia's Volga-Kama Region, 1827–1905.* Ithaca, NY: Cornell University Press, 2002.

Werth, Paul W. *The Tsar's Foreign Faiths: Toleration and the Fate of Religious Freedom in Imperial Russia.* Oxford: Oxford University Press, 2014.

Whittaker, Cynthia H. "The Ideology of Sergei Uvarov: An Interpretive Essay." *RR* 37.2 (1978): 158–76.

Whittaker, Cynthia H. *The Origins of Modern Russian Education: An Intellectual Biography of Count Sergei Uvarov, 1786–1855.* DeKalb: Northern Illinois University Press, 1984.

Williams, Brian Glyn. *The Crimean Tatars: From Soviet Genocide to Putin's Conquest.* London: C. Hurst and Co., 2015.

Williams, Brian Glyn. "Hijra and Forced Migration from Nineteenth-Century Russia to the Ottoman Empire." *Cahiers du monde Russe.* 41/1 Janvier-Mars (2000): 79–108.

Williams, Gavin. *Hearing the Crimean War: Wartime Sound and the Unmaking of Sense.* Oxford: Oxford University Press, 2019.

Wirtschafter, Elise. *From Serf to Russian Soldier.* Princeton, NJ: Princeton University Press, 1990.

Wortman, Richard. *The Development of a Russian Legal Consciousness.* Chicago, IL: University of Chicago Press, 1976.

Wortman, Richard. *Scenarios of Power: Myth and Ceremony in Russian Monarchy.* Princeton, NJ: Princeton University Press, 2000.

Zakharova, O. Iu. *Svetleishii Kniaz' M. S. Vorontsov.* Simferopol: Biznes-Inform, 2008.

Zaionchkovskii, A. M. *Oborona Sevastopolia: podvigi zashchitnikov, kratkii istoricheskii ocherk.* St. Petersburg: tip. Ekspeditsii zagotovleniia gos. bumag, 1904.

Zaionchkovskii, A. M. *Vostochnaia Voina, 1853–1856.* 2 vols. St. Petersburg: Ekspeditsiia izgotovleniia gosudarstvennykh bumag, 1908–1913.

Zaionchkovskii, P. A. *The Abolition of Serfdom in Russia*, edited and translated by Susan Wobst, introduction by Terrence Emmons. Gulf Breeze, FL: Academic International Press, 1978.

Zaionchkovskii, P. A. *Voennye Reformy 1860–1870.* Moscow: Moscow University Press, 1952.

Zatler, F. K. *Zapiski o prodovol'stvii voisk v voennoie vremia*, 3 vols. St. Petersburg: tip. Torgovogo doma S. Strugovshikova, 1860.

Zelenkevich, V. "Napadenie na Balaklavu." In *Materialy dlia istorii krymskoi voiny i oborony Sevastopolia,.*, edited by N. F. Dubrovin, 3: 128–35. St. Petersburg: Tip. Departmenta Udelov, 1872.

Zorin, Andrei. *Kormia Dvuglavogo Orla . . . Literatura i gosudarstvennaia ideologiia v rossii v poslednei treti XVIII-pervoi treti veka.* Moscow: novoe literaturnoe obozrenie, 2001.

Zweiniger-Bargielowska, Ina, Rachel Duffett, and Alain Drouard, eds. *Food and War in Twentieth-Century Europe.* Farnham, England: Ashgate, 2011.

INDEX

Page numbers followed by *f* and *t* refer to figures and tables, respectively.